Demystifying
Crime
and
Criminal Justice

Robert M. Bohm
University of Central Florida

Jeffery T. Walker
University of Arkansas, Little Rock

Roxbury Publishing Company
Los Angeles, California

Library of Congress Cataloging-in-Publication Data

Demystifying crime and criminal justice / [edited by] Robert M. Bohm, Jeffery Walker.
   p.   cm.
Includes bibliographical references and index.
ISBN 1-933220-16-3 (alk. paper)
1. Crime. 2. Law enforcement. 3. Criminal justice, Administration of. 4. Corrections. I. Bohm, Robert M. II. Walker, Jeffery T. III. Title.

HV6251.D45 2006
364—dc22

2005018534
CIP

DEMYSTIFYING CRIME AND CRIMINAL JUSTICE

Publisher: Claude Teweles
Managing Editor: Dawn VanDercreek
Production Editor: Nina M. Hickey
Copy Editor: Virginia Hoffman
Proofreader: Christy Graunke
Typography: Pegasus Type, Inc.
Cover Artist: Marnie Kenney
Cover Art: Elizabeth Deacon

Printed on acid-free paper in the United States of America. This book meets the standards for recycling of the Environmental Protection Agency.

ISBN 1-933220-16-3

ROXBURY PUBLISHING COMPANY
P.O. Box 491044
Los Angeles, California 90049-9044
Voice: (310) 473-3312 • Fax: (310) 473-4490
Email: roxbury@roxbury.net
Website: www.roxbury.net

Dedication

This book is dedicated to all our students, from whom we learn as much as teach. You push us to continue to seek knowledge as we endeavor to improve criminal justice and, ultimately, the overall quality of life worldwide. We are especially indebted to those students who go on to work in criminal justice and matriculate to doctoral programs—eventually joining us as colleagues and helping us prepare future generations of criminal justice and criminology students and practitioners. We hope you will join us in our quest.

—Robert M. Bohm and Jeffery T. Walker

Acknowledgments

We would like to thank the people who have helped us with this book. Thanks first to our families for their love, support, and understanding; and to the chapter authors for their willingness to be part of this project, their knowledge of the subject matter, and their good humor during the process. We would also like to thank the following reviewers for their insightful reviews and helpful suggestions: Roger C. Barnes, University of the Incarnate Word; Ellen Cohn, Florida International University; Rhonda R. Dobbs, University of Texas at Arlington; Jerry C. Jolley, Lewis-Clark State College; Charis Kubrin, George Washington University; Mitch Miller, University of South Carolina; César J. Rebellón, University of New Hampshire; and Jeffrey P. Rush, University of Louisiana at Monroe. And finally, our thanks to the staff at Roxbury Publishing Company: Scott Carter, Nina M. Hickey, and especially Claude Teweles—whose vision, ideas, and perseverance helped make this book possible. ✦

About the Editors

Robert M. Bohm is professor of criminal justice and legal studies at the University of Central Florida in Orlando. Besides being co-editor of *Demystifying Crime and Criminal Justice* and the author or co-author of numerous journal articles and book chapters, he is the author of *Deathquest II: An Introduction to the Theory and Practice of Capital Punishment in the United States*, 2nd ed., and *A Primer in Crime and Delinquency Theory;* the co-author of *Introduction to Criminal Justice*, 4th ed.; an editor of *America's Experiment With Capital Punishment: Reflections on the Past, Present, and Future of the Ultimate Penal Sanction*, 2nd ed., and *The Death Penalty in America: Current Research*. He served as president of the Academy of Criminal Justice Sciences and received the Southern Criminal Justice Association's Outstanding Educator of the Year award, as well as the Academy of Criminal Justice Sciences Founder's award. He is also a fellow of the Academy of Criminal Justice Sciences.

Jeffery T. Walker is professor of criminal justice and criminology at the University of Arkansas, Little Rock. He currently serves as the graduate coordinator for the Master of Arts in Criminal Justice program and as the advisor for the Criminal Justice track in the Public Policy Ph.D. program—jointly administered by the University of Arkansas, Fayetteville. He holds joint appointments with the University of Arkansas, Fayetteville, and the University of Arkansas Medical School. He is the president-elect of the Academy of Criminal Justice Sciences, and has served as the editor of the *Journal of Criminal Justice Education* and of *ACJS Today*, as well as the editor-in-chief of the *Journal of Critical Criminology*. Previous publications include articles in the *Journal of Quantitative Criminology, Journal of Criminal Justice Education, Journal of Gang Research*, and the books *Leading Cases in Law Enforcement*, 6th ed., *Statistics in Criminal Justice and Criminology: Analysis and Interpretation*, and *Policing and the Law*. ✦

About the Contributors

James R. Acker is a distinguished teaching professor at the School of Criminal Justice, University at Albany. He is co-editor of *America's Experiment With Capital Punishment: Reflections on the Past, Present, and Future of the Ultimate Penal Sanction*, 2nd edition, and presently is co-editing a forthcoming volume focusing on victim-based perspectives on the death penalty. He has written extensively about legal and social science issues related to capital punishment and other aspects of criminal justice.

Brandon Applegate is an associate professor at the University of Central Florida, where he teaches undergraduate and master's courses in criminal justice as well as doctoral courses in public affairs. He has published numerous articles on punishment and rehabilitation policy, correctional treatment, juvenile justice, public views of correctional policies, jail issues, and decision-making among criminal justice professionals. He also co-authored *Offender Rehabilitation: Effective Correctional Intervention*.

Bruce A. Arrigo teaches crime, law, and justice courses at the University of North Carolina at Charlotte. Some of his recent books include *Psychological Jurisprudence, Police Corruption and Psychological Testing,* and *Criminal Behavior: A Systems Approach*. He is the editor of the *Journal of Forensic Psychology Practice*, and book series editor of *Critical Perspectives in Criminology* and *Criminal Justice and Psychology*. He is a fellow of the American Psychological Association and the Academy of Criminal Justice Sciences.

David E. Barlow is a professor and chair in the Department of Criminal Justice at Fayetteville State University. His research interests include multicultural issues in policing, white-collar crime, and the history, ideology, and political economy of crime control in the United States. He is the author of numerous articles in professional journals, co-editor of two books, *Classics in Policing* and *Police in America: Classical and Contemporary Readings,* and co-author of the book, *Police in a Multicultural Society: An American Story*. He is currently working on a new book, *The Police in America: Theory and Practice*.

Melissa Hickman Barlow is a professor of criminal justice and the assistant dean in the College of Basic and Applied Sciences at Fayetteville State University. She has published articles on the history and political economy of crime control policy, crime and justice in the media, and race and class issues in criminal justice, and is co-author of *Police in a Multicultural Society: An American Story*. She is currently engaged in research on community justice and public health.

Donna M. Bishop is professor of criminal justice at Northeastern University. Her major research interests include juvenile justice policy reform, race and gender bias in justice processing, and the etiology of delinquency. Recent publications have appeared in *Crime and Justice: A Review of Research, Criminal Justice and Behavior;*

Criminology and Public Policy; and *Crime and Delinquency.* Her current research is focused on the dynamics of "due process oriented" juvenile courts.

Curtis Blakely is assistant professor of criminal justice at the University of South Alabama. His publications on correctional thought, prison privatization, and community and police partnerships have appeared in *Criminal Justice Policy Review, American Journal of Criminal Justice,* and *Federal Probation.*

Henry H. Brownstein is senior vice president and director of the Substance Abuse, Mental Health, and Criminal Justice Studies Department at NORC at the University of Chicago. He has published articles and book chapters on drug-related violence, homicide by women, and the social construction of public policy and social problems. His most recent book is *The Problems of Living in Society,* and he is co-editor of *Violence: From Theory to Research.*

Michael Buerger is an associate professor of criminal justice at Bowling Green State University. He has alternated between the practice of policing and the study of policing throughout his career, including nine years as a police officer. He was the director of the Minneapolis Office of the Crime Control Institute during the RECAP Experiment and the Hot Spots of Crime Experiment (1987–1990). He was a member of the Urban Institute's team that conducted the national evaluation of the "100,000 Cops On The Street" initiative under Title 1 of the 1994 Crime Bill.

Jacqueline Buffington-Vollum is a forensic psychology fellow at the University of Virginia's Institute of Law, Psychiatry, and Public Policy. Her primary areas of clinical expertise are forensic assessment, particularly of psychopathy and violence risk.

Her recent work has been published in *Law and Human Behavior, Criminal Justice and Behavior,* and *Justice Quarterly.*

Jennifer L. Bullock is a psychotherapist in the Washington, DC area, where she has worked with a variety of clinical and criminal populations. Her areas of research interest address the intersection of criminal justice and mental health and include criminal responsibility, the right to refuse psychiatric care, and competency to be executed. She has written articles for the *Journal of Forensic Psychology Practice* and has written a chapter on solitary confinement in the forthcoming *U.S. Penitentiary–Marion.*

Gary Cordner is a professor of police studies at Eastern Kentucky University where he also serves as director of the International Justice and Safety Institute and director of the Regional Community Policing Institute. He is co-author of the books *Planning in Criminal Justice Organizations and Systems, Police Administration,* and *Police and Society* and co-editor of four police anthologies. His articles have appeared in such journals as *Criminology and Public Policy, Criminology, Journal of Criminal Justice, Police Studies,* and the *Journal of Police Science and Administration.*

Charisse T. M. Coston is an associate professor and graduate coordinator in the Department of Criminal Justice at the University of North Carolina at Charlotte. Her current research interests include victimology and the fear of crime within and between vulnerable populations, serial murder, deviance, and critical theory in gender studies. Praeger Press has recently published *Victimizing Vulnerable Groups: Images of Uniquely High-Risk Crime Targets.*

Francis T. Cullen is distinguished research professor of criminal justice and sociology at the University of Cincinnati. He is the author of *Rethinking Crime and Deviance Theory: The Emergence of a Structuring Tradition*, the co-author of *Reaffirming Rehabilitation; Corporate Crime Under Attack: The Ford Pinto Case and Beyond; Criminology; Combating Corporate Crime: Local Prosecutors at Work;* and *Criminological Theory: Context and Consequences*, and the co-editor of *Offender Rehabilitation: Effective Correctional Intervention; Contemporary Criminological Theory; Criminological Theory: Past to Present–Essential Readings;* and *Taking Stock: The Status of Criminological Theory*.

David O. Friedrichs teaches in the Department of Sociology and Criminal Justice at the University of Scranton in Pennsylvania. He is the author of *Trusted Criminals: White Collar Crime in Contemporary Society* and *Law in Our Lives: An Introduction*, 2nd edition, and the editor of *State Crime: Volumes I and II*. He has also published numerous journal articles, book chapters, encyclopedia entries, and professional publication essays on a range of criminological, sociolegal, and sociological topics.

Russ Immarigeon is a town court justice in Hillsdale, New York, as well as an editor of *Offender Programs Report* and *Women, Girls and Criminal Justice*. He edits *VOMA Connections*, the national newsletter of the Victim-Offender Mediation Association, is co-editor of *After Crime and Punishment: Pathways to Offender Reintegration*, and the editor of the forthcoming, tentatively titled *Women, Girls and Criminal Justice*.

Richard Janikowski is an associate professor and the chair of the Department of Criminology and Criminal Justice at the University of Memphis. He has published on issues concerning criminal law, criminal procedure, and criminology. He is the co-editor of *Legality and Illegality*, and is currently completing a book on constitutional criminal procedure.

Mark Jones is a professor of criminal justice at East Carolina University in Greenville, North Carolina. His primary teaching interests are community corrections, organized crime, and criminal justice history. He has published in *Crime and Delinquency, The Prison Journal*, and the *Journal of Criminal Justice Education*. He recently conducted a study on community corrections strategies for organized crime offenders, published in *Corrections Compendium*, and is the author of *Community Corrections* and *Criminal Justice Pioneers in U.S. History*.

Michael Kenney is assistant professor of public policy at the School of Public Affairs, Pennsylvania State University, Capital College. In 2004, he was a postdoctoral scholar in Organizational Learning for Homeland Security with the Center for International Security and Cooperation at Stanford University. His research interests include the Colombian drug trade, counter-narcotics law enforcement, terrorism, intelligence, and organization theory. His published work has appeared in *Survival, International Journal of Intelligence and Counterintelligence, Transnational Organized Crime*, and the *Wall Street Journal*.

Joseph B. Kuhns III is an assistant professor at the University of North Carolina at Charlotte, where he teaches policing/community policing, research methods, and drugs, crime, and criminal justice to undergraduate and graduate students. His work has been published in a variety of professional outlets, including *Journal of*

Research in Crime and Delinquency, Violence and Victims, and *The American Journal of Public Health.* He is currently working on an international project to reduce drug-related homicides and violence in Trinidad and Tobago.

Paul Leighton teaches criminology in the Department of Sociology, Anthropology, and Criminology at Eastern Michigan University. He is co-editor of *Criminal Justice Ethics* and co-author of *Class, Race, Gender and Crime.* Leighton was the North American editor of *Critical Criminology: An International Journal,* and worked with Mark Hamm to put together *Teaching and Understanding Sept 11,* available online at *http://www.StopViolence. com.*

Kim Lersch is an associate professor in the Department of Criminology at the University of South Florida. Her primary research interests focus on police practices, especially police deviance. She has published two books: *Space, Time, and Crime* and *Policing and Misconduct,* and has authored numerous book chapters and journal articles. Recent works have appeared in the *Journal of Criminal Justice, Policing: An International Journal of Police Strategies and Management,* and *Western Criminology Review.*

Dennis R. Longmire is a professor of criminal justice at Sam Houston State University, where he also directs the College of Criminal Justice's Survey Research Program. He has served on the advisory boards of the Houston/Harris County Chapter of Murder Victim's Families for Reconciliation, the *Texas Death Row Journal,* and the Texas Coalition to Abolish the Death Penalty. As a resident of Huntsville, he regularly holds a vigil on the evening of each execution and was featured in the *Contemporary Justice Review's* "Justice Profile" for his work in this area.

Stephen D. Mastrofski is the director of the Administration of Justice Program and the Center for Justice Leadership and Management at George Mason University. Research interests include control of police discretion, police performance measurement, police reform, and field research methods. His work has appeared in such journals as *Annals of the Academy of Political and Social Science, Criminology, Criminology and Public Policy, Journal of Research in Crime and Delinquency, Justice Quarterly,* and *Law and Society Review.*

Marilyn McShane is currently a professor of criminal justice at the University of Houston–Downtown and director of the university's Community Justice Institute. Her writing has appeared in numerous publications, including two encyclopedias, more than a dozen books, and numerous journal articles. Her most recent work includes *The Encyclopedia of Juvenile Justice* and *Criminological Theory,* 4th edition, and articles on management issues, fear of crime, and parolee recidivism.

Raymond Michalowski is a sociologist and Arizona Regents Professor in the Department of Criminal Justice at Northern Arizona University. He has authored numerous writings on crime, punishment, elite wrongdoing, criminological theory, comparative criminology, and the politics of memory, including *State-Corporate Crime: Wrongdoing at the Intersection of Business and Politics; Critical Perspectives on Crime, Power, and Identity; The New Primer in Radical Criminology; Run for the Wall: Remembering Vietnam on a Motorcycle Pilgrimage; Radkikale Kriminologie;* and *Order, Law and Crime.*

Mary Parker serves as the administrative head of the Department of Criminal Justice at the University of Arkansas at Little Rock. She is a member of the Board of Corrections, which oversees all adult correctional activities in the state of Arkansas. She is an acknowledged expert on corrections in Arkansas, having authored the legislation that supports the current adult correctional configuration, and continues to be a recognized expert by all branches of government.

Eugene A. Paoline III is an assistant professor in the Department of Criminal Justice and Legal Studies at the University of Central Florida. His research interests include police socialization and culture, occupational attitudes of criminal justice practitioners, and theoretical development in criminal justice. He is the author of *Rethinking Police Culture: Officers' Occupational Attitudes*, and his most recent work has appeared in *Criminology, Justice Quarterly, Police Quarterly, Journal of Criminal Justice, Punishment and Society, Women and Criminal Justice*, and *Policing: An International Journal of Police Strategies and Management*.

Beth Pelz is an associate professor of criminal justice and the dean of the College of Public Service at the University of Houston–Downtown. Her research and publications have focused on inmate social organization, prison gangs, youth gangs, and juvenile delinquency. Her current research agenda includes the relationship between sensory processing and delinquency prevention.

Hal Pepinsky teaches criminal justice at Indiana University, Bloomington, and at Walden University. His most recent book is available online for free reading and use at: *http://www. critcrim.org/critpapers/ pepinsky-book.htm.*

Katheryn Russell-Brown is a professor of law and the director of the Center for the Study of Race and Race Relations at the University of Florida. Her interests are in the areas of criminal law, sociology of law, and race and crime. Her article, "The Constitutionality of Jury Override in Alabama Death Penalty Cases," was cited in *Harris v. Alabama*, 513 U.S. 504 (1995). She is the author of *The Color of Crime* and *Underground Codes: Race, Crime, and Related Fires*. She also co-edited *Petit Apartheid in the U.S. Criminal Justice System*.

Kathryn E. Scarborough is a professor of criminal justice and police studies at Eastern Kentucky University, as well as the director for research, evaluation, and testing for the Justice and Safety Center. Her research interests include criminal investigation, law enforcement technology, cybercrime and security, and police administration. She has contributed to journals such as *Police Quarterly, Thomas Jefferson Law Review, American Journal of Criminal Justice*, and *Crime Prevention and Community Safety: An International Journal*. She has co-authored textbooks on workplace violence, police administration, and women in law enforcement.

Barbara Sims is an associate professor of criminal justice at Penn State at Harrisburg, as well as the coordinator for both the undergraduate and graduate criminal justice programs. She has published numerous articles in such journals as *Journal of Crime and Delinquency, Crime and Delinquency, The Prison Journal, Police Quarterly, Criminology and Public Policy*, and *The Justice Professional*. Her recent works include an edited volume of manuscripts that address the problem of treating substance addicted offenders, and a forthcoming handbook on juvenile law and justice.

Paula Smith is an assistant professor of criminal justice and the assistant director of the Corrections Institute at the University of Cincinnati. Her publications have focused on offender assessment, program evaluation, and developing an empirically-based theory of effective correctional intervention.

John Ortiz Smykla is the chair of criminal justice and legal studies at the University of West Florida. He is co-author of *Executions in the United States, 1608–2003: The Espy File,* 3rd edition, and *Corrections in the 21st Century,* 3rd edition. His publications on corrections, capital punishment, and drug courts have appeared in *Justice Quarterly, Journal of Criminal Justice, Criminal Justice Review,* and *American Journal of Criminal Justice.*

Scott Vollum teaches in the Department of Justice Studies at James Madison University. His research interests include death penalty attitudes, violence in prison, and violence against animals. His recent work has been published in *Justice Quarterly, The Prison Journal,* and *Society and Animals.* He is co-author of *The Death Penalty: Constitutional Issues, Commentaries and Case Briefs.*

David Weisburd is the Walter E. Meyer professor of law and criminal justice at the Hebrew University in Jerusalem and a professor of criminology and criminal justice at the University of Maryland, as well as a senior fellow at the Police Foundation and a fellow of the American Society of Criminology and the Academy of Experimental Criminology. He is the author or editor of numerous books and articles that cover a range of criminal justice research topics.

Frank P. Williams III is a professor of criminal justice at the University of Houston–Downtown, and director of the university's graduate Security Management Program. His recent publications include *Imagining Criminology,* an encyclopedia, and journal articles or book chapters on drug use, gangs, processing females in the criminal justice system, and parolee recidivism.

James J. Willis is an assistant professor of sociology at the University of Massachusetts–Boston. Research interests include police organizations, police reform, and penal change. Recent publications on COMPSTAT and convict transportation in eighteenth- and nineteenth-century Britain have appeared in *Justice Quarterly* and *Law and Society Review.* His latest project is on COMPSTAT and community policing.

Peter B. Wood is a professor of sociology and director of the program in criminal justice and corrections at Mississippi State University. He is also the current president of the Southern Criminal Justice Association, a research fellow at the Social Science Research Center, and a research associate at the Center for Computer Security Research at Mississippi State University. His work has appeared in *Crime and Delinquency, Justice Quarterly, Criminology, The Prison Journal, Journal of Offender Rehabilitation, Social Science Quarterly,* and *Journal of Criminal Justice.* ✦

Table of Contents

    Robert M. Bohm and Jeffery T. Walker

    Hal Pepinsky
    The myth that crime statistics accurately show what
    crimes are being committed and what crimes are most
    harmful.

    Jennifer L. Bullock and Bruce A. Arrigo
    The myth that most criminals—especially the dangerous
    ones—are mentally ill.

    David O. Friedrichs
    The myth that white-collar crimes do not hurt anyone.

    Katheryn Russell-Brown
    The myth that minorities commit more crime, especially
    more violent crime.

    Joseph B. Kuhns III and Charisse T. M. Coston
    The myth that serial killers are middle-aged, white
    males.

Section 2: Law Enforcement

Introduction

Robert M. Bohm and Jeffery T. Walker

About two decades ago, one of the editors of this book wrote that "the task of debunking myths about crime, criminals, and crime control policy has received only limited attention. Myths continue to be perpetuated" (Bohm 1986:193).[1] Those words are as true today as they were then.[2] The purpose of this book is to debunk or to demystify—that is, to correct misconceptions or to "set the record straight"—many of the current myths about crime and criminal justice. In this book, a "myth" refers to:

> a credible, dramatic, socially constructed representation of perceived realities that people accept as permanent, fixed knowledge of reality while forgetting (if they were ever aware of it) its tentative, imaginative, created, and perhaps fictional qualities. (Nimmo and Combs 1980:16)

Myths have also been called simply "exaggerations of reality" (Kappeler, Blumberg, and Potter 2000:85).

For some, debunking myths is a controversial and presumptuous practice because it assumes that the debunker's conception of reality is the correct one, while the believer of the myth conceives reality incorrectly. Thus, it should not be surprising that many of the "truths" or "realities" in this book are themselves considered myths requiring demystification (see, for example, Logan and DiIulio 1992, reprinted in Kraska 2004:31). Who is right? Is "reality" simply tentative, socially constructed, and personal? Is one person's "myth" another person's "reality," and vice versa? Or are people sometimes deceived? Can people be falsely conscious of the world in which they live, intentionally misled by lies, distortions, and propaganda? We believe people can be falsely conscious of the world in which they live. From our point of view, the relationship between myths and reality is not a trivial matter because, as described below, beliefs in myths have practical and, in many cases, undesirable consequences.

The perpetuation of crime and criminal justice myths has resulted in at least two undesirable consequences for the majority of Americans. First is a myopic focus on short-term interests of dubious value and a near total obliviousness to long-range interests, which promise greater relief from crime. Obliviousness to future interests makes exploitation easier. "Exploitation," in this context, refers to the activity of one group preventing another group from "getting what they may as yet have no idea of, and therefore do not desire, but would prefer to their present condition if only they knew about it" (Plamenatz 1963:322). A second undesirable consequence for most Americans is the contradictions that occur when actions are based on myths. Though not inevitable, contradictions, when they arise, sometimes adversely affect both short- and long-term interests. For many people, control policies based on myths result in an exacerbation of harm and suffering.

Myths about crime and criminal justice are perpetuated because they serve a variety of interests. "Interests," refer to "what it makes sense for people to want and do, given their overall situation" (Ollman 1976:122). Among the interests served by crime and criminal justice myths are those of the general public, the media, politicians, criminologists, criminal justice officials, and social elites. One of the problems with discussions of crime-related mythology is the emphasis on the way elite interests are served. Early on, Marx and Engels opined that "the ideas of the ruling class are in every epoch the ruling ideas . . ." (1970:64). They noted that for the ruling class to carry out its ideas, it is necessary

> to represent its interest as the common interest of all the members of society, that is, expressed in ideal form: it has to give its ideas the form of universality, and represent them as the only rational, universally valid ones. (Marx and Engels 1970:65–66)

This, of course, includes ideas about crime and criminal justice.

A problem with Marx and Engels' observations is that they failed to distinguish between short- and long-term interests. While in the long-run, elite interests are served by myths about crime and criminal justice, and the general public is duped into believing that their long-run interests are also served, it is unlikely that the myths could find such universal appeal if they did not also serve real short-term interests of the general public. It is maintained here that myths about crime and

criminal justice are perpetuated because they actually do serve the general short-term interest, as well as long-term elite interests.

In the following paragraphs some of the ways myths serve both general and elite interests are examined. Also considered are some of the contradictions and consequences of beliefs and policies based on myths. While there is obvious overlap in groups served by myths (e.g., members of the media, politicians, criminologists, criminal justice officials, and elites are also part of the general public), the ways that each group contributes to and is served by myths are a little different. For this reason, each group is considered separately.

The Public

The public contributes to its own myth-laden conception of crime and criminal justice in at least four ways. The first is by over generalizing from personal experience. If people have been crime victims, for example, they may consider their own experience typical or representative of crime in general. A problem is that it is unlikely that there is such a thing as "typical" crime, and the crime most people know and experience is not representative of crime in general. A second way the public contributes to myths is by relying on inaccurate communication. Some people embellish crime experiences, and thus distort their own conceptions or the conceptions of those to whom they communicate. A third way the public contributes to myths is by relying on atypical information. For those who are not aware that they have experienced crime, part of their conceptions of crime may come from atypical and unrepresentative experiences, embellished or otherwise, of family or friends, who may or may not have been victims themselves. Finally, the public contributes to myths through a lack of consciousness. There are many cases where the public has no knowledge of victimization. For example, in cases of consumer fraud or medical negligence, people may never know that a crime has been perpetrated against them. In such cases, it would be difficult to conceptualize such actions as criminal.

The public perpetuates myths about crime and criminals because they serve at least three short-term interests: (1) they offer identities; (2) they aid comprehension by creating order; and (3) they help forge common bonds, creating and reinforcing a sense of community. Implicit in each of these interests, however, are important contradictions. Myths about "criminals" and "law-abiding citizens" offer identities. For many people, it is comforting to conceive of themselves as law-abiding citizens. Given the daily temptations to violate the law, those who do not, even in the face of great material deprivation, demonstrate a moral courage and a self-control that often forms the basis of their self-identities. Additionally, many consider abiding by the law as an aspect of patriotism. This does not mean that law-violators necessarily consider themselves unpatriotic, but only that to be law-abiding and patriotic is an important part of many people's identities. This facet of patriotism is an emotion that politicians find advantageous to exploit. For these reasons, many people find it in their interests to believe in and perpetuate the myth of the criminal and law-abiding citizen.

In reality, however, many self-conceived, law-abiding citizens are engaging in self-delusion. No doubt there are a few paragons of virtue, but not many. Most people manifest common human frailties. For example, evidence suggests that more than 90 percent of all Americans have committed some crime for which they could be incarcerated (see, for example, Bohm and Haley 2004:48; Gabor 1994). This is not to imply that most Americans are murderers or robbers, for they are not. Criminality is a relative (and political) phenomenon. In his discussion of delinquency, Matza (1964) captured this relativity when he wrote that juveniles drift between law-abiding and law-violating behavior. Whether a juvenile actually engages in a delinquent act depends on a host of factors, not the least of which is available opportunity. There are few delinquents or criminals whose entire life orientation is centered on delinquent or criminal activities. Consequently, it makes little sense to label an individual a "delinquent" or a "criminal" who occasionally gets into a fight, steals from a store, exceeds the speed limit, or cheats on income taxes. While these are "criminal" acts, the people who commit them are not "criminals."

A contradiction is that the criminal role offers a different kind of identity to another segment of the population. For some, the criminal label is actively sought. The literature on juvenile delinquency is replete with examples of juveniles whose identity is based on their "rep" (reputation) for toughness, sexual prowess, institutional experience, etc. Many of those who assassinate or attempt to assassinate famous people are likely seeking a public identity that could not be achieved legitimately. This applies as well to many "notorious" criminals. A problem with labeling theory, in this regard, is an overemphasis on the negative consequences of the label or stigma—that individuals actively seek to avoid it. In many cases, as noted above, individuals actively seek the label as a goal. Myths offer identities, criminal or otherwise, real or imagined;

and people find it in their interest to believe in and perpetuate the myth of the criminal and law-abiding citizen.

Another way in which myths about crime and criminals contribute to identity is through the reinforcement and perpetuation of the myth of the individual. The concept of "individual," as used here, does not deny "individualism" but only refers in a limited sense to the idea of the "free-willed" being who acts on society without being acted on by society. Although the myth of the individual has informed philosophical and criminological thought at least since the Enlightenment, it became a part of popular consciousness and identity through existentialism and the human potential, and other movements of the 1960s. It began influencing criminal justice policy again significantly in the mid-1970s.

However, as Foucault (1977:194) explains, "The individual is no doubt the fictitious atom of an 'ideological' representation of society. . . ." The idea of the individual, as used here and portrayed in existentialism, for example, is an illusion precisely because human beings are necessarily social. Not only are human beings social by virtue of the social nature of self-identity and of relations with others, but also because of the social component (e.g., language) in the ability of human beings to conceive of anything at all (Ollman 1976; Mead 1972).

The idea of the "free-willed individual" finds characteristic expression in the current politically conservative interpretation of the "criminal" and his or her behavior. In this view, the criminal is considered an isolated being whose social environment is generally inconsequential or, at least, legally irrelevant to his or her criminal actions. Kennedy (1976:39) maintains that the notion of the criminal as individual was the product of a histori-

cal transformation from "the ethic of shared responsibility for individual conduct (the cooperative ethic) to the ethic of individual responsibility." He adds that this transformation "was fundamental to the birth of crime and penal sanction" and "to political, economic, religious, and familistic transformation generally. . . ." Thus, states Kennedy (1976:38), "individualism as an attitude of self is basic to guilt, and as a premise of both civil and criminal law it is elemental to the whole legal practice of incrimination." A consequence is that the belief that the individual, alone, is responsible for his or her conduct diverts attention away from the structural elements in society that inevitably contribute to criminal behavior. (This last point will be discussed further in another context later.)

Another reason that myths find popular support is that they aid comprehension by creating order. Myths aid comprehension in two ways. They reduce contradictions and simplify complex phenomena.

As previously noted, myths about crime and criminals create a simple dichotomy that separates the "good guys" from the "bad guys." Quinney (1977:14) maintains that the myth of crime "provides the metaphor for our human nature; crime represents human nature in its less attractive form." Consequently, for many people, the "criminal" is conceived as abnormal, irrational, evil, or untrustworthy, while the "law-abiding citizen" is normal, rational, good, and trustworthy. While dichotomies such as these can be useful heuristic devices, they necessarily abstract and distort reality.

Myths also aid comprehension by reducing contradictions, which is especially important when it comes to public conceptions about crime and criminal justice. One of American society's major contradictions is that despite being one of the wealthiest and technologically advanced countries in the world, it still contains widespread poverty, unemployment, and crime. Historically, a myth that has been perpetrated to resolve this contradiction is that crime is an individual problem, the result of personal defect—especially of poor, young males between the ages of 15 and 24. Conceived of in this way, it follows that there is no social or structural solution to the problem of crime.

Another contradiction that perplexes many Americans is that during times when more effort is expended and more money is spent on crime control, the problem remains, or even worsens. Myths help people cope with the knowledge that crime-control efforts have not lived up to expectations. For example, during the heyday of the Law Enforcement Assistance Administration (LEAA) in the 1970s, when billions of dollars were presumably spent on crime control, crime became, in the minds of many, epidemic. However, when LEAA was disbanded and the monies expended on crime control were greatly reduced, the crime problem, according to official statistics, decreased. No doubt other factors were operating, but the impression given to many people must have been that the more we do, the worse we fail, which for many is a very disconcerting observation. Another example is the "war on drugs." Between 1980 and 2003, the United States spent more than $300 billion on federal, state, and local antidrug efforts. In 2002, the federal government alone spent nearly $20 billion to combat illegal drugs (Bohm and Haley 2004:51). Yet, between 1981 and 2000, cocaine and heroin prices steadily declined and the level of purity of both drugs increased, indicating that the "war on drugs" has failed to significantly reduce either supply or demand (Reiman 2004: 39–40).

It is likely that the current punitive attitude of a large segment of the public, and the return to a punishment model in crime control, can be attributed at least in part to the simple solution the punishment model offers to seemingly intractable problems. A result is that the United States currently holds the distinction of incarcerating more of its citizens than any other country in the world, and it is among one of the last countries outside of Africa and Asia to impose the death penalty.

Finally, crime myths contribute to public fear, which helps forge common bonds and creates and reinforces a sense of community. Fear of crime makes people feel that they share the same situation. Crime crosses social barriers. In reality, however, the chance of actual victimization from the crimes most people fear is very unevenly distributed among social groupings. Nevertheless, that matters little, because it is the abstract fear that helps unite people. Fear of crime also creates and reinforces a sense of community. Neighborhood watch programs and vigilantism are two examples of the way that fear of crime unites people.

A contradiction is that fear of crime also inhibits community. Because of fear, people are afraid to leave their homes and are suspicious of strangers. It is fear of crime, moreover, that politicians play upon in their "law and order" campaigns. Weighed together, it is likely that factors inhibiting community are more influential than those creating community.

The Media

Perhaps the most important source of common conceptions and myths of crime and criminal justice is the media. As Vold observed, "crime waves are now and probably always have been products of newspaper headlines" (1935:803; also see Fishman 1978; Kappeler, Blumberg, and Potter 2000:29). One thing is certain: the media presents a distorted crime picture to the public. According to one study, the factors that influence crime news selection are the seriousness of the offense, whimsical or unusual elements, sentimental or dramatic aspects, and the involvement of famous or high-status persons (Roshier 1973:34–35; also see Graber 1980; Sheley and Ashkins 1981).

The entertainment media has a particularly distorting effect on public conceptions of crime and criminal justice. Crime and criminal justice–related television programs, for example, have been conservatively estimated to account for about one-fourth to one-third of all prime time television shows and, at times, perhaps as much as 80 percent of all television programming (Surette 1998:24 and 37; Dominick 1973). Crime is "the largest single subject matter on television" (Surette 1998:36). Information that the public receives from these shows is anything but accurate. Studies have indicated that (1) the least committed crimes, such as murder and assault, appear more frequently than those crimes committed more often, such as burglary and larceny; (2) violent crimes are portrayed as caused by greed or as attempts to avoid detection, rather than by passion accompanying arguments, which is more typical; (3) the necessary use of violence in police work is exaggerated; (4) the use of illegal police tactics is seemingly sanctioned; (5) police officers are unfettered by procedural law; and (6) the police nearly always capture the "bad guys," usually in violent confrontations (Dominick 1973; Pandiani 1978; Gitlin 1979; Surette 1998).

Perhaps the principal reason why the entertainment media perpetuates such myths is that they attract a large viewing audience, which, in turn, sells advertising and generates profit. Whether more accurate presentations would be less appealing, however, is an empirical question yet to be answered. In any event, whether intentional or not, crime myths perpetuated by the media often serve elite interests by, among other things, portraying crime in a particular manner (other ways in which crime myths serve elite interests are examined in a later section). The fact that most of the mass media in the United States are either owned by large corporations or are dependent on corporate advertising has been taken as evidence of a conspiracy among the elite to control the public consciousness (Miliband 1969; Halberstam 1979; Dreier 1982; Evans and Lundman 1983). While such a view has a certain intuitive appeal, and some empirical evidence to support it, the fact remains that the mass media, particularly of late, has been at the vanguard in exposing elite malfeasance. Whether the effort is sincere or merely an attempt to legitimate the media as an institution that serves the interests of the public—as was the case with the federal regulation of corporate crime—is not clear. Intentions aside, there is no question that the mass media conveys a false conception of crime and criminal justice to the public.

Another, though subtle, way the media influences common conceptions about crime and criminal justice is through public-opinion polls. Erskine (1974) argued that the public's conception of crime may be the result of categories selected by pollsters. Erskine reported that 1965 was the first year (since 1935, when Dr. George H. Gallup polled his first respondent) that crime appeared as a response to the question: "What do you think is the most important problem facing this country today?" The crime response, however, did not appear alone as a single category, but was grouped in a category that included "immorality, crime and juvenile delinquency." Crime did not appear again as a response when the same question was asked until 1968 when it was grouped in a category of "crime and lawlessness, including riots, looting, and juvenile delinquency." The importance of the category in which crime is grouped, in generating a response, was underscored by Erskine who noted, "When categories such as unrest, polarization, student protest, moral decay, drugs, and youth problems began to be itemized separately, crime 'per se' began to rank relatively lower than it had previously" (1974:131). Furthermore, in response to the Harris Survey question— "In the past year, do you feel the crime rate in your neighborhood has been increasing, decreasing, or has it remained about the same as it was before?"—the conception of crime appeared to be tied to a variety of events such as racial violence, assassination, war protest and campus unrest, as well as criminal activity (Erskine 1974:131–132). In short, it is conceivable that people who were polled in both Gallup and Harris Surveys were responding either to noncriminal problems (e.g., unrest, polarization, student protest, moral decay, etc.) arbitrarily grouped together in a category that also included crime, or to dramatic social events that artificially raised people's conception of the crime rate.

Politicians

A third source of crime-related myths is politicians. As members of the public, politicians derive much of their knowledge in the same way as does the rest of the public. However, unlike much of the public, politicians also get knowledge about crime and criminal justice from criminologists and, especially, criminal justice officials. Since "law and order" rhetoric is often politically advantageous (for reasons already discussed), many politicians find it difficult not to disseminate popular myths.

Criminologists and Criminal Justice Officials

A fourth source of crime-related myths is criminologists and criminal justice officials. Like politicians, they are members of the public, and thus derive part of their conception of these subjects from their own experiences. However, if blame is to be leveled at any one group for perpetuating myths, then it should fall here, because criminologists and criminal justice officials should and often do know better. They are in the best position to dispel the myths. There are several reasons why they do not.

Many criminologists find it in both their short- and long-term interests to perpetuate myths. These interests, moreover, may be either cognitive or structural. Regarding the former, many criminologists, like other members of the general public, have internalized the myths as part of their social "reality." To challenge the myths would be, for many, to undermine long-established and fundamental conceptions of society. For many criminologists, what is considered a myth in this book simply makes sense or attunes with preconceived ideas. To question the myths might create cognitive dissonance.

Other criminologists perpetuate myths because it is in their structural interests to do so. Platt (1975:106–107) suggested that this is because of academic repression and cooptation. In some places, prestigious university appointments and promotions in general typically go to those academics whose work does not fundamentally challenge myths supportive of the status quo. It appears that some prestigious journals rarely publish articles that radically deviate from an accepted, often myth-laden, perspective (though this may reflect considerations other than ideology). Similarly, major research grants generally seem to be awarded to academics whose proposals do not fundamentally undermine privileged positions or deviate from preconceived, often myth-laden, wisdom. Whether myths are perpetuated because of academic repression and cooptation, academic life at some institutions is generally more pleasant for those who do not make waves.

Criminal justice officials perpetuate myths for at least four reasons. First, employment and advancement often depend on responsiveness to the interests of political and economic elites. Administrators, in particular, are generally either elected to their positions or appointed to them by politicians. Since political election or appointment often depends on the support of political and economic elites, those who would dispel myths that serve the interests of political and economic elites are not likely to find support forthcoming.

Second, for police administrators, prison officials, judges, and prosecutors, the myths of increasing crime or crime epidemics—or the threat of mythical predators such as random stranger-killers or juvenile "superpredators"—are used to justify larger budgets, more personnel, and higher pay (Kappeler, Blumberg, and Potter 2000:39, 41, 45; Pepinsky and Jesilow 1984:16–17, 30). Those myths also sustain a large and expanding private crime-control industry (Kappeler, Blumberg, and Potter 2000:44). Third, as was the case with the public, myths also provide order to the potentially chaotic role of police officer or other criminal justice position. They allow police officers and other criminal justice personnel to believe they can do the job (i.e., prevent or control crime). Finally, as was also the case with the public, myths provide police officers and other criminal justice personnel with a basis of solidarity, common purpose, and collective unity in the face of a hostile and potentially threatening environment.

Social Elites

As part of the public, social elites contribute to the perpetuation of myths in much the same ways as do other members of the public. It is doubtful, moreover, that political and economic elites conspire to perpetuate myths, primarily because it is unnecessary for them to do so. Because myths serve at least the short-term interests of virtually all members of society, myths of crime and criminal justice probably would be perpetuated whether they served the interests of social elites or not. Nevertheless, social elites receive more significant and long-lasting advantages from the myths than any other social grouping. Social elites are also less influenced by the adverse consequences of the myths.

The principal way myths about crime and criminal justice serve elite interests is by helping to secure and legitimate the social status quo with its gross disparities of wealth, privilege, and opportunity (Reiman 1979:5, 2004:4). Two interrelated means by which myths help to accomplish this are by providing a scapegoat and by redirecting and defusing dissent.

In the first place, the "crime problem" in general as well as a variety of specific crimes in particular have been used as scapegoats for increasing political and economic distress (Quinney 1977:6; Parenti 1999:239). Even the occasional prosecution of corporate crime has its advantages for social elites. It serves as a symbolic gesture that reinforces the belief that the law is applied uniformly to all persons (Pearce 1976:90). Secondly, by focusing public attention on particular forms of crime (e.g., crimes of the poor), the belief that such crime is the basic cause of social problems obscures "the conditions of inequality, powerlessness, institutional violence, and so on, which lie at the bases of our tortured society" (Liazos 1977:155; Parenti 1999:239).

A major result of scapegoating is the polarization of the population into a "confident and supportive majority" and an "alienated and repressable minority" (Clements 1974). By creating a readily identifiable criminal group through scapegoating, willing obedience and popular support of the "noncriminal" majority are made less problematic, thus reducing the need for compulsion. If polarization were not accomplished, or if people (e.g., the poor) were not divided through a fear of being criminally victimized, for example, then they might unite to the detriment of social elites to press for the realization of their common interests (Wright 1973:21; Chambliss 1976:7; Pearce 1976:90; Quinney 1979).

Another result of scapegoating, and another way that myths serve the interests of social elites, is by redirecting or defusing dissent. One means by which dissent is redirected is the perpetuation of the myth that crime is primarily the work of the poor. Belief in this myth diverts the attention of the poor from the social and economic exploitation they experience to the criminality of their own class (Chambliss 1976:8). Furthermore, the myth "deflects the discontent and potential hostility of middle America away from the classes above them and toward the classes below them" (Reiman 1979:5, 2004:4; also see Pepinsky and Jesilow 1984:42). In both cases, myth has the effect of directing attention away from the sources of crime that have the most detrimental consequences for society.

A primary way dissent is defused is by supervising or institutionalizing potential dissidents. As Gordon (1976:208) related, "If the system did not effect this neutralization, if so many of the poor were not trapped in the debilitating system of crime and punishment, then they might otherwise gather the strength to oppose the system which reinforces their misery." Thus, the criminalization of the poor negates their potential "for developing an ideologically sophisticated understanding of their situation . . . and by incarcerating them it is made difficult for them to organize to realise their ideas" (Pearce 1976:81).

Ultimately, the success or failure of redirecting or defusing dissent depends on the degree to which the public accepts myths of crime and criminal justice as accurate descriptions of reality. Fortunately for social elites, myths are likely to be uncritically accepted by the public for the following reasons (besides those already noted): First, the ethic of individual responsibility, a "legal fiction" which is both socially and psychologically insupportable, obscures the state's causal role in crime (Kennedy 1976:48). Second, most individuals have been socialized, to varying extents, to behave in conformity with the law (Schumann 1976:292). Third, most criminal behavior represents impulsive reactions to unspecific social conflicts, which rarely victimize the opponent in the underlying conflict, thus obscuring the "real" sources of social conflict (Schumann 1976:292). Ironically, for the exploited, "much, if not most, crime continues to victimize those who are already oppressed . . . and does little more than reproduce the existing order" (Quinney 1977:103). Fourth, most individuals who commit crimes attempt to conceal their illegal behavior from others, and, thus, remain isolated instead of attempting to develop solidarity with others (Schumann 1976:292). Finally, most individuals are insulated from any abridgment of justice so that interpretations of justice made by the state are credible. For example, "systematic elimination or incarceration of a certain 'criminal element' must always be the objective and professional pursuit of the rule of law. . ." (Clements 1974:176).

In sum, as the chapters in this book will show, common conceptions of crime and criminal justice are to a rather large degree informed by myths. The myths are perpetuated not only because they serve elite interests, but also because they serve the short-term interests of much of the public.

Because myths serve elite interests by helping to secure and to legitimate the social status quo, and because social elites are less influenced by the crimes most people fear, social elites have little incentive to dispel myths or to reduce crime. Ironically, social elites are the one group that could have a profound effect on changing the system that creates these problems (cf. Reiman 1979, 2004).

The real irony is that the rest of the public helps perpetuate myths that inhibit the reduction of those actions or inactions that cause them harm and suffering. While myths do serve, in a perverted way, short-term interests of the public, in the long run, they inhibit comprehension of the fundamental changes necessary to bring about a reduction in harm and suffering. The poor, as a result, bear the bulk of the blame while continuing to be the most victimized; and the middle class, also victimized, must bear the bulk of the costs of policies that do not provide them the protection and the security they are seeking.

There are people who would like to perpetuate the myth that nothing can be done to significantly reduce crime in the United States. If the ameliorative reforms of the past are the sole indication, they may be right. However, there remains the possibility that a significant reduction in crime could be achieved through fundamental social change. Although the details of such a program are beyond the scope of this introduction, a first step may be demystifying the myths that are inhibiting fundamental social change. It is hoped that this book contributes to that effort.

Plan of the Book

The book is divided into four major sections: (1) Crime Myths, (2) Law Enforcement Myths, (3) Administration of Justice Myths, and (4) Corrections Myths. To enhance continuity, we asked contributors to follow an outline consisting of the following subheadings: (1) The Myth, (2) The Kernel of Truth, (3) The Truth or Facts, (4) Interests Served by the Myth, and (5) Policy Implications of Belief in the Myth. In the first section of each chapter, "The Myth," authors describe a myth or a set of myths about a particular subject. (Some authors begin their chapters with a brief introduction.) In the second section, "The Kernel of Truth," authors identify accurate aspects of the myth or myths. This is included because for myths to be believable and accepted, they generally must contain at least a kernel of truth. In the third section, "The Truth or Facts," authors debunk the myth or myths by providing the best available evidence on the subject. The fourth section, "Interests Served by the Myth," continues the argument developed in the introduction to the book that myths are created and perpetuated because they serve the interests of particular groups. In each of the chapters, authors explain the specific interests served by the myth or myths they have analyzed. Finally, the fifth section, "Policy Implications of Belief in the Myth," also augments a theme addressed in the introduction to the book that myths have practical and often undesirable consequences. The practical consequences of the myth or myths are explained in each chapter.

None of the analyses in this book should be uncritically accepted. They should be discussed and debated. We encourage readers to think of other crime and criminal justice myths, to try and debunk them, and to identify the interests served by the myths and the policy implications of belief in the myths. Unfortunately, for those seeking an accurate understanding of crime and criminal justice, there are many myths from which to choose.

Notes

1. Most of the introduction is from this source.
2. Regarding the debunking or demystification of crime and criminal justice myths (besides this book), three recent and notable exceptions are Kappeler, Blumberg, and Potter (2000), Reiman (2004), and Bohm and Haley (2004).

References

Bohm, R. M. 1986. Crime, criminal, and crime control policy myths. *Justice Quarterly* 3:193–214.

Bohm, R. M., and K. N. Haley. 2004. *Introduction to criminal justice,* 4th ed. New York: McGraw-Hill.

Chambliss, W. J. 1976. Functional and conflict theories of crime: The heritage of Emile Durkheim and Karl Marx. In *Whose law what order?* eds. W. J. Chambliss and M. Mankoff. New York: Wiley.

Clements, J. M. 1974. Repression: Beyond the rhetoric. In *The criminologist: Crime and the criminal,* ed. C. E. Reasons. Pacific Palisades, CA: Goodyear.

Dominick, J. R. 1973. Crime and law enforcement on prime-time television. *Public Opinion Quarterly* 37:241–250.

Dreier, P. 1982. The position of the press in the U.S. power structure. *Social Problems* 29:298–310.

Erskine, H. 1974. The polls: Fear of violence and crime. *Public Opinion Quarterly* (Spring):131–145.

Evans, S. S., and R. J. Lundman. 1983. Newspaper coverage of corporate price-fixing: A replication. *Criminology* 21:529–541.

Fishman, M. 1978. Crime waves as ideology. *Social Problems* 25:531–543.

Foucault, M. 1977. *Discipline and punish.* New York: Pantheon.

Gabor, T. 1994. *Everybody does it! Crimes by the public.* Toronto: University of Toronto Press.

Gitlin, T. 1979. Prime time ideology: The hegemonic process in television entertainment. *Social Problems* 26:251–266.

Gordon, D. M. 1976. Class and the economics of crime. In *Whose law what order?* eds. W. J. Chambliss and M. Mankoff. New York: Wiley.

Graber, D. A. 1980. *Crime news and the public.* New York: Praeger.

Halberstam, D. 1979. *The powers that be.* New York: Knopf.

Kappeler, V. E., M. Blumberg, and G. W. Potter. 2000. *The mythology of crime and criminal justice,* 3rd ed. Prospect Heights, IL: Waveland Press.

Kennedy, M. C. 1976. Beyond incrimination. In *Whose law what order?* eds. W. J. Chambliss and M. Mankoff. New York: Wiley.

Kraska, P. B. 2004. *Theorizing criminal justice: Eight essential orientations.* Long Grove, IL: Waveland.

Liazos, A. 1977. The poverty of the sociology of deviance: Nuts, sluts, and perverts. In *Criminology: Power, crime and criminal law,* eds. J. F. Galliher and J. L. McCartney. Homewood, IL: Dorsey.

Logan, C., and J. J. DiIulio, Jr. 1992. Ten deadly myths about crime and punishment in the U.S. *Wisconsin Interest* 1:21–35.

Marx, K., and F. Engels. 1970. *The German ideology.* New York: International Publishers.

Matza, D. 1964. *Delinquency and drift.* New York: Wiley.

Mead, G. H. 1972. *On social psychology.* Chicago: The University of Chicago Press.

Miliband, R. 1969. *The state in capitalist society.* New York: Basic Books.

Nimmo, D., and J. E. Combs. 1980. *Subliminal politics: Myths and mythmakers in America.* Englewood Cliffs, NJ: Prentice Hall.

Ollman, B. 1976. *Alienation,* 2nd ed. Cambridge: Cambridge University Press.

Pandiani, J. A. 1978. Crime time TV: If all we know is what we saw. . . . *Contemporary Crises* 2:437–458.

Parenti, C. 1999. *Lockdown America: Police and prisons in the age of crisis.* New York: Verso.

Pearce, F. 1976. *Crimes of the powerful.* London: Pluto Press.

Pepinsky, H. E., and P. Jesilow. 1984. *Myths that cause crime.* Cabin John, MD: Seven Locks.

Plamenatz, J. 1963. *Man and society,* Vol. 2. New York: McGraw-Hill.

Platt, T. 1975. Prospects for a radical criminology in the USA. In *Critical criminology,* eds. I. Taylor, P. Walton, and J. Young. Boston: Routledge and Kegan Paul.

Quinney, R. 1977. *Class, state and crime.* New York: David McKay.

———. 1979. *Criminology,* 2nd ed. Boston: Little, Brown.

Reiman, J. H. 1979. *The rich get richer and the poor get prison: Ideology, class, and criminal justice.* New York: Wiley.

———. 2004. *The rich get richer and the poor get prison: Ideology, class, and criminal justice,* 7th ed. Boston: Allyn and Bacon.

Roshier, B. 1973. The selection of crime news by the press. In *The manufacture of news,* eds. S. Cohen and J. Young. Beverly Hills: Sage.

Schumann, K. F. 1976. Theoretical presuppositions for criminology as a critical enterprise. *International Journal of Criminology and Penology* 4:285–294.

Sheley, J. F., and C. D. Ashkins. 1981. Crime, crime news, and crime views. *Public Opinion Quarterly* 45:492–506.

Surette, R. 1998. *Media, crime, and criminal justice: Images and realities,* 2nd ed. Belmont, CA: Wadsworth.

Vold, G. B. 1935. The amount and nature of crime. *American Journal of Sociology* 40:496–803.

Wright, E. O. 1973. *The politics of punishment.* New York: Harper Colophon. ✦

Section 1

Crime

Chapter 1
The Myth That Crime and Criminality Can Be Measured

Hal Pepinsky

The Myth

Chapters on defining and measuring crime are virtually universal to criminology and criminal justice texts. Since the early nineteenth century, expanding crime counts have been used to justify the expansion of the crime control industry and a global explosion in incarceration rates (Christie 2004; Pepinsky 1976). Today, in the United States, indicators of whether we are in greater or lesser social danger are increasingly consolidated in national justice department reports; specifically, in the Bureau of Justice Statistics reports (*http://www.ojp.usdoj.gov/bjs*).

Somehow the idea took hold that the proper authorities and their advisers could take counts and determine how safe or dangerous communities might be. Crime counts in Europe and in the United States began in the early nineteenth century with two primary counts: Crime was first counted as officially recorded convictions, and criminality was first measured as differences between prisoners and others. As of World War II, adults in the United States were already self-reporting near-unanimous, repeated law violations on questionnaires. However, after the U.S.

Department of Justice took over national crime victim surveys in the mid-1970s, the number of crimes reported by victims consistently dropped, even during times when police reported increases in crime, especially in violent crime. This is ironic because, when they were commissioned, the first national victim surveys showed, in a narrow range of legal categories, that much more crime was being committed than appeared in official police reports.

In the United States during the mid-1970s, incarcerated populations started to grow to the point where a country with about 1/25th of the world's population records holding one-quarter of the entire world's prisoners on any given day (see Pepinsky 1976, for a history of crime counting). Those who opposed this trend in U.S. punitiveness argued that too many people were incarcerated at a time when victim surveys showed that crime was declining. On the other hand, those who championed the value of incarcerating and otherwise punishing more offenders interpreted the data to indicate that retribution against offenders was successful. When crime goes up because crime rates rise, or criminality expands as measured by arrests, the prevailing conclusion is that criminals are not being punished hard enough. The measurement of crime and criminality in the United States, that is now largely centralized in the Bureau of Justice Statistics, becomes an advertisement for the growth of law-and-order whether crime and criminality indices rise or fall in the process.

At the same time, myths about the differences between criminals and law-abiders perpetuate the typology that initially emerged when characteristics of prisoners were first identified in criminological literature: criminals are poor. In the United States and other areas dominated by the European legacy of crime

3

counting, violent criminality is believed to be especially concentrated among poor young men of color, both as victims and as offenders.

The latest Bureau of Justice Statistics (BJS) results provide facts and figures across an array of issues, from characteristics of prisoners (including whether they were under the influence of drugs when they were caught and what age they were when they were arrested), to broader crime trends, and to the most serious trend—homicide. The front page of the December 1, 2003, BJS report, *Homicide Trends in the U.S.*, reads as follows:

> The homicide rate doubled from the mid-1960s to the late 1970s. In 1980, it peaked at 10.2 per 100,000 population and subsequently fell off to 7.9 per 100,000 in 1985. It rose again in the late 1980s and early 1990s to another peak in 1991 of 9.8 per 100,000. Since then, the rate has declined sharply, reaching 5.5 per 100,000 by 2000. Blacks are disproportionately represented in both homicide victims and offenders. Males represent three-quarters of homicide victims and nearly ninety percent of offenders. Approximately one-third of murder victims and almost half the offenders are under the age of 25.

This passage illustrates the myth of measuring crime: Crime and criminality counts confirm that the categories of people we imprison—notably young dispossessed people—are the kind of people who need to be held down hardest to preserve what there is of social order. Globally, the biggest myth of all in criminology is that poverty causes crime, mostly among those who have already been caught and punished for crime. The dominant science of counting crime and criminality shows, with sharper focus and more refinement,

who the dangerous classes are so that they can become the targets of efforts to remove them from society.

The Kernel of Truth

If effort alone counted, we would be far closer to knowing the size and direction of crime and criminality problems than we were two centuries ago. For instance, once telephone and personal interviews yielded more crimes than were reported by law enforcement agencies in pilot studies for the President's Commission on Law Enforcement and Administration of Justice, the Department of Justice began conducting a national crime victim survey on an annual basis that today is one of the major projects of the Bureau of Justice Statistics. Elaborate efforts were made to refine questions, to train and monitor interviewers, and to clean data to ensure interview reliability. Yet, the Bureau of Justice Statistics acknowledges and wrestles with contradictions among data sets as no government agency has before. One major contradiction is that, since the advent of national crime victim surveys in 1974, rates of crime, according to the surveys, have generally and steadily dropped; while during several periods, police-recorded crime rates have increased. Given these contradictory results, Bureau of Justice Statistics analysts have carefully attempted to determine which counts are closer to the truth.

The same is true of criminologists who do not trust official crime counts which purportedly show who the real criminals are (and by extension and contrast, who is really law-abiding and hence, presumably, an asset rather than a threat to social order). Clearly, many people commit offenses and are not caught. The bias created by counting only those who get caught inflates the crime counts of lower-class people. Self-report crime surveys have attempted to correct for this bias; however, confessing to offenses is embarrassing. To get people to confess as freely as possible, seemingly nonjudgmental ways of asking people to confess have to be used, such as asking: "Have you ever taken something worth more than $5 or $10 that did not belong to you?" This is presumably better than asking a survey respondent whether she or he is a thief.

More recently, the results of self-report crime surveys tend to mirror official crime counts. For example, students who report disobeying their parents and check off more offense categories are those who most frequently get into trouble at school and with the legal system. These data confirm what police crime counts have always shown, that the class of teenagers who self-report having committed the most crime, especially serious crime, and who are institutionalized and officially labeled *delinquent*, are from the same class as the biggest social troublemakers described in previous criminological literature. The kernel of truth is that criminologists using sophisticated research methodologies continue to find that poor, young, people of color—mostly men, but women in increasing numbers—commit the most crimes and especially the most serious crimes.

The Truth or Facts

The truth is that most crime, and most violence, still goes unrecognized and uncounted, which distorts the picture of what offenders are really like. For the Ph.D. dissertation in sociology I finished in 1972, I rode with police patrol officers in a reputed high-crime neighborhood of Minneapolis to see how, in response to calls for service, officers decided whether or not to file crime reports. At the time,

police crime reports were the only nationally available basis for measuring crime rates and trends. I found that whether officers reported offenses depended overwhelmingly on whether dispatchers named offenses or not (e.g., "check a burglary" versus "see a party at . . . "). When dispatchers named no offenses in calls for service, the officers never reported offenses, even when they confronted evidence similar to that which they had cited in other offense reports.

I later participated in a study of 30 years of police-reported crime trends in Indianapolis (1948–1978), and studied 10 years of police-recorded crime trends in Sheffield, England (1973–1983). Based on these findings, I called for a moratorium on crime counting (Pepinsky 1987; see also Pepinsky 2001, chapter 1). To me, then and now, the only thing that could be shown to explain crime and criminality trends was shifts of behavior among those who collected and coded crime and criminality reports. Although examples used here are about crime and criminality counting in the United States, my British field experience supports an argument that changes in police mobilization affect crime trends in parallel ways worldwide.

Currently, there are essentially four sources of crime data. Police, via the Federal Bureau of Investigation, control two of the four primary data sources: "crimes known to the police," which refers to crimes both reported to and officially recorded by the police, and data on who is arrested. The U.S. Department of Justice, of which the FBI is a part, also oversees the Bureau of Justice Statistics, which manages the third source of primary crime data: the National Crime Victimization Survey (NCVS). The fourth source of crime data is the self-report crime survey, which was discussed previously. Following are some of the ways each of these sources of crime data, alone and in combination, distorts what the public believes about crime and criminality.

A problem with determining whether crime and criminality are increasing or decreasing is illustrated by a recurrent way crime trends known to the police interact with arrest trends. When arrests go up, police-recorded crime (i.e., "crimes known to the police"), frequently goes down. This is a result of the organizational dynamics of crime recording. I found this to be true both in Sheffield and in the United States. Internally, an arrest report counts as much as a crime report as evidence of an officer's crime-fighting activity. So, when police arrest people for public-order offenses (which account for most police arrests), felonies, or even for "technical violations" of parole or probation, their arrests go up. Officers take as much time to fill out arrest or violation reports as they do crime reports, and when aggressive public-order maintenance is in political favor, arrests go up.

Arrest trends generally go in the opposite direction from police-recorded crime trends. For example, during waves of proactive policing—such as when police focus on clearing apparently homeless people off city streets—gaps in responding to citizen complaints become more obvious. As public outcry over the failure of police to respond seriously to citizen complaints rises, police are pressed to take more crime reports. The more time they spend in these responses to citizen complaints, the less time they spend in public-order enforcement. Therefore, as police-recorded crime rates on the whole go up, arrests go down. When arrests increase, crime reports tend to drop.

As for the national crime victimization surveys, which were first conducted by the BJS in 1973, there was a general rise in national trend figures between 1973 and 1974; and on the whole, the rates of reported victimization have fairly consistently dropped since. The initial increase in the victimization rates may have been partly due to the novelty of the surveys for interviewers and respondents, and the subsequent drop in the rates may have been partly due to the survey having lost its novelty. After all, each time an interviewer records that an informant has reported a victimization, pages of details regarding the offense and its effects are added to the interview. As with declines in police time and enthusiasm for writing offense reports, it only takes a marginal decrease in propensity to fill out reports to lead to a decline of several percentage points in overall reporting rates. This may help explain why rates of victim reporting have fallen steadily for three decades, with scattered exceptions.

Offenses known to the police and victim survey reports often concern crimes in which offenders are unknown. They, therefore, are seldom used to describe criminals, although victim survey respondents who report having been robbed, raped, or assaulted are asked for some perceptions of their alleged offenders, such as whether the offenders seemed to be under the influence of alcohol or drugs. The most common official counts of trends in offender populations are, literally, trends in arrest rates. So, for example, data on the age of persons arrested is used to infer the modal age of offenders, and trends in juvenile arrests are reported as trends in juvenile crime. However, these data reveal more about police behavior—about the behavior of those who are making the arrests—than it does about who is actually committing crimes. Who gets arrested is a function of where and how police find people to arrest. Recall, for instance, the recurring pattern that as police pull back from arrests that are mostly for public order offenses, they devote more attention to complaints received in calls for service and, hence, report rising crime. This often follows criticism that police are not responsive enough to calls for service. Then, when crime rates rise and arrests fall, police are criticized for lagging behind in solving and fighting crime, and a period of increased arrests and dropping offense rates follows. I call this a roller-coaster effect in the politics of police crime reporting.

Researchers also persist in using data on who is convicted or incarcerated to estimate characteristics of offenders. This assumes that those who get in trouble with the law are an unbiased sample of criminals from the larger populace. Obviously, though, getting caught breaking the law (or for that matter, getting in legal trouble even when innocent) is a function of where and how police look for criminality. For instance, young or apparently intoxicated people hanging out on inner-city streets are more likely to get caught than older people committing crimes in corporate suites or in single-family dwellings in wealthy suburbs. Just as crime victim surveys are designed to tap "the dark figure" of crimes not recorded by the police, so self-report crime surveys are designed to tap unrecorded criminality.

The number of crimes reported and the proportion of people reporting their own criminality rises dramatically in self-report crime surveys from what is found in arrest data and other official crime data. Currently, self-report crime data are largely collected from schoolchildren and address limited categories of offenses, such as those found in national surveys of illicit drug and alcohol use. The main problem with these data is with the validity of responses. Attempts are made to check the validity, for example, by comparing who reports offenses to who gets in

trouble in school or with the law. As I try to interpret these results, I imagine myself a respondent, filling out a questionnaire for researchers I do not know. If I am someone who commonly gets in trouble with adults, I may be more willing than other respondents to admit to what I have done, and may even tease researchers (as I might be angry enough to do with all adult authority figures) by exaggerating how bad I am. If I am invested with the image of being the obedient child and good student, I may be marginally more reluctant to recall and admit to illicit activity. Or if I am being asked how much I use drugs at a time when drug enforcement and intolerance in my school environment has increased, I may be more reluctant to admit drug use to anyone. Self-report crime researchers presume that because respondents do not know them, respondents have no stake in hiding or lying about what they have done. Likewise, it seems to me, respondents have no particular stake in telling the truth or in recalling accurately what they have or have not done to strangers.

Some criminologists have argued that, for all we may not know about crime and criminality, we at least have pretty good counts on murder. I am not so sure. Police-recorded murders began dropping dramatically in New York City when a new recording system called "CompStat" was initiated. Under this system, precinct commanders had to account weekly for crime counts, and were told they were subject to replacement if their precinct figures did not show steady declines, especially for serious crimes like murder. Notably, the first year, murder reports fell by around 20 percent and suicide reports increased by more than 40 percent (see Pepinsky 2001, chapter 1).

Within FBI instructions for recording homicide, there is plenty of room for discretion as to whether to report human deaths as crimes. There may be ambiguity about whether a death is natural, accidental, suicidal, or homicidal. For instance, when a body of a homeless person is found on the streets, or when a crib death is reported, policy and practice may change as to whether an autopsy is ordered or the possibility of homicide is considered. Under FBI rules, the death of someone killed while committing a felony is not reportable as criminal homicide, which might be applied to someone found to have died while using an illegal drug. Also not reportable as criminal homicide is killing deemed justifiable or excusable. All this presumes that police are honestly and literally following FBI reporting rules, which is questionable considering that the external training in and monitoring of each law-enforcement agency's bookkeeping is minimal.

The point is that no one has a way of getting at the truth of whether crime and personal violence are really increasing or decreasing, let alone of being able to profile those who most often rape and kill. Crime and criminality counters only touch briefly on people's lives. Their reports often show their inability to get strangers to disclose crime and violence that is most deeply personal, scary, and shameful. The more personal crime and violence become, the less likely we are to know about them. Most rape and much, if not most, murder is probably not reported.

Interests Served by the Myth

In 1986, while doing research on Norwegian incarceration trends, I discovered that as of 1840, Norway had an incarceration rate as high as that in the United States in 1960, which at the time was at a record high for the country. By the end of the nineteenth century, incarceration rates in Norway had dropped by more than two-thirds to approximately the same rate as today—among the world's lowest. A generation before 1840, Norway had sent combat troops abroad for the last time. That is, a generation after Norwegians gave up foreign combat, they turned away from a form of civil war—their own war on crime.

Then, examining U.S. incarceration trends, I noticed that, since the mid-nineteenth century, the only periods in which incarceration rates leveled off or dropped where when the United States had major forces engaged in overt combat, beginning with the Civil War and ending with the war in Vietnam. Over time, people in the United States have become more warlike, and foreign wars have become the only relief we have had from mounting bigger and wider domestic wars on crime (see Pepinsky 2001). The crime control industry (Christie 2000) increased rapidly in the United States when the Soviet Union, U.S. public enemy number one, collapsed. Interestingly, now, when the United States has more than 100,000 troops engaged in combat in Iraq and in Afghanistan, some state incarceration rates are beginning to drop, and legislatures and even the U.S. Supreme Court are talking about cutting back on mandatory sentencing and extending sentence length. As spending on foreign military operations increases, state and local governments feel the federal budget decreasing dramatically, and suddenly, even conservative legislators begin to think they cannot afford such a heavy criminal justice burden. So, perhaps, we are seeing the beginning of another break in the growth of the criminal justice–industrial complex.

One can point to various agencies and interest groups for fueling the war on crime, but the problem appears to be bigger than any single group of criminal justice entrepreneurs. "Growth" has become a global imperative. The presumption is especially strong in the heart of the global military empire, the United States, that growth is good—growth in consumption, organization, and expansion. Why should it be any different for a police force, a prosecutor, or a community corrections program—public or private?

Moreover, in a militarized society such as the United States, politicians tend to hang onto their jobs by creating public enemies and by appealing for popular unity against threats to public security. Being tough on foreign enemies and tough on crime is a proven path to political success. Keep the people scared, mobilize them to war, and they will stand behind their leaders.

A Norwegian friend, who was visiting the United States as the 1991 Gulf War broke out, observed that if the Norwegian prime minister ever talked about Norwegian national greatness—about Norway being number one—Norwegians would rapidly force him or her out of office as a threat to national security, raising the specter of the national militarism that led the Germans to occupy Norway during World War II. Or take the case of South Africa, emerging from apartheid, where the national intelligence service has been dismantled and the concept of terrorism is seen as laughable because the two postapartheid presidents and many of their fellows in the African National Congress were once the apartheid government's "terrorists." The implication seems to be that wars on domestic enemies can only abate during major foreign wars unless the political culture tires of war altogether, unless and until militarism itself comes to be seen by the body politic as a national danger, rather than as a source of national security.

Policy Implications of Belief in the Myth

On its face, the war on crime and criminality is immoral. Reiman (2003) is the most widely known scholar arguing the thesis that "The Rich Get Richer and the Poor Get Prison." It is not only that the amounts stolen and the lives taken and maimed in white-collar and state crime (crimes committed by government agents) are believed to far outweigh the toll taken by the street criminals most often punished. We are also coming to a realization that the greatest threat to life and limb is domestic violence against women and children, which for all we know is as rampant among families of means as it is among the poor. Even though enforcement is almost entirely directed against poor young offenders, we are beginning, grudgingly, to recognize how commonplace violence against children is among professionals, such as priests. Meanwhile, as we near having one out of every thousand U.S. inhabitants in jail or prison each day, about one in ten young men of color is spending the day there, and the dramatic increase in incarceration of women is largely composed of young women of color incarcerated for drug offenses. Circumstances have not changed since Korn (1971) observed that the norm in responding to white-collar offenses is to settle them privately or informally, and that violence among persons of means is normally, and legally, invisible.

Since crime and criminality cannot accurately be measured, there is no way to know whether people have become safer from violence and predation as the U.S. war on crime has escalated; but, it is easy to see that over the past three decades, people have become more concerned about the danger of crime and are investing more in protecting themselves against it—e.g., locking their homes, offices, and cars more religiously and more securely, paying more for public and private security, and having more invasive surveillance, security screening, and drug testing. People are constantly admonished to be vigilant against the threat of random attacks. No amount of reporting of decreases in crime rates seems to slow the political trend of getting tougher on criminals and actual, or potential, enemies. And because wars on crime often focus on politically convenient offenders, the great bulk of the risk we suffer of being victimized goes unrecognized and unaddressed. In the process, gaps between the rich and the poor—between the powerful and the weaker members of society—grow larger. Those who are targeted by law enforcement become more marginalized; and those whose wealth and privilege grow also become less secure, demanding even more protection and advantage to hold their positions.

The problem is that monitoring and controlling the crime and criminality we count puts the focus on identifying problem individuals instead of identifying problems in human relations. The problem of human relations that threatens the security of the rich and poor alike, is the problem of relying on violence to "solve" human problems. When we go after criminals, we use violence to respond to violence. The law of *lex talionis*, popularly known as the law of an eye for an eye, was an early recognition of this problem. When, for instance, someone violated a member of another family, it might have been normal for that family to retaliate, in escalating cycles of violence and vengeance. *Lex talionis* prescribes that those

who retaliate for violence should take no more than an eye for an eye, so that the cycle of violence and vengeance might end instead of becoming an enduring and bloody feud. Essentially, the challenge of transforming violent or predatory relations into safe and secure social relations is transforming contests of might into cooperative, democratic relationships of mutual respect and dignity. In the realm of criminal justice, much of the recent attempt to achieve this transformation has come under the heading of *restorative justice*—holding mediation sessions among offenders, victims, and community members to work out arrangements for offender safety and restitution to victims, and for offenders to make amends and establish safe, trustworthy community ties in the wake of violence and predation. This can be seen as part of a larger social movement to turn hierarchical human relationships into cooperative, democratic relationships, such as between parents and children, teachers and students, employees and their managers, and former colonizers and their subjects (Sullivan and Tifft 2001). It is not so much a matter of knowing how to build peace in the face of violence, as it is a matter of letting go of the conviction that right has to be made with sheer might. When attention turns from identifying, isolating, and subduing offenders and other public enemies to working out democratic mechanisms for redressing violence and predation, we all become safer; and our compulsion to identify and measure crime and criminality loses its grip on our criminological imagination.

References

Bureau of Justice Statistics (BJS). 2003. *Homicide Trends in the United States*. Washington, DC: Government Printing Office.

Christie, N. 2000. *Crime control as industry.* 3rd ed. London/New York: Routledge.

———. 2004. *A suitable amount of crime.* London/New York: Routledge.

Korn, R. 1971. Of crime, criminal justice, and corrections. *San Francisco Law Review* 6:27–75.

Pepinsky, H. E. 1976. The growth of crime in the United States. *Annals of the American Academy of Political and Social Science* 423:23–30.

———. 1987. Explaining police recorded trends in crime in Sheffield. *Contemporary Crises* 11: 59–73.

———. 2001. A criminologist's quest for peace. Website of the Critical Criminology Division of the American Society of Criminology and the Academy of Criminal Justice Sciences, *http://www.critcrim.org/critpapers/pepinsky-book.htm.*

Reiman, J. 2003. *The rich get richer and the poor get prison: Ideology, class, and criminal justice.* 7th ed. New York: Pearson, Allyn and Bacon.

Sullivan, D., and L. Tifft. 2001. *Restorative justice: Healing the foundations of our everyday lives.* Monsey, NY: Criminal Justice Press. ✦

Chapter 2
The Myth That Mental Illness Causes Crime

*Jennifer L. Bullock and
Bruce A. Arrigo*

The stereotype of the dangerous mentally ill person is pervasive in American society. Some of the most popular entertainment media feature this stereotype. Movies such as *The Silence of the Lambs, Psycho,* and *Slingblade* depict frightening images of fictitious "mental patients" committing violent acts, and do a great deal to reinforce the notion that the mentally ill are dangerous. Researchers (Monahan and Arnold 1996; Torrey 1994) who have conducted content analyses of television dramas and print media have found that characters with mental illness are much more likely to be portrayed as violent than characters who are not mentally ill. Newspapers regularly report terrible and even bizarre crimes committed by people who were later identified as suffering from a mental illness or who declared that they were "insane" (a legal term, not a psychiatric diagnosis) when they committed the crime. Occasionally, these crimes are so infamous that they dominate national news, such as the case of Andrea Yates, who drowned her children in the bathtub in her home in Texas, or John Hinckley, who was acquitted by reason of insanity for his attempt to assassinate then-President Reagan.

After being confronted with so much media exposure, it is no wonder the public believes that people with mental illness are more dangerous than "normal" people. Public opinion research confirms that this belief is widely held among the general public. A poll conducted by the Field Institute in 1984, for example, found that almost two-thirds of respondents probably or definitely agreed that people who were diagnosed with schizophrenia were more likely to commit a crime than a normal person (Monahan and Arnold 1996). Another poll, conducted by the DYG Corporation for the Robert Wood Johnson Foundation Program on Chronic Mental Illness in 1996, found that 24 percent of its respondents agreed with the statement, "People with chronic mental illness are, by far, more dangerous than the general population" (Monahan and Arnold 1996). Finally, in a poll conducted by Mark Clements Research in 1993, 57 percent of respondents answered "yes" to the question, "Do you think the mentally ill are more likely to commit acts of violence?" (Monahan and Arnold 1996).

It seems as though we are repeatedly confronted with evidence that mental illness is strongly linked to violence. The reality is that the perception that mental illness causes violent crime is largely a myth.

The Myth

The prevalent belief in American society that people with mental illness are more likely to commit acts of criminal violence than other people is a belief that has, for the most part, been uncritically accepted by the public. In addition, the acceptance of this belief serves to support existing practices. This is an important point that will be discussed later in this chapter. For now, it is sufficient to point out that the uncritically accepted belief that the mentally ill are dangerous as a group is inaccurate, and it is incorrect to patently assert that persons with psychiatric disorders are more dangerous than their nonmentally ill counterparts (Arrigo 2006). The reality is that most people with mental illness are not violent, and most people who are violent are not mentally ill (APA 1998). The myth that mental illness causes violent crime, however, is not totally false, either. Like many myths, it contains some kernel of truth that may have led to its acceptance in the first place.

The Kernel of Truth

At one time, advocates for people with mental illness maintained that there was no more than a chance association between mental illness and violence (Monahan 1992; Monahan and Arnold 1996). At the time, no empirical evidence existed to the contrary, and it was believed that people with mental illness were no more likely to be violent than people in the general population. Research conducted in the 1990s on the relationship between mental illness and violence, however, is superior methodologically to past research. This new research has identified a modest but consistent relationship between violence and mental disorder (APA 1998; Link, Andrews, and Cullen 1992; Monahan 1992; Mulvey 1994; Swanson et al. 1990). The increased risk of violence associated with mental disorders is small, however, and is attributable to the presence of certain active symptoms or conditions, such as active symptoms of psychosis (APA 1998; Link, Andrews, and Cullen 1992; Mulvey 1994; Torrey 1994) or neurological impairment (APA 1998; Torrey 1994). Also, substance abuse has been shown to significantly increase the risk of violence among people with mental disorders, just as it has been shown to increase the risk of violence among members of the general population (Arrigo 2006; APA 1998; Mulvey 1994; Torrey 1994).

The Truth or Facts

Several pieces of research have increased our understanding about the nature of the relationship between mental illness and violent behavior. One study by Swanson and his colleagues (1990) used data from the Epidemiologic Catchment Area (ECA) survey to examine the relationship between violence and psychiatric disorders among adults living in the community. The Epidemiologic Catchment Area survey, conducted by the National Institute of Mental Health, is a large community study of psychiatric disorders in the United States. The ECA focuses on an assessment of randomly selected community residents. In the study by Swanson and his colleagues, data on 10,000 respondents from three surveyed communities (Baltimore, Raleigh-Durham, and Los Angeles) were used to examine (1) whether psychiatric disorders increase the risk of assaultive behavior; (2) whether people in the community with untreated mental illness and those seen in treatment settings are equally prone to violence; (3) the relative probabilities of violence being associated with specific disorders; and (4) whether the connection between violence and mental illness is conditioned by other variables, such as socioeconomic status. Diagnoses examined in this study included schizophrenia, major depression, mania or bipolar disorder, alcohol abuse or dependence, drug abuse or dependence, obsessive-compulsive disorder, panic disorder, and phobia. Five items from the Diagnostic Interview Schedule (DIS) were used to assess violence, including: (1) Did you ever hit or throw things at your wife/husband/partner? (2) Have you ever spanked or hit a child hard enough so that he or she had bruises or had to stay in bed or see a doctor? (3) Since age 18, have you been in more than one fight that came to swapping blows, other than fights with your husband/wife/partner? (4) Have you ever used a weapon like a stick, knife, or gun in a fight since you were 18? (5) Have you ever gotten into physical fights while drinking? Respondents were counted as violent if they endorsed at least one of these items and said that the behavior occurred during the 12 months preceding the interview.

The study found that individuals in the community with psychiatric disorders, as a whole, were more likely to engage in self-reported violence than those without mental illness or substance use. Substance abuse was the most prevalent diagnosis by far among those respondents who were violent. Affective (mood) disorders and schizophrenia or schizophreniform (symptom-like schizophrenia, especially including delusions and hallucinations) disorders were three times more common among respondents who were violent than respondents who were not. As would be expected, being young, male, and of lower socioeconomic status increased the risk of violence apart from psychiatric illness. The presence of more than one psychiatric problem increased rates of violence. The combination of substance abuse and major mental illness significantly increased the risk of violence.

Link, Andrews, and Cullen (1992) examined the limitations of earlier research comparing the arrest rates of psychiatric patients to the arrest rates of the general public. In this study, Link and his colleagues compared psychiatric patients with community residents who had never received psychiatric treatment for official and self-reported measures of violent and illegal conduct. They found that psychiatric patients had consistently higher rates of both official and self-reported violence and illegal behavior than a control group of community residents who had never received psychiatric treatment. Social variables such as age, sex, ethnicity, level of education, and living in a violent neighborhood were significantly related to violent and illegal behavior, but did not fully explain the association between psychiatric patient status and violence. It is important to note, however, that only those psychiatric patients who were experiencing current psychotic symptoms were found to have elevated rates of violence.

In their investigation on whether particular types of psychotic symptoms were more likely to be associated with violent behavior, Link and associates (1999) concluded that "threat/control-override" (TCO) delusions were strongly associated with violence among individuals suffering from major mental illness. TCO delusions are false beliefs that cause persons who suffer from them to believe others are threatening them or wish to harm them (threat), or that their minds are being influenced or controlled by some source outside themselves (control override). Link and his colleagues concluded that TCO symptoms play a key role in explaining the association between mental illness and violence because these symptoms influence how individuals suffering from them define their situation. Individuals who are suffering from these symptoms typically feel threatened, and people who feel threatened may be more prone to respond with violence. Still, Link and his colleagues noted that, even among individuals who experience high levels of TCO symptoms, only a minority of them engages in violence.

Although Link and associates (1999) found an elevated risk of violence associated with TCO symptoms, a second study by Appelbaum, Robbins, and Monahan (2000) found no significant differences in rates of violence between delusional and nondelusional patients. Additionally, no significant association was found between the presence of threat/control-override delusions and violence. Data for the study by Appelbaum and his colleagues (2000) were drawn from the MacArthur Violence Risk Assessment Study, a prospective, multisite study of violent behavior in recently discharged psychiatric inpatients. The authors compared their methodology with that of the previous study by Link and his associates (1992) in an attempt to explain why their findings differed. Appelbaum, Robbins, and Monahan (2000) suggested that previous studies relied on the subjects' self-report of threat/control-override delusions, while the present study probed subjects' responses to self-reports and examined other data—such as the patients' medical records—to determine whether the patients were actually delusional. In this manner, the later study eliminated a substantial number of subjects who were initially identified as delusional.

Another type of delusion that may be associated with violent behavior is the delusion of misidentification. Silva et al. (1992) identified several types of misidentification delusions. Capgras syndrome, or "the syndrome of doubles," causes the sufferer to believe a person, usually someone close, has been replaced psychologically by a physically identical imposter. Fregoli syndrome causes the sufferer to believe another person has changed his or her physical identity while his or her psychological identity remains the same. The syndrome of intermetamorphosis causes the sufferer to believe another person has undergone radical physical and psychological changes. The "syndrome of subjective doubles" causes the sufferer to believe there are one or more physical duplicates of the person, and that these duplicates are psychologically different from the self. Silva and his colleagues (1992) note that misidentification syndromes in general are associated with anger and suspiciousness toward the misidentified other. Hostility and paranoid ideation directed toward the misidentified object have the potential to lead to violence and have been associated with completed homicides.

In addition to examining the clinical factors that increase the risk of violence among people with serious mental illness, it is important to examine the social context in which such violence occurs. People with serious mental illness are frequently of lower socioeconomic status. They may live in impoverished neighborhoods with high crime rates, lack stable employment or other purposeful activity, live in relative social isolation, abuse drugs and alcohol, and are often visibly disabled and vulnerable (Silver 2001). Violence often occurs within the homes and neighborhoods of the disadvantaged communities where many chronically mentally ill people live. Given these circumstances, it is not surprising that people with serious mental illness, as a group, have higher lifetime rates of violent victimization than the general population (Hiday et al. 2001). The experience of victimization may in turn contribute to violent behavior. Recent research shows that victimized people may feel more threatened and engage in violence to protect themselves, or they may feel angry and engage in reactive violence. Hiday and her colleagues (2001), for example, studied a sample of people who were involuntarily hospitalized at a psychiatric institution and then placed in outpatient commitment (court-ordered outpatient psychiatric treatment). The study found that only substance abuse was a stronger predictor of violence than criminal victimization. Thus, among people with serious mental illness, substance abuse and a history of being a violent crime victim are strongly predictive of future violent behavior. Again, it is important to emphasize that most people who have these risk factors will not be violent.

This relationship, however, begs the question of whether victimization raises the probability of future violence, or violence raises the probability of future victimization. It may be that these variables are reciprocal. People with mental illness, like other people, are more likely to be violent toward people with whom they have regular contact (Hiday et al. 2001), such as relatives or caretakers. Additionally, many violent relationships involve mutual violence between people who are known to each other, and it is not always clear who is the aggressor and who is the victim. Violence by a person with serious mental illness is less likely to be inflicted on a stranger than on a person known to the perpetrator (APA 1998).

Estroff and her colleagues (1994) examined the social support networks of people with mental illness who had been violent, and found that the quality of the mentally ill person's relationships with other people in his or her social support network is an important factor to consider when assessing that individual's risk for violence (see also Shipley and Arrigo 2004). Mentally ill people who behaved violently perceived and experienced hostility in their relationships with others, and mentally ill people who made threats of violence felt threatened themselves. Estroff and associates (1994) found that mothers are at particularly high risk for becoming targets of repeated violence by their mentally ill adult children. This is because mothers frequently become the caretakers of their mentally ill children when they grow up.

The emotionally intimate nature of their relationship and close proximity to the person with mental illness fosters the social context in which the experience of perceived hostility is likely to occur. In the general population, spouses are far more likely to become victims of violence than are any other types of relatives, but people with severe and persistent mental illness tend not to marry, and for this reason may be more likely to direct their violence toward their parents or siblings (Estroff et al. 1994).

Interests Served by the Myth

Thus far we have identified the myth that mental illness causes criminal violence and explored the facts about mental illness and violence. We know that most people with mental illness are not violent, but that certain mental illnesses do pose a modest risk of violent behavior. This risk is associated only with the presence of active psychotic symptoms, and is significantly enhanced by substance abuse. Although we know that people with mental illness contribute only a small amount of violence to the overall level of violence in society, the myth that the mentally ill are dangerous is persistent and prevalent. It warrants examination, therefore, to determine whose interests are served by accepting and maintaining the myth that mental illness causes violent crime.

Despite declining rates of violent crime, people are surrounded by images of violence. Both television and newspapers routinely report such stories as a man who shot his boss, a woman who left her newborn baby to die, or a child who disappeared on the way home from school. Attributing societal violence to the mentally ill provides the community with an explanation they can understand, as well as a source of blame for the violence. Unfortunately, this view does nothing to solve the problem of societal violence or to protect the public, and it inflicts untold harm on people who suffer from mental illness.

Maintaining the myth that mental illness causes violent crime provides justification for discrimination against people with mental illness (Arrigo 2002; Perlin 2000). Institutionalized discrimination against the mentally ill is the traditional practice supported by the myth in this case. Discrimination against people with mental illness takes many forms. If people suffering from mental illness are presumed to be dangerous, it increases their existing state of isolation and reduces their already deficient social supports. Other people are likely to respond to them with fear or anger. Their displays of emotion are likely to be scrutinized. Employers may be reluctant to hire people who have received mental health treatment services. People may feel justified in criminally victimizing the mentally ill, who are already in a vulnerable position. Community groups may oppose the establishment in their neighborhoods of group homes or community treatment programs for people with mental illness. Thus, the myth of the dangerous mentally ill significantly influences how people informally respond to and interact with people who have mental illness.

Perlin (2000) characterizes these mistaken and discriminatory beliefs about people with mental illness in the context of "sanism" and "pretextuality." A preconceived commitment to what is sane (and what is not) establishes an institutional pretext by which behaviors are judged. There is evidence of this in a host of mental health law practices from determinations of competency to stand trial to the execution of the psychiatrically disordered. Arrigo (2002) argues that sanism and pretextuality represent unconscious

beliefs about punishing difference and privileging sameness that assume symbolic form. However, once spoken, these beliefs become institutionalized through clinical and legal decision-making practices taken de facto to be fair, inclusive, just, and equitable. In this way, the psycholegal community legitimizes, perpetuates, and reinforces its own ideological truths and circumscribed knowledge about the mentally ill.

Policy Implications of Belief in the Myth

Maintaining the myth of the dangerous mentally ill person has important legal and public policy implications as well. One ominous consequence of presuming that the mentally ill are dangerous is that coercive forms of social and ideological control seem justified (Williams and Arrigo 2002). Laws and policies regulating the control and treatment of people with mental illness include civil commitment laws, which allow a person to be confined in a psychiatric hospital against his or her will. In some cases, these laws allow the forced administration of psychotropic medication. Newer civil commitment laws allow outpatient commitment, which is a court order mandating that an individual attend outpatient appointments for treatment at a mental health center and comply with the recommended treatment plan. It is important to note that "dangerousness to others" is a prominent element in evaluating whether an individual meets the criteria for civil commitment. What is questionable is whether the presence of a mental disorder creates enough of a risk factor for violence to warrant special treatment under the law (Mulvey 1994). Civil commitment can amount to a form of preventive detention, in which an individual is confined for something he or she might do, rather than for something he or she has already done. This sort of coercive social control is a serious infringement on a person's civil liberties. It would not be tolerated if applied widely to the population as a whole, but it seems justifiable for the mentally ill as a class because they are presumed to be a threat to society.

A second important public policy stemming from the myth of dangerous mentally ill people is the "direct threat" exception to the employment protection afforded by the Americans with Disabilities Act (ADA). The ADA requires that people with disabilities, including mental disabilities, have equal access to employment and various government programs, services, and activities. Employers and programs may not, however, be required to provide access to individuals with mental disabilities, especially if the applicant is believed to pose a "direct threat" to the health or safety of others (Rubin and McCampbell 1995). The "direct threat" exception to the ADA is an example of a public policy that resulted from the commonly held belief that people with mental disorders are likely to pose a threat of violence to others.

In conclusion, endorsing the myth that people with mental illness are violent creates obstacles for the social acceptance and legal rights of people with mental illness as a class. Maintenance of the myth serves only to reinforce the stigma that people with mental illness and their families already endure. Monahan (1992) noted that there is a modest and limited relationship between mental illness and violence; however, this association need not have negative implications for mental health advocacy, mental health law, and the provision of mental health treatment. Despite the limited relationship between violence and mental disorder, the majority of people with mental illness are not vio-

lent. The risk of violence associated with mental disorder is small when compared to other risk factors such as male gender, young age, and lower socioeconomic status. Finally, it is important to remember that violence by people with mental disorders is grounded in a social context. When we respond to people with mental illness with fear, anger, and hostility, we are helping to create the kind of context in which violence is likely to occur. By taking the time to educate ourselves about mental illness, we can better understand our neighbors and act as communities to help care for our most vulnerable and different citizens.

References

American Psychiatric Association. 1998. Fact sheet: Violence and mental illness. January.

Appelbaum, P. S., P. C. Robbins, and J. Monahan. 2000. Violence and delusions: Data from the MacArthur Violence Risk Assessment Study. *American Journal of Psychiatry* 157:566–572.

Arrigo, B. A. 2002. *Punishing the mentally ill: A critical analysis of law and psychiatry.* Albany: State University of New York Press.

———. 2006. *Criminal behavior: A systems approach.* Upper Saddle River, NJ: Prentice Hall.

Estroff, S. E., C. Zimmer, W. S. Lachicotte, and J. Benoit. 1994. The influence of social networks and social support on violence by persons with serious mental illness. *Hospital and Community Psychiatry* 45(7):669–678.

Hiday, V. A., J. W. Swanson, M. S. Swartz, R. Borum, H. R. Wagner. 2001. Victimization: A link between mental illness and violence? *International Journal of Law and Psychiatry* 24(6):559–572.

Link, B. G., H. Andrews, F. T. Cullen. 1992. The violent and illegal behavior of mental patients reconsidered. *American Sociological Review* 57:275–292.

Link, B., J. Monahan, A. Stueve, and F. Cullen. 1999. Real in the consequences: A sociological approach to understanding the association between psychotic symptoms and violence. *American Sociological Review* 64:316–331.

Monahan, J. 1992. Mental disorder and violent behavior: Perceptions and evidence. *American Psychologist* 47:511–521.

Monahan, J., and J. Arnold. 1996. Violence by people with mental illness: A consensus statement by advocates and researchers. *Psychiatric Rehabilitation Journal* 19(4):67–70.

Mulvey, E. P. 1994. Assessing the evidence of a link between mental illness and violence. *Hospital and Community Psychiatry* 45(7):663–668.

Perlin, M. L. 2000. *The hidden prejudice: Mental disability on trial.* Washington, DC: American Psychological Association.

Rubin, P. N., and S. W. McCampbell. 1995. The Americans with Disabilities Act and criminal justice: Mental disabilities and corrections. *Research in Action* July NCJ 155061.

Shipley, S. L., and B. A. Arrigo. 2004. *The female homicide offender: Serial murder and the case of Aileen Wuornos.* Upper Saddle River, NJ: Prentice Hall.

Silva, J. A., K. K. Sharma, G. B. Leong, and R. Weinstock. 1992. Dangerousness of the delusional misidentification of children. *Journal of Forensic Sciences* 37:830–838.

Silver, E. 2001. *Violence and mental illness: The importance of neighborhood context.* New York: LFB Scholarly Publishers.

Swanson, J. W., C. E. Holzer, V. J. Ganju, and R. T. Jono. 1990. Violence and psychiatric disorder in the community: Evidence from the epidemiologic catchment area surveys. *Hospital and Community Psychiatry* 46:761–770.

Torrey, E. F. 1994. Violent behavior by individuals with serious mental illness. *Hospital and Community Psychiatry* 45(7):653–662.

Williams, C. R., and B. A. Arrigo. 2002. *Law, psychology, and justice: Chaos theory and the new (dis)order.* Albany: State University of New York Press. ✦

Chapter 3
The Myth That White-Collar Crime Is Only About Financial Loss

David O. Friedrichs

The Myth

The fear of crime has been a persistent theme of American social life for many decades, having intensified significantly from the 1970s on. It is especially pronounced for Americans who live in an urban setting. This fear is focused most strongly on crimes of interpersonal violence, such as murder, rape, and assault (Beckett 1997:82). Glassner (2000) observed that people often fear most those events that are least likely to happen. People are far more likely to be physically injured by using a lawnmower than by the actions of a terrorist, but people are also far more likely to fear terrorists than lawnmowers. And people are generally more fearful of a stranger lurking in an alleyway than of corporate executives operating out of office buildings, but the decisions of such executives may have more negative consequences than do the actions of conventional offenders.

Perceptions of violence and fear are often shaped by the media. Conventional forms of violence are pervasively featured in film, television, newspapers, and most other media (Surette 1998). The public has been socialized to think of violent crime principally in terms of either individual offenders or a small group of offenders (e.g., a gang); violent crimes are disproportionately associated with deranged or manifestly evil offenders, and are most readily thought of in terms of murder, rape, or felonious assault. Overall, it has been easier to portray the crimes of individual psychopaths than those of corporations, and such crime makes for much more colorful copy than corporate crime. When the media expose unsafe, harmful, and destructive activities of corporations, they risk, as well, losing advertising revenue from such corporations; this is only one of the more obvious reasons why the media focus on conventional violence.

Powerful entities in society all too often have been able to shield themselves in various ways from being labeled criminals. The term "crime" itself has been defined in quite different ways (Henry and Lanier 2001); but many of the activities of powerful entities, including corporations, can legitimately be characterized as criminal by virtue of violations of international law, human rights protocols, or laws of the state itself. More broadly, the activities of these powerful entities have demonstrably harmful effects that are avoidable, and in this sense alone should be defined as criminal.

Criminologists, as well, have devoted most of their attention to conventional forms of crime and violence. In part, this reflects their own professional socialization; that is, they have been largely educated to think of crime and violence in conventional terms. In part, it reflects the fact that funding for research has been available principally, if not exclusively, to sponsor research on conventional forms of crime and violence (Simpson 2003).

Perhaps as well, the relative lack of criminological attention to the crimes of wealthy and powerful corporations reflects the greater complexity of their crimes. That said, the number of criminologists studying some form of white-collar crime has grown in recent times.

The Kernel of Truth

White-collar crime is driven mainly by financial considerations. The pursuit of illegal financial gain, or law breaking to minimize or avoid financial losses, is a central defining element of the most widely recognized forms of white-collar crime (Helmkamp, Ball, and Townsend 1996). Such crime typically is viewed as driven by rational calculation, not by emotions or irrational factors. It is true that white-collar crime, as typically defined, does not include physical harm to human beings as an intentional objective. Nevertheless, as shall be documented in this chapter, an immense amount of physical harm—and violence on many different levels—is one of the major consequences of corporate crime, and occupational crime as well.

If white-collar crime has focused principally on extending financial advantage or minimizing financial loss, the scope of financial losses that result is immense, and dwarfs the size of such losses as a consequence of conventional crime, however those losses are measured. It is difficult to measure accurately the financial losses due to any form of crime, and the difficulties are compounded in the case of white-collar crime. It has been estimated that economic losses due to white-collar crime, broadly defined, may exceed $1 trillion annually in the United States alone (Schlegel 2000). Losses to workers and investors as a consequence of the collapse of Enron were estimated at up to $50 billion (Greider 2002). By even the most conservative estimates, the annual financial losses due to white-collar crimes are in the hundreds of billions of dollars. Any such estimation dwarfs financial losses attributable to conventional forms of property crime.

White-collar crime differs from conventional crime in a number of important dimensions (Friedrichs 2004). The perpetrators are more likely to be middle class or wealthy, and some of the perpetrators are exceedingly wealthy. While it is true that a certain proportion of white-collar offenses—e.g., some employee thefts, or frauds—are committed by individuals of modest means, and some murderers and rapists—and even burglars—are privileged members of society, the proportional representations differ greatly. White-collar crime is also distinctive because much of the most consequential crime is committed on behalf of, and by means of the resources available to, an organization (e.g., a corporation). While some proportion of conventional crime is committed by "organizations" in the form of gangs or mobs, conventional crime is more likely to be an individual enterprise, or carried out with one or more partners. It is because corporate crime is carried out on behalf of an entity with vast resources that its consequences can be so widespread and substantial.

The Truth or Facts

The recognition that corporations cause great physical harm to people is hardly new. In the late nineteenth century, for example, Engels ([1895] 1958) claimed that factory owners engaged in murder because they were aware that the working conditions in their factories would kill some of their workers. They did not specifically intend to kill their workers, and probably hoped workers would not die in their factories; but this was still murder in Engels' view. The premature deaths were a function of the owners' privileging of profit over the health and lives of their workers.

Parallel claims can be advanced about contemporary corporations. It is certainly true that corporations today no longer kill people—be they citizens, consumers, or workers—on the same scale they did in the nineteenth century. Throughout the twentieth century, in particular, a series of laws were adopted, and regulatory regimes were established, to enforce on corporations attention to health and safety concerns. These endeavors came about principally in response to the exposé of corporate practices by muckrakers, widespread public outrage, the efforts of labor unions, the establishment of environmentalist and consumer groups, and other such forces. For the most part, tougher safety and health standards were imposed involuntarily on corporations. Corporations throughout much of the twentieth century strongly resisted these initiatives, at least in cases where they seemed to threaten profits. Corporations have only been amenable to adopting higher standards and safety measures when they identified a competitive advantage to doing so. In the latter part of the twentieth century, there was often an almost comical spectacle of corporations trumpeting the safety features of their products—e.g., automobile seat belts—they had long resisted adopting and only adopted under pressure.

It is common for corporations to cut corners on safety and health concerns to maximize profits. When claims of harm begin to surface—for example, that a significant number of people are dying unnecessarily due to unsafe drugs, or unsafe tires—the corporation attempts to conceal this information or "stonewall" the claims. Corporations have often made the conscious choice to address claims of harm and injury within the context of civil lawsuits, ideally by offering legitimate claimants out-of-court settlements, conditioned upon their silence about the terms of the settlement, rather than acknowledge the harm inherent in their practices, product design, or workplace conditions. This choice is based on the calculation that it will be less costly to the corporation to settle claims or address civil lawsuits than to modify practices, products, or conditions.

Despite the safety measures adopted in the recent era, corporate activities continue to lead to significant injuries, enduring health problems, and premature or traumatic death. By some estimates, more than 30,000 Americans die annually from work-related diseases and accidents, and nearly 3 million workers suffer other significant physical harm in the workplace (Reiman 2004). If one accepts such estimates, the American labor force is more vulnerable to injury from corporations than from conventional offenders, with much of the injury being avoidable. In one case, Manville and other corporations exposed their workers to asbestos for decades, although they knew this exposure had devastating consequences for the health and life span of these workers (Brodeur 1985; Labaton 2000). An investigative report in 2003 on McWane, Inc., revealed that it was one of the most dangerous employers in America (Barstow and Berman 2003a; 2003b). In the previous seven years, nine workers had been killed in McWane foundries, and at least 4,600 were injured, often seriously. Some industries—such as mining—have especially high mortality rates due to occupational trauma. Conditions in "sweatshops" operated by American multinationals in developing countries, with a disproportionately large number of women and children as workers, are especially likely to be unsafe (Wonders and Danner 2002). Criminal prosecutions for exposing workers to dangerous conditions are rare.

Consumers in large numbers have also been injured or killed by decisions made by corporate executives. Tens of thousands of Americans are alleged to die annually from product-related accidents, and millions more suffer disabling injuries. Food products (e.g., unsafe meat), pharmaceutical products (e.g., unsafe drugs such as Thalidomide and unsafe devices such as the Dalkon Shield), and transportation products (e.g., unsafe cars, such as the Ford Pinto, and unsafe tires, such as Firestone radials), are among the most well-documented examples of such harm. In the Dalkon Shield case, the A. H. Robins Company sold an intrauterine device that rendered large numbers of women sterile, and killed a few of them (Mokhiber 1988). In the Ford Pinto case, the auto company produced a vehicle with a gas tank located in the rear, prone to a deadly explosion in rear-end accidents (Cullen, Maakestad, and Cavender 1987). Year after year the Federal Trade Commission and other entities continue to identify unsafe products major corporations have manufactured and sold to the public.

Citizens have also been victims of the unsafe environmental practices of corporations. Corporations have frequently dumped toxic wastes in sites (or waters) to which citizens are exposed, with possible devastating consequences in terms of emerging health problems. In one case, the Hooker Chemical Company dumped toxic waste near Love Canal adjacent to Niagara Falls, with alleged miscarriages, birth defects, and liver ailments as a consequence for those living near the canal (Mokhiber 1988). The air pollution practices of many corporations have surely contributed to elevated cancer rates and respiratory illnesses, although direct cause-and-effect is not always so easily established (Grant, Jones, and Bergesen 2002; Regenstein 1986). Corporations have typically denied responsibility for the harmful consequences attributed to their polluting practices, and have resisted changing these practices until forced to do so (Barstow and Bergman 2003a; 2003b). Again, criminal prosecutions in even the most egregious cases of pollution have been uncommon.

Finally, in this context, it should be noted that corporations have even been complicit in the destruction of entire communities, such as when unsafe practices have led to dam breaks (Stern 1976). When the Buffalo Creek dam burst in February 1972, the town of Saunders, West Virginia, was demolished, and 125 community members died.

State-corporate crime is also complicit in a significant amount of physical harm to people. State-corporate crime has been defined as the illegal or harmful actions that emanate from cooperative state and corporate activities (Kramer and Michalowski 1990). In one case of state-corporate crime, the IG Farben chemical corporation in Nazi Germany was found after World War II to have supplied poison gas for the Nazi death camps, and to have exploited massive numbers of slave laborers in concentration camps established by the Nazi regime; at least 25,000 of these laborers died prematurely as a consequence of the conditions in these camps (Borkin 1978). The 1996 crash of ValuJet Flight 592 in the Florida Everglades, which killed more than a hundred passengers, has been characterized as state-corporate crime because the Federal Aviation Administration (FAA) failed to adequately enforce safety regulations and a private airline cut costs by contracting maintenance to a company (Sabretech) that placed an improperly inspected oxygen canister (which caught fire and exploded) on the flight (Matthews and Kauzlarich 2000).

To date, white-collar crime scholars have paid little attention to what can be labeled "crimes of globalization." Such crimes are harmful consequences emanating from the policy decisions of international financial institutions such as the World Bank and the International Monetary Fund (Friedrichs and Friedrichs 2002). For example, the World Bank provided loans to build dams in developing countries (Caufield 1996; Johnson 2000). In addition to destroying the livelihood of large numbers of people, anti-dam protesters have in some cases been massacred. However well intended they may be, projects funded by international financial institutions have too often had negative effects on the health and well-being of people in developing countries.

Corporate violence, and related forms of violence identified in the preceding section, is real. It represents a broad and ongoing threat to the health and lives of large numbers of people.

To the extent that the violent dimension of white-collar crime has received attention, much of this attention has focused on corporate violence (e.g., Hills 1987; Mokhiber 1988; Punch 1996). But many activities committed within a legitimate occupational context, and outside of a corporate context, can have violent consequences. In one case of occupational crime, a Kansas City pharmacist was sentenced to prison for systematically diluting cancer drugs prescribed for customers in the interest of greatly enhancing his profits (Jones 2002). He accumulated millions of dollars, while some of the cancer patients who acquired their drugs from him suffered unnecessary pain and possibly premature death.

Much evidence suggests that many retail food businesses engage in health-threatening practices of altering expiration dates, concealing food spoilage, and handling food in an unhygienic manner (Bellafante 1997; Blumberg 1989). An incalculable amount of illness—possibly even death in some cases—results from such practices.

Fraudulent repairs are quite common for a range of products. When products such as automobiles are involved, accidents occur, sometimes with fatal consequences (Belsky 1996). In one case, a pool mechanic allegedly failed to install a $1.44 plastic exhaust pipe, leading to the death by carbon monoxide poisoning of a prominent tennis player staying at a friend's guest house by the pool (Carvajal 1995).

Some people—e.g., nursing home patients and the mentally ill—are especially vulnerable to mistreatment and exploitation (Levy 2003; Mendelson 1974; Payne and Gray 2001). In a significant number of cases, cost-cutting measures by operators of nursing homes and homes for the mentally ill lead to injury, avoidable health problems, or premature death for residents of these homes.

A significant number of people every year suffer from illnesses, injuries, and premature death as a consequence of medical practices driven by the objective of maximizing profit as opposed to minimizing the possibility of harm to patients. By one account, some 16,000 patients die annually in the United States from unnecessary operations (Reiman 2004). Although malpractice suits against physicians are not uncommon, criminal prosecutions for causing physical harm to patients are rare (Nossiter 1995). For one thing, criminal intent is difficult to establish in such cases.

Even research scientists may engage in fraudulent activities resulting in physical harm. In a highly competitive environment for research grant funding and professional recognition, a certain proportion of researchers engage in fraud, although there is some dispute over whether such fraud is common (Brainard 2000; LaFollette 1992). In one admittedly rare case, a research scientist was sentenced to jail for falsifying data pertinent to controlling the behavior of mentally retarded children, on the premise that the fraudulent research provided a basis for treatment that was in fact harmful to such children (Davis 1989). Similarly, a Canadian researcher was accused of falsifying data in a study of breast cancer that influenced treatment strategies for women with cancer (Altman 1994). A research laboratory affiliated with an American university engaged in research directly implicated in the death of an experimental subject, and possible harmful effects for other experimental subjects (Associated Press 2001). Altogether, much avoidable physical harm is inflicted on many members of society by a wide range of individuals and entities operating out of a legitimate occupational context, including in some cases highly prestigious professionals.

Interests Served by the Myth

If indeed it is a myth that violent crime is carried out predominantly by lower-class conventional offenders, and disproportionately by young, inner-city males of color, this myth is certainly beneficial to the established interests. Reiman (2004) advanced the notion of "Pyrrhic defeat" to explain this benefit. As long as so much concern and anger about violent crime is focused on the activities of conventional offenders—"street criminals" and the like—it is deflected from focusing on the forms of harm inflicted by the rich and powerful. Many Americans regard the sale and distribution of illicit drugs such as heroin and cocaine as harmful activities, and certainly some undesirable consequences can be associated with use of such drugs. American prisons are filled with drug offenders, a disproportionate number of whom come from disadvantaged segments of American society. It is far from clear that on balance these offenders have inflicted more demonstrable harm on Americans than have corporate executives and others who hold legitimate occupational statuses; but few corporate offenders go to prison for the actions undertaken within the context of their occupation that have demonstrably harmful consequences.

The criminal justice system may also be said to benefit from the disproportionate focus on conventional forms of violence. On balance, it is generally easier to investigate and prosecute conventional forms of violence than is the case with corporate violence and violence emanating out of the activities of professionals or others holding a legitimate occupational status. Accordingly, career-related rewards are more easily obtained in conjunction with pursuing conventional violence than would be true of pursuing corporate violence and the violence of professionals. The criminal justice system is more easily able to obtain funding from the political system for combating conventional forms of violence—and such high-profile forms of violence as terrorism—than for pursuing corporate violence. The public, which translates into voters as far as politicians are concerned, is generally more responsive to initiatives addressing forms of violence that seem especially direct, dramatic, and frightening, than the less visible, less tangible, and less immediate forms of violence associated with the activities of corporations. Furthermore, corporate executives—to say nothing of physicians—simply do not fit the common image of "violent criminals." And politicians depend upon the generosity of corporations, businesspeople, and professionals as supporters of their political campaigns, and may be wary of attacking those associated with these categories. Perhaps even criminologists may benefit from an ongoing focus on conventional violent offenders. It is easier, for all the reasons suggested above, to obtain research funding to study such offenders. It may be easier, as well, to describe and explain such offenders, and to offer policy recommendations for effectively responding to their activities. Accordingly, mainstream criminologists may also benefit from privileging conventional forms of violence over corporate forms of violence, or violence emanating out of white-collar crime generally.

Policy Implications of Belief in the Myth

If the problem of violent crime is viewed principally in terms of the acts of conventional offenders or deranged individual offenders, then it follows that policy initiatives in response to violent crime are directed principally toward such offenders. In recent times, such widely publicized initiatives as "Three Strikes and You're Out" and "Megan's Law" were inspired by, in the first case, a repeat felony offender who abducted, sexually assaulted, and murdered a 12-year-old girl (Polly Klaas), and in the second case by a paroled sex offender who molested and murdered a young child (Megan Kanka) (Gest 2001). Such heinous crimes understandably inflame the public, and politicians can garner much favorable

attention and support by sponsoring legislative initiatives against the types of offenders involved. In the case of both of these initiatives, some critics contended that these laws, passed in a politically charged environment, may in fact be counterproductive and may fail to have the intended effect of deterring or preventing violent crimes of this nature (Beckett 1997; Robinson 2002). But for the most part, the violence emanating out of corporate activities, or the activities of professionals and others operating within a legitimate occupational context, have not been the focus of such policy initiatives. Geis (1996) argued that a "Three Strikes and You're Out" policy could be more appropriately applied to white-collar offenders. White-collar violence, however, is recognized to be fundamentally different in character from conventional forms of violence, and accordingly may not be as effectively addressed by criminalization (Simpson 2002). Certainly, the first line of response to white-collar crime has to be the adoption of policies that foster and promote safe practices across the spectrum of corporate, professional, and occupational activities. Ideally, then, prevention and deterrence of such violence is the goal. When prevention and deterrence fail, the criminal prosecution of such white-collar offenses is fully warranted.

References

Altman, L. 1994. Researcher falsified data in breast cancer study. *New York Times* October 1, A12.

Associated Press. 2001. Johns Hopkins is investigating study in India by professor. *New York Times* February 9, A14.

Barstow, D., and L. Bergman. 2003a. At a Texas foundry, an indifference to life. *New York Times* January 7, A1.

———. 2003b. A family's fortune, a legacy of blood and tears. *New York Times* January 9, A1.

Beckett, K. 1997. *Making crime pay: Law and order in contemporary American politics.* New York: Oxford University Press.

Bellafante, G. 1997. Hide and go Sue. *Time* January 13, 81.

Belsky, G. 1996. Steer clear of these car repair ripoffs. *Readers Digest* (December) 134–137.

Blumberg, P. 1989. *The predatory society: Deception in the American marketplace.* New York: Oxford University Press.

Borkin, J. 1978. *The crime and punishment of I. G. Farben.* New York: Free Press.

Brainard, J. 2000. As U.S. releases new rules on scientific fraud, scholars debate how much and why it occurs. *Chronicle of Higher Education* December 8, A26.

Brodeur, P. 1985. *Outrageous misconduct: The asbestos industry on trial.* New York: Pantheon Books.

Carvajal, D. 1995. Gerulaitis death attributed to short pipe. *New York Times* May 24, B5.

Caufield, C. 1996. *Masters of illusion: The World Bank and the poverty of nations.* New York: Henry Holt & Co.

Cullen, F., W. Maakestad, and G. Cavender. 1987. *Corporate crime under attack: The Ford Pinto case and beyond.* Cincinnati: Anderson Publishing Co.

Davis, M. S. 1989. The perceived seriousness and incidence of ethical misconduct in academic science. Ph.D. Dissertation. Ohio State University.

Engels, F. [1895] 1958. The condition of the working class in England. Translated by W. O. Henderson and W. H. Chaldner. Stanford, CA: Stanford University Press.

Friedrichs, D. O. 2004. *Trusted criminals: White collar crime in contemporary society.* Belmont, CA: Thomson/Wadsworth.

Friedrichs, D. O., and J. Friedrichs. 2002. The World Bank and crimes of globalization: A case study. *Social Justice* 29:13–36.

Geis, G. 1996. A base on balls for white-collar criminals. In *Three strikes and you're out: Vengeance as public policy,* eds. D. Shichor and D. Sechrest. Thousand Oaks, CA: Sage.

Gest, T. 2001. *Crime and politics: Big government's erratic campaign for law and order.* New York: Oxford University Press.

Glassner, B. 2000. *Fear: Why Americans are afraid of the wrong things.* Boulder, CO: Perseus.

Grant, D., A. Jones, and A. Bergesen. 2002. Organizational size and pollution: The case of the U.S. chemical industry. *American Sociological Review* 67:389–407.

Greider, W. 2002. William Lerach's legal crusade against Enron and infectious greed. *The Nation* (August 5–12):11–15.

Helmkamp, J., R. Ball, and K. Townsend, eds. 1996. *Definitional dilemma: Can and should there be a universal definition of white collar crime?* Morgantown, WV: National White Collar Crime Center.

Henry, S., and M. Lanier, eds. 2001. *What is crime? Controversies about the nature of crime and what to do about it.* Lanham, MD: Rowman and Littlefield.

Hills, S. L. 1987. *Corporate violence.* Totowa, NJ: Rowman and Littlefield.

Johnson, B. T. 2000. The World Bank does not provide effective development programs. In *The third world: Opposing viewpoints,* ed. L. K. Egendorf. San Diego: Greenhaven Press.

Jones, C. 2002. Pharmacist admits diluting drugs. *USA Today* February 27, 3a.

Kramer, R. C., and R. J. Michalowski. 1990. State-corporate crime. A paper presented at the annual meeting of the American Society of Criminology, November 7–12 in Baltimore, MD.

Labaton, S. 2000. Top asbestos makers agree to settle 2 large lawsuits. *New York Times* January 23, A22.

LaFollette, M. C. 1992. *Stealing into print: Fraud, plagiarism, and misconduct in scientific publishing.* Berkeley: University of California Press.

Levy, C. 2003. U.S. indicts doctor in fraud at state homes for mentally ill. *New York Times* January 7, A1.

Matthews, R., and D. Kauzlarich. 2000. The crash of ValuJet flight 592: A case study in state-corporate crime. *Sociological Focus* 3: 281–298.

Mendelson, M. A. 1974. *Tender loving greed.* New York: Random House.

Mokhiber, R. 1988. *Corporate crime and violence: Big business power and the abuse of the public trust.* San Francisco: Sierra Club Books.

Nossiter, A. 1995. A mistake, a rare prosecution, and a doctor is headed for jail. *New York Times* March 16, A1.

Payne, B. K., and C. Gray. 2001. Fraud by home health care workers and the criminal justice response. *Criminal Justice Review* 26:209–232.

Punch, M. 1996. *Dirty business: Exploring corporate misconduct.* London: Sage Publications.

Regenstein, L. 1986. *How to survive in America the poisoned.* Washington, DC: Acropolis Books.

Reiman, J. 2004. *The rich get richer, and the poor get prison.* Boston: Allyn & Bacon.

Robinson, M. 2002. *Justice blind? Ideals and realities of American crime and justice.* Upper Saddle River, NJ: Prentice Hall.

Schlegel, K. 2000. Transnational crime. *Journal of Contemporary Criminal Justice* 16:365–385.

Simpson, S. 2002. *Corporate crime, law and social control.* New York: Cambridge University Press.

———. 2003. The criminological enterprise and corporate crime. *The Criminologist* 28:1, 3–5.

Stern, G. M. 1976. *The Buffalo Creek disaster.* New York: Vintage.

Surette, R. 1998. *Media, crime, and criminal justice: Images and realities.* Belmont, CA: Wadsworth Publishing Co.

Wonders, N., and M. Danner. 2002. Globalization, state-corporate crime, and women: The strategic role of women's NGOs in the new world order. In *Controversies in white collar crime,* ed. Gary Potter. Cincinnati, OH: Anderson. ✦

Chapter 4
The Myth of Race and Crime

Katheryn Russell-Brown

The Myth

Some of us grew up believing in Santa Claus. We believed he was real because that is what we were told and because there was an abundance of "evidence" that he existed. Santa Claus was brought to life in the stories told by family members, what we saw on television, and in the person we saw dressed up in a red Santa suit at the mall or discount store. At some point, however, we were told the truth: Santa Claus is fiction, a myth presented to us in the spirit of protecting our childhood innocence.

Interestingly, at the same time that millions of children are told the myth of Santa Claus, they are also being exposed to images, stories, and representations that enhance the myth of Black criminality.[1] This myth is spread in print and visual media—for example, through newspapers, magazines, television shows, commercials, the news, and music videos. In homes, images of Black deviance are transmitted through words, gestures, actions, and even silence. However, unlike the myth of Santa Claus, which is typically abandoned as evidence to the contrary presents itself, the myth of crime and race lingers on in the minds of most people.

The media's representation of young Black men as criminal perpetrators is so uniform that most people treat them as imagined bogeymen. Studies indicate that Whites, Latinos, Asian Americans, American Indians, and African Americans believe they are most likely to be victimized by Black men. This is the myth of the *criminalblackman* (Russell 1998:3). That this myth is contrary to fact—people are most likely to be victimized by someone of their same race—apparently is not a part of the national consciousness.

It is not enough to observe that the media associates crime with blackness, though certainly it does. The media routinely portrays Black men as the quintessential criminals. Mass media, however, do not operate in a vacuum. The public adopts the images presented and then incorporates them, often wholesale, from the way we dress, the way we talk, the jokes we tell, where we decide to live, who our friends are, and how we vote.

The *criminalblackman* myth is both simple and complex. In its simplest form, it holds that blackness and deviance are joined. It presents a basic algebraic equation: a + b = c (Black + man = crime). This crude deduction leaves little room for other variables.

The myth's complexity exists on two levels. First, the association of Black men with criminality does not present itself as a myth. Messages and images of Black men as criminals are not introduced as anecdotes. Rather, they are presented as the truth. This explains why the myth is so difficult to dispel: People do not typically question what they believe to be fact.

Second, recognizing it as a myth is difficult because of its encumbrances. For the myth to resonate and take hold, there are many other, smaller myths that must first be accepted. These "petit myths," some of which are listed here, have to be taken as fact for the *criminalblackman* myth to appear to be true.

- Whites do not commit many serious crimes.
- Blacks commit most crime.
- White fear (of Black men in particular) is justified by high Black crime rates.
- Street crime is more serious than white-collar crime.
- Blacks may be innately prone to commit crime.
- The police and court systems fairly mete out justice.

One or more of the above statements must be taken as fact for one to believe that particular racial groups—e.g., African Americans—are intrinsically prone to commit crime. Petit myths are important to identify because they establish social parameters. The decision to label a particular group as criminal predetermines the treatment accorded and solutions society adopts for the group. Therefore, if Blacks are viewed as "social problems," it is easy to predict they will be subjected to a harsher fate within the justice system.

The Kernel of Truth

It is true that, based on their percentage in the population, Blacks are disproportionately overrepresented in the offender population. The high rate of Black offending is well known and widely cited. However, without further illumination this disproportionality explains very little. This raises several concerns. First, Blacks offend at a disproportionate rate for *some* crimes. That is, Blacks are overrepresented in the offender population for some crimes, primarily "street" crimes, also known as index offenses (e.g., robbery, aggravated assault).

Second, a "race only" view does not take into consideration other factors that affect involvement in crime. An intersec-

tional analysis, however, takes into account race along with other variables such as socioeconomic status. As a group, Blacks are disproportionately poor and as a group poor people are more likely to commit, be convicted of, and serve time for street crimes.

Third, while it is true that African Americans are arrested for a disproportionate share of index crimes, as Table 4.1 indicates, the *majority* of crimes are not committed by African Americans (Department of Justice 2003). Disproportionate offending and majority offending are two separate issues. These concepts, however, are routinely confused. Further, the fact that a group is disproportionately involved in the criminal justice system does not mean the group is innately prone to crime. A complete picture of race and crime requires looking at race, gender, and class. It is important to separate the kernel of truth from the myth and the petit myths that surround it.

The Truth or Facts

As a society, we are lazy in thinking about crime. Distinct concepts have been confused, there has been a hesitance to acknowledge and challenge the racial images presented by the mass media, and we have inadequately considered how those portrayals might influence thinking on the link between crime and race. One ex-

Table 4.1
Overall Percentage of Arrests by Race, 2003 (includes index and non-index offenses)

Whites	70.7
Blacks	26.9
American Indians	1.3
Asian Americans	1.1

Note: Hispanics are classified as an ethnicity, not a race.
Source: Department of Justice 2002a.

ample of this lazy thinking is the way crime is defined.

"Crime" is primarily used to reference street crime. It is rarely used to indicate white-collar crime, such as embezzlement, fraud, insider trading, or corporate mismanagement. Related to this, the race and crime connection has been employed as shorthand for "Blacks and crime." "Race and crime" is almost never used to refer to "Whites and crime" (Russell 1998: 110). The reality is that "race and crime" has become synonymous with "Blacks and crime," instead of being a reference to whether and how race is linked with crime.

Further, the routine depiction of Black male deviance is almost impossible to avoid. As a result, it is difficult—even for those who know better—not to be influenced by these negative images. The majority of people, across race, think Black men pose the greatest crime threat. Most people believe this even though it is contrary to the facts (see next section). It is important to acknowledge the degree to which people are exposed to and influenced by media representations of blackness as criminal. Leaving these images unchecked can have racially explosive consequences, such as the racial hoax.

A racial hoax occurs when someone fabricates a crime and blames it on another person because of his or her race or, when an actual crime has been committed, the perpetrator falsely blames someone because of his or her race (Russell 1998:69). The majority of the reported hoaxes involve someone White falsely accusing someone Black of a crime. Well-known cases include Susan Smith and Charles Stuart. Racial hoaxes are successful precisely because so many people have adopted the dominant narrative that dark skin is synonymous with crime. One way to move beyond the *criminalblackman*

myth is to acknowledge some foundational facts.

To begin with, there must be some knowledge of the racial breakdown of the U.S. population, which is presented in Table 4.2 (U.S. Census Bureau 2003).

These percentages are important because they determine whether a particular racial group's involvement in the justice system is proportionate or disproportionate. For example, if Whites are less than 73 percent of the people arrested or convicted each year, then Whites are said to be disproportionately underrepresented in arrests and convictions. By contrast, if Blacks are more than 12 percent of the people arrested or convicted each year, then Blacks are said to be disproportionately overrepresented in arrests and convictions. The population percentages provide the base rates for statements about a racial group's degree of involvement in the criminal justice system.

Victimization rates are also important in this discussion because, in the United States, people of color have disproportionately high rates of violent victimization. As Table 4.3 indicates, this is particularly true for American Indians, African Americans, and Hispanics (Department of Justice 2002b:2). Violent victimization rates are particularly important because they dispel the commonly held perception that Whites are the group most likely to be victims of violent crime. One of the most

Table 4.2
U.S. Population, Percentage by Race

Whites	73
Blacks	12
Hispanic	12.5
Asian American	3.6
American Indian	less than 1

Source: U.S. Census Bureau 2000.

surprising findings is that an American Indian is more likely to be a victim of a violent crime than a person of any other race. It is also noted that the overwhelming majority of crime is intraracial—most crime involves an offender and victim who are of the same race. According to the 2003 Uniform Crime Reports, approximately 80 percent of all murders are intraracial (Department of Justice 2003).

Given that drug offenses make up a large percentage of crimes committed in the United States, drug use and punishment are also integral to this discussion. Under the federal crack law, the possession of five grams of crack cocaine is punished as severely as the possession of 500 grams of powder cocaine—each one is subject to a five-year mandatory minimum sentence. Most notably, there is no medical rationale for the 100:1 disparity between powder and crack cocaine. Pharmacologically, they are the same. The 1986 law was quickly passed following the death of Len Bias, a star basketball player at the University of Maryland. Just days after being selected as the number one NBA draft pick, Bias died of what was widely believed to be a crack cocaine overdose. Within a few months of Bias' death, the U.S. Congress passed the federal crack law. This is relevant to the discussion at hand because Blacks are 85 percent of the offenders who are convicted under the federal crack law. Data on crime indicate, however, that there is a dramatic difference between the use of drugs and arrest for possession of drugs. There are more Whites in the United States who use crack cocaine than Blacks (National Household Survey on Drug Abuse 1998).

Table 4.4 summarizes how various racial groups are involved in the criminal justice system (U.S. Department of Justice 2001; 2002). As indicated, African Americans are disproportionately subject to prison, jail, probation, and parole. Blacks are 12 percent of the population and 36 percent of people under the control of the correctional system (Russell-Brown 2004: 136).

Whites are 73 percent of the population and 48 percent of the correctional population. The 15 percent control rate for Hispanics nearly matches their near 13 percent in the population. Both Asian Americans and American Indians are disproportionately underrepresented in the correctional system. A report by the Sentencing Project indicates that one-third of all Black men between the ages of 20 and 29 are under the supervision of the crimi-

Table 4.3
Violent Victimization Rates, by Race

	Rate, per 1,000 [within each racial group]
American Indian	52.3
Black	34.1
Hispanic	27.9
White	26.5
Asian	8.4

Source: Department of Justice 2002.

Table 4.4
Control Rates by Race Within the Justice System

	Percentage of Total Corrections Population*
White	48
Black	36
Hispanic	15
American Indian	less than 1
Asian American	less than 1

*Includes prison, jail, probation, and parole
Source: Russell-Brown 2004.

nal justice system (Mauer and Huling 1995:2).

Based on these statistics, it is no surprise that African Americans are the racial group with the greatest probability of spending time behind bars. Of all the race and gender groups, Black men have the highest lifetime likelihood of going to prison (32.2 percent). For Blacks overall, the rate is 18.6 percent; for Whites, the overall rate is 3.4 percent; and for Hispanics, the overall rate is 10 percent (Department of Justice 2003).

Criminal offenses, ranging from fraud, bribery, tax crimes, and money laundering, to consumer fraud and corporate malfeasance, are primarily committed by Whites. These are offenses that are typically overlooked in discussions of race and crime, which primarily focus on street crime. Further, when compared with data on street crime, information on white-collar crime is not easy to locate. For instance, the only white-collar crimes included in the FBI's Uniform Crime Reports are fraud and embezzlement. To develop a comprehensive picture of white-collar offending, data must be culled from numerous sources. As Table 4.5 reports, Whites comprise the majority of people serving time in federal prison for white-collar offending (U.S. Department of Justice 2001a:526).

Table 4.5
White-Collar Offenders
in Federal Prison, by Race

Offense Type	White	Black	Hispanic
Tax	71%	11.9%	10.4%
Gambling	70.7%	10.1%	14.1%
Fraud	54.1%	28.1%	12.7%
Embezzlement	56.3%	28.2%	8.4%

Source: U.S. Department of Justice 2001a.

As indicated, Whites comprise the majority of offenders sentenced for tax, gambling, fraud, and embezzlement offenses. Notably, for tax and gambling crimes, the percentage of Whites approximates their percentage in the population.

The use of "race and crime" to refer to "Blacks and crime" has meant that the incidence and prevalence of "White crime" has been overlooked (Russell 1998:110). By doing this, a message is sent that White crime is not important. At the same time, the association between Blacks and crime is reinforced.

The facts outlined above represent a very small part of the race and crime issue. As indicated, though Blacks are disproportionately involved in the justice system, they do not comprise the majority of offenders. Further, the high rates of incarceration for Blacks are not strictly correlated with rates of offending. Many factors influence the sentencing decision, including type of crime, location of offense (e.g., state), race of victim, and type of counsel.

Interests Served by the Myth

For many reasons, the myth of the *criminalblackman* persists. First, it is always difficult to challenge conventional wisdom. The idea that there is a link between race and crime is based on longstanding and deeply rooted beliefs. This argument also ties in with the earlier discussion of the kernel of truth. Many people conclude that the way things are represents the way things ought to be. Further, there is the problem of collective ignorance. Society is often hesitant to address issues of race, and this extends to discussing the even more volatile subject of race and crime.

Second, it is hard to see the myth at work. Discussions of the criminal justice system are often couched in the language of objectivity. For example, television crime news, featuring crime scenes and mug shots which overwhelmingly feature African Americans, sends the message that Blacks are criminals. Based on these presentations, the public is expected to believe that the reporters are simply providing the facts—that neither race nor racism plays a role in who is targeted, brought into, and sentenced within the justice system. This pretense of neutrality encourages faith in the myth.

A more subtle application of the myth occurs in general discussions of crime. For instance, we routinely hear about the high rates at which African Americans, particularly young African American males, are involved in the criminal justice system. These reports of disproportionate victimization and offending are so common they no longer provoke either interest or surprise. These stories are treated as statements of how the world is, rather than as statements of what is wrong with how the world works. This alone suggests the myth has taken hold. All told, the dominant message that comes through the media is that the myth is real. Therefore the myth is easy to believe.

Finally, the *criminalblackman* myth appears to satisfy a collective need to have a target to blame—a convenient bad guy. It enables society to label one particular group a criminal threat. As noted earlier, the existence of racial hoaxes attests to this need for a national bogeyman.

It is important to observe not only that the myth remains but that all of us are "myth traffickers." We all play a part in keeping the mythic association of blackness with crime alive. This occurs through passive acceptance or active engagement in perpetuating the myth. If this is true, do we all have something to gain by keeping the myth alive? Are we traffickers and stakeholders?

There are at least two different kinds of stakeholders. First, there are those who are the emotional keepers of the myth. Most people fall into this category. Everyone has something to lose if there is a paradigm shift in thinking about crime and race. So long as we believe that what we are told about race and crime is true, we do not have to do anything. No action on our part is required. This allegiance to the status quo symbolizes the comfortable myth of race and crime.

Second, there are those who are financial stakeholders. This includes investors who literally buy stock in the justice system, hoping to strike it rich. These stakeholders, including some within the media and those who have invested in private prisons, benefit from the exponential increase in the prison population. This increase has been built on the back of the *criminalblackman* myth.

Whether we gain emotionally or financially by preserving the status quo, we are all stakeholders. Leaving this state of ignorance is not easy. Most of us do not confront the maze of historical, empirical, and legal reasons why crime is linked with blackness. Learning new information that contradicts earlier learning presents a mammoth challenge.

Policy Implications of Belief in the Myth

Regarding race and crime, there are clear policy implications for proceeding with business as usual. The criminal stigma associated with African Americans affects policy and social outcomes. First, it is used to support the exponential growth in the prison population—what has been called the "prison industrial complex." Related to this, the *criminalblackman* myth supports current policing and punishment schemes that disproportionately impact African Americans.

Second, policies supporting prison growth support other forms of government actions related to criminal justice. These include supporting the elimination of financial aid for prisoners (e.g., Pell grants), felony disenfranchisement, stiffer sentencing laws (e.g., mandatory minimums) and a de-emphasis on drug recovery, mental health programs, and re-entry programs.

Third, the prevalence of the myth further alienates African Americans from the justice system. As a group, Blacks are more likely to experience and believe they are subject to racial targeting and unfair processing through the system. This in turn influences the relationship between the police and communities of color.

A final harmful consequence of the *criminalblackman* myth is its potential labeling effect on young African Americans, particularly young Black men. The message that Black men are criminals and people to be feared and loathed is troubling. It further encourages Black men to question their place in society and the fairness of the criminal justice system. It also tells young Black men that they are expected to engage in crime. In this way, the mythic Black criminal further marginalizes an already marginalized population.

Conclusion

We do not know how much is at stake because there is still so much we do not know. Consider what the average person's reaction would be to a picture of Santa Claus in prison stripes. First, this image does not fit the common perception of Santa Claus. Second, it challenges our belief system on a fundamental level—it goes against how we believe the world operates. We think to ourselves, "Santa Claus is a good guy. He's safe. He's not a criminal." I argue that this deductive reasoning is analogous to how we process the image of Blacks and crime. As a result of early conditioning and exposure, we readily perceive blackness as deviant and as justifiably linked to crime. Thus, for most of us "Blacks" and "crime" are linked in very personal, intricate ways, and have been for most of our lives. Therefore, we do not question the association of Blacks with crime because it fits in neatly with what we believe to be true. The challenge is before us. Do we continue believing what we now know to be unfounded, or do we reject the myth of Santa Claus?

Note

1. Black and White are used here as racial terms and thus capitalized.

References

Mauer, M., and T. Huling. 1995. *Young African Americans and the criminal justice system: Five years later.* Washington DC: The Sentencing Project.

National Household Survey on Drug Abuse. 1998. *Population estimates 1998.* SAMSHA.

Russell, K. 1998. *The color of crime: Racial hoaxes, white fear, black protectionism, police harassment, and other macroaggressions.* New York: New York University Press.

Russell-Brown, K. 2004. *Underground codes: Race, crime, and related fires.* New York: New York University Press.

U.S. Census Bureau. 2000. *www.census.gov/population/wwwcen2000/briefs.html.*

———. 2003. *Prevalence of imprisonment in the U.S. population, 1974–2000.* Washington, DC: U.S. Government Printing Office.

U.S. Department of Justice. 2001a. *Sourcebook of criminal justice statistics 2000.* Washington, DC: U.S. Government Printing Office.

———. 2001b. *Prison and jail inmates at midyear 2000.* Washington, DC: U.S. Government Printing Office.

———. 2002a. *FBI, uniform crime reports.* Washington, DC: U.S. Government Printing Office.

———. 2002b. *Hispanic victims of violent crime.* Washington, DC: U.S. Government Printing Office.

———. 2002c. *Prisoners in 2001.* Washington, DC: U.S. Government Printing Office.

———. 2002d. *Probation and parole in the United States, 2001.* Washington, DC: U.S. Government Printing Office.

———. 2003. *FBI uniform crime reports, 2002.* Washington, DC: U.S. Government Printing Office. ✦

Chapter 5
The Myth That Serial Murderers Are Disproportionately White Males

Joseph B. Kuhns III
and Charisse T. M. Coston

The Myth

Prior to recent acts of domestic and international terrorism, perhaps no criminal phenomenon held the attention of the general public, the media, and the criminal justice system to the extent of serial murder. Towns have been gripped in terror, society has been engrossed with curiosity, the media frequently turned the phenomenon into a frenzied circus, and law enforcement quickly responded by developing a national computer-based data system to assist in the investigation and apprehension of serial murderers and other serial violent offenders throughout the United States.

Despite the ongoing fascination with serial murder, a common myth persists and remains relatively unexplored and unchallenged: Most citizens, media representatives, scholars, and even law enforcement officers tend to agree that serial murderers are disproportionately white males. However, there is a growing body of evidence that counters this belief and points to more than 100 African-American serial murderers who have been largely ignored by the media and society. The evidence indicates that the proportion of African-American serial murderers may closely parallel their proportion of the population. In this chapter, we explore the myth of the white-male serial murderer, provide some evidence that there have been many African-American serial murderers throughout recent history, and discuss some reasons why these murderers have not achieved the notoriety of their white counterparts.

Holmes and DeBurger (1988) estimated that as many as 35 serial murderers claim between 3,500 and 5,000 lives annually, although such estimates are rather speculative and based on unfounded conjecture according to some (see, for example, Hinch and Hepburn 1998). More importantly, the probability that any particular individual will fall victim to a serial killer is extremely low; statistically, a person is more likely to be struck by lightning. Regardless, serial murder remains frightening because of its extreme violence and seemingly apparent randomness, and because it often victimizes women, children, the homeless, prostitutes, and others who are less able to adequately protect themselves, or whose untimely deaths may remain unnoticed for long periods of time.

According to a number of media sources, serial murderers are disproportionately white males in their 20s and 30s. The following quotes from various Internet sites on serial and mass murder generally agree on this common descriptive profile:

- "Serial killers tend to be white, heterosexual males in their twenties and thirties who are sexually dysfunctional and have low self-esteem" (*www.mayhem.net*).

- "A serial killer is a typical white male, 20–30, and most of them are usually in the USA" (*www.fortunecity.com*).

- "Serial killers are primarily handsome white males in their 20s and 30s" (*www.geocities.com*).

- "He is usually male, between the ages of 25–30, and he is usually white" (*www.macalester.edu*).

- "He is usually male, between the ages of 25–35, and he is usually white" (*www.isuisse.ifrance.com*).

- "Most are white males in their 20s or 30s, with varying levels of intelligence" (Fox 2004).

Further, many "true crime" books seem to perpetuate this general description by providing graphic case histories of white-male serial killers (The Editors of Time Life Books 1992; Publications International 1991), and recent popular movies such as *Silence of the Lambs, Manhunter*, and a series of movies on Ted Bundy and others continue to suggest that serial murder is generally a "white-male phenomenon." In fact, the number of movies that focused on serial murderers steadily increased in the twentieth century, and increased dramatically in the 1990s (Main 1997). There are even sets of trading cards depicting serial and mass murderers that further sustain the stereotype (Jones and Collier 1992), and video games have also been developed using white-male serial killers (Take-Two Interactive 2004).

The Kernel of Truth

This popular description of the serial murderer is not limited to online sites, popular culture, and Hollywood films. Many noted serial-murder scholars have also offered a general profile of a serial murderer consistent with the "white male between 20 and 30" description, both

within the United States (Holmes and DeBurger 1985, 1988; Prentky et al. 1989; Leibman 1989; Hickey 1997) and in other countries, including Australia (Pinto and Wilson 1990), Britain (Grover and Soothill 1999), and Germany (Harbort and Mokros 2001).

Based on a comprehensive encyclopedia of serial killers, Newton (1990) found that 82 percent of twentieth century American serial murderers were white and 85 percent were male. The gender of another 7 percent of his sample was unknown because the killers were not captured. All else being equal, presumably 85 percent of that remaining 7 percent was also male and a corresponding proportion would be white, which would raise the percentages of white-male serial killers slightly.

Internationally, Harbort and Mokros (2001) studied 61 convicted serial murderers in Germany, all of whom were German citizens. Although racial composition was not examined, 91 percent of this German sample was male. Further, 12 of 14 (86 percent) convicted serial killers in Australia from 1900 to 1987 were also male; although again, race was not examined in this study (Pinto and Wilson 1990). In sum, the literature in the United States and abroad supports the contention that a serial murderer is most likely to be a white male, both within the United States and in other countries.

The Truth or Facts

As a basis of comparison, consider murder and population demographics in general. In 2002, there were 15,813 murders committed in the United States (murder and most crimes decreased in the late 1990s and early 2000s). Among murders for which the gender of the offender was known, males committed 90 percent of them. As such, it is probably fair to suggest that murderers are likely to be males (Federal Bureau of Investigation 2002).

A racial breakdown of U.S. murderers in 2002 for which the race of the offender is known indicates that 48 percent of murders were committed by white offenders and 50 percent were committed by black offenders (Federal Bureau of Investigation 2002). Therefore, it would be inaccurate to conclude that murderers in general were more likely to be white or black. In fact, murderers in the United States in 2002 were just as likely to be white as they were to be black.

Finally, it is important to keep in mind that murders are typically intraracial, such that white offenders kill white victims and black offenders kill black victims. In 2002, for example, in cases where the race of the offender and the victim were known, 84 percent of white victims were murdered by white offenders and 91 percent of black victims were murdered by black offenders (Federal Bureau of Investigation 2002). As such, it seems reasonable to conclude that murderers are likely to take the life of someone within their own race.

In 2000, the United States had an estimated population of 281 million citizens: 75.1 percent were white, 12.3 percent were African American, and 12.5 percent were Latino (U.S. Census Bureau 2000). Given these demographics and comparing the percentages with homicide statistics, it is rather apparent that African-American murderers are significantly overrepresented relative to their population figures. Blacks represented approximately 12.3 percent of the 2000 population (population figures are not collected each year, so the most recent 2000 Census figures were used), but accounted for 50 percent of the 2002 murders for which the race of the offender was known. Disproportionately

high black homicide rates have been the subject of study by many scholars (see, for example, Hawkins 1986). Whites, on the other hand, were underrepresented in murder statistics, accounting for 75 percent of the 2000 population while committing 48 percent of the 2002 murders. Latinos were not distinguished in the Uniform Crime Reports so comparisons within that group are not possible here.

Considering serial murderers, specifically, Newton (1990) determined that about 85 percent of serial murderers were male, and 88 percent of Hickey's (1997) sample of known serial murderers were male, although that number decreased to 84 percent in a later, but much broader, assessment of known serial killers from 1800 to 1995 (Hickey 2002). Since the population is roughly split 50/50 by gender, it is apparent that males are overrepresented among known serial murderers. Therefore, it is probably reasonable to assume that serial murderers are likely to be male, although scholars have spent considerable time studying female serial murderers as well (Keeney 1994, 1995; Hickey 2002).

Further review of Newton's (1990) encyclopedia of serial killers in the United States suggests that approximately 82 percent of his sample was white, 15 percent was African American, and another 2.5 percent was Latino. Hickey (1997) indicated that 85 percent of his sample of known serial murderers were white and 13 percent were African America, although his broader sample indicated that as much as 20 percent of 399 known male and female serial murderers were black (Hickey 2002:243).

In contrast to murder in general, it appears that the proportion of white and black serial murderers is slightly higher than their corresponding representation in the population. Specifically, about 75 percent of the U.S. population is white, while 80–85 percent of serial murderers are white. Blacks accounted for about 12 percent of the 2000 U.S. population and from 13–20 percent of serial murderers in the United States, depending on the source used or the timeframe examined. Finally, Latino serial murderers may be somewhat underrepresented, accounting for 12.5 percent of the population but only 2.5 percent of serial murderers. Given the small numbers of serial murderers overall, the percentage differences could and should be considered insignificant, because smaller samples yield larger percentage differences when making comparisons among groups. Nevertheless, the proportion of white serial murderers and black serial murderers in the United States appears to closely parallel their overall demographic representation in the population. So, if white serial murderers and African-American serial murderers appear in numbers that roughly correspond to their respective proportions in the general population, is it reasonable and responsible to assume that serial murderers are disproportionately white?

Instead, it may be more accurate to conclude that race, in and of itself, provides little help in distinguishing who may be serial murderers in the United States and, perhaps, abroad. Therefore, it seems prudent to eliminate racial descriptions from the typical profile of a serial murderer altogether (more discussion about this later). Some experts, including former FBI agent Robert Ressler, who spent several decades chasing down serial murderers, determined that there is no such thing as a "typical" serial killer (Sunde 2002). It follows that there may not be a typical serial murderer profile. Therefore, to create and perpetuate such a profile has both investigative and societal implications that merit further attention.

Interests Served by the Myth

Perpetuation of this myth may intentionally or unintentionally serve a variety of interests. This recurring stereotype was most likely created from and further perpetuated by several sources, including (1) historical and contemporary attempts by psychologists, psychiatrists, and law enforcement to profile serial murderers; (2) mass media attention on specific and extreme or spectacular cases of white serial murderers, notwithstanding comparable cases of spectacular black serial murderers; and (3) a possible failure of law enforcement to link black victims of homicide to possible serial murder investigations.

Criminal Profiling

The Federal Bureau of Investigation's Violent Criminal Apprehension Program (VICAP) uses psychological profiling strategies to identify and apprehend serial offenders, including serial killers. The basic purpose of psychological profiling is to construct a personality sketch, based on evidence derived through investigation of the crimes, for use in the investigation and subsequent prosecution. A personality sketch (it is assumed) provides information about an individual's behavior, genetic make-up, cultural characteristics, sexual patterns, victim preferences, and historical experiences. Much of the information on which profiles are based comes directly from crime scenes. Crime scenes can be very informative, yielding not only physical evidence (e.g., DNA), which can link an individual to a crime scene, but other indirect abstract evidence that can be psychologically and forensically analyzed.

Criminal profiling has been used extensively in serial murder investigations (Holmes and DeBurger 1988; James 1991;

Keppel 1989; Norris 1988); however, it is important to note that criminal or psychological profiling has some significant limitations. The accuracy and reliability of profiling has yet to be determined. In fact, some historical evidence suggests criminal profiling helped identify a primary suspect in only 17 percent of 192 cases for which profiles were developed (FBI 1980). For example, in the case of Albert Desalvo, "The Boston Strangler," for example, the criminal profile suggested the killer was a homosexual who was unable to express hatred toward his mother and was likely well-acquainted with the victims. In fact, Desalvo was married, had an insatiable heterosexual appetite, and in most cases the victims were strangers. Unfortunately, such inaccurate profiles are fairly common, although profiling has certainly helped capture some serial killers and serial rapists over the years. Focusing exclusively on white serial killers provides law enforcement and the media with a finite construct that makes investigating the serial murderer phenomenon easier, similar to focusing a sexual assault investigation on men exclusively, and subsequently ignoring potential women offenders (of which there are few).

Media Attention

Media attention regarding the issue of serial murder has also perpetuated the myth of the white-male serial murderer. As discussed previously, the number of films on serial murder increased steadily over the last 50 years or so, and increased significantly in the 1990s. Many films have focused on serial murder in general, but there were also a number of films and documentaries that examined specific serial killers including Jack the Ripper, Ted Bundy, Jeffrey Dahmer, Albert Desalvo, Henry Lee Lucas, and other white serial murderers. Recently, *Monster: The Life*

and Death of a Serial Killer was one of the first movies focusing on a female serial murderer (Aileen Wuornos), who also happened to be white.

We are unaware of any popular movies that depict fictional or nonfictional accounts of black serial killers, and if such movies do exist they are few in number. Jenkins (1993) provided some explanations for this apparent absence, including Hollywood concerns with creating movies categorized exclusively as "Black interest" (which may limit the audience and the subsequent box-office draw), or filmmaker concerns with the fear of being accused of depicting crude or controversial racial stereotypes. Jenkins pointed out that there were many cases of "spectacular" black serial killers (those who claimed more than eight victims). He identified 13 such cases from 1960 to 1987, but those cases have been largely ignored by the mass media and perhaps by scholars as well. Further, an incomplete and unpublished work in progress by Ellington (2004) identified as many as 115 black serial murderers in the twentieth and early twenty-first centuries, and additional cases were identified recently (CNN News 2004). Using Jenkin's indicator regarding the number of victims, as many as 31 (27 percent) of the black offenders in Ellington's preliminary study would be considered spectacular serial killers, or those who have claimed at least eight victims.

Selective or Ineffective Law Enforcement

Finally, Jenkins (1993) noted that law enforcement may have unintentionally failed to link cases of serial murder within black communities, and that African-American serial homicide may be a largely underrecognized phenomenon. Because murder in general occurs at disproportionately higher rates among blacks than would be expected, given their proportion of the population, law enforcement may systematically, but unintentionally, fail to consider that murders in black communities could be linked to cases of serial murder. Again, murder is most often intraracial. The majority of serial murder victims in Hickey's (2002) sample were white, as was the majority of his sample of serial murderers. Nevertheless, a serial murderer that chooses black male (or more likely black female) victims may end up eluding capture for long periods of time if investigators are not attentive and open-minded to the possibility that any given homicide may be one in a series of murders. For example, Henry Louis Wallace, a black serial murderer who operated in Charlotte, North Carolina, was arrested and convicted of nine killings of black females. Local law enforcement was initially informed by the FBI that there was no serial killer. This example shows that a number of stereotypes, including racial assumptions, can inadvertently hamper an investigation. Whether the failure of law enforcement to recognize potentially related cases and limitations associated with profiling serial killing impedes linking investigations on a larger scale should be the focus of future research.

Policy Implications of Belief in the Myth

The issue of addressing racial profiling related to serial murders is further complicated by recent media and legal attention to racial profiling by police. As the fiftieth anniversary of *Brown v. Topeka Board of Education* is celebrated, the United States remains focused on race relations, and racial profiling has become a major concern within the law enforcement community and across the country. Using a suspect's race as part of a criminal

profile has met with severe scrutiny within the court system, among law enforcement agencies (McMahon et al. 2002), and within cities and towns as an attempt is made to move away from unfair historical practices and toward a community policing style (Peak and Glensor 2002).

The irony of the white-male serial murderer myth is that this "profile" of the serial murderer may represent an obvious example of majority racial profiling. By "majority" racial profiling, we simply mean that the profiling impacts the *majority* race as opposed to a *minority* race. In this case, suggesting and commonly accepting that serial murderers are white should be no less of a concern than suggesting that murderers are black. However, there appears to be little concern within the community, among scholars, or within the media about describing serial murderers as white males. On the other hand, attempts to describe murderers as black males might quickly make the front page of the newspaper, and be followed by civil suits alleging racial discrimination or racial profiling.

If serial murder is unrelated to race (as evidence tends to suggest) and if murder and serial murder are primarily intraracial crimes (notwithstanding racially-based hate crimes), then law enforcement investigators should be particularly attentive to local community demographics during homicide investigations. There is evidence which suggests that some serial murderers kill locally; in fact, Hickey's (2002:137) research suggested that more than half (55 percent) of his sample of serial murderers killed locally, and 65 percent of the murderers never killed outside of the state in which they began their killing. This evidence also tends to refute the common notion of a serial killer as a loner who travels across the country in search of random victims. Many serial killers do seek out victims who are strangers; however, those strangers are often not that far away from his or her home.

The implications of this analysis for law enforcement are important. If serial murderers are more often racially representative of the population, more likely to seek victims of their own race (the majority of offenders and victims are white, although more specific racial patterns were not discussed [2002:249]), and likely to be local jurisdictional killers, then law enforcement should use these patterns to assist and facilitate investigations. Further, given the disproportionate numbers of homicides among African Americans, investigators should be mindful of the potential for local homicides involving black victims to be linked to serial murder cases.

References

CNN News. 2004. Man charged in 12 killings of women and girls. Accessed online April 19, 2004: *http://www.cnn.com/2004/LAW/04/19/ kc.serial.killings.ap/index.html.*

Editors of Time Life Books. 1992. *True Crime: Serial Killers.* Edited by L. Foreman. Alexandria, VA: The Time Inc. Book Company.

Ellington, K. 2004. *African American serial killers.* Unpublished and incomplete work in progress (Master's thesis). University of North Carolina at Charlotte.

Federal Bureau of Investigations (FBI). 1980. Offender profiles: A multidisciplinary approach. *Law Enforcement Bulletin* 49:16–20.

———. 2002. Crime in the United States—2002. Washington, DC: U.S. Department of Justice. Accessed online at: *http://www.fbi.gov/ucr/ 02cius.htm.*

Fox, J. 2004. What do we know about serial murder in America? Accessed online May 4, 2004: *http://www.cj.neu.edu/faculty_and_staff/ faculty_experts/what_do_we_know_about_ serial_murder_in_america/index.php.*

Grover, C., and K. Soothill. 1999. British serial killing: Towards a structural explanation. *The British Society of Criminology* 2:1–18.

Harbort, S., and A. Mokros. 2001. Serial murderers in Germany from 1945 to 1995. *Homicide Studies* 5(4):311–334.

Hawkins, D. 1986. *Homicide among black Americans.* New York: University Press of America, Inc.

Hickey, E. 1997. *Serial murderers and their victims,* 2nd ed. Belmont, CA: Wadsworth.

———. 2002. *Serial murderers and their victims,* 3rd ed. Belmont, CA: Wadsworth.

Hinch, R. and C. Hepburn. 1998. Researching serial murder: methodological and definitional problems. *Electronic Journal of Sociology.* Accessed online May 10, 2004: *http://www. sociology.org/content/vol003.002/hinch_d. html.*

Holmes, R., and J. DeBurger. 1985. Profiles in terror: The serial murderer. *Federal Probation* 49(September):29–34.

———. 1988. *Serial murder.* Newbury Park, CA: Sage Publications.

James, E. 1991. *Catching serial killers: Learning from past serial murder investigations.* Lansing, MI: International Forensic Services, Inc.

Jenkins, P. 1993. African Americans and serial homicide. *American Journal of Criminal Justice* 17(2):47–60.

Jones, V., and P. Collier. 1992. *True crime series two: Serial killers and mass murders* (trading cards). Jon Bright Eclipse Enterprises: Forestville, CA.

Leibman, F. 1989. Serial murderers: Four case histories. *Federal Probation* 49:41–45.

Keeney, B. T. 1994. Gender differences in serial murderers: A preliminary analysis. *Journal of Interpersonal Violence* 9(September):383–398.

———. 1995. Serial murder: A more accurate and inclusive definition. *International Journal of Offender Therapy and Comparative Criminology* 39(Winter):298–306.

Keppel, R. 1989. *Serial murder: Future implications for police investigations.* Cincinnati, OH: Anderson Publishing.

Main, V. 1997. *The changing image of serial killers in film: A reflection of attitudes toward crime from 1929–1995.* Master's Thesis. California State University, Fresno.

McMahon, J., J. Garner, R. Davis, and A. Kraus. 2002. *How to correctly collect and analyze racial profiling data: Your reputation depends on it!* Washington, DC: U.S. Department of Justice, Office of Community Oriented Policing Services.

Newton, M. 1990. *Hunting humans: An encyclopedia of modern serial killers.* Port Townsend, WA: Loompanics Unlimited.

Norris, J. 1988. *Serial killers.* New York: Doubleday.

Peak, K., and R. Glensor. 2002. *Community polic-ing and problem solving: Strategies and prac-tices.* 3rd ed. New Jersey: Prentice Hall.

Publications International. 1991. *Serial killers and murderers.* A PI Book, Signet Special. Illi-nois: Publications International.

Prentky, R. A., A. Burgess, F. Rokous, A. Lee, C. Hartman, R. Ressler, and J. Douglas. 1989. The presumptive role of fantasy in serial ho-micide. *American Journal of Psychiatry* 146(7): 887–891.

Pinto, S., and P. Wilson. 1990. *Serial murder.* Aus-tralian Institute of Criminology: Trends and Issues in Crime and Criminal Justice No. 25.

Schmemann, S. 1992. 'Citizen Ch.': Russia opens files on serial killings. *New York Times, Inter-national* April 4:3–4.

Serial Killer Hit List. 2004. Accessed online May 11, 2004: *http://www.mayhem.net/Crime/serial1.html.*

Serial Killers. 2004. Accessed online May 11, 2004: *http://www.macalester.edu/~psych/whathap/UBNRP/serialkillers/serialkillers.html.*

Serial murder: An introduction. 2004. Accessed online May 11, 2004: *http://www.fortunecity.com/roswell/streiber/273/inf_smintro.htm.*

Serial murder. 2004. Accessed online May 11, 2004: *http://www.geocities.com/serialmurderers/serialmurder.html.*

Sunde, S. 2002. Ex-FBI profiler: No such thing as a "typical" serial killer. Accessed online May 5, 2004: *http://www.seattlepi.nwsource.com/local/54980_profilers18.shtml.*

Take-Two Interactive. 2004. *Manhunt.* New York: Rockstar North.

U.S. Census Bureau. 2000. All across the USA: Population distribution and composition, 2000. In *The population profile of the United States: 2000* (Internet Release). Accessed on-line at: *http://www.census.gov/population/www/pop-profile/profile2000.html.*

Who is a serial killer? 2004. Accessed online May 11, 2004: *http://www.isuisse.ifrance.com/emmaf/base/who_ser.html.* ✦

Chapter 6
The Myth of Drug Users as Violent Offenders

Henry H. Brownstein

Speed kills. The poet Allen Ginsberg, in an underground newspaper interview in 1965 (Kunkin 1965), was one of the first to warn us, and in 2003 it was affirmed by the Office of National Drug Control Policy (ONDCP). Describing the effects of methamphetamine use, the ONDCP (2003) reported, "Chronic methamphetamine abuse can lead to psychotic behavior including intense paranoia, visual and auditory hallucinations, and out-of-control rages that can result in violent episodes." This conclusion was based on a variety of research reports published by a variety of federal agencies. It is not in itself false. The problem is that it serves as the foundation for a myth about the link between methamphetamine use and violence, and this myth is a variation of a broader social myth about the relationship between drug use and violence.

The Myth

The myth about drug use and violence can be simply stated: drug use leads to violent outcomes. That sounds simple, and perhaps even reasonable, but only until further examined. Drugs may all be psychopharmacological agents, but there are many different drugs. In both body and mind, people naturally react differently to different drugs, and different people may react differently to the same drug. Different drugs, and even the same drug, are used for different purposes and under different circumstances, some socially acceptable and some not. So the conclusion that drug use inevitably leads to violence is not so certain.

In recent years, concern among Americans about methamphetamine use has grown. Newspaper articles about methamphetamine users and the dangers of methamphetamine laboratories have become commonplace. On September 9, 2003, an article in the *Memphis Commercial Appeal* started, "Welcome to the crazed, violent world of methamphetamine." A few days later, a headline in the *Honolulu Advertiser* read, " 'Violent reality' of ice outlined in Waipahu." Much of the concern and related fear are grounded in a belief that methamphetamine use inevitably results in violent behavior.

The stories of violence resulting from methamphetamine use are told in terms of different contexts of violence; focusing on gangs, drug dealers, and particularly the link between methamphetamine use and domestic violence. In Arizona, there is the story of a woman who ran from her home with her children because her partner, "high on methamphetamine, was flying into rages more and more often" (*Arizona Republic* December 19, 2003). In California, a woman was found guilty of murder for poisoning her husband so he would not expose her to methamphetamine use (*San Diego Union-Tribune* November 13, 2002).

To say that such stories have a mythological dimension is not to say they are necessarily false, nor is it to say that particular incidents of violence are never related to methamphetamine use. Rather, it is to say that the truth of such a relationship in particular ways or in specific cases is not enough to suggest that the relationship will regularly be found on a broad societal level. Not everyone who uses methamphetamine becomes violent, and people who use methamphetamine and do become violent do not necessarily do so every time.

The stories about methamphetamine use are only the most recent myth about drug using and violence, and are not even the most compelling. Perhaps more interesting are the myths about violence as it relates to marijuana and crack cocaine.

In 1936, a film released in theaters opened with a warning to viewers that what they were about to see was a work of fiction, but that it was based on "actual research." They were told that, while the film might startle them, it was necessary to "sufficiently emphasize the frightful toll of the new drug menace which is destroying the youth of America in alarmingly increasing numbers. *Marijuana* [emphasis in the original] is the drug—a violent narcotic [sic]—an unspeakable scourge—the Real Public Enemy Number One!" *Reefer Madness* was a story about high school friends, how they were lured into marijuana use, and how they lost control over themselves. Eventually in the story, a young girl is murdered. Her killers, identifiable by their tousled hair and maniacal stares, are—naturally—marijuana users.

Marijuana is found in nature. Crack cocaine was developed. According to one account, "Crack was not invented; it was created by a sharp crowd of sinister geniuses who took a simple production technique to make a packaged, ready-to-consume form of a product with a low unit price to entice massive numbers of consumers" (Witkin 1991). There was an overabundance of cocaine in the United States in the early 1980s (Office of National Drug Control Policy 1989). The market for ex-

pensive powder cocaine was too small to absorb it all. Crack was a way for cocaine distributors to expand their market to the poor, who were known to be heavy drug users but were unable to afford cocaine in powder form (Williams 1992).

After just a few years on the market, in the late 1980s, stories about a crack cocaine epidemic "literally destroying the nation" became commonplace (Reinarman and Levine 1989). Violence in general, and in particular murder and child abuse, were all linked to the use of crack. Crack was even called a "uniquely evil drug" (Martz et al. 1989). Other news accounts told a similar story. An article in the *New York Times* told how crack had "fueled" a 25-percent increase in the homicide rate in Queens, New York, the city's most "middle-class" borough. The *Daily News* in New York reported an increasing homicide rate. The *Albany Times Union* had an article called " 'Crack' gives birth to new horror of abused young."

The Kernel of Truth

Myths typically grow from a kernel of truth. For the myth about drug using and violence, that kernel is found in social life and experience. Most people living in the United States routinely use drugs purchased legally through pharmacies and even supermarkets (see Brownstein 2000a). On any given day, millions of people in the United States also use illicit drugs, or use legal drugs in illegal ways (Substance Abuse and Mental Health Services Administration 2003). Evidence shows that some of these drug users do violent things (Roth 1994), but most of them do not (Currie 1993; Inciardi 1992). For example, in a study of heroin users in New York City and in Baltimore, Nurco and his colleagues (1991) found that only a small proportion of heroin users in their sample used violence with any regularity. In addition, they found that the same small group of people, within the study, were responsible for most of the violent acts committed.

Data on drug using among people who get arrested show that people engaged in criminal offending use drugs more often than do other people (National Institute of Justice 2003a). That finding is consistent across the world (National Institute of Justice 2002); however, closer examination of international data show that violent offenders are less likely than property offenders to have been using drugs at the time of their arrest (Taylor et al. 2003). The point is that while drug using and crime and violence are often found together, drug using does not always end in violence.

In 1937, Congress passed the Marijuana Tax Act. Prior to its passage, Harry Anslinger, former head of the Federal Bureau of Narcotics, was quoted as having said, "How many murders, suicides, robberies, criminal assaults, hold-ups, and deeds of maniacal insanity [marijuana] causes each year, especially among the young, can be conjectured?" (cited in Kaplan 1971:92). It was a good question. At the time, social science had not yet provided any evidence on whether marijuana was related to crime or violence. This lack of evidence did not deter Anslinger from turning his claims into a kernel of truth. Kaplan (1971:92) wrote:

> In weighing the evidence on the connection between marijuana and aggression, one is struck by two things: one is the relatively large number of statements made by policy-making committees, medical societies, and public officials as compared with the relatively small number of studies that actually bear on this issue; the other is the even more striking fact that the

studies and evidence relied on in these statements are of extremely weak probative value.

Current research about the relationship between drugs and violence (National Institute of Justice 2003b) runs contrary to the kernel of truth and what was once believed about this relationship.

The Truth or Facts

A considerable body of research was conducted in the later years of the twentieth century about the relationship between drugs, alcohol, and violence. In the early 1950s, Wolfgang and Strohm (1956: 416) studied 588 homicides committed in Philadelphia between 1948 and 1952. They found that alcohol had been consumed by 64 percent of the victims. In a follow up to that study in the late 1960s, Hepburn and Voss (1970) observed similar patterns of intoxicant use by homicide victims in Philadelphia and Chicago.

In an analysis of homicide victims and the use of drugs other than alcohol, Zahn and Bencivengo (1974) found that homicide was the leading cause of death among drug users in Philadelphia in 1972, and that drug users accounted for 31 percent of homicide victims in the city that year. Reidel, Zahn, and Mock (1985:19) later conducted a nationwide study of homicide records and found that in most cases drugs were not detectable in the bodies of the victims after death, and in those cases that a drug was detected, it was most often alcohol or narcotics.

Haberman and Baden (1978) used autopsy and toxicological data from New York City during the 1970s to study people "thought to have died unnaturally." They found that, "apart from substance abuse, homicide was the leading cause of death of narcotics abusers, alcoholics, and those with both conditions" (8). In a later study of autopsy data from New York, Tardiff and Gross (1986:426) concluded, "victims of drug-related homicides were more likely to have only drugs present in their blood, victims of robberies were more likely to have neither alcohol nor drugs, and victims of disputes had alcohol either with or without drugs." In Los Angeles in the 1980s, a study of autopsy data for homicide victims found that between 1980 and 1987, "cocaine has gone from a rarely detected drug [in homicide victims] to the second most frequently detected drug (second only to alcohol)" (Budd 1989: 377).

Because toxicological data on homicide victims are more easily available than data on violent offenders, who may or may not be apprehended, most of the research on the relationship between drugs and violence has involved homicide victims. Nonetheless, there have been studies of violent offenders and drug using. Gary (1986) studied homicide data from U.S. cities during the 1980s and found a strong relationship among black males between the commission of homicide and the use of alcohol. Wieczorek and his associates (1990) examined survey data for 1,887 incarcerated homicide offenders in the early 1980s and found that 56 percent reported having been under the influence of a drug, usually alcohol, at the time of their offending. In 1985, Ladouceur and Temple studied rapists and found that fewer than half were under the influence of drugs at the time of their offense. They concluded, "If there are connections between substance abuse and crime, the links are probably not as direct as has been previously thought" (1985:288).

Goldstein (1985) suggested that, theoretically at least, drugs and violence could be related in three different ways: violence could be the direct result of drug ingestion, it could be a product of the instability or disorder of drug-market organization or activity, or it could be the consequence of people acting out because of a compulsive need for drugs or money for drugs (Goldstein 1985). Research by Goldstein and associates (1989, 1992) and Brownstein and associates (1992) found that homicides related to crack cocaine were usually the product of market instability or disorder and rarely the result of drug ingestion.

Based on an extensive review of the literature on alcohol, drugs, and violence, Parker and Auerhahn (1998:291) concluded, "Despite a number of published statements to the contrary, we find no significant evidence suggesting that drug use is associated with violence." Other recent reviews of the literature have similarly discounted the claim that drug using causes violence (Brownstein 2000b; Chaiken and Chaiken 1990; Fagan 1990; National Institute of Justice 2003b; White and Gorman 2000). When drug use is found to have a connection to violent outcomes, the drug is almost always alcohol (Parker and Auerhahn 1998). So while particular studies do show a connection between drug use and violence, a more careful reading of the literature suggests the kernel of truth should not be confused with a bushel of chaff. Consideration of the social, historical, and political context within which the myth about drug using and violence was constructed will help to explain why this kernel became a myth in the first place.

Interests Served by the Myth

According to Musto (1997:23), the late 1800s in the United States was a period of "wide availability and unrestrained advertising" for drugs. From the period of the Revolution through the end of the nineteenth century, Americans preferred home remedies to medical practices for dealing with pain and illness (Inciardi 1992:3). Without government regulation, manufacturers of widely available medicines did not report their ingredients, which often included derivatives of cocaine or opium (Inciardi 1992:4). In 1885, a new soft drink called Coca-Cola was introduced, which contained extracts of coca to give it a stimulant effect; in 1897, the Sears Roebuck catalogue advertised hypodermic kits for morphine users; and around that same time Bayer and Company began selling a new product for coughs and chest ailments under the trade name Heroin (Inciardi 1992:5–9).

It was during this period of drug manufacturing and drug using that the potential for addiction was first observed. Given the respectability of most drug users and the limited knowledge about drugs at the time, the medical community in the United States emphasized its own interests, defined heroin and cocaine addiction as health problems, and proposed medical solutions (Inciardi 1992:15). In 1906, in response to what was then considered by the media and politicians to be an epidemic, Congress passed the Pure Food and Drug Act, which imposed standards for "quality, packaging, and labeling" of all food and drug products. Then, in 1914, the Harrison Narcotics Act was passed and, in 1937, the Marijuana Tax Act. Together, these acts gave the federal government authority to regulate and control drug production, importation, sale, purchase, and distribution. What was first considered a normal pattern of behavior and then a health problem was transformed into a crime problem (Falco 1989; Kaplan 1971; Musto 1997; Smith 1988).

Throughout the twentieth century, there were those who continued to argue that drug using was not only normal but perhaps even desirable behavior, a way to relieve the pain and monotony of everyday life (Huxley 1954; Weil 1972). And there were those who continued to argue for the medical value of drugs and drug using (Trebach 1982; Schur 1962; Zimmer and Morgan 1997). Nonetheless, the predominant view throughout the century was, and still is, that drug using is criminal and causes further crime and violence. The ascendance of this latter view can be explained in terms of the cultural, social, and political tensions of the times (Bakalar and Grinspoon 1984; Musto 1973), as well as the personal interests of government officials (McWilliams 1990).

Musto (1973) observed that the forces driving drug control and prohibition policy in the twentieth century were related to tensions among categories of people with socioeconomic and cultural differences. For example, marijuana use was legal and considered socially acceptable in the late nineteenth century when users were middle-class, but came to be seen as a crime problem in the 1920s and 1930s when its use became "visible among members of minority groups—blacks in the South and illegal alien Mexicans in the Southwest" (Inciardi 1992:21). Focusing on legal and moral forces, Duster (1970: 20) similarly observed that the evolution of drug policy over this period was related to the fact that most drug addicts in 1900 were middle-class and middle-aged white women, while most addicts in the later years of the century were young, lower- and working-class black males. He argued, "the point is simply that America's moral hostility comes faster and easier when directed toward a young, lower-class Negro male, than toward a middle-aged white female" (Duster 1970:21).

In the context of these cultural, social, and political tensions, a lack of scientific evidence about the relationship between drugs and violence did not deter Anslinger from using the myth to build a career and an agency in his own interest (Inciardi 1992; Kaplan 1971; McWilliams 1990). There are other cases (see, for example, Brownstein 1996:69), but perhaps none so interesting and transparent as Anslinger's.

In 1937, Congress held hearings on a bill called Taxation of Marijuana. At the time Anslinger was the commissioner of narcotics, in the Bureau of Narcotics, in the Department of the Treasury—a petty bureaucrat in a lesser bureau of a major federal agency. He had no evidence from research, but he did have what has since become known as his "gore file," a collection of unsubstantiated but horrifying stories about what happened to people who used marijuana (Kaplan 1971; Sloman 1979). With them, he appeared before Congress and was influential in passing the bill into law (McWilliams 1990; Sloman 1979). Between the 1930s and 1960s, Anslinger remained in office and became one of the most powerful drug policy officials in the United States.

Currently, the war on drugs is sustaining a huge bureaucracy, employing thousands of people, and costing billions of dollars. A tool in the war on drugs is *asset forfeiture*, from which law enforcement agencies have received millions of dollars in money, property, or goods associated with illegal-drug trafficking. Trafficking in illegal drugs is big business. Americans spend billions of dollars a year on illegal drugs. In short, the war on drugs is currently serving the interests of tens of thousands of people, especially drug traffickers and drug-law enforcers.

Policy Implications of Belief in the Myth

In the competition for resources, bureaucrats and program managers, who are responsible for drug prevention and treatment and control programs, compete with each other and with those responsible for other types of programs. Having a good story to tell helps, and the myth that drug using causes violence is a good story. It can attract and hold public attention. It suggests immediate public risk, and so demands an allocation of public resources. As the lessons of the stories of methamphetamine, marijuana, and crack cocaine have shown, it is not an easy story to ignore.

Assuming that drug using and violence are directly related encourages policymakers to design, propose, and implement a particular set of policies. Those policies in turn lead to a particular set of programs. Then, despite the fact that those programs are based on a false premise, they consume resources that could be used productively elsewhere.

In its annual National Drug Control Budget report for fiscal year 2005, the White House Office of National Drug Control Policy proposes a budget of $12.6 billion to reduce illegal drug use in the United States. According to official crime data, there were 13,741,438 people arrested in the United States in 2002, of whom 1,538,813 (11 percent) were arrested for drug abuse violations (Federal Bureau of Investigation 2003). From 1995 to 2002, the total number of arrestees increased by 21 percent and the number of arrestees for drug offenses increased by 38 percent. Between 1995 and 2002, the number of incarcerated persons sentenced for a drug offense in state prisons increased by about 15 percent and in federal prisons by about 49 percent (Harrison and Beck 2003). The Federal Bureau of Prisons estimates the average annual cost of incarceration per federal inmate is about $22,000 (Federal Register 1999). Using that figure for all inmates, the estimated cost for housing 325,000 people in state and federal prisons for drug offending in 2001 was $7 billion.

According to official drug use data, in 2002, an estimated 2,013,000 people in the United States received substance-abuse treatment for any illicit substance (Office of Applied Studies 2003:Table 5.38A). In a report on the costs of drug abuse in the United States, the ONDCP (2001:87) estimated that in 2000, the total costs for health care for drug abusers amounted to about $15 million. That figure includes the total cost of community-based and federally-provided drug treatment, estimated with all support service costs at about $6 million.

The fact that incarceration is so much more expensive than drug treatment for the same number of people is not the important point here. If drug users are people who are prone to violence against other people, then perhaps there is no cost too great to incapacitate them. But if they are not particularly likely to be violent or to commit other crimes—and research has shown they are not—then perhaps it would be wiser to allocate resources in a way that would place more drug users into treatment. From research, we know that for at least some people using certain drugs, treatment does work (National Institute of Justice 2003b). In 2000, there were an estimated 4.5 million people in the United States who were drug dependent or drug abusers (Office of Applied Studies 2002). The need for treatment is even greater among arrestees (Crossland and Brownstein 2003). Scarce resources should be allocated to programs where they can do the most good. To do that, policies and programs should be developed on the basis of knowledge and not on the basis of myth.

References

Bakalar, J., and L. Grinspoon. 1984. *Drug control in a free society*. Cambridge: Cambridge University.

Brownstein, H. 1996. *The rise and fall of a violent crime wave: Crack cocaine and the social construction of a crime problem*. Guilderland, NY: Harrow and Heston.

———. 2000a. Drug distribution and sales as a work system. In *Encyclopedia of criminology and deviant behavior—Volume IV: Self destructive behavior and disvalued identity*, ed. C. D. Bryant. London: Taylor and Francis.

———. 2000b. *The social reality of violence and violent crime*. Boston: Allyn and Bacon.

Brownstein, H., H. R. Baxi, P. J. Goldstein, and P. Ryan. 1992. The relationship of drugs, drug trafficking, and drug traffickers to homicide. *Journal of Crime and Justice* 15:25–44.

Budd, R. 1989. Cocaine abuse and violent death. *American Journal of Drug and Alcohol Abuse* 14:375–382.

Chaiken, J., and M. Chaiken. 1990. Drugs and predatory crime. In *Drugs and crime*, ed. M. Tonry. Chicago: University of Chicago Press.

Crossland, C., and H. Brownstein. 2003. Drug dependence and treatment. In *Annual report 2000: Arrestee drug abuse monitoring*, ed. National Institute of Justice. Washington, DC: U.S. Department of Justice.

Currie, E. 1993. *Reckoning drugs, the cities, and the American future*. New York: Hill and Wang.

Duster, T. 1970. *The legislation of morality law, drugs, and moral judgment*. New York: Free Press.

Fagan, J. 1990. Intoxication and aggression. In *Drugs and crime*, ed. M. Tonry. Chicago: University of Chicago Press.

Falco, M. 1989. *Winning the war on drugs: A national strategy*. New York: Priority Books.

Federal Bureau of Investigation (FBI). 2003. *Crime in the United States: 2002 Uniform Crime Reports*. Washington, DC: Federal Bureau of Investigation.

Federal Register. 1999. Notices. Vol. 64, no. 154 (August 11):43882 [FR Doc. 99-20651].

Gary, L. 1986. Drinking, homicide, and the black male. *Journal of Black Studies* 17:15–31.

Goldstein, P. 1985. The drugs/violence nexus: A tripartite conceptual framework. *Journal of Drug Issues* 15:493–506.

Goldstein, P., H. Brownstein, and P. Ryan. 1992. Drug–related homicide in New York City: 1984 and 1988. *Crime and Delinquency* 38:459–476.

Goldstein, P., H. Brownstein, P. Ryan, and P. Bellucci. 1989. Crack and homicide in New York City, 1988: A conceptually-based event analysis. *Contemporary Drug Problems* 16: 651–687.

Haberman, P., and M. Baden. 1978. *Alcohol, other drugs and violent death*. New York: Oxford University Press.

Harrison, P., and A. Beck. 2003. *Prisoners in 2002, Bureau of Justice Statistics bulletin*. NCJ 200248. Washington, DC: U.S. Department of Justice.

Hepburn, J., and H. Voss. 1970. Patterns of criminal homicide: A comparison of Chicago and Philadelphia. *Criminology* 8:21–45.

Huxley, A. 1954. *Doors of perception*. New York: Harper and Row.

Inciardi, J. 1992. *The war on drugs II*. Mountain View, CA: Mayfield.

Information Canada. 1973. *LeDain Commission: Final report*. Ottawa, Canada: Information Canada.

Kaplan, J. 1971. *Marijuana: The new prohibition*. New York: Pocket Books.

Kunkin, A. 1965. Interview with Allen Ginsberg in Los Angeles. *Free Press* December.

Ladouceur, P., and M. Temple. 1985. Substance use among rapists: A comparison with other serious felons. *Crime and Delinquency* 31:269–294.

Martz, L., M. Miller, S. Hutchinson, T. Emerson, and F. Washington. 1989. The tide of a killing drug. *Newsweek* January 16:44–45.

McWilliams, J. C. 1990. *The protectors: Harry J. Anslinger and the Federal Bureau of Narcotics*. Newark: University of Delaware.

Meisler, S. 1996. The first drug czar. *Drug Policy Letter* 29:13–17.

Musto, D. 1973. *The American disease*. New Haven: Yale University.

———. 1997. Opium, cocaine and marijuana in American history. In *Drugs, crime, and justice: Contemporary perspectives*, eds. L. K. Gaines and P. Kraska. Prospect Heights, IL: Waveland.

National Institute of Justice. 2002. *I-ADAM in eight countries: Approaches and challenges*, ed. B. Taylor. Washington, DC: United States Department of Justice.

———. 2003a. *Annual report 2000: Arrestee drug abuse monitoring*. Washington, DC: United States Department of Justice.

———. 2003b. *Toward a drug and crime research agenda for the 21st century*. Washington, DC: United States Department of Justice.

Nurco, D. N., T. F. Hanlon, M. B. Balter, T. W. Kinlock, and E. Slaght. 1991. A classification of narcotics addicts based on type, amount, and severity of crime. *Journal of Drug Issues* 2:429–448.

Office of Applied Studies. 2002. *National household survey on drug abuse 2000: Volume 1, findings*. Washington, DC: Substance Abuse and Mental Health Services Administration.

———. 2003. *National survey on drug use and health, 2002*. Washington, DC: Substance Abuse and Mental Health Services Administration.

Office of National Drug Control Policy (ONDCP). 1989. *National drug control strategy*. Washington, DC: Executive Office of the President.

———. 2001. *The economic costs of drug abuse in the United States 1992–1998*. Washington, DC: Executive Office of the President.

———. 2003. *Methamphetamine fact sheet*. Washington, DC: ONDCP Drug Policy Information Clearinghouse. Accessed online December, 2003: *http://www.whitehousedrugpolicy.gov/publications/factsht/methamph/index.html*.

Parker, R., and K. Auerhahn. 1998. Alcohol, drugs, and violence. *Annual Review of Sociology* 24:291–311.

Reidel, M., M. Zahn, and L. Mock. 1985. *The nature and patterns of American homicide*. Washington, DC: National Institute of Justice.

Reinarman, C., and H. G. Levine. 1989. Crack in context: Politics and media in the making of a drug scare. *Contemporary Drug Problems* 16: 535–577.

Roth, J. A. 1994. *Psychoactive substances and violence*. Washington, DC: National Institute of Justice—Research in Brief (February).

Schur, E. 1962. *Narcotic addiction in Britain and America: The impact of public policy*. Bloomington: Indiana University.

Sloman, L. 1979. *Reefer madness: Marijuana in America*. New York: Grove.

Smith, M. A. 1988. The drug problem: Is there an answer? *Federal Probation* 52:3–6.

Substance Abuse and Mental Health Services Administration. 2003. *Overview of findings from the 2002 national survey on drug use and health*. Rockville, MD: Office of Applied Studies, NHSDA Series H-21, DHHS Publication No. SMA 03-3774.

Tardiff, K., and E. M. Gross. 1986. Homicide in New York City. *Bulletin of the New York Academy of Medicine* 62:413–426.

Taylor, B. G., H. Brownstein, C. Parry, A. Pluddemann, T. Makai, T. Bennett, and K. Holloway. 2003. Monitoring the use of illicit drugs in four countries through the International Arrestee Drug Abuse Monitoring (I-ADAM) program. *Criminal Justice: An International Journal of Policy and Practice* 3:269–286.

Trebach, A. S. 1982. *The heroin solution.* New Haven: Yale.

Weil, A. 1972. *The natural mind: An investigation of drugs and higher consciousness.* Boston: Houghton Mifflin.

White, H., and D. Gorman. 2000. Dynamics of the drug-crime relationship. In *Criminal justice 2000: Volume 1, The nature of crime: Continuity and change,* ed. G. LaFree. Washington, DC: National Institute of Justice.

Wieczorek, W., J. Welte, and E. Abel. 1990. Alcohol, drugs, and murder: A study of convicted homicide offenders. *Journal of Criminal Justice* 18:217–227.

Witkin, G. 1991. The men who created crack. *U.S. News & World Report* August 19:44–53.

Williams, T. 1992. *Crackhouse: Notes from the end of the line.* New York: Penguin.

Wolfgang, M., and R. Strohm. 1956. The relationship between alcohol and criminal homicide. *Quarterly Journal of Studies on Alcohol* 17:411–425.

Zahn, M., and M. Bencivengo. 1974. Violent death: A comparison between drug users and nondrug users. *Addictive Diseases* 1:283–296.

Zimmer, L., and J. P. Morgan. 1997. *Marijuana myths, marijuana facts: A review of scientific evidence.* New York: Lindesmith Center. ✦

Chapter 7
The Myth of Drug Decriminalization

Barbara Sims and
Michael Kenney

Historically, advocates for drug decriminalization or legalization were typically associated with individuals on the fringes of left-wing politics (MacCoun and Reuter 2001). By the 1990s, however, more moderate individuals and groups (for example, Ann Landers, former Secretary of State George Schultz, and the editorial boards of several major newspapers) began to call for reconsiderations of current drug laws and/or policies (MacCoun and Reuter 2001). The debate over the issue of drug decriminalization can be understood in terms of two underlying philosophical arguments. On the one hand, opponents of drug decriminalization argue that to do so would put U.S. society in peril, opening a Pandora's box and thus loosening all the evils associated with drug use. Proponents of decriminalization, however, argue the contrary. They suggest that it was, in fact, criminalizing drugs in the first place that created a new class of criminals and cost the United States an inordinate amount of resources that could be better spent in other social arenas (families, schools, and so forth).

The purpose of this chapter is to discuss several myths typically associated with the issue of drug decriminalization. An attempt is made here to address the basic arguments of both sides and to examine the policy implications of the more punitive approach to illicit drug use cur-

rently stressed by society and the criminal justice system. We note up front a distinction between drug *legalization*, which would mean repealing most existing laws addressing illicit drug possession and use, and drug *decriminalization*, which calls for a more relaxed policy related to drug possession and use without a blanket policy legalizing such behavior.

The Myth

There are several absolutist positions and myths to which opponents of drug decriminalization hold fast. For one, opponents argue that decriminalization would result in an exponential increase in the number of drug users and/or addicts. They point to the devastating financial and human costs associated with the legal use of alcohol and tobacco as a comparison. Alcohol, for example, is involved in the deaths of about 320,000 people each year in the United States compared with about 3,500 drug-related deaths. Further, crime reports indicate that approximately 23 percent of offenders were under the influence of alcohol at the time of their crimes (Engs and Hanson 1994). Some opponents of decriminalization argue that if the use of illicit drugs is decriminalized, the number of drug-related deaths might soon rise to a level similar to alcohol-related levels. They further maintain that more people would be under the influence of currently illicit drugs, which could lead to an increase in crime victimizations.

A second myth is related to the relationship among drug use, race, and crime. The "crack scare" of the 1990s, for example, was sensationalized by the media in such a way as to convince the American public that urban areas, primarily associated with young, black males, were war zones. This view consisted of perceptions that crime was being committed disproportionately by young, black males high on a drug that transformed them into madmen with superhuman strength. Opponents of decriminalization argue that decriminalization will only exacerbate this problem.

A third myth is related to the rise of *drug cartels.* Eager for profitable news copy, investigative journalists often repackaged the law enforcement line into exciting biographical accounts detailing the rich and infamous lifestyles of such figures as Pablo Escobar, Gonzalo Rodriguez Gacha, Carlos Lehder, and other so-called cocaine kingpins. As numerous transnational trafficking networks increased their penetration of U.S. drug markets in recent decades, a popular misconception developed that the international cocaine trade was run by a handful of massive, vertically integrated cartels that restricted global cocaine production and set international market prices.

One final myth espoused by opponents of decriminalization is that drug use is nothing more than an attempt by individuals to alter their mental states for recreational purposes. Drug use is often attributed to people who are weak and void of moral character. This way of thinking about drug use calls for repressive actions against drug users in an effort that, for all intents and purposes, saves individuals from themselves. Further, punishing drug users becomes deeply embedded in a social control model of law enforcement, with the government willing to invest billions of dollars in police and prisons. This promotes the myth that such an approach will, in turn, create a more morally responsible citizenry.

The Kernel of Truth

Data from the 2003 National Household Survey on Drug Abuse reveal that 19.5 million Americans, age 12 or older, reported using some illicit drug in the month prior to the survey (SAMHSA 2004). This represents approximately 8.2 percent of the U.S. population within that same age category. Further, approximately 3.8 million people were classified with substance dependence in 2003 (SAMHSA 2004).

Opponents of drug decriminalization are correct in their assumption that Americans use illicit drugs on a somewhat regular basis, even in light of the current "get tough" rhetoric and policies that have come to be associated with the nation's war on drugs. They are also correct in their argument that problems associated with abusing substances can wreak havoc on abusers, family members, and friends. According to Lyman and Potter (2003), the substance-addicted individual may resort to stealing from family and friends in order to support his or her habit. Families and friends may provide financial support for their family members who are unable to provide for themselves because of addiction. In worst case scenarios, family members and friends may be called upon to assist with legal or other fees related to problems with the criminal justice system. Attempts at continuing to emotionally and financially support substance-addicted individuals can become extremely draining over time, weakening the familial bond and destroying friendships.

The Office of National Drug Control Policy (ONDCP 1996) reports that the cost of illegal drug use to society is about $110 billion annually. Lyman and Potter (2003) report that some states spend about 13 cents of every budget dollar on drug abuse. They report further that about 77.6 billion dollars in lost earnings annually are associated with drug abuse (Lyman and Potter 2003).

In a study of drug addicts admitted to a residential detoxification center in an urban location, DeAlba, Samet, and Saitz (2004) found that a marjority of them presented with no primary medical care across the life span. Of those admitted, 45 percent were diagnosed with a chronic illness and 80 percent reported having had prior medical hospitalizations (DeAlba, Samet, and Saitz 2004). With the addict having no personal means of obtaining needed healthcare, the costs of treating him or her often falls to other members of society.

This means that both direct and vicarious harm is associated with drug addiction. Not only is harm inflicted on the abuser, family, and friends; the extended community is harmed as well. Proponents of maintaining legal restrictions on the use of illicit drugs point to these facts and argue that decriminalization will only increase the social ills associated with their use.

The Truth or Facts

Many advocates of decriminalization concede that following decriminalization, drug use is likely to increase, leading to many of the same problems associated with alcohol and tobacco use. However, studies show that the majority of illicit drug users experiment and then desist from use altogether after a relatively short period of time (Shedler and Block 1990).

Sometimes, as noted by Inciardi (1991), proponents of decriminalization begin by demonstrating the failed experiment with prohibited alcohol use. Certainly one of the most violated laws in the history of the United States, prohibition set up a black market supply operation, driving up costs of the much-desired product and creating wars among competing illegal distributors for a slice of the profits. Decriminal-izing drugs would most certainly interrupt the black market associated with drug distribution and cut drastically into profits from drug sales. In turn, it could be argued that much of the violence connected with turf wars over illicit drug distribution could be reduced.

Furthermore, there is little evidence to suggest that should drugs be decriminalized there will be large numbers of Americans eager to use them. In the United States, for example, levels of drug use in nineteenth-century America, before laws making drug use illegal, were about what they are today. According to Inciardi (1991), when marijuana use was decriminalized in 12 states in the 1970s, there was no significant increase in the number of marijuana users. In the Netherlands, after decriminalizing the use of marijuana, use of that drug has actually declined (Inciardi 1991). Comparably, not all Americans drink alcohol and not all Americans smoke cigarettes. The U.S. government, health professionals, and grassroots organizations have continued campaigns about the dangers of both, and have regulated their use for decades now. Educational programs and warnings by the U.S. Surgeon General, for example, have deterred many from smoking or have convinced those who do smoke to quit.

Proponents of decriminalization argue that the same thing can happen if illicit drugs are made legal. Careful targeting of educational programs can convince individuals to refrain from what they have learned can be damaging to their health. Treatment programs can be made available to the individual who abuses cocaine, heroin, and other drugs to the extent that Alcoholics Anonymous has assisted people who abuse alcohol. Taken together, proponents argue that decriminalizing drugs will not have the long-term affect of increasing drug use, and may actually reduce it.

The relationship between drug use and crime is not as easy to address. Research shows that many people commit criminal or delinquent acts while under the influence of drugs. Data from a Bureau of Justice report suggests that 36 percent of local jail inmates were under the influence of some drug at the time of their offense, with the most common drug being marijuana (18 percent) followed by cocaine/crack (15 percent) and then heroin (6 percent) (Wilson 2000). But the presence of drugs in a personís system does not necessarily mean the drug caused the criminal or delinquent behavior. Recall the number of self-reported illicit drug users in American society reported above. It is important to point out that only a small number of those users ever become involved in crime, other than, of course, the drug possession and use itself. Further, many police officers argue that if one wants to make a connection between violent behavior and drug use, attention should be focused on the legal drug (except for minors), alcohol. As for the "which came first" argument, it is difficult to determine whether drug use precedes crime or whether involvement in criminal or delinquent activities comes before drug use. Some have even suggested the two occur simultaneously (Walker 1994). Others suggest drug use and crime are totally unrelated, and some individualsí involvement with crime would likely continue even if they ceased using drugs (BJS 1992).

To be sure, a number of independent enterprises transacted with one or more of the cocaine cartels, investing money or merchandise in drug shipments. Small and large trafficking groups in Colombia also cooperated to reduce their exposure to U.S. and Colombian law enforcers.

During the 1980s, a risk-sharing mechanism known as *la apuntada* developed in which smaller groups and individual investors piggybacked their cocaine loads onto larger shipments coordinated by the Medellin or Cali cartel. By pooling resources and using diverse means to export cocaine to the United States, *la apuntada* reduced the risks facing individual financiers (Krauthausen and Sarmiento 1991). But coordination does not equal cartelization.

Not all drug use is for recreational or nefarious purposes. Drugs currently defined as illegal have historically been used for medicinal purposes. Drugs that occur naturally from an unrefined organic source (e.g., opium from the poppy plant, cocaine from coca leaves, etc.) have been consumed for thousands of years to alleviate the symptoms of various medical conditions. Opium is known for its ability to alleviate both physical and psychological suffering, and cocaine has been used to treat fatigue and depression and, in some cases, to ease withdrawal symptoms for individuals addicted to opiates (Levinson 2002). In nineteenth-century America, marijuana was often used to alleviate pain from migraine headaches and as an anticonvulsant and relaxant (Levinson 2002). Proponents of decriminalization argue that those currently illegal drugs could be inexpensive substitutes for more expensive prescription drugs that address the same problems, as well as others.

Interests Served by the Myth

One controversial policy issue associated with current expenditures on corrections, especially prison costs, is privatization. Major corporations now listed on the New York Stock Exchange (Corrections Corporation of America and Wackenhut, for example) boast of profits made from the prison industry. As suggested by Whitehead, Pollock, and Braswell (2003), it is unlikely that an industry in the business of making profits from prisons would want the current trend of locking up more people to decline. This is particularly important as it relates to the number of prisoners locked up for drug crimes. Austin and Irwin (2001) examined the increase in the percent of the U.S. prison population who were incarcerated for drug crimes. Among whites, the percentage in 1960 was only 5 percent, and for nonwhites, 32 percent. By 1996, those percentages equaled 53 percent and 30 percent, respectively. Further, between the years 1987 and 1998 the number of inmates in privately owned prisons increased from 3,100 to 132,000 (Austin and Irwin 2001). The profit being made by these corporations is related to this increase, with much of it tied directly to an increase in the locking up of more and more people for drug-related crimes.

There are some segments of society that see attempts at stopping people from using illicit drugs as their moral responsibility. Certain "moral entrepreneurs" in society, to use a term coined by Becker (1963), are served by having the use of illicit drugs criminalized. This is because these types of restrictions on members of society push the agenda of some religious groups who believe that drug use will bring about the downfall of society in general. Many religious zealots have been able to influence the voting electorate and their elected representatives, and any attempt to decriminalize illicit drug use in the United States is likely to be met with the full force of their organizations.

The mass media, especially television and the movie industry, are well served by keeping drug use illegal. As was noted above, for example, it has been the media that have kept images of young, black males engaged in drug crimes before the American public. With an increasing move toward news as entertainment, negative stereotypes of drug users are regularly displayed on the nightly news or on news magazine shows. Further, the movie industry has made a considerable amount of profit portraying similar images, and the same can be said of the television industry. If drug use were decriminalized in the United States, and after some period of adjustment, these stereotypes would no longer be a big deal, and thus not fodder for a consuming public that has grown less and less interested in the subject matter.

In 1992, building on previous investigation successes, the Drug Enforcement Administration (DEA) introduced a major initiative that quickly became the agency's signature counternarcotics program: to go after the drug kingpins. This expanded greatly the jurisdiction of the DEA; and just after a year and a half of operation, the DEA reported the seizure of $210 million in drug proceeds and the confiscation of 144 aircraft and 91 boats, trucks, and cars (Nieves 1997). Such an expansion of government operations creates thousands of jobs for law enforcement agencies and produces a never-ending supply of resources for those agencies. The Assets Forfeiture Fund established by the Comprehensive Forfeiture Act of 1984 allows for the sharing of seized assets with cooperating state and local law enforcement agencies. According to Vecchi and Sigler (2001), this could set up the possibility of abuse with local law enforcement agencies becoming more interested in asset hunting than in narcotics policing. In a survey of both federal and local drug enforcement officers, for example, Vecchi and Sigler (2001) found that financing the agency was more important for local police officers than for federal officers. If drugs were decriminalized, many of the resources funneled to these agencies through asset forfeitures would vanish.

Keeping the myth of evil drug cartels and kingpins alive in the minds of the American people serves well federal, state, and even local law enforcement communities. Nevermind the fact that most forfeitures are not associated with members of higher-level dealers; rather, they are more often connected with local citizens who have gotten caught up in small time drug dealing.

Policy Implications of Belief in the Myth

Prior to the 1800s in the United States, there were no government interventions operating to curtail the use of drugs such as opium, cocaine, or marijuana. Early attempts at curbing drug use were directed toward immigrant groups, in particular the Chinese. Willing to work for low wages, this group soon came to be seen as a threat to U.S. citizens. Laws were passed, first in the San Francisco area in about 1875, to make it a crime to smoke opium (Levinson 2002).

Inciardi (1991) and others (Gray 2001; Nadelmann 1991) have attempted to frame the history of public policies and/or legislation enacted and put into place to curb the use of drugs in American society. Responding to changing attitudes toward the use of narcotics, Congress passed the Pure Food and Drug Act in 1906. This new law required that all patent medicines, commonly referred to as elixirs or snake oil, label the ingredients used to make the medicine. The business community became involved in pushing for reform because the "new machine age demanded reliable and efficient employees" (Levinson 2002:14). Much like passing laws against vagrancy has been seen as an at-

tempt by government to force workers into factories during the industrial revolution, laws against drug use could be viewed as a similar attempt.

As noted by Levinson (2002), major campaigns against marijuana use and distribution began to take place in the 1930s. Although the stalk of the marijuana plant, or hemp, had a rich history of noningested uses in the United States (parchment paper, sails for ships, ropes, paint oils, etc.), marijuana came to be connected with "jazz musicians, petty crooks, the avant garde, and Mexican immigrant agricultural workers who were smoking dope and becoming violent" (Levinson 2002:18). So strong was the rhetoric, that Congress reacted and passed the Marijuana Tax Act in 1937, and marijuana became yet another prohibited substance in the United States.

Through the decades of the 1940s, 1950s, and 1960s, heroin use increased primarily in large urban areas, but young people from various backgrounds were experimenting more and more with cocaine, LSD, and marijuana (Levinson 2002): The media played a major role in how Americans viewed drug use by young people, convincing most adults that drugs were destroying an entire generation. In 1965, the Federal Bureau of Narcotics was renamed the Bureau of Narcotics and Dangerous Drugs. Four years later, then-President Richard Nixon called for extra efforts by law enforcement agencies to block the entry of drugs into the United States from foreign countries and to eradicate drugs from American society or else risk losing an "entire generation" (Massing 1998:97).

In 1970 Congress passed the Comprehensive Drug Abuse Prevention Act, trumping all previous legislation dealing with illicit drugs. Under this act, grounded in the U.S. Constitution's Commerce Clause, overseeing violations was to be handled by the law enforcement community, more specifically, the Department of Justice. The Drug Enforcement Administration (DEA) was eventually established and became the agency most responsible for overseeing the enforcement of the country's drug laws. Less than a decade later, in 1979, Congress acted again by passing asset forfeiture legislation (as discussed previously) allowing the DEA to seize certain assets of suspected drug traffickers, and within a short period of time, expanded legislation to cover drug paraphernalia as well (Levinson 2002).

In the 1980s, then-President Ronald Reagan called for total abstinence and appropriated significant funding for law enforcement crackdowns. President Reagan "increased the enforcement part of the federal drug control budget from one half to two thirds" (Levinson 2002:27). During this time period, crack cocaine hit the U.S. market and soon produced another public outcry for the government to intervene. The Anti-Drug Abuse Act of 1986 established an unprecedented $4 billion for the war on drugs. It also established mandatory minimum sentences, creating an exponential growth in prison populations.

Just two years later, the legislative assault on drug users and sellers continued with the passage of the Omnibus Drug Act, increasing penalties that also called for the seizing of assets such as homes, cars, boats, etc. It also created the White House Office of National Drug Control Policy, and the director of that organization is often referred to as the nation's drug czar. During the Administration of Bush the father, the drug-related rhetoric continued with the new president going so far as to invade Panama and capturing and placing on trial Manuel Noriega for violating America's drug laws (Levinson 2002).

The DEA's kingpin strategy was premised on the assumption that by removing their leaders, the drug cartels would collapse. This never happened, in part because these enterprises took the form of fluid, interorganizational networks composed of multiple production, transportation, and distribution nodes. While policy makers can design more effective counter-drug enforcement programs, the structure and adaptability of the drug trade suggests that supply reduction strategies as currently conceived and executed will not work.

The war on drugs has continued to the present; but law enforcement's ability to get to the root of the American drug problem has not proved successful, and many argue that, instead, it has created a major social crisis. In short, the nation's war on drugs has not met its goals to stamp out drug use within American society, and the rhetoric surrounding the war is not subsiding.

Drug-related legislation and U.S. policies toward the use and distribution of illicit drugs sought to make illegal certain acts that were previously considered under the purview of individual choice. In turn, this created a new class of criminals; and as is the case with any other type of criminal behavior, social control mechanisms had to be put into place to deal with them. Drug use and its trafficking would be seen as major social problems and behaviors that had to be curtailed by the full force of the criminal justice system and other government entities (e.g., the Treasury Department).

Largely as a result of the war on drugs, the nation's incarceration rate has grown from 124 per 100,000 citizens in 1978, to 313 in 1985, and to 470 in 2001 (Whitehead, Pollock, and Braswell 2003). Although other explanations for the dramatic increase in the incarceration rate are increased sentences and the public's outrage over crime, most researchers agree that it is the country's legislative approach to dealing with America's drug problem that has resulted in the locking up of more people (Whitehead, Pollock, and Braswell 2003). In turn, as a result of locking up more people, the costs associated with building and maintaining prisons has skyrocketed. In California, for example, the 2002 state budget showed that 18 percent was spent on corrections, with only one percent spent on higher education (Whitehead, Pollock, and Braswell 2003).

Proponents of decriminalization argue that the better approach to reducing drug consumption would be to implement a series of demand-side initiatives: high-quality, public treatment on demand; scientifically based school prevention programming spread over numerous years; greater funding for research on understanding the nature of drug addiction and the organizational structure of drug trafficking, etc. Decriminalization would remove the criminal penalties that users face for their drug use. On the other hand, because the supply of drugs would remain illegal, it would not address the profit paradox and organizational adaptability that drives drug production and distribution.

Addressing the future of illicit drugs, MacCoun and Reuter (2001:76) argued, "The key consequentialist policy question, though not the only one, is whether, notwithstanding increases in use, there would be a net increase or decrease in drug-related harms." MacCoun and Reuter (2001) provided a description of such harms, along with a discussion of who bears the harm and/or risk for them. They also included a discussion framed as the primary source of harm. An abbreviated version of MacCoun and Reuter's (2001) grid suggests the following:

- There are several health-related harms due to illicit drug use and that the user him/herself bears the harm, along with intimate others, and that the source of the harm is the user;

- Social and economic harm is multifaceted, and although the user and his/her intimates bear the brunt of harm, society in general (e.g., employers and local neighborhoods) may be harmed as well; the primary sources of these types of harm are the user, the illegal status of the drug, and enforcement strategies to control use;

- Safety and public order harm (accidents on the job or on the highways, violent behavior, reduced property values, etc.) are most harmful to local neighborhoods and society in general; the primary sources of this type of harm are the user coupled with the drug's illegal status and social control mechanisms to control its use; and,

- Criminal justice institutions are harmed through increased costs, overcrowded jails and prisons, backed up court systems, etc., with society as a whole bearing the burden of paying for it all; the primary source of harm for this category is law enforcement strategies to curtail the sale and use of illicit drugs.

Proponents of decriminalization argue that many of these harms would be greatly reduced if illicit drugs were legalized or, at the very least, there was an effort to find some compromise through decriminalization. The reality is that Americans engage in illicit drug use for a variety of reasons. There is also evidence that the general public is still in favor of current drug laws and that illicit drugs have a long way to go before they will receive the same level of acceptance as have alcohol and tobacco.

As stated earlier, the debate over decriminalization is likely located on a philosophical continuum, with drugs intrinsically evil on one end and drug use as a matter of private choice on the other end. Both of these positions are probably so absolutist in nature that there is not likely to be much movement of either side. This is unfortunate because it is possible to reach a compromise, as has been the case with alcohol and tobacco products. Instead, the evidence pointing to a conclusion that prohibition does not work is lost in today's drug-related rhetoric. So is the scientific evidence indicating that strategic, well-designed educational programs, along with carefully implemented treatment modalities for substance addicted individuals, can work. More likely than not, the supply-side approach to drug eradication will continue for some time.

References

Becker, H. S. 1963. *Outsiders: Studies in the sociology of deviance.* New York: Free Press of Glencoe.

Bureau of Justice Statistics (BJS). 1992. *Drugs, crime, and the justice system.* Washington, DC: Government Printing Office.

De Alba, I., J. H. Samet, and R. Saitz. 2004. Burden of medical illness in drug and alcohol dependent persons without primary care. *American Journal of Addiction* 13:33–45.

Drug Enforcement Administration (DEA). 1993. *U.S. drug threat assessment: 1993.* Washington, DC: DEA Headquarters, September.

Engs, R. C., and D. J. Hanson. 1994. Boozing and bawling on campus: A national study of violent problems associated with drinking over the past decade. *Journal of Criminal Justice* 22(2):171–180.

Gray, J. P. 2001. *Why our drug laws have failed and what we can do about it: A judicial indictment of the war on drugs.* Philadelphia: Temple University Press.

Inciardi, J. A. 1991. American drug policy and the legalization debate. In *The drug legalization debate*, ed. James A. Inciardi, 7–15. Thousand Oaks, CA: Sage.

Krauthausen, C. and L. F. Sarmiento. 1991. *Cocaína y co.: Un mercado ilegal por dentro.* Bogota, Colombia: Tercer Mundo.

Levinson, M. H. 2002. *The drug problem: A new view using the general semantics approach.* Westport, CT: Praeger.

Lyman, M. D., and G. W. Potter. 2003. *Drugs in society: Causes, concepts, and control.* 4th ed. Cincinnati, OH: Anderson.

MacCoun, R. J., and P. Reuter. 2001. *Drug war heresies: Learning from other vices, times and places.* Cambridge, MA: Cambridge University Press.

Massing, M. 1998. *The fix.* New York: Simon and Schuster.

Nadelmann, E. A. 1991. The case for legalization. In *The drug legalization debate*, ed. James A. Inciardi, 17–44, Thousand Oaks, CA: Sage.

Nieves, R. J. 1997. *Colombian cocaine cartels: Lessons learned from the front.* Washington, DC: National Strategy Information Center.

Office of National Drug Control Policy (ONDCP). 1996. *National drug control strategy.* Washington, DC: U.S. Government Printing Office.

Shedler, J., and J. Block. 1990. Adolescent drug use and psychological health: A longitudinal inquiry. *American Psychologist* 45:612–630.

Substance Abuse and Mental Health Services Administration (SAMHSA). 2004. *Results from the 2003 National Survey on Drug Use and Health: National findings.* Rockville, MD: Office of Applied Studies, NSDUH Series H–25, DHHS Publication No. SMA 04–3964.

Vecchi, G. M., and R. T. Sigler. 2001. Economic factors in drug law enforcement decisions. *Policing* 24(3):310–330.

Walker, S. 1994. *Sense and nonsense about crime and drugs: A policy guide.* 3rd ed. Belmont, CA: Wadsworth.

Whitehead, J. T., J. M. Pollock, and M. C. Braswell. 2003. *Exploring corrections in America.* Cincinnati, OH: Anderson.

Wilson, D. J. 2000. *Drug use, testing, and treatment in jails.* Washington, DC: Bureau of Justice Statistics, U.S. Department of Justice. ✦

Chapter 8
Demystifying Terrorism: "Crazy Islamic Terrorists Who Hate Us Because We're Free?"

Paul Leighton

The Myth

"September 11 changed everything" is an observation that is heard frequently along with discussions of a "post–9/11 world." Yet before the terrorist attacks, criminology had only a "grudging acceptance of terrorism" (Rosenfeld 2002:1), and the situation has changed surprisingly little. Certainly, many criminology students will find employment and increased opportunities in security and related fields, but the discipline has made little movement to build on its understanding of violent crime and hate crimes to better understand the mass murders committed by terrorists. Indeed, serial killers are still a trendy topic, with much interest in psychological profiling and "mind hunting." Getting inside the head of Bundy, Gacy, or Dahmer is still more popular than understanding Osama bin Laden (who has killed far more people than those serial killers combined).

While there are some patterns to understanding serial killers, much of what people find fascinating relates to aspects of individual pathology. In contrast, terrorism is political violence, and thus requires knowledge of social and political issues. International terrorism requires some understanding of global politics and history, which are not popular topics in the United States. Even after September 11, few Americans increased their consumption of international news. Anti-American terrorism is more difficult to study. Following the attacks on the World Trade Center and Pentagon, the emphasis was on creating solidarity rather than understanding—and seeing the world through the eyes of—"the enemy."

Further, those who do try to understand anti-American terrorism and to see the world as the terrorists do, run the risk of seeming unpatriotic and of appearing to blame the victims, even though those who do the same with serial killers never hear such accusations. Indeed, one university that simply wanted to require all incoming freshmen to read a book about Islam found itself sued in federal court and berated by a range of conservative groups and Christian evangelists. One news analyst compared the assignment to teaching *Mein Kampf* in 1941, and questioned the purpose of making freshmen study "our enemy's religion." However, one freshman, demonstrating a much better grasp of the issues, commented: "After the terrorist attacks, I was so angry that I really didn't care to learn anything about Muslims. But I know now that refusing to learn is what causes more anger and confusion" (Johnson 2002:A2).

The author of a book about Islam also noted the importance of understanding, because the United States is likely to have continuing conflicts with Islamic nations and militants. Ignorance is no longer an option. Indeed, without understanding and a willingness to explore uncomfortable issues like anti-Americanism, myths and distortions are likely to flourish. Given the complexity of terrorism and strong mixed feelings about the war on terrorism, there are many myths and problematic simplifications that this chapter could address. The focus, however, will be on several fundamental myths. The first goes to the basic character of terrorists—the belief that they are insane psychopaths bent on evil. The second and third are about terrorists' politics and worldview—the beliefs that they hate us because we're free and that they are only motivated by anti-Americanism. Revealing the kernel of truth in these statements facilitates a better understanding of terrorism and enables criminology to be more relevant to the issues facing America in the twenty-first century.

The Kernel of Truth

Many discussions on the character of terrorists engage in labeling rather than explanation: terrorists have done evil, therefore they are evil (and vice versa). People do not understand—or do not want to understand—so the terrorism is seen as senseless and irrational, and people thus assume the terrorists are crazy. Likewise, the mass violence of terrorism seems similar to mass murder, so people assume terrorists must be similar to psychopaths and serial killers. While these characterizations are circular and flawed, the important fact is that terrorists are fanatics, or what Hoffer (1951) called "true believers." Not all true believers endorse violence, writes Hoffer, but "their innermost craving is for a new life—a rebirth—or, failing this, a chance to acquire new elements of pride, confidence, hope, a sense of purpose and worth by an identification with a holy cause" (21). True believers and fanatics see the world in very clear-cut

terms, so they feel a high degree of moral certainty or righteousness about their position. When combined with a sense that something sacred is threatened, the stage is set for action—action which often includes violence.

Terrorists working on their own are considered more likely to have personality disturbances than those working as a team. Occasionally two psychopaths will work together, and frequently one will be clearly dominant. So there is some basis for believing that terrorists can be explained by personality disorders. But, as discussed below, psychopaths are too egocentric to work together in groups for a larger political or social cause. More generally, personality plays a role in shaping terrorists, especially in terms of how it interacts with events in life that serve as catalysts to terrorism. The role of mental illness and diagnosable personality disorders is ultimately a small contribution to explaining terrorism, and a focus on those subjects diverts attention from social issues that are the basis for terrorism's political violence.

The political issues of Al-Qaeda and other Islamic fundamentalists certainly include anti-Americanism, which is evident from bin Laden's speeches and his fatwa (religious decree) about the "Zionist-Crusader Alliance." Although Europeans waged the Crusades that ravaged Muslim countries, militants see the Crusades as a timeless battle between Islam and forces of western imperialism, which the United States currently seems to embody. But the fatwa's title also suggests that anti-Semitism, or at least anti-Zionism, is part of the motivation. And furthermore, explaining the terrorism of bin Laden's followers also involves understanding his reasons for a number of acts that have happened in Arab lands and have taken the lives of many fellow Muslims.

To the extent that Islamic extremism is anti-American, the reasons include—and go beyond—American freedom in the abstract. Summarizing a global attitudes survey, the Pew Center (2003:40) found "a pattern of support for democratic principles combined with the perception that their nation is currently lacking in these areas is characteristic of many Muslim nations." People in countries around the world endorse American democratic values, although they also believe that the social, political, and economic freedoms in the United States lead to behaviors that are decadent and materialistic. Islamic militants seize on ambivalent reactions to America in the Muslim community, especially in terms of sexuality, abortion, women's rights, and homosexuality. Ironically, some of these issues are also concerns of the survivalist right in the United States, a male-dominated movement that—while not monolithic in its beliefs—tends to endorse very traditional roles for women, bombs abortion clinics, and views homosexuality and interracial mixing as signs of moral decline that must be fervently resisted.

The Truth or the Facts

When attempting to make sense of the character of terrorists, the proper context is research showing that "normal" people participate in executions, lynch mobs, military massacres, and genocide. For example, a key figure in the Nazi extermination of Jews was Adolph Eichmann, who was examined by six psychiatrists who proclaimed him "normal." "More normal, at any rate, than I am after having examined him," one of them is said to have exclaimed, while another found that Eichmann's whole psychological outlook, his attitude toward his wife and children, mother and father, brothers, sisters, and

friends, was "not only normal but most desirable" (Arendt 1964:25–26). While Nazis are different from Islamic terrorists and American lynch mobs, what links them is that they all involve normal people acting together to combat what they see as a dangerous threat. The fight against that threat is viewed by them as an important and eternal version of "The Good."

In a wide-ranging literature review, Hudson (1999) finds no support for an explanation based on mental illness or abnormality in any of the studies of individual terrorists and terrorist groups. The elaborate timing and planning that go into "successful" terrorism are inconsistent with mental disorders. Hudson concludes that terrorists are not psychologically different from the nonterrorist. What distinguishes terrorists from nonterrorists is childhood development and radicalizing events, like war or insurrection, which combine with belief systems that are projected on to ever changing regional and global conflicts (Hamm and Leighton 2002).

Some of the arguments above do not apply to psychopaths, who are capable of elaborate planning to carry out serial murder. But the majority of serial killers work by themselves, and the majority of team killers only involve two members (Hickey 1997). Even in such teams, psychopaths exhibit narcissism and self-absorption; their motives for killing lie in fantasy, especially sexual fantasies. In contrast, terrorists are focused on a larger social or political cause and suppress much of their individual autonomy—in the extreme, carrying out suicidal attacks—to further these ends. Further, one of the hallmarks of Al-Qaeda is multiple, simultaneous attacks that require elaborate planning. One senior CIA official commented that "two [attacks] at once is not twice as hard—two at once is a hundred times as hard" (Reeve 1999:200). Al-Qaeda's September 11 operation involved four separate teams and could not have been completed by self-absorbed people pursuing individual fantasies.

In terms of the social and political issues involved with Islamic terrorism, Benjamin and Simon (2002) provide a helpful starting point. The authors were both directors of the National Security Council, and write about the "root causes" of terrorism. They argue:

> The United States is resented for its cultural hegemony, global political influence, and overwhelming conventional military power. Its cultural reach threatens traditional values, including the organization of societies that privilege males and religious authority. It offers temptation, blurs social, ethical, and behavioral boundaries, and presages moral disorder. America's political weight is seen as the hidden key to the durability of repressive regimes that fail to deliver prosperity while crushing dissent. Its support is cited to explain the power of Israel to oppress Muslims and degrade Islam. American military prowess is used to kill Muslims, as in Iraq, or is withheld to facilitate their extermination, as in Bosnia. The American cultural challenge to Islamic societies stands for a broader Western commitment to secularization, the relegation of religion to the private sphere, and a focus on the here and now instead of on either a hereafter for individuals, or a messianic era in which the righteous as a collective will partake. (2002:407)

This lengthy quote is important because it concisely identifies a range of issues that need to be examined instead of individual pathology. It recognizes that anti-Americanism is a significant factor for reasons that include—and go beyond—American freedoms. The root causes examined in this quote help explain terrorist attacks perhaps directed at Western targets but which also kill large numbers of Arabs and fellow Muslims, such as the 2003 bombings in Saudi Arabia and Bali. Ultimately, the question "Why do they hate us?" is "too self-centered and exclusionary a reflex. Those who hate in this way hate much more than us" (Hoagland 2003:B7).

As Benjamin and Simon (2002) note in the quote above, part of the motivation for terrorism is a desire to bring to life a new messianic era involving an Islamic superpower ruled by Islamic law. Muslims who put man's law above God's law are as despised as America and Israel. The militants hope to restore an Islamic caliphate, which is "an integral part of Islam's glory," a "divinely mandated leader whose forces lead a lightning conquest of much of the known world for the faith" (Benjamin and Simon 2002:47).

This goal may be new information to many, but this part of bin Laden's quest has roots that go back to medieval Muslim theologian Ibn Taymiyya. His writings included issues that we now discuss in terms of the separation of church and state, which for Ibn Taymiyya centered on the secularization of government and the consequent subordination of religion to the state. He felt that rulers needed to enforce sharia, Islamic teachings that have been codified into law, and exhibit personal piety: "To obey a leader who violated the percepts of Islam would be to reject the word of God and be guilty of apostasy oneself" (Benjamin and Simon 2002:48). Ibn Taymiyya wanted to purify Islam, and a crucial aspect of this task was jihad—holy war—and not just the "inner" jihad or individual struggle to become more devout. Jihad was against enemies, but not just the ones at the political borders: "By asserting that jihad against apostates within the realm of Islam is justified—by turning jihad inward and reforging it into a weapon for use against Muslims as well as infidels—he planted a seed of revolutionary violence in the heart of Islamic thought" (Benjamin and Simon 2002:50).

This line of reasoning from Ibn Taymiyya is handed down through the Crusades, European conquest, and colonialism—all of which Muslims found humiliating—to bin Laden. Al-Qaeda and its supporters view less-militant interpretations of Islam as coming from the paid lackeys of apostate leaders bought off by the United States. Indeed, such governments tend to be more Western, more secular, and thus not only place human judgment over the divine, but also lead Muslims away from the true faith. For bin Laden, the overthrow of such governments is an important step to securing rule by those such as the Taliban, who govern in accordance with Islamic law. The ultimate goal is to create an Islamic superpower and resurrect the glory days when Islam was a powerful force, united under a divinely appointed ruler. To this end, bin Laden is willing to engage in violence against a wide range of people who stand in the way of this vision, and has indicated that acquiring a nuclear weapon is a religious duty (Benjamin and Simon 2002:140, 160).

Interests Served by the Myth

Hudson (1999) notes that many terrorism experts are skeptical of explanations that rely on mental illness or psychopathy because these explanations hide social and political issues the terrorists take very seriously. This point is crucial for understanding September 11 because bin Laden is a "terrorist hero," similar to the Western outlaws and urban gangsters Kooistra

(1989) writes about. Indeed, after September 11, The Pew Center's global attitudes survey asked people around the world which leader they "had confidence in to do the right thing in world affairs." Osama bin Laden received substantially higher ratings than President Bush or British Prime Minister Blair in six countries whose combined population is almost 500 million people (Pew Center 2003). This survey is consistent with earlier information that "scores of Pakistanis have named their newborn sons Osama," highlighting that the terrorists may be on the fringe "but those who applaud are the disenfranchised Muslims everywhere" (Reeve 1999: 203). Believing that the September 11 suicide terrorists were crazy or had questionable pathologies might be comforting but disguises an important issue about how widespread support for bin Laden is.

Kooistra (1989:52) suggests that hero status occurs when people find "some symbolic meaning in his criminality"—or his political violence, in the case of bin Laden. With criminals, support for the symbolic meaning happens when substantial segments of the public feel " 'outside the law' because the law is no longer seen as an instrument of justice but as a tool of oppression wielded by favored interests" (1989:11). In terms of terrorism, the message sent by the political violence finds support when large segments of the population feel disenfranchised within the social, political, and economic order of the world.

The analysis of disenfranchisement points back to the above excerpt of the root causes of terrorism by Benjamin and Simon (2003): Muslims feel oppressed because of America's military might, foreign policy, and the invasive spread of American culture and values. While discussions of these issues do occur, they do not follow from beliefs about crazy terrorists, so one of the interests served by the myth is a general one of American hegemony in the world. American hegemony refers to American dominance and all the ways it is maintained, from the use of military force to unexamined beliefs about the superiority of U.S. values. Exposing the myth of crazy terrorists who hate us because we're free does not mean relinquishing power, but rather being more open to thinking about how the rest of the world sees us and how our presence influences others.

The rhetoric of crazy, freedom-hating terrorists also serves the interests of the president in his attempt to rally support for whatever actions he believes should be taken, even when those actions and strategies are problematic. The division of *us* (rational freedom-lovers) versus *them* (crazy freedom-haters), when combined with rhetoric emphasizing the stark choice of "with us" or "against us," minimizes legitimate debate in favor of unquestioning support. While national unity and secrecy can be important at times, people should be free to raise questions or oppose plans they consider to be flawed, without accusations of being unpatriotic or giving comfort to terrorists. Partisan interest, not democracy, is more likely to be hurt by full information and robust debate.

Further, whether a president is using terrorism for partisan purposes is a question that should be asked regardless of which party holds the office. The best interests of politicians (especially around election time) may or may not be the same as the country's long-term best interest; patriotic titles on legislation may or may not be an accurate reflection of the bill's content.

Policy Implications of Belief in the Myth

A belief that terrorists are crazy or irrational may lead to an overemphasis on security to deal with the relatively small number of terrorist organizations, rather than taking a more holistic approach to the root causes of terrorism. The belief that terrorists are driven by anti-Americanism and hatred of freedom reinforces the idea that terrorism is an accumulation of the irrational or "sick" beliefs of a few, rather than the militant wing of a substantive political agenda that may receive widespread support, including financial aid. The myth that terrorists are mainly motivated by anti-Americanism ignores the violence they have done to other Muslims, and sets up Islam as the enemy rather than highlighting potential alliances with Arab leaders.

Further, the belief that terrorists are simply evil implies that the threat requires unprecedented presidential power, even going beyond the scope of powers prescribed by the Constitution during a time of declared war. The ability to detain people and declare them outside of both the U.S. criminal law and the protections of international law is a problematic way to defend democratic freedoms (Leighton 2004), and, when used against Muslims, adds to their feelings of persecution. Declaring that well-established international law does not apply, adds to perceptions that the United States thinks it is above the laws it frequently insists other countries obey. Ignoring international law at this juncture also undercuts policies favoring the development of international law to deal with a growing number of disputes caused by a shrinking and increasingly interconnected global village.

This chapter has argued for a more complex understanding of terrorism that includes an uncomfortable examination of the social issues raised by Al-Qaeda's political violence (Hamm and Leighton 2002). Indeed, criminology does not only focus on security to prevent crime, but attempts to examine the causes of crime and believes that certain social conditions are important factors. Dealing with school violence only through metal detectors and surveillance cameras is limited, unimaginative, and could benefit from serious inquiry into the mindset of students who show up at school ready to massacre their classmates. While many people would like to believe simply that such students are crazy, the emerging picture suggests it has more to do with the dynamics of exclusion and marginalization, and that these students reflect aspects of the society that shaped them. While terrorism is not exactly like school violence, the analogy helps illustrate the problems with the current myths surrounding terrorism.

Unfortunately, following the suggestions in this chapter will not end terrorism, and it is unrealistic to expect any policy to bring an end to terrorism—or crime. Crime prevention policies are not expected to end crime but instead are judged by the amount of victimization and suffering they can reduce in relation to the resources they require. Terrorism prevention policies are still in development, but should be judged by the same standard rather than discounted because they will not end terrorism. Reducing the frequency, severity, and support for terrorism are important goals, and ones that should not be left only to political scientists, psychologists, and security personnel. Criminology has an important role to play in helping confront the problem of international terrorism, and should take up the uncomfortable challenges of pursuing a deeper understanding.

References

Arendt, H. 1964. *Eichmann in Jerusalem: A report on the banality of evil.* New York: Viking Press.

Benjamin, D., and S. Simon. 2002. *The age of sacred terror.* New York: Random House.

Hamm, M., and P. Leighton, eds. 2002. Teaching and understanding Sept 11. Accessed online: *http://stopviolence.com.*

Hickey, E. 1997. *Serial murderers and their victims,* 2nd ed. Belmont: Wadsworth.

Hoagland, J. 2003. Fighting for the soul of Islam. *Washington Post* July 13, B7.

Hoffer, E. 1951. *The true believer.* New York: Harper & Row.

Hudson, R. 1999. *The sociology and psychology of terrorism: Who becomes a terrorist and why?* Washington, DC: Federal Research Division, Library of Congress and U.S. Dept. of Commerce, National Technical Information Service.

Johnson, D. 2002. N.C. University students discuss readings in Islam: Christian group sought to bar assignment on Koran. *Washington Post* August 20:A2.

Kooistra, P. 1989. *Criminals as heroes: Structure, power and identity.* Bowling Green: Bowling Green State University Popular Press.

Leighton, P. 2004. The challenge of terrorism to free societies in the global village. In *Terrorism and counter-terrorism: Criminological perspectives,* ed. Mathieu Deflem. Amsterdam: Elsevier Science.

Pew Center. 2003. *View of a changing world.* Washington DC: The Pew Research Center for The People and The Press. Accessed online: *http://people-press.org/.*

Reeve, S. 1999. *The new jackals: Ramzi Yousef, Osama bin Laden and the future of terrorism.* Boston: Northeastern University Press.

Rosenfeld, R. 2002. Why criminologists should study terrorism. *The Criminologist* 27(6):1, 3–4. ✦

Section 2

Law Enforcement

Chapter 9
The Myth That the Role of the Police Is to Fight Crime

David E. Barlow and
Melissa Hickman Barlow

The Myth

The most common perception about the police is that their role is to fight crime and protect citizens from harm. This seems obvious. Stories about the crime-fighting activities of the police are abundant in newspapers and on the evening news in scenes of police officers taking dangerous suspects into custody or leading them into the courtroom. Both news and entertainment media perpetuate the view of police as crime fighters, and they do so with help from police agencies. News media are usually only interested in police stories when they involve notable criminal activity because this is the aspect of policing deemed most newsworthy. Similarly, fictional crime dramas on television and in the movies typically depict police in a crime-fighting role (Kappeler, Blumberg, and Potter 1996). Even some of the scholarship on police uncritically incorporates the notion that the role of the police is to fight crime. For example, Iannone (1994, 201) states that the proper way to evaluate the success of a police department is "by its ability to suppress unlawful activity." Critics of the police (see, for example, Murphy 1993) attribute their problems and shortcomings to a failure to adequately embrace and fulfill the crime-fighting role. They proclaim that "American policing is a failure. Its first responsibility is to prevent crime. The police have misunderstood their role" (Murphy 1993: 113). Therefore, police scholars confirm the common-sense view of police as crime fighters, stating that "the core mission of the police is to control crime," and underscoring the point by arguing that "no one disputes this" (Moore, Trojanowicz, and Kelling 1988:1).

The Kernel of Truth

There is certainly a kernel of truth to the argument that the function of the police is to control crime. Every day in cities all across the country, crimes are reported to the police and the police record information on these crimes and the potential suspects involved. In addition, the police investigate crimes, seek out suspects, arrest offenders, and provide physical evidence and testimony that may lead to the conviction and sanction of criminals. It is a myth, however, that these activities constitute the fundamental role of the police in the United States. The crime-fighting role of police is only a surface reality.

This surface reality, though, is the only reality ever experienced by many citizens when it comes to the police. For the majority of people in the United States, the view of police as crime fighters reflects all they know of police through a very narrow range of personal experience and from the media. Their reality is one limited by the fact that they rarely encounter the police in the performance of their duties. There are many people in society whose only contact with police comes when they are victims of crime and police come to their aid. Most white, middle-class children

73

are taught that the police officer is their friend and protector, a safe haven from "stranger danger." And when members of the white, middle-class majority come into contact with police because they are suspected of a crime, this too is a context in which the police are engaged in their crime-fighting function.

Most individuals who choose to become police officers do so because they want to fight crime and protect citizens from harm. After all, police departments are the agencies to which crimes are reported and it is police officers who are responsible for apprehending and arresting criminal offenders. What many of those seeking their first job as a police officer fail to realize is how small a proportion of a police officer's time is spent on crime-fighting activities. They are attracted to the job because of the surface reality. Underneath what appears on the surface, the truth about policing is that, throughout the history of our country, it has served as a mechanism of social control designed to preserve the status quo in relations of power in society.

The Truth or Facts

In contrast to those whose limited experience with police gives them no reason to question the surface reality of the crime-fighting role, there are subgroups of U.S. citizens who have not commonly found a safe haven in police. Racial and ethnic minorities, people who are poor, abused children, immigrants, and battered women are groups whose typical experiences with police expose the ethnocentrism of the assumption that the role of police is to fight crime and to protect the citizenry from harm. In fact, most policing in the United States takes place in poor neighborhoods with high concentrations of racial and ethnic minorities. Most police are as-

signed to these locations; therefore people living in these areas have regular contact with the police. Yet the perspectives of citizens living in these areas are rarely incorporated into our understanding of the police and their role in society. For example, Wright (1945:157) described a reality not reflected in the myth that the role of police is to fight crime:

> One morning, while I was polishing brass out front, the boss and his son drove up in their car. A frightened black woman sat between them. They got out and half dragged and half kicked the woman into the store. White people passed and looked on without expression. A white policeman watched from the corner, twirling his night stick; but he made no move. I watched out of the corner of my eyes, but I never slackened the strokes of my chamois upon the brass. After a moment or two I heard shrill screams coming from the rear of the store; later the woman stumbled out, bleeding, crying, holding her stomach, her clothing torn. When she reached the sidewalk, the policeman met her, grabbed her, accused her of being drunk, called a patrol wagon and carted her away.
>
> When I went to the rear of the store, the boss and his son were washing their hands at the sink. They looked at me and laughed uneasily. The floor was bloody, strewn with wisps of hair and clothing. My face must have reflected my shock, for the boss slapped me reassuringly on the back. "Boy, that's what we do to niggers when they don't pay their bills," he said.

The core mission of the police officer in this event seems confused. There is no evidence he was acting in a deviant manner; rather he was performing what he perceived to be his normal duty. His normal duty, though, was not to protect this woman from violent crime, but, rather, to maintain the existing racist social order.

More recently, Scott (1993) referred to the Los Angeles Police Department as just another gang. According to Scott's accounts, even the police referred to themselves as a gang identified by their precinct, calling themselves the "Seventy-seventh Street gang." In the following excerpt, Scott (1993:175) described police activities during a war between the "Eight Trays" (Scott's gang) and a rival gang known as the "Sixties," activities that are nearly unimaginable to most Americans:

> Our missions were successful largely because we had logistical help from the LAPD CRASH units. For four nights in a row now, we had been getting helpful hints from "our friends" in blue—as they liked to refer to themselves. "But," they'd quickly add, "we are from the Seventy-seventh Street gang, which just happens to not get along with the Rollin' Sixties."
>
> Ignorant, very eager, and filled with a burning hatred for the "enemy," we ate that shit up. We never realized that the Seventy-seventh Street gang didn't get along with anybody in the New Afrikan community.
>
> "Hey, Monster," a tomato-faced sergeant said, "I tell you them goddamn Sixties are talking about murdering you on sight."
>
> "Oh yeah, who?"
>
> "Peddie, Scoop, Kiki, and a few others. If I were you I'd keep my gun close at hand, 'cause those boys seem mighty serious."
>
> "Yeah, well fuck the Sixties. They know where I'm at."
>
> "Yeah, but do you know where they are? I mean right now?"
>
> "Naw, you?"
>
> Then, calling me to the car in a secretive manner he said, "They on

Fifty-ninth Street and Third Avenue. All the ones I just mentioned who've been bad-mouthing you. I was telling my partner here that if you were there they'd be scared shitless. If you get your crew and go now, I'll make sure you are clear. But only fifteen minutes. You got that?" he added with a wink and a click of the tongue.

> "Yeah, I got it. But how I know you ain't setting me up?"
>
> "If I wanted to put you in jail, Monster, I'd arrest you right now for the gun in your waistband."
>
> Surprised, I said, "Righteous," and stepped away from the car.
>
> We mounted up and went over to Fifty-ninth and Third Avenue. Sure enough, they were there. And just as he had said, we encountered no police.

Although this type of police behavior seems unconscionable, Scott's experiences are real. Scott provides a view of the police role that many of us are not privileged to experience first hand. Perhaps it is in communities where the police are most active and most aggressive that their core mission is laid bare (Chambliss 1994; Kraska and Kappeler 1997; Barlow and Barlow 2000).

Even evidence from scientific research on police does not support the claim that their primary role is to fight crime. Most studies indicate law enforcement comprises no more than 15 percent of a patrol officer's time. In a cross-cultural analysis of police in four different democratic societies, Bayley (1994) calculated the percentage of police officers' time devoted to law enforcement at less than 5 percent. Even if the proportion of time devoted to enforcing the law is as high as 15 percent, that still leaves 85 percent of their time maintaining the social order. In response to the question of what police do, Bayley (1994) notes that only between 7 and 10 percent of their time is spent handling requests involving crime. Even less of their time is spent in the battle against violent crime. Most of their time is spent "restoring order and providing general assistance," not by invoking the criminal law, but by using their "intervention authority" (Bayley 1994:18). According to Bayley (1994), the majority of the patrol officer's time is spent preparing for war. The prime directive of police managers is to always have enough officers available on patrol to be deployed to respond to major disturbances. Although in small ways each police officer is continuously maintaining order in his or her own area of patrol, the quantity and quality of police responses to citizens' requests and to everyday street crime are secondary to the ability of the police department as a whole to respond in force to primary threats to the social order.

If the core mission of the police were truly to fight crime and protect victims from assaults by violent offenders, then the response to one of the most common types of violent assault resulting in calls for assistance, domestic violence, would be completely different than history reflects (Barlow and Barlow 2000). Before the early 1980s, the primary police response to woman battering, which often results in serious injury and, in some cases, the death of the victim, was to take as little action as possible. The most frequent police responses were to take no action or to advise the victim to temporarily leave the home so the offender could not continue to attack her at that time. At most, the officer might do some emergency counseling or inform the victim that, if she wanted to press charges, she could swear out a warrant before a judge on the next weekday. Rarely was a report taken, much less an arrest made for spousal assault. The common police prac-

tice of not taking official action in response to domestic violence changed only because a major social and political movement within the United States weakened patriarchal power and empowered women to influence the law and its enforcement. As the Women's Movement enhanced women's rights and participation in the political process, women began to file lawsuits against police and to lobby to force the police to enforce the laws against domestic assault. Even with these changes, women's organizations continue to struggle with police departments to get them to provide an adequate response to domestic violence and to treat its victims as deserving of protection by police. Historically, standard police procedure in domestic violence cases maintained the social order—a patriarchal and repressive social order, particularly hard on women who are poor and thus more vulnerable to becoming trapped in abusive relationships. Sympathy, compassion, and protection were rarely given to an abused spouse, particularly if that spouse was poor or a member of a racial minority (Dobash and Dobash 1979; Pleck 1987; Hirschel et al. 1992; Feder 1999; Chesney-Lind 2002; Robinson and Chandek 2000).

In a sense, each action by individual police officers, as they exercise their intervention authority, resolve conflicts, and keep open the lines of commerce, is part of the larger effort to preserve social order. Thus, if we develop a single definition of the role of police based on what they do, as identified by Bayley's (1994) research, as known to police officers, as experienced by the white middle class, as experienced by victims of domestic violence, and as described by Wright (1945) and Scott (1993), the primary role of the police is not to fight crime but to maintain order. However, a review of the history of police in the United States illustrates that the police do not preserve just any order, but the social order, with all its current class, race, and gender power relations (Barlow and Barlow 2000). Moreover, they have played this role throughout U.S. history. Although it is true that one element of the order-maintenance activities of police is to fight crime, definitive statements by police scholars that the core mission of the police is crime control deny historical and cultural controversy about this issue. Police have not continued to endure as a vital and growing component of our society despite their failure to control crime, as Murphy (1993) and others have suggested, but because of their success in their core mission of maintaining order (Barlow and Barlow 2000; Reiman 2004). To understand the role of police in our society, we must look beyond the rhetoric. We must look at what police do and have done throughout the history of our society. We must look closely at what they do in all segments of society and at how their activities vary depending on location, time, circumstances, and population. By examining the interests that were served by the types of police departments formed during each era in the history of policing in the United States, we are able to gain insight into the interests that are served by the myth that the role of the police is to fight crime.

Interests Served by the Myth

Each stage in the historical development of police in the United States demonstrates that the core mission of police is not to fight crime but to maintain the social order. Barlow and Barlow (1999, 2000) argue that the first municipal police departments in the United States were created in Southern cities in the mid-1700s, and their primary function was to preserve the racist social order based

upon slavery. Preindustrial police protected the "private property" of slave owners by not allowing slaves to run away. They punished slaves who challenged the status quo, and were especially harsh on those who took part in slave rebellions. In these respects, the police played an instrumental role in helping to ensure that the economy of the pre-Civil War South remained profitable for rich and powerful plantation owners (Barlow and Barlow 1999, 2000).

The police agencies that were formed during the era of industrial policing (also commonly referred to as the "political era" of policing) played the same role as the preindustrial police, only in the context of a different economic order. Industrial police departments, formed first in the industrial Northeast, were charged with the regulation and control of large populations of recent German and Irish immigrants, as well as some free blacks migrating from the South. The large numbers of immigrants who moved to major U.S. cities during the Industrial Revolution in search of a better life found themselves struggling with the realities of poverty, hunger, and the harsh working conditions of factory employment and, thus, had the least to lose and the most to gain should existing power relations be altered. As a result, mass movements of social unrest during the late 1800s and early 1900s posed a significant challenge to the social order based on industrial capitalism. Industrial police began as private police employed by factory owners and later came to be publicly funded. Both as private and as public police, though, industrial police fulfilled the function of breaking strikes and suppressing riots. In doing so, the police were central to the success of leaders of business and industry in maintaining the profitability of their companies.

Over time the industrial police came to be connected with the political machines that dominated most major cities in the Northeast and Midwest in the nineteenth century. Police personnel commonly obtained their jobs through political patronage and also played a key role in ensuring the political boss in power won elections. In effect, police departments became criminal rackets designed to collect both votes and money for their political bosses, operating more like criminal organizations than agencies devoted to suppressing criminal activity (Haller 1976). Few of the daily activities of police in this era suggested that the role of police in society was to investigate crimes, catch criminals, or protect the innocent from harm. Ultimately, their disregard for the rule of law made it impossible for police to maintain their legitimacy. As the legitimacy of the industrial police was undermined, so was their effectiveness in preserving the social order in the face of significant social unrest in the latter part of the nineteenth century. As a result, changes were implemented and police departments were transformed into bureaucratic agencies characterized by greater discipline, better organization, and advances in technology.

The era of modern police is often referred to as the era of police professionalism, and it was professionalization that restored legitimacy to police departments, allowing them to effectively and efficiently maintain order in society. Police re-created themselves as professional crime fighters in the modern era, and this transformation carried police departments from the latter nineteenth century through the first half of the twentieth century. It was not until police were faced with the social unrest associated with the social movements of the 1960s that they once again confronted challenges to their legitimacy as agents of social control (Barlow and Barlow 1999, 2000).

The latest stage in the historical development of police, which we refer to as postmodern policing, began in the 1960s as police departments faced the challenges to social order posed by numerous and often overlapping social movements, such as the Civil Rights Movement and student protest movements for free speech and against the Vietnam War. Violent police clashes with demonstrators seeking to change the social order were brought into the homes of American citizens in a way that had not been possible prior to the advent of television. As a result, what many viewed as the "traditional" style of policing came under serious criticism as too repressive, largely ineffective, or both. Out of such criticism arose the beginnings of a critique of the professional model of policing, leading to new forms of policing in the decades since the 1960s. These new forms of policing—variously known by such names as community policing, problem-oriented policing, team policing, and quality of life policing—place paramount importance on improving police-community relations and enhancing the image of police departments among those who are policed. In the present historical context, close examination of what police do indicates that those who are policed most heavily in society are racial minorities and the poor, and that regulating these marginalized populations remains a central component of the role and function of police (Websdale 2001; Robinson and Chandek 2000; Feder 1999; Kraska and Kappeler 1997; Chambliss 1994). Just as professionalization enabled the police to preserve the social order in the modern era, image management has become a critical factor in the ability of police to maintain the social order in a media-saturated postmodern society (Barlow and Barlow 1999, 2000).

Policy Implications of Belief in the Myth

Examination of the history of policing in the United States consistently demonstrates order maintenance as the most consistent duty of police in varied social and political contexts. Crime-fighting functions do not define the police, nor can they explain all or even most police activities. Belief in the myth that the role of the police is to fight crime, when in fact their primary role is to maintain the social order, has important implications for public policy.

Perhaps the most important policy implication is this: Believing the myth that the role of police is to fight crime lends legitimacy to a range of police activities that would otherwise be questioned in a democratic society. It is true that under the directive to fight crime police officers investigate reported criminal activity, gather evidence of criminal wrongdoing, apprehend suspects, and arrest criminal offenders. But under this same directive, police also investigate potential insurrections, infiltrate dissident groups, and gather intelligence on individuals who are suspected of conspiring to disrupt the social order. Finally, in the name of fighting crime, police engage in a level of surveillance and control among racial minorities and the poor different from that experienced by more privileged members of our society. Believing in the myth that the role of the police is to fight crime leads many to support giving police departments whatever resources they need to do their job. It also leads many to argue that as few restrictions as possible should be imposed on the police in the performance of their duties. Disposing of this myth would

allow informed decisions not only about levels of support or degrees of restriction for police, but also about whether there might be ways to change the role of police in society.

Furthermore, looking beyond the myth makes it possible to understand the actions police have taken to preserve a social order that at times was unimaginably and inhumanely racist, along with being discriminatory with respect to gender and class. The police activities observed by Wright (1945) and Scott (1993) were illegal and, therefore, cannot be understood as efforts to fight crime. However, if the role of police is understood as maintaining a racist social order, then these activities become logical within a racist and inhumane logic. Knowing that the core mission of police is to preserve the status quo in relations of power helps to explain why the crime-fighting activities of police have commonly not protected racial and ethnic minorities, immigrants, people who are poor, children who are abused, and women who are battered to the same degree as those in more privileged positions in society. Understanding that the core mission of police is not to fight crime but to preserve the social order makes it possible to comprehend why many citizens of the United States have not been able to count on the police to take action to protect them from harm.

All of this being said, we are compelled to conclude our discussion by saying that to identify that the core mission of police is not to fight crime but to maintain the social order does not negate the fact that there are many good, humane, and ethical police officers. It is our belief that most individuals who choose to become police officers do so because they view policing as a profession in which they can make a positive contribution to society. Many become heroes, putting their own lives at risk to protect their fellow citizens. Many struggle with the contradictions posed by the conflict between the sentiments that led them to choose police work and the job they find themselves doing. We hope that this discussion will not be viewed as an attack on police officers, but rather a critique of the contradictions of policing in a democratic, yet unequal society. Such critique is a necessary first step toward imagining and creating a democratic society in which the role of police is truly to provide equal protection for all.

References

Barlow, D. E., and M. H. Barlow. 1999. A political economy of community policing. *Policing: An International Journal of Police Strategies and Management* 22(4):646–674.

———. 2000. *Police in a multicultural society: An American story.* Prospect Heights, IL: Waveland Press.

Bayley, D. H. 1994. *Police for the future.* New York: Oxford University Press.

Chambliss, W. J. 1994. Policing the ghetto underclass: The politics of law and law enforcement. *Social Problems* 41(2):177–194.

Chesney-Lind, M. 2002. Criminalizing victimization: The unintended consequences of pro-arrest policies for girls and women. *Criminology and Public Policy* 2:81–90.

Dobash, R. E., and R. Dobash. 1979. *Violence against wives: A case against patriarchy.* New York: Free Press.

Feder, L. 1999. Police handling of domestic violence calls: An overview and further investigation. *Women and Criminal Justice* 10:49–68.

Haller, M. H. 1976. Historical roots of police behavior: Chicago, 1890–1925. *Law and Society Review* 10:303–323.

Hirschel, D., I. Hutchinson, C. Dean, and A.-M. Mills. 1992. Review essay on the law enforcement response to spouse abuse: Past, present, and the future. *Police Quarterly* 9:247–283.

Iannone, N. F. 1994. *Supervision of police personnel.* 5th ed. Englewood Cliffs, NJ: Prentice Hall.

Kappeler, V. E., M. Blumberg, and G. W. Potter. 1996. *The mythology of crime and justice.* 2nd ed. Prospect Heights, IL: Waveland Press.

Kraska, P. B., and V. E. Kappeler. 1997. Militarizing American police: The rise and normalization of paramilitary units. *Social Problems* 44(1):1–18.

Moore, M. H., R. C. Trojanowicz, and G. L. Kelling. 1988. *Crime and policing.* Washington, DC: National Institute of Justice.

Murphy, P. V. 1993. Organizing for community policing. In *Issues in policing: New perspectives,* ed. John W. Bizzack, 113–128. Lexington, KY: Autumn House.

Pleck, E. 1987. *The making of American social policy against family violence from colonial times to the present.* New York: Oxford University Press.

Reiman, J. 2004. *The rich get richer and the poor get prison: Ideology, crime and criminal justice.* 7th ed. Boston: Allyn and Bacon.

Robinson, A. L., and M. S. Chandek. 2000. Differential police response to black battered women. *Women and Criminal Justice* 12:29–61.

Scott, K. 1993. *Monster: The autobiography of an L.A. gang member.* New York: The Atlantic Monthly Press.

Websdale, N. 2001. *Policing the poor: From slave plantation to public housing.* Boston: Northeastern University Press.

Wright, R. 1945. *Black boy.* New York: Harper & Brothers Publishers. ✦

Chapter 10
The Myth of a Monolithic Police Culture

Eugene A. Paoline III

The Myth

A part of common folklore about police is that there is a single unifying culture (or subculture) that exists among officers. The attitudes, values, and norms of this culture are said to arise as a mechanism for helping police officers buffer the strains of their job. These strains are largely the result of the central features of the occupational (i.e., the street) and organizational (i.e., the department) environments. The coping mechanisms that police officers supposedly learn from this culture, in response to these environments, have drastic consequences for the ways officers interact with citizens and supervisors. What follows is a discussion of the monolithic culture of policing. Figure 9.1 presents this model in terms of the environments, coping mechanisms, and outcomes (for more detail on the monolithic model, see Paoline 2003).

One aspect of the police environment is the occupational (or street) environment, where officers interact with their main clientele—citizens. One defining characteristic of this environment is danger (Skolnick 1966). Few would discount the fact that policing is a dangerous, or potentially dangerous, job. A second prominent feature of the occupational environment is the coercive authority officers display over citizens, which often reinforces the notion that the environment is dangerous (Bittner 1974). Police are unique in that they have been granted the legitimate use of coercion, although they constantly have to manage how much to use as well as when to use it.

The second aspect of the police work environment is the organization, which is characterized by the interactions between officers and their supervisors. One issue that officers confront in this arena is unpredictable and punitive supervisory oversight (Skolnick 1966). A large degree of uncertainty exists between officers and their supervisors, as officers are expected to enforce laws but are often second-guessed for their procedural approaches (Brown 1988). Officers learn that when supervisors comment about their work it is usually for something they have done wrong (procedurally) instead of something they have done well (substantively). A second feature of the organizational environment is the role ambiguity that management perpetuates. Officers are expected to perform three roles on the street (law enforcement, order maintenance, and service), yet they find that they are only officially recognized for one—law enforcement (Fielding 1988). Performance evaluations, training, the creation of specialized divisions, and promotions all reinforce the crime-fighting role that police perform (Bittner 1974). The two environments, occupational and organizational, create stress and anxiety for police officers which is relieved, according to the myth, by the collective coping mechanisms of the culture.

The myth posits two primary coping mechanisms/prescriptions for the issues officers confront in the occupational environment. First, largely as a result of the danger that exists, officers are suspicious of citizens (Reiner 1985). This assists

Figure 9.1
The Monolithic Police Culture Model

Environments		Coping Mechanisms/ Prescriptions		Outcomes
Occupational				
Danger		Suspiciousness		
	⇒ Stress and Anxiety ⇒		⇒	Social Isolation
Coercive Authority		Maintaining the Edge		
Organizational				
Supervisor Scrutiny		Lay Low/CYA		
	⇒ Stress and Anxiety ⇒		⇒	Loyalty
Role Ambiguity		Crime Fighter Orientation		

officers in reducing or controlling the amount of uncertainty associated with a dangerous environment. Second, the coercive authority officers are expected to wield, as well as the environmental danger, result in the need for police to "maintain the edge" or be "one up" on citizens during encounters (Rubinstein 1973). Again, these two coping mechanisms assist officers in dealing with the strains of the occupational environment.

The organizational environment also produces coping mechanisms/prescriptions that help officers deal with supervisory issues, according to the myth. One consequence of police supervisors' focus on rule violations is the "lay low" or "CYA" ("cover your ass") approach to policing, whereby officers are discouraged from engaging in efforts that might bring undue attention to them (Ericson 1982; Van Maanen 1974). Essentially, the mantra is

the more you do, the more chances you have to do something wrong. The second coping mechanism, the crime fighter role orientation, results from the role ambiguity that management perpetuates (Klockars 1985). Here, officers pragmatically realize that one role is "officially" recognized, so this is where efforts should be concentrated. As such, the police culture is said to stress crime fighting or "real" police work over order maintenance and service roles. The issues officers confront in their primary work environments, as well as the coping mechanisms prescribed by the police culture, cumulatively produce two outcomes—social isolation and group loyalty.

In sum, the myth suggests that the universally shared attitudes, values, and norms of the police culture serve to manage the strains created by the nature of police work and the punitive practices of police management and supervision. Such attitudes, values, and norms include a distrust and suspiciousness of citizens, a prescription to maintain the edge over people and situations in terms of their potential threat, a "lay low" or "CYA" orientation to police work, a strong emphasis on the law enforcement elements of the police role, an "us versus them" attitude toward citizens, and strong loyalty to their peer group. These shared occupational outlooks are said to transcend both time and place. For example, Crank (1998:26) argues that "street cops everywhere tend to share a common culture because they respond to similar audiences everywhere." The characterization of a monolithic police culture still tends to dominate empirical and textbook explanations of the police, despite evidence to the contrary.

The Kernel of Truth

The idea of a monolithic police culture is based largely on ethnographic police research conducted more than fifty years ago. Studies conducted by William Westley and Jerome Skolnick highlighted many of the themes found in the preceding discussion of a single culture. Westley's (1970) research in Gary, Indiana, in the 1950s noted the strains officers confront on the street, finding that police and citizens were hostile toward each other and officers were a secretive, tight-knit group. Skolnick's (1966) research in Oakland, California, in the 1960s added the notion that the police organization is an equally stressful and dangerous place because officers must constantly appear efficient in the eyes of supervisors. To each of the authors' credit, they were among the first to break the research barriers that existed between police departments and academics. Their aim, although independent of one another, was to shed light on

some of the informal aspects of policing. To this end, their research was successful.

Westley's and Skolnick's contributions to the understanding of police culture was partially a product of their research methodology. Both ethnographic studies attempted to summarize the empirical world but, in doing so, may have glossed over some complexities, such as differences in the ways officers respond to their work environment—an issue that cannot be addressed after the fact. On the other hand, officers may have been very similar to one another during the earlier time periods. This is a plausible assumption because police officers fifty years ago shared many of the same characteristics (i.e., they tended to be white, blue-collar, male, with a high school education). However, the important issue is not whether a monolithic police culture existed in the 1950s and 1960s, but rather the extent to which a monolithic police culture exists today. This is especially salient because of the changing demographic characteristics of police officers, in terms of race, sex, and education, and philosophies of policing, such as community policing (Paoline, Myers, and Worden 2000).

During the 1970s and 1980s, when police officers' demographic characteristics were changing, researchers began to develop typologies of police that illustrated stylistic differences among officers. These typology studies, as well as more current research, found one group of officers that closely resembled the officers of the monolithic police culture. In this sense, there may be a "kernel of truth" regarding the monolithic police culture.

The Truth or Facts

Police typology research also found additional styles or types of officers, indicating that not all officers respond to their environments in the same way. This suggests that there might be multiple police subcultures. This section of the chapter represents a review of police typologies, including findings that offer a more comprehensive and contemporary examination of officer types and subcultures.

Despite different research sites and samples, and across different points in time, a number of American police researchers (e.g., Broderick 1977; Brown 1988; Muir 1977; White 1972) have described very similar police officer styles. Worden (1995) synthesized this research and concluded with five groups of officers. A first group, the "Tough-Cops," represents many of the values depicted in characterizations of the monolithic police culture. For example, these officers are hostile toward citizens and supervisors, and endorse an aggressive approach to fighting crime on the street. A second group is the "Clean-Beat Crime-Fighters," who are similar to "Tough-Cops" in their disdain for citizens and supervisors, though unlike "Tough-Cops," they believe in pursuing all types of crimes (not just felonies) while placing a premium on the due process rights of citizens (unlike "Tough-Cops"). "Avoiders" represent a third group. These officers are detached from citizens, supervisors, and police work in general. "Avoiders" are characterized as cynical, burnt-out officers who are doing just enough on the job to get by. "Problem-Solvers" are citizen-oriented officers who believe in using their discretionary powers to assist the community they serve. As such, these officers are not aggressive in their pursuit of enforcing laws and place a high regard on the due process rights of citizens. The "Professionals"—the last group—embody the ideals of the professional reform movement that started in policing during the early part of the twentieth century (White 1972). According to Worden (1995), these officers are willing to accept the changes/innovations that occur in policing; hold favorable opinions toward citizens, supervisors, procedural guidelines, and police work in general; and have one of the broadest role orientations of all officers (i.e., they accept order maintenance and service roles along with law enforcement).

Worden's (1995) review of typology studies that were conducted during the 1970s illustrates that the attitudes, values, and norms officers endorse are not all the same. What is interesting is that during the time these studies were conducted, most officers were still primarily white, high-school educated, male, military veterans, and from working-class backgrounds (Van Maanen 1974). Although cultural fragmentation was noted, it begs the question of how different officers are now that the demographics and philosophies of police departments have changed. That is, officers now work in police departments that are more representative in terms of females, racial minorities, and college-educated officers, and are exposed to a different philosophy of policing that endorses frequent contacts with citizens. The answers to these questions were addressed in the work of Paoline (2001). What follows is a brief summary of the main findings of that study.

Based on an analysis of survey data collected as part of the Project on Policing Neighborhoods (POPN), seven groups of police officers were identified (recall that Worden's typology study discovered five groups of officers). This study differed from the earlier typology research in two fundamental ways. First, in developing a classification scheme of officers, it was possible to analyze ten separate attitudinal dimensions simultaneously, whereas earlier typology researchers focused only on two or three dimensions at a time. The attitudinal dimensions examined were all prominent features of police culture. More specifically, groups of officers were formed based on views of citizen cooperation, citizen distrust, first line supervisors, district management, procedural guidelines, law enforcement functions, order maintenance role functions, community policing functions, aggressive patrol, and selective enforcement of the law. Second, unlike the qualitative nature of most typology studies, this research was quantitative.

The findings of this study mirrored some of the same conclusions drawn from typology work conducted some twenty-five years before. Of particular relevance is that, like "Tough-Cops" of the 1970s, a group of officers emerged that espoused many of the values associated with the traditional monolithic police culture. As such, the "Traditionalists" appear to still be a part of contemporary police departments. More importantly, other groups were found that closely mirror their older typology counterparts (in parentheses): "Law Enforcers" ("Clean-Beat Crime-Fighters"), "Old-Pros" ("Professionals"), "Peacekeepers" ("Problem-Solvers"), and "Lay-Lows" ("Avoiders"). Besides the five groups that closely resemble earlier types, there were also two additional groups, suggesting that cultural fragmentation may be even more pronounced among contemporary officers. The first group, "Anti-Organizational Street-Cops," share some of the same attitudes of "Lay-Lows" and "Traditionalists," although they are distinguished by their extremely negative views of supervisors and their very strong positive attitudes toward citizens. A second group, "Dirty Harry Enforcers," resemble parts of "Law Enforcers" and "Tra-ditionalists," and are characterized by their belief in a strong, aggressive pursuit of crime and disorder, while favorably endorsing the occasional violation of citizens' due process rights. Interestingly, the attitudinal groups of officers identified by Paoline (2001) were relatively indistinguishable with respect to the factors that served as the impetus for the study. More specifically, there was not a group of officers that were predominantly female, college educated, nonwhite, etc.

The results of this research, as well as the research conducted in the 1970s, suggest that officers do not uniformly respond to the strains of their work environment in the same ways. While there was a group that resembled the characterization of the monolithic police culture (i.e., "Tough-Cops" of the 1970s and more contemporary "Traditionalists"), there were also additional groups. This is not to say there are no officer similarities. For example, it is rather naive to doubt that officers are loyal to one another, like members of other occupational systems (e.g., firefighters). But, the extent to which officers uniformly view central components of their occupational world (e.g., citizens, supervisors, procedural guidelines, role orientation, and policing tactics) is certainly debatable, largely as a result of the empirical evidence presented in this chapter.

Interests Served by the Myth

The belief in a monolithic police culture serves the general interests of four groups: the media, police officers, police researchers/academics, and police administrators. Both the news and entertainment media gain from the myth. Newspaper and television news accounts of police often attribute the disconnection between police and citizens to the values of the culture. The rogue crime-fighting cop who clashes with citizens and supervisors is also a common portrayal of police in the entertainment media. Television shows and movies alike often glorify this depiction of American police. In all, this serves the economic interests of both media outlets, as bad news and violence sell.

Besides the media, police officers also benefit from the police culture myth. The perception of a close-knit brotherhood that is fighting a war on crime often serves to glorify an occupation that, in many ways, is rather mundane and reactive in nature. The common conduits for this glorification are police officer stories and media portrayals of police work. The isolation from citizens, coupled with the aggressive crime-fighting role orientation associated with the culture can be a misguided avenue for officers to mistreat citizens both physically (i.e., improper and excessive force) and verbally (i.e., name calling). In this sense, belief in the myth may offer an officer a behavioral excuse for inappropriate actions. The myth also has other benefits for officers. For example, officers may feel less stress and uncertainty about the occupation by the perceived mutual protection (i.e., loyalty) from other officers, regardless of whether it is true.

Police researchers and academics gain by believing that a monolithic police culture exists. First, the idea that there is one, and only one, culture helps to simplify the empirical world. The notion that police officers are coping with the stress of their occupation in the same way in Florida, Maine, Washington, and Texas, for example, is more manageable from a research point of view than conceiving of a fragmented occupational group. Ethnographic summary accounts of police collectiveness may be a much less daunting task from a statistical modeling perspective, compared to endeavors that seek to tease out individual differences and statistically control for additional explanatory factors. Second, the collective loyalty and isolation from citizens associated with the monolithic culture is a useful explanatory factor for many of the negative things that police do (e.g., excessive force, corruption, etc.). It follows that police administrators can also use the same rationale for explaining the behavior of their subordinates.

In terms of day-to-day police activity, administrators use the collective culture myth to their advantage. For example, when officers get into trouble, administrators can explain their inability to effectively investigate the problem by pointing to the lack of cooperation among the officers. When police officers use excessive force, the crime-fighting aggressiveness and the "us versus them" values of the culture are reasonable explanations for police administrators who can stress the need for additional officer training (e.g., cultural sensitivity). When reform efforts (e.g., community policing) stall or fail to work altogether, the myth of an impenetrable, resistant police culture gives management a useful "out." In this sense, assuming that there is a monolithic culture among officers that is virtually untouchable serves the interests of administrators who may be indirectly responsible for inappropriate behavior (i.e., lack of proper training and/or supervision).

Policy Implications of Belief in the Myth

If, in fact, the monolithic police culture is true, there are important policy implications to consider. As previously noted, social isolation and group loyalty are two outcomes associated with "the police culture." Officers are isolated from citizens, largely as a result of the dangerous work environment and the coercive power they possess (Kappeler, Sluder, and Alpert 1998). The prescription to be suspicious of citizens also works to separate the police and the public. In terms of the uncertainty and scrutiny of supervisors and managers, officers learn they can only rely on and trust other officers, who mutually protect one another from organizational stress (Westley 1970). This strong group loyalty helps to protect officers from unreasonable and unpredictable supervisors, who are often viewed as making officers' lives more difficult.

Social isolation and group loyalty are problematic for the daily operation of police departments. Officers who are detached from the public they serve stymie the proper development of police-citizen partnerships, which are a vital component of contemporary policing philosophies. Likewise, strong intergroup loyalty, while effective in forging a bond among occupational members, sometimes has the unintended effect of separating police officers from management. Moreover, attempts to control police misconduct, in ensuring accountable police practice, may be hindered because of officers' unwillingness to sever the bond in reporting peer misbehavior.

In sum, there is a common myth that exists in policing. This myth assumes that there is a single police culture that imparts universal attitudes, values, and norms across all occupational members. These attitudes, values, and norms are said to be a collective way of dealing with the stress and anxiety of the police profession. Evidence has been presented here illustrating that some officers may cope with the strains of policing in this manner, but others respond in very different ways. The monolithic police culture myth tends to serve the interests of the media, police officers, and researchers/academics alike. Finally, in terms of police policy and practice, belief in the myth can lead to a police force that is detached from both citizens and supervisors.

References

Bittner, E. 1974. Florence Nightingale in pursuit of Willie Sutton: A theory of the police. In *The potential for reform of criminal justice*, ed. H. Jacob. Beverly Hills: Sage.

Broderick, J. J. 1977. *Police in a time of change.* Morristown, NJ: General Learning Press.

Brown, M. K. 1988. *Working the street: Police discretion and the dilemmas of reform.* 2nd ed. New York: Russell Sage Foundation.

Crank, J. P. 1998. *Understanding police culture.* Cincinnati, Ohio: Anderson Publishing Company.

Ericson, R. 1982. *Reproducing order: A study of police patrol work.* Toronto: University of Toronto Press.

Fielding, N. G. 1988. *Joining forces: Police training, socialization and occupation competence.* London: Routledge.

Kappeler, V. E., R. D. Sluder, and G. P. Alpert. 1998. *Forces of deviance: Understanding the dark side of policing.* 2nd ed. Prospect Heights, IL: Waveland Press.

Klockars, C. B. 1985. Order maintenance, the quality of urban life, and police: A different line of argument. In *Police leadership in America: Crisis and opportunity*, ed. W. A. Geller. New York: Praeger.

Muir, W. K., Jr. 1977. *Police: Streetcorner politicians.* Chicago: University of Chicago Press.

Paoline, E. A., III. 2001. *Rethinking police culture: Officers' occupational attitudes.* New York: LFB Publishing.

———. 2003. Taking stock: Toward a richer understanding of police culture. *Journal of Criminal Justice* 31:199–214.

Paoline, E. A., III, S. M. Myers, and R. E. Worden. 2000. Police culture, individualism, and community policing: Evidence from two police departments. *Justice Quarterly* 17:575–605.

Reiner, R. 1985. *The politics of the police.* New York: St. Martin's Press.

Rubinstein, J. 1973. *City police.* New York: Farrar, Straus, and Giroux.

Skolnick, J. H. 1966. *Justice without trial: Law enforcement in democratic society.* New York: John Wiley.

Van Maanen, J. 1974. Working the street: A developmental view of police behavior. In *Police leadership in America: Crisis and opportunity,* ed. W. A. Geller. New York: Praeger.

Westley, W. A. 1970. *Violence and the police: A sociological study of law, custom, and morality.* Cambridge, MA: MIT Press.

White, S. O. 1972. A perspective on police professionalization. *Law & Society Review* 7:61–85.

Worden, R. E. 1995. Police officers' belief systems: A framework for analysis. *American Journal of Police* 14:49–81. ✦

Chapter 11
The Myth of Policewomen on Patrol

Kim Lersch

The Myth

It has been more than three decades since the passage of the 1972 Equal Opportunity Act that opened the way for women to enter law enforcement, but female police officers are still haunted by the myth—both internally and externally—that they simply cannot perform as well as male police officers (Austin and Hummer 1999). In fact, policing has been described as one of the most hostile, resistant careers in accepting women as competent, equal professionals (Belknap and Shelley 1992). This chapter explores the myth that women are not suited for patrol work.

The Kernel of Truth

When actually combating crime, it is sometimes useful for police officers to be large, imposing, and aggressive individuals (Haarr 1997). For many years, police agencies screened for these characteristics. First, applicants for positions as law enforcement officers had to meet a minimum height requirement to be considered for employment. For the majority of agencies, the minimum height was 5'8". This was significantly taller than the average height for females, thereby eliminating the majority of women from employment

consideration (President's Commission on Law Enforcement and Administration of Justice 1967; Walker and Katz 2002; Holladay 2002). Even if a woman was tall enough to meet the minimum standards, she would then face a rather imposing physical-ability test, which for years overemphasized upper body strength. Applicants were asked to complete a variety of military-style physical challenges in a specified amount of time, such as pushups, sit-ups, and bench-presses of one's own weight. Women failed these exams at significantly higher rates than their male peers, and were thus eliminated from the "qualified" applicant pool (Hale and Wyland 1993; Swanson, Territo, and Taylor 1998).

Hale and Wyland (1993) discussed the major arguments raised against women serving as patrol officers. First among the arguments was that women are not as strong and aggressive as men, which would therefore make them less effective as patrol officers. The reality is that, generally speaking, women are not as big or as strong as men. The average woman is 5'4" tall and weighs 152 pounds, while the average man is 5'9" tall and weighs 180 pounds. Because of the physical disparities, women and men do not compete in athletic competitions against each other (Holladay 2002; Maglione 2002). However, as Maglione (2002:22) asserts, "Physical differences are a fact of nature, not a point of equity." This is especially true in policing, where agencies have had a difficult time demonstrating that physical strength is a legitimate factor necessary for job performance (Swanson, Territo, and Taylor 1998). In fact, the majority of the old screening mechanisms based solely on strength were dropped because those criteria could not be demonstrated as critical to the performance of a police officer's duties. Although officers do need to be able to react quickly, research suggests that brute force and long-term endurance are among the most infrequent, noncritical physical tasks required of police officers (Booth and Hornick 1984). Furthermore, physical strength has not been positively linked to overall job performance or even the ability to handle dangerous situations (Bell 1982; Sherman 1973).

Differences in aggression also contain a kernel of truth. The reality is that we live in a patriarchal society in which boys and girls are treated differently based on their gender. Boys are expected to be aggressive and tough, while girls are socialized to be more submissive and peaceful. It has been argued that because of the differing socialization of men and women, one should see marked differences in how male and female police officers interact with citizens and perform their duties (Martin and Jurik 1996; Worden 1993). In some of the early studies on the effectiveness of women as patrol officers, women were found to be less assertive than their male co-workers, as indicated by a lower number of arrests, fewer citizen contacts, and fewer citizen complaints (Bartlett and Rosenblum 1977; Bloch and Anderson 1974; Steffensmeier 1979). For example, in an analysis comparing the work of male and female patrol officers in St. Louis County, Sherman (1975) reported that female officers were less aggressive and pro-active in their patrol activities than male officers and ultimately made fewer arrests. Some researchers have found no appreciable differences in the behavior of male and female police officers (see, for example, Price 1974; Snortum and Beyers 1983), while others have concluded that female police officers are less authoritarian, less brutal, more nurturing, better communicators, and possess a greater pacifying quality than do their male counterparts (Bell 1982; Grennan 1987; Lersch 1998; Rivlin 1981; Van Wormer 1981; Weldy 1976).

It is reasonable, therefore, to accept the kernel of truth that women are smaller and weaker then men. It can also be accepted that there may be differences in aggressive behavior due to differential socialization of men and women. The question, then, is whether these tendencies automatically mean women cannot be good police officers. In this era of community-oriented policing, the answer must be a resounding "No!"

The Truth or Facts

The myth that women cannot serve as effective patrol officers is largely based on erroneous assumptions about the everyday duties of a patrol officer. The public often assumes that police work is dangerous, violent, and unpredictable (Austin and Hummer 1999). Popular movies and television shows regularly portray officers in precarious situations dealing with criminals who are often brutal and dangerous. Normally, these shows also feature gunfire or a fight during which the officer must wrestle the suspect to the ground. Similarly, in their quest for ratings, newspapers and television news shows overemphasize the violent aspects of policing. Officer-involved shootings are front-page news stories, fueling the belief that police work is much more dangerous than it actually is. Of course, police officers themselves tend to exaggerate the danger of their work, telling and retelling "war stories" and focusing their conversations on crime and violence (Manning 1977; Skolnick and Currie 1970; Westley 1970).

Walker and Katz (2002) describe this phenomenon as "the myth of police officers as crime fighters." In reality, instead of being focused on fighting crime, most police work is concerned with service-related issues (Hale and Wyland 1993). In an analysis of more than 26,000 calls for service to three metropolitan police agencies, only 2 percent of the calls were related to what would be considered serious violent crime: murders, rapes, robberies, etc. Conversely, a third of the calls were related to various information or minor assistance problems, such as citizens needing directions, complaints over barking dogs, or other relatively trivial, often noncriminal events (Walker and Katz 2002; see also Scott 1981). Far from the image of police officers constantly battling violent criminals, most patrol officers go their entire careers without discharging their weapon. Many students decide against a career in policing after the completion of an internship with a local agency, not from the fear and danger they experience, but from the boredom.

Despite the persistent belief that policing is too violent, too gritty, and simply not women's work, consistent research findings point to the contrary view: Women are extremely capable as police officers, and in some respects, outperform their male peers. In a recent Department of Justice report (Bureau of Justice Assistance and National Center for Women and Policing 2000), six advantages were discussed for the hiring, retention, and promotion of women in law enforcement. The findings of the report are summarized below (18–23).

Female officers are as competent as their male counterparts. Research does not show any consistent differences in how male and female patrol officers perform their duties. In some areas, women out-perform their male peers. Women in law enforcement careers have higher levels of education and, when promoted to supervisory positions, have been shown to be more assertive, confident, creative, and flexible than males in similar positions. Citizens, supervisors, and patrol officers all agree that female officers are more effective than male patrol officers in handling domestic violence calls.

Female officers are less likely to use excessive force. Female patrol officers are less likely to be involved in high-speed pursuits, incidents of deadly force, and the use of excessive force. Women generally use a less authoritarian style of policing that is less dependent on the use of force to back up commands. Female officers are more capable at calming potentially violent situations through communication, and also demonstrate heightened levels of caution. The report cited studies showing that many citizens prefer the presence of a female officer in potentially violent circumstances because of their interpersonal skills.

Female officers can help implement community-oriented policing. The popularity of community-oriented and problem-solving policing has grown exponentially over the past twenty years. Because this form of policing is built on communication and mutual respect between officers and local citizens, female officers are especially suited for this type of work (but no less suited for work in departments that do not emphasize community policing). Studies have shown that female officers are more supportive of the community-policing philosophy than are their male counterparts. Furthermore, because community policing is based on the assumption that community police officers should reflect the relevant demographic characteristics of the neighborhoods they serve, women should not be forgotten when agencies actively recruit minorities and other underrepresented populations.

Female officers can improve law enforcement's response to violence against

women. Among the most common calls for police services are those related to domestic violence. For decades, police agencies have struggled with the best course of action for these types of problems. If the call is not handled appropriately, victims may be deterred from reporting future acts of abuse to the police. Agencies may also risk lawsuits and other legal remedies when they fail to adequately respond to a complaint. Studies have shown that female officers are more patient and understanding in handling domestic-violence calls. Furthermore, female victims of domestic violence are more likely to provide positive evaluations of female officers than their male counterparts.

Increasing the presence of female officers reduces problems of sex discrimination and harassment within an agency. The majority of women in law enforcement have reported incidents of sexual harassment, which include being the target of inappropriate jokes and sexually-charged comments, being exposed to pornography, and experiencing unwanted sexual advances (Haarr 1997; Martin 1980, 1992; National Center for Women and Policing 1999). To substantially alter the boys-only clubhouse mentality that continues to exist in many departments, agencies must hire, promote, and retain more females.

The presence of women can promote beneficial changes in policy for all officers. When agencies take steps to recruit, retain, and promote females within their ranks, these agencies must often reexamine their recruiting materials, screening mechanisms, selection criteria, performance evaluations, and other personnel management tools. In many cases, these tools place too much emphasis on the crime-fighting aspect of law enforcement. Agencies may take advantage of this opportunity to recruit and evaluate all employees based on what officers actually do, as opposed to perpetuating the myth of police as crime fighters.

Interests Served by the Myth

As discussed above, there is a great deal of evidence that refutes the myth that women are not capable police officers. Why does the myth persist? On a very practical level, the interests of men who aspire to be police officers and male police officers who seek advancement within the profession are served by the myth. By denying females the opportunities of seeking careers and promotions in law enforcement occupations, men are guaranteed these positions.

Prior to the early 1970s, women and minorities were denied equal access to many occupations and opportunities. The 1972 Equal Employment Opportunity Act (EEOA), which extended the protections provided by the 1964 Civil Rights Act to state and local governments, marked the beginning of a new era in many law enforcement agencies (Martin and Jurik 1996). The legislation prohibited discrimination based on race, color, and gender. The act opened many doors to persons of color and to women who wished to pursue a law-enforcement career. Some police scholars believe that without the benefit of the 1972 EEOA mandate and other protections such as affirmative action, women would not be allowed to perform patrol duties (Hale and Lanier 2002).

Despite the EEOA protections, women continue to be underrepresented as police officers. According to recent findings, women hold only 14.3 percent of all sworn law-enforcement positions in this country (National Center for Women and Policing 1999). In a study of the distribution of women in Florida police agencies, Poulos and Doerner (1996) found that 20 percent of the smaller agencies in the state did not employ a single female officer. Even when agencies do open their doors to women, the women are usually confined to lower, nonsupervisory ranks or in nonsworn, lower paying civilian positions. In a 1999 survey of larger police agencies, women held more than 66 percent of lower-paying civilian positions, and 65 percent of the agencies did not currently have a woman serving in a higher-level supervisory position (National Center for Women and Policing 1999). At the highest levels, representation of women is even worse. Currently, there are about 125 women serving at the rank of chief, which accounts for approximately 1 percent of police chiefs (Polisar and Milgram 1998; Schulz 2002). It is important to view these findings in light of the fact that women comprise 46.5 percent of the adult labor market (Harrington 2000).

Although there have been gains in the representation of women in law enforcement, the growth has been slow, with an average annual increase of 0.5 percent (Bureau of Justice Assistance and National Center for Women and Policing 2000). In 1972, women held 4.2 percent of sworn positions. In the mid-1990s, the percentage increased to about 9 percent (Lanier 1996). If the representation of women continues to grow at this same slow rate, it will take about 70 years for women to reach equal standing with men in the police profession (Bureau of Justice Assistance and National Center for Women and Policing 2000). Obviously, if women are not holding law enforcement positions, the jobs are being held by men.

On a more abstract level, the myth of women as ineffective police officers perpetuates a patriarchal system in which women are subservient to men. Traditionally, through laws and cultural standards, men have had the power to dictate which positions women were allowed to hold (Bartollas and Hahn 1999; Martin and Jurik 1996). It was not long ago that women were not allowed to attend college, own property, manage their own financial affairs, or vote. Although great advancements for women have been made, there is still room for improvement. This is especially true in the field of policing. When women first entered patrol work, they were met with open hostility and organized resistance from their male peers. It was not unheard of for male supervisors to refuse to train female recruits, or for female officers to be denied backup in dangerous situations (Hunt 1984; Martin 1980; Martin and Jurik 1996).

Today, many female officers continue to face discrimination and prejudice in the workplace (Barker 1999; Haarr 1997; Hale and Lanier 2002; Hunt 1990; Martin 1994). Barker (1999), in a 20-year ethnographic study of the Los Angeles Police Department, observed that officers noted clear distinctions between the "Old Police," or those hired prior to 1972, and the "New Police." The New Police, which included many women and minority officers, were viewed by the Old Police as being less competent, not as committed, and less qualified to hold their positions. Barker's findings are typical. In fact, the literature is consistent with respect to reports of prejudice and disparate treatment of women in patrol by their male counterparts. Despite the gains made by women, male co-workers and supervisors continue to resist females on patrol (Hale and Wyland 1993; Lanier 1996). The hostility has been so great that a report published by the U.S. Department of Justice concluded that "research consistently demonstrates that the negative attitude of male colleagues is the single most significant problem reported by female officers" (Bureau of Justice Assistance and National Center for Women and Policing 2000:22).

It has been argued that the reason for this continued hostility and opposition stems from the threat women pose to the traditional policing culture, a culture that is based on masculinity, danger, authority, and solidarity (Skolnick 1966; Westley 1970). According to this view, and in a patriarchal society, men have had total ownership of the policing occupation and, more importantly, the formal means of social control. Men openly resist the entry of women into policing because they do not wish to relinquish their exclusive ownership of the right to maintain order and enforce the laws of society (Heidensohn 1992; Martin and Jurik 1996). By welcoming women into the policing occupation, men would be handing over the power and control they have owned for hundreds, even thousands of years.

Policy Implications of Belief in the Myth

Agencies that continue to buy into the myth that women cannot be effective law enforcement officers do so at their own peril. Under the protections provided by the 1972 Equal Employment Opportunity Act, if an agency causes, condones, or fails to stop unfair treatment of women, the agency may be held liable. Such litigation can be expensive; if a complaint of sexual harassment goes to trial, the legal fees alone can be as high as $700,000. This figure does not reflect any fines, lost wages, or other punitive assessments charged against the agency (Bartollas and Hahn 1999; Swanson, Territo, and Taylor 1998).

Beyond the direct legal expenses, there are other costs as well. If women do not feel accepted in the workplace, voluntary turnover will be higher. Agencies that do not retain their officers incur additional

training and replacement costs, which can run into the tens of thousands of dollars. Furthermore, there are expenses associated with workshops and other training activities related to sensitizing officers to sexual harassment issues. Finally, agencies may lose critical community support if female officers file lawsuits for discrimination and harassment, or if an agency has a reputation for being hostile and unwelcoming towards women (Bartollas and Hahn 1999).

Agencies that are serious about hiring, retaining, and promoting women can do something about the problem. For example, North Carolina's Charlotte-Mecklenburg Police Department (CMPD) initiated a mentoring program for female recruits, which included workshops on practical problems encountered by female officers. Because of its proactive efforts, the agency uncovered a number of gender-specific problems facing female officers. For example, uniforms had only been available in men's sizes. This meant that pants, ties, shirts, and duty belts did not fit the women properly. Representatives from the CMPD were able to work with the uniform vendors to provide more comfortable, better-fitting attire for the women (Maglione 2002). As a result, the CMPD has had better retention and promotion rates for their female officers. A number of other agencies, including the Fairfax County, Virginia, Police Department, the Lakewood, Colorado, Police Department, and the Nassau County, New York, Police Department have adopted similar mentoring programs (Kranda 1998).

Other agencies have had success by developing women-specific, targeted marketing materials. For example, the San Jose, California, Police Department increased the percentage of female academy recruits from 8 percent to 50 percent after the agency included a "women in policing" link on its departmental web page that featured photos and biographies of currently employed female officers (Milgram 2002). Recruitment posters for the Michigan State Police include advertisements reading "Trooper. Wife. Mother." Similar gender-specific marketing tools have been used by the New York State Police, whose slogan is "Protecting My Family, Protecting Yours" (Prussel and Lonsway 2001).

If an agency needs help in its recruitment and retention efforts, chiefs and administrators can find assistance from such organizations as the Institute for Women in Trades, Technology and Sciences; the National Association of Women Law Enforcement Executives; or the International Association of Women Police. These organizations provide training materials, seminars, and newsletters to assist agencies that wish to review their current personnel practices (Milgram 2002).

The myth that women cannot be effective officers has resulted in a severe underrepresentation of women in policing agencies. Women can bring special attributes to policing that are especially conducive to successful community policing efforts. Agencies that effectively communicate the message that women are welcome and respected among the ranks and that there are opportunities for advancement will, in time, diversify their work force.

References

Austin, T., and Hummer, D. 1999. What do college students think of policewomen? An attitudinal assessment of future law enforcement personnel. *Women and Criminal Justice* 10:1–24.

Barker, J. 1999. *Danger, duty, and disillusion: The worldview of Los Angeles Police Officers.* Prospect Heights: Waveland Press.

Bartlett, H., and A. Rosenblum. 1977. *Policewoman effectiveness.* Denver: Civil Service Commission and Denver Police Department.

Bartollas, C., and L. Hahn. 1999. *Policing in America.* Boston: Allyn and Bacon.

Belknap, J., and J. K. Shelley. 1992. The new Lone Ranger: Policewomen on patrol. *American Journal of Police* 12:47–75.

Bell, D. 1982. Policewomen: Myths and realities. *Journal of Police Science and Administration* 10:112–120.

Bloch, P., and D. Anderson. 1974. *Policewomen on patrol: Final report.* Washington, DC: Police Foundation.

Booth, W. S., and C. W. Hornick. 1984. Physical ability testing for police officers. *The Police Chief* 1:39–41.

Bureau of Justice Assistance and National Center for Women and Policing. 2000. *Recruiting and retaining women: A self-assessment guide for law enforcement.* Washington, DC: United States Department of Justice.

Grennan, S. 1987. Findings on the role of officer gender in violent encounters with citizens. *Journal of Police Science and Administration* 15:78–85.

Haarr, R. 1997. Patterns of interaction in a police patrol bureau: Race and gender barriers to integration. *Justice Quarterly* 14:53–85.

Hale D., and M. Lanier. 2002. New millennium: Women in policing in the twenty-first century. In *Visions for change: Crime and justice in the twenty-first century*, 3rd ed., eds. R. Muraskin and A. R. Robers. Upper Saddle River, NJ: Prentice Hall.

Hale, D., and S. Wyland. 1993. Dragons and dinosaurs: The plight of patrol women. *Police Forum* 3:1–6.

Harrington, P. 2000. *Hiring and retaining more women: The advantages to law enforcement agencies.* Arlington: National Center for Women in Policing.

Heidensohn, F. 1992. *Women in control? The role of women in law enforcement.* New York: Oxford University Press.

Holladay, A. 2002 (December). Wonderquest. Accessed online February 1, 2004: *http://www.wonderquest.com/size-women-us.htm.*

Hunt, J. 1984. The development of rapport through negotiation of gender in field work among police. *Human Organization* 43:283–296.

———. 1990. The logic of sexism among police. *Women and Criminal Justice* 1:3–30.

Kranda, A. 1998. Women in policing: The importance of mentoring. *The Police Chief* 65:54–56.

Lanier, M. 1996. Evolutionary typology of women police officers. *Women and Criminal Justice* 8: 35–57.

Lersch, K. 1998. Exploring gender differences in citizen allegations of misconduct: An analysis of a municipal police department. *Women and Criminal Justice* 9:69–79.

Maglione, R. 2002. Recruiting, retaining, and promoting women: The success of the Charlotte-Mecklenburg Police Department's women's network. *The Police Chief* 69:19–24.

Manning, P. 1977. *Police work.* Cambridge: MIT Press.

Martin, S. 1980. *Breaking and entering: Policewomen on patrol.* Berkeley: University of California Press.

———. 1992. The changing status of women officers: Gender and power in police work. In *The changing role of women in the criminal justice system,* ed. I. L. Moyer. Prospect Heights, IL: Waveland.

———. 1994. Outsider within the station house: The impact of race and gender on black women police. *Social Problems* 41:383–400.

Martin, S., and N. Jurik. 1996. *Doing justice, doing gender: Women in law and criminal justice occupations.* Thousand Oaks, CA: Sage.

Milgram, D. 2002. Recruiting women to policing: Practical suggestions that work. *The Police Chief* 69:23–29.

National Center for Women and Policing. 1999. Equality denied: The status of women in policing. Accessed online January 15, 2004: *http://www.womenandpolicing.org/Final_1999 StatusReport.htm.*.

Polisar, J., and D. Milgram. 1998. Recruiting, integrating, and retaining women police officers: Strategies that work. *The Police Chief* 65: 42–52.

Poulos, T., and W. Doerner. 1996. Women in law enforcement: The distribution of females in Florida police agencies. *Women in Criminal Justice* 8:19–33.

President's Commission on Law Enforcement and Administration of Justice. 1967. *Task force report: The police.* Washington, DC: United States Government Printing Office.

Price, B. R. 1974. A study of leadership strength of female police executives. *Journal of Police Science and Administration* 2:219–226.

Prussel, D., and K. Lonsway. 2001. Recruiting women police officers. *Law and Order* 49:91–96.

Rivlin, G. 1981. The last bastion of macho. *Update on Law-Related Education* 5:22–24, 65–67.

Schulz, D. 2002. Law enforcement leaders: A survey of women police chiefs in the United States. *The Police Chief* 69:25–27.

Scott, E. 1981. *Calls for service: Citizen demand and initial police response.* Washington, DC: U.S. Government Printing Office.

Sherman L. 1973. A psychological view of women in policing. In *Police roles in the seventies: Professionalization in America,* ed. J. Kinton. Ann Arbor: Edwards Brothers.

———. 1975. Evaluation of policewomen on patrol in a suburban police department. *Journal of Police Science and Administration* 3:434–438.

Skolnick, J. 1966. *Justice without trial.* New York: John Wiley & Sons.

Skolnick, J., and E. Currie. 1970. *Crisis in American institutions.* Boston: Little Brown.

Snortum, J., and J. Beyers. 1983. Patrol activities of male and female officers as a function of work experience. *Police Studies* 6:36–42.

Steffensmeier, D. 1979. Sex role orientation and attitudes toward female police. *Police Studies* 2:39–42.

Swanson, C., L. Territo, and R. Taylor. 1998. *Police administration: Structures, processes, and behavior,* 4th ed. Upper Saddle River, NJ: Prentice Hall.

Van Wormer, K. 1981. Are males suited to police patrol work? *Police Studies* 3:41–44.

Walker, S., and C. Katz. 2002. *The police in America: An introduction,* 4th ed. Boston: McGraw-Hill.

Weldy, W. 1976. Women in policing: A positive step toward increased police enthusiasm. *The Police Chief* 43:46–47.

Westley, W. 1970. *Violence and the police.* Boston: MIT Press Books.

Worden, A. P. 1993. The attitudes of women and men in policing: Testing conventional and contemporary wisdom. *Criminology* 31:203–241. ✦

Chapter 12
The Myth of Racial Profiling

Michael Buerger

The Myth

"Racial profiling" is the corruption of a legitimate law-enforcement practice of profiling. Profiles consist of a group of related attributes and behaviors that collectively signify an elevated probability that the individuals (or groups) displaying those characteristics are or have been engaged in criminal activity. The original context was the drug-courier profile used by the United States Customs Service to identify airplane passengers who might be smuggling illegal drugs into the country (see, for example, *United States v. Soko-low*). The Operation Pipeline highway-courier profile, developed by the Drug Enforcement Administration in the 1980s based upon intelligence about the nature of drug-distribution networks within the United States, was an offshoot of the customs profile. On the opposite end of legality, racial profiling occurs when a single factor—the race or ethnicity of an individual—is used as the sole or primary indicator of criminal behavior, in relation to other specific characteristics in the original profile.

The ongoing debate over what is called "racial profiling" involves a set of interrelated myths. On the community side, the term *racial profiling* embodies long-held suspicions that police actions are based largely on racial bias. There is an attendant myth, less supported by hard evidence, that some police engage in illegal means to search vehicles for drugs, or merely to harass minority citizens. On the police side, there are two myths. The primary myth is that minority citizens (primarily African Americans and Latinos) are far more likely to engage in criminality than are other groups. A corollary myth is that those groups have a greater involvement in drug trafficking. Mixed in with these beliefs are others more general to the police occupation, particularly the belief in a "sixth sense" which can distinguish individual criminality.

The Kernel of Truth

Race was a factor in the original drug-courier profile of Operation Pipeline, the DEA program for highway interdiction of bulk drugs. At the time, intelligence indicated that bulk drugs were being transported from the import points in Florida to the distribution cities in the north by a particular method. "Drug mules"—persons with no formal involvement in the drug trade, and thus theoretically beyond anti-drug surveillance and intelligence measures—were hired from the streets of poor neighborhoods in the south. They were given a car with the drugs locked in the trunk, or otherwise concealed in the vehicle, and a map with instructions and checkpoints. Their job was essentially to drive to the destination without stopping, to follow the interstate highway system (the fastest, most direct route), and to deliver the drugs in as short a time as possible. From this basic scheme, the highway drug-courier profile emerged.

The profile involved a car moving at a fast rate of speed, driven by two young males (ages 18–25 usually) of African American or Latino origin. The vehicle might contain many fast-food wrappers (the timetable left no room for a leisurely meal), blankets and pillows (for sleeping in shifts while driving straight through), and perhaps a strong detergent or other pungent substance to hide the smell of drugs from human or canine noses. A map would have cities and times circled on them, indicating the points at which the couriers were to check in with their employer to verify the product was on schedule. The car might contain tools or other evidence of alterations for hidden compartments. The key might be a valet key, which would run the car but provide no access to the trunk (Webb 1999).

Taken together, these facts and circumstances were suggestive of drug transport. They did not constitute probable cause to search the car, but were a tip-off to officers to investigate further and attempt to obtain permission to search inside the car. Successful stops based on this profile resulted in important seizures of drugs, and provided validation that the drug-courier profile was accurate.

The community side is anchored in two truths, one historical and one contemporary, both strongly opposing the police assertion that enforcement actions are race-neutral. The first lies in the historical police role, the enthusiastic enforcement of the Jim Crow laws and continued enforcement of racist social attitudes after legal segregation was overturned. The contemporary truth is experiential and incorporates a large body of anecdotal evidence. African-American drivers speak of "driving while black," and of being stopped by the police for seemingly no reason other than to harass them or to inquire if they are carrying drugs. Descriptions of many of these events do not resemble the drug-courier profile in any way. These stops involve single persons, families with children, individuals of color singled out from a line of traffic moving at the same speed, individuals

stopped numerous times and asked about drugs but never cited, etc. In many of the cases, the only salient element of the drug-courier profile present was the race of the driver.

The Truth or Facts

Two court cases brought the issue of racial profiling to the public's attention. A 1996 New Jersey appellate case, *State of New Jersey v. Pedro Soto, et al.*, established the "fact" of racial profiling. Soto and other defendants claimed that their convictions for drug possession—all of which involved small amounts of drugs—were based on illegal searches because they were stopped for no reason other than their race. The defense demonstrated that African-American drivers were almost five times as likely to be stopped as were white drivers. African Americans represented 15 percent of the highway traffic, but constituted 46 percent of the persons stopped by a drug-interdiction team working the southern stretch of the New Jersey Turnpike. The court ruled that the unexplained statistical disparity constituted a prima facie case of racial discrimination. Following the decision, the United States Department of Justice opened an investigation, and the state police undertook an internal review of its own practices.

The *Soto* case might have disappeared quietly but for an April 1998 incident on the northern New Jersey Turnpike. Two New Jersey troopers stopped a southbound van carrying four young men on their way to a basketball camp. Accounts of the stop vary widely (see Buerger and Farrell 2000), but at one point the van rolled backwards toward the troopers, who fired into the vehicle, wounding three of the four occupants. No drugs were found in the vehicle.

In the wake of the shooting, the state revived its earlier internal probe begun after the *Soto* decision. Among its findings were more instances of disparate stops of minority motorists, as well as training records and internal memoranda appearing to support the accusation that the New Jersey State Police targeted motorists based upon their race. Shortly thereafter, the state of New Jersey entered into a consent decree with the Department of Justice: it acknowledged the practice of racial profiling, and committed the state police to a series of corrective measures.

The civil case of *Wilkins v. Maryland State Police* also involved highway drug-interdiction methods, but arose from a stop in which no drugs were found. An analysis of Maryland State Police stops was compared to a study of the highway user population. That analysis revealed that African-American drivers constituted 17 percent of the highway users, but accounted for 73 percent of the searches. White drivers, by contrast, made up 75 percent of the highway population, but only 20 percent of the searches.

More telling, and more fatal to the myth of disparate drug use by minorities, was the fact that the "hit rate" (the rate at which illegal drugs were discovered as a result of a vehicle search) was almost the same for both white and black drivers: 28.4 percent of black drivers and 28.8 percent of white drivers were found to be carrying drugs in their vehicles. The amount of drugs found is not mentioned in any of the case materials and appears to be small amounts for personal use, not the bulk drugs of the Operation Pipeline drug-courier profile (the New Jersey Attorney General's report acknowledged that the amounts of drugs seized in the stops were small).

One other aspect of the myth was a sideshow in the New Jersey case. The commander of the New Jersey State Police was fired by the governor after an interview published in the *Star-Ledger* of Newark. The commander had said, in part:

> Two weeks ago, the president of the United States went to Mexico to talk to the president of Mexico about drugs. He didn't go to Ireland. He didn't go to England. . . . Today with this drug problem, the drug problem is cocaine or marijuana. It is most likely a minority group that's involved with that. . . . If you're looking at the methamphetamine market, that seems to be controlled by the motorcycle gangs, which are basically, predominantly white. . . . If you're looking at heroin and stuff like that, your involvement there is more or less Jamaicans. . . . (Associated Press 1999)

Police interpreted the firing as political correctness run amok, because it had long been established that some of the drug gangs were indeed organized around tight-knit groups of a particular ethnicity. However, there is a disconnect between that truth and the conclusion that if the upper echelons of a particular drug network are of a particular race or ethnicity, then every person who shares only that characteristic should be suspected of drug involvement. Were that the case, the police should search the cars of all white motorists for methamphetamines. That they do not is testimony both to the power of the minority-drug myth, and the different levels of political clout wielded by the two communities.

Once the New Jersey and Maryland cases were resolved by consent decrees, a number of jurisdictions conducted analyses of their own traffic-stop data, using basically the same formula as the highly publicized cases. Most of the major studies found racial disparities, though none were as severe as those in the flagship cases (see Engel, Calnon, and Bernard 2002, for a summary). Even more than in the New Jersey and Maryland contexts, there is a need for explanations of why those disparities exist.

To the community, the disparities represent further evidence that racially biased police actions are widespread. Within the police context, the lower rates leave open the possibility that the disparities validate the police belief in greater minority participation in crime. The current generation of aggregate data analysis does not provide sufficient explanatory power, because details concerning the contexts of the stops are not recorded.

Interests Served by the Myth

The myth of disproportionate involvement in the drug trade serves the interests of the police. Belief in the myth that certain races are predominately involved in certain types of drug trafficking provides law enforcement the pretext to stop and search for illegal drugs among certain types of drivers. Their interests are served when they perceive themselves as becoming more efficient and effective in their job (in this case, stopping drugs). Likewise, the myth of racial profiling itself serves the interests of critics of the police. The statistical evidence of the *Soto* and *Wilkins* cases—and the subsequent actions by the courts—gave concrete grounding to the belief that widespread racially biased practices continue to be visited on minority citizens by the police.

The myth also fosters aggressive antidrug campaigns, which are politically useful for obtaining support and additional finances (e.g., funds for overtime, which benefit individual officers, and seizure funds, which benefit agencies and munici-

palities). If no careful distinction is made between drug couriers and those who have some drugs in their possession, then the myth supports an inflation of the actual efficacy of the campaigns, giving the impression that every profile-based arrest yields huge amounts of drugs (and other contraband, such as unlawful guns) that are still occasionally found in vehicles during roadside stops.

Policy Implications of Belief in the Myth

Police belief in a disproportional minority role in the drug trade is part and parcel of a belief in the war on drugs, and on crime. The secondary justification, the overrepresentation of minorities in the criminal justice system, is derived in part from experience and in part from a surface reading of official statistics. It enters into the realm of "police experience" that is part of the justification for officer-initiated actions. For the police, "racial profiling" does not exist; they define their actions as "criminal profiling."

The myth of greater involvement in drugs embedded within the Operation Pipeline drug-courier profile gave the police a quasi-legitimate reason to stop vehicles they wanted to "check out." With a small number of visible factors, the police could go on a "fishing" expedition: stop the car on a pretext, look within it, question the occupants, and perhaps persuade them to open the trunk or other concealed portions of the vehicle. Since most vehicles stopped under those conditions were released without charges, and with fairly minimal delay, the negative consequences were relatively few. Until the consent decrees that followed *Soto* and *Wilkins*, review of police officers' actions began only *after* an arrest was made.

The ability to discern criminals on sight is a prized, and perhaps mythical, ability of police officers. Intermittent successful interdictions of large drug shipments self-validates the profile and the reliance upon it, while ignoring the much larger number of failed searches. The link between "the profile" and the successful seizures then rationalizes a new generation of enforcement actions aimed at replicating the success. In the absence of an Operation Pipeline mother-lode seizure, the police substitute individual seizures of smaller amounts of drugs as evidence that the profile works. Either perspective justifies the continued use of profiling, substituting anecdotal successes for a more robust assessment of the efficacy of the profile.

The complementary myth is far more powerful. For the community, the "fact" of racial profiling that was established in the *Wilkins* and *Soto* cases encapsulates and validates the long history of complaints of racist and race-based actions by the police. The statistics documenting racial disparities in traffic stops in the flagship cases, and by many (though not all) of the subsequent studies, are prima facie evidence that the minority communities' long-standing complaints of disparate treatment are matters of fact, not perception. In *Soto*, in the absence of a justification of the disparities, the court considered the differences alone to be strong enough evidence to warrant dismissal of the case. *Soto* also carried judicial censure of enforcement practices based upon racially established inferences, rather than observed conduct.

The finding that a few major drug dealers share a common racial or ethnic heritage does not validate widespread intrusion into the lives of citizens who share only that one attribute. Likewise, the fact that a few police agencies engage in racial profiling does not validate the suspicion that all police routinely engage in racially-prejudiced actions. The fact that these roles are reversed is an irony lost on most observers.

Soto was lost for lack of a credible explanation of the disparities. Had the state of New Jersey been able to demonstrate that African-American drivers were transporting (or possessing) drugs at a rate significantly higher than Caucasian drivers, the convictions might have stood. Had the state introduced evidence that African-American drivers were more likely to transport bulk drugs than white drivers, the appeals might have been denied. But the weak statistical analysis that was possible with the New Jersey statistics indicated no significant difference in the rate of drug possession, and the drugs seized were usually small "personal use" amounts. Even the elevated seizure numbers of the *Wilkins* case demonstrated that blacks and whites carried drugs in equal proportion.

In the remainder of the chapter, we will look at policy implications that attend the debunking of the myth. These policy implications are relatively simple, at least for the police: racial profiling is an invalid practice and must be avoided. Naturally, this is more easily said than done. Organizations remain vulnerable to problems arising from subtle biases in the matters of race. The belief that minorities are more crime-prone than others enters police departments through prior uncritical learning. These attitudes are often reinforced by similar existing attitudes that manifest themselves in the police socialization process, and occasionally in police training.

The first practical implication lies in the area of training. Clear and unequivocal messages that race-based decision making is unacceptable constitute the first step, but are not themselves sufficient. Training (both recruit and continuing in-service) must give officers the tools to establish legitimate probable cause. Equally essential is the development of written and verbal skills, so that officers can convincingly convey the bases of their reasonable suspicions and the elements of probable cause to supervisors, prosecutors, judges, and juries. The agency's supervisory structure must also ensure that the lessons of training are solidified into practice, consistently expected, and reinforced by review and instruction.

At the same time, it is incumbent upon police managers to know what their agency is doing in practice. Failure to do so has produced major scandals in various cities at various times, such as the Rampart's CRASH situation and the Rodney King incident in Los Angeles, the Moellen and Knapp Commission corruption investigations in New York City, the River Cops in Miami, and the cases discussed above.

While public outrage often fuels reform, proactive control of employee behaviors is preferable, and less expensive. When damning information is revealed under adversarial conditions (as it was in the *Soto* trial and the *Wilkins* suit), the result is embarrassment to the agency and considerable costs to the taxpayers. Professional and fiscal responsibilities dictate that agencies avoid such situations where possible. A systematic review of the data on activities, conducted on an ongoing basis, should illuminate problematic trends well in advance of scandal, allowing for corrective measures to be made that will avoid public spectacle entirely.

The data analysis in the *Soto* and *Wilkins* cases was conducted by outsiders, as most of the subsequent studies have been. The results demonstrated patterns of conduct that should already have been known to supervisors of the respective agencies. At the same time, the rarified conditions of highway drug interdiction cannot be applied to the multiple missions that attend municipal policing.

Highway drug interdiction focuses on a single activity, driving a vehicle from point A to point B. All individuals using the limited-access Interstate highways are engaged in that one activity, and the interdiction teams look for anomalous features that suggest the covert drug activity piggybacked with such travel. The simple racial disparities of *Soto* and *Wilkins* are enough to capture the patterns of police activity under these circumstances.

The same technique, however, cannot serve as well in the arena of city policing, when motor-vehicle stops arise from traffic enforcement, criminal investigation, roadside safety and sobriety checks, responses to particular complaints, and general community concerns (among other sources). Elevated rates of stops may reflect legitimate police service in response to community concerns, or it may reflect racial bias. Aggregate statistics cannot tease out legitimate practices from illegitimate ones (if there are any); patterns will vary within jurisdictions by zone and neighborhood. As the highway cases indicate, officers operating in small groups may engage in prejudicial behaviors; if their actions are not representative of agency practices, the bias may be masked statistically by larger agency patterns. The influence of those actions on minority citizens will remain, however, and the gap between what is experienced and what is demonstrated statistically will remain a cause of friction.

In the past, agencies lacked the ability to conduct systematic analysis of their day-to-day operations because paper-based files presented immense logistical obstacles to meaningful examination.

Today, however, investment in computerized records and communications equipment provides the capacity to expand administrative oversight into many other areas.

Though police analysts tend to focus on crime patterns, the statistical techniques for crime- and geography-specific pattern analysis are similar to those needed for officer- and unit-specific activity analysis. Internal analysis can provide considerably more insight into local conditions than outsiders can: knowledge of neighborhood conditions, initiatives undertaken in partnership with the community or in response to specific complaints about area problems, market fluctuations in drug-dealing and attempted purchases, etc. Stops related to criminal activity and citizen complaints can be separated from officer-initiated activity at the local level, and both legitimate and questionable patterns of activity identified. Similarly, agency supervisors will certainly know more than outside analysts who the individuals on the job are whose attitudes and performance may be problematic in this regard.

The vivid disparities of the *Soto* and *Wilkins* cases stand out readily, and leave little doubt as to the corrective actions needed. Such cases tend to be rare, however, as the subsequent research has demonstrated. The more subtle variations of racial bias, hidden amidst the large volume of legitimate police activity, are more difficult to discern. That is the ongoing challenge for police administration in the coming years.

References

Associated Press. 1999. N.J. state police head fired for remark on minorities. *Boston Globe* March 1, A3.

Buerger, M. E., and A. Farrell. 2000. The evidence of racial profiling: Interpreting documented and unofficial sources. *Police Quarterly* 5(3):272–305.

Engel, R. S., J. M. Calnon, and T. J. Bernard. 2002. Theory and racial profiling: Shortcomings and future directions in research. *Justice Quarterly* 19(2):249–273.

State of New Jersey v. Pedro Soto, et al. 1996. 324 N.J.Super. 66, 734 A.2d 350.

United States v. Sokolow. 1989. 490 U.S. 1.

Webb, G. 1999. DWB. *Esquire* April, 118–127.

Wilkins v. Maryland State Police. 1993. Civil Action No. CCB-93-483 (D.Md.). ✦

Chapter 13
The Myth That Science Solves Crimes

Gary Cordner and
Kathryn E. Scarborough

The Myth

Solving crimes with science has long been part of the vision of better policing and better criminal justice. This explains the century-old popularity of the fictional character Sherlock Holmes and the current popularity of the television series *CSI* (Crime Scene Investigation). The ideal of scientific crime solving is best understood and appreciated by reference to the opposite situation—when crimes are solved through the use of human evidence from informants, suspects, and eyewitnesses. Human evidence is known to have high rates of error because people lie, forget, exaggerate, and make other kinds of mistakes in the process of listening, seeing, remembering, and describing events. Science, by contrast, is considered objective, precise, and honest—it does not lie.

The myth is that most crimes are solved with science. In fact, most crimes are never solved. The relatively few crimes that are solved (about 20 percent of those reported to the police) owe their solution to human evidence and mundane investigative work more often than to science. Although scientific crime solving has been an important social and legal ideal for well over 100 years, the degree to which it

has been achieved is disappointing. TV shows such as *CSI* notwithstanding, most detectives still rely more on informants, witnesses, and confessions than on forensic science.

The Kernel of Truth

Of course, some crimes are solved using science. Fingerprints found at a crime scene can be matched to a suspect, proving that she was there. Blood found on a victim can be matched with a suspect's blood, proving that it is his. Fibers found on a victim can be matched to the carpet in a suspect's house, suggesting the victim may have been in contact with that carpet (or another carpet from the same manufacturer's batch). The victim's hair can be found in the trunk of the suspect's car. Blood spatter analysis can contradict a suspect's version of events, suggesting he is lying. In these and many other ways, science can provide very important information in an investigation, helping prove a particular suspect did it.

Moreover, forensic science has obviously progressed in the last 100 years. Reliable data are surprisingly hard to obtain, but it seems certain that more crimes are being solved with science today than was true in the past.

The Truth or Facts

In the earliest days of policing, solving crime depended solely on information gathered from people—victims, witnesses, criminals, and other police officers. One of the earliest uses of science and technology was anthropometry, a system that used body measurements to aid in the identification of criminals. Another early development, dactylography (fingerprinting), had and continues to have a substantial influence on criminal investigation. Historically, the primary contribution of fingerprinting was for criminal identification—taking fingerprint impressions from persons who had been arrested to determine the person's correct identity.

The use of latent fingerprints for crime solving had a smaller influence until recently. Latent prints are those found at a crime scene. Police developed the capacity to "lift" such prints long ago, but before computers it was extremely difficult to figure out to whom the latent print from the crime scene belonged. If a suspect was identified through some other means (such as an eyewitness), then that suspect's fingerprints could be compared to the latent print and it could usually be determined whether there was a match or not. However, if no suspect was identified by witnesses or other means (which was the most common situation), it was almost impossible to conduct a "cold search" of fingerprint files to find a match with the latent print from the crime scene.

The historical situation with respect to other types of physical evidence (blood, semen, hair, fiber, etc.) was even worse. Take blood as an example. Until recently (pre-DNA), if police found blood at a crime scene, they could study it for evidence about how the assault or injury occurred (blood spatter analysis), and they could collect the blood and submit it to a crime lab for analysis. That analysis, though, could only establish the blood type. Thus, the police might learn that the blood at the crime scene was Type A- with certain other characteristics. With that information, the police could rule out certain people—they might be able to conclude it was not the victim's blood, for example, or not a particular suspect's blood. If the suspect had the same blood type and other blood characteristics, however, the police could only say it could be the suspect's blood found at the crime scene—they could not know for sure. And even more frustrating, knowing the type of blood found at the crime scene was of absolutely no value at all to the police in finding a suspect, since no databases of individuals' blood types existed; and even if they did, thousands or millions of people would have had the same blood type as that found at the crime scene.

Legal considerations. During the Due Process Revolution of the 1960s and 1970s, police work changed dramatically. Starting with *Miranda v. Arizona* in 1966, the U.S. Supreme Court applied more restrictive provisions of the U.S. Constitution to state and local police work, forcing police to reexamine how they conducted interrogations, searches, and other aspects of criminal investigation. Also, twentieth century case law influenced the use of scientific evidence in court, including *Frye v. United States* (1923) and *Daubert v. Merrell Dow Pharmaceuticals, Inc.* (1993). The *Frye* case established that before a specific technique could be admissible in court, the technique had to have gained acceptance in its particular field. In *Daubert*, the Supreme Court ruled that specific criteria have to be met before scientific evidence is admissible in court, including not only acceptance in its field, but also that it has been tested, that it has been subject to peer review within its scientific field, and that it has a known error rate.

Research. The relatively minor role played by physical evidence in real-life crime solving was demonstrated in an early study in Berkeley, California (Parker and Peterson 1972). Two of the revealing findings of the study are that only 4 out of 3,303 Part I crimes involved laboratory examination of physical evidence; and that 88 percent of burglary crime scenes had physical evidence, yet in less than 5 percent was there even a request for laboratory services.

The seminal work examining the process of criminal investigation was the Rand study by Greenwood, Chaiken, and Petersilia (1975). This study found that 80 percent of serious crime cases were never solved, and of those that were solved, most of the "credit" belonged to witnesses and patrol officers rather than to detectives or forensic science. It also found that physical evidence was often collected at crime scenes, but most of it was never analyzed and it was rare for physical evidence to lead the police to a suspect.

A subsequent study by Eck (1983) and the Police Executive Research Forum (PERF) came to similar conclusions. Eck's work examined robberies and burglaries in three jurisdictions. He found that follow-up work performed by detectives did contribute to solving some cases. Use of physical evidence, though, while readily available, was still limited. The detective activities that contributed the most to crime solving were searching for additional witnesses, contacting informants, talking to other officers, and using police records—not using physical evidence or forensic science.

These major studies of criminal investigation were completed over 20 years ago, before the advent of considerable science and technology, especially computerized fingerprint searching and the development of DNA analysis for individual identification. It is to these two topics the discussion now turns.

AFIS. The use of fingerprints as physical evidence has increased significantly in the last two decades due to modern technology, yet also illustrates some of the barriers that can limit the impact of science and technology on law enforcement (Schwabe, Davis, and Jackson 2001). Automated Fingerprint Identification Systems (AFIS) are now operated at the local, regional, state, and federal levels. With these systems, latent fingerprints from crime scenes can be electronically scanned, digitized, and checked against existing databases of fingerprints. That means that latent prints from crime scenes can now be used to identify suspects who would otherwise be unknown to the investigator—a significant new investigative capacity. Thousands of suspects have been identified through the use of AFIS and IAFIS, which is the national system that ties together the various AFIS systems and databases of fingerprints around the country and even internationally (Swanson, Chamelin, and Territo 2003).

These AFIS systems have not reached their potential, however. One problem is cost—not all jurisdictions can afford the equipment or the staff time to scan fingerprints. Some police agencies have been disappointed by the technology when there are few "hits" from scanned latent prints. Ironically, this is caused mainly by poor quality fingerprints in the database. AFIS cannot match a latent print from a crime scene to a suspect's fingerprints in its database if those fingerprints are so smudged that their characteristics are obscured. Of course, this is not really a technology failure but rather human failure on the part of the officers who took the fingerprints when the person was previously arrested. Another human factor that has limited the impact of AFIS is the failure of detectives and officers to look for and recover latent prints at crime scenes. This results from the outdated but enduring belief within police work and criminal investigation that physical evidence, and especially fingerprints, is not very useful in solving crimes. Old habits die hard, even when the science on which they were originally based has dramatically changed.

DNA. In 1985, deoxyribonucleic acid (DNA), a person's genetic blueprint, was first used successfully in a criminal case in England. The United States shortly followed suit. The analysis of DNA previously took much time and large samples of the human tissue evidence. Now, due to advancements in technology, the utility of DNA has dramatically increased.

By 1998, DNA evidence had gained such prominence in the United States that Attorney General Janet Reno created the National Commission for the Future of DNA Evidence to "provide the Attorney General with recommendations on the use of current and future DNA methods, applications and technologies in the operation of the criminal justice system, from the crime scene to the courtroom" (National Institute of Justice 2004). The Commission's work resulted in the publication of three reports, a pamphlet, and two training CDs on the collection of DNA evidence.

The use of DNA has developed much like the use of fingerprints in criminal investigations. As with IAFIS, the FBI's Combined DNA Index System (CODIS) serves as a national database for DNA. Legislation in 1994 formalized the FBI's authority to establish a national DNA index for law enforcement purposes (Federal Bureau of Investigation 2004). However, unlike AFIS, there are numerous challenges with CODIS resulting from the inconsistency of state laws concerning submissions to the database. For example, Louisiana permits the collection of DNA evidence from all felons, some misdemeanants (as specified), arrestees, suspects, juvenile offenders, and other individuals in the state corrections system. By contrast, Missouri only permits DNA collection from sex offenders, murderers, and some individuals within the corrections system.

In addition, as reported by Franzen (2004), many states lag behind in analyzing DNA samples already collected from crime scenes and offenders. For example, Oregon has 20,000 unprocessed inmate DNA samples. This situation is improving, though. In Michigan, a 10-year backlog was recently eliminated, as reported by Bailey (2004), and other states have also made significant progress recently. The President's FY 2004 budget included $232.6 million for Advancing Justice Through DNA Technology, and requested more than $1 billion for the next five years (Smith Alling Lane 2004).

In contrast to the situation in the United States, the potential of DNA technology is more advanced in the United Kingdom, specifically in England and Wales. England, in fact, is touted as the most advanced country in these efforts. Significant improvements in evidence collection, practice, and more efficient laboratory analyses have characterized the United Kingdom's (UK) endeavors. In 1994, the Criminal Justice and Public Order Act (CJPOA) established the authority for the creation of a DNA database. While the CJPOA has numerous provisions related to DNA evidence collection, perhaps the most notable is its authorization of the police to collect saliva and mouth samples without the necessity of consent. Previously, saliva and mouth samples were considered "intimate" and could only be collected with a police supervisor's permission. Samples are collected using buccal swabs, which make processing and analysis much less expensive. In 2001, another act was passed that provided for the indefinite retention of DNA samples from all individuals who provided either voluntary written consent or became a suspect in a criminal case.

Pending legislation would allow routine sampling of all arrestees.

The broad application of DNA technology in England and Wales is such that evidence is routinely collected at crime scenes for a variety of offenses. Potential DNA evidence is collected not only at the scenes of serious violent crimes, such as murder and rape, but also at the scenes of "volume crimes" including burglary, car theft, criminal damage, and other less violent offenses. The expectation is that the collection of DNA evidence will eventually become commonplace for all types of crimes, suspects, and offenders.

The National DNA Database of England and Wales is widely recognized as the most effective and efficient DNA database in the world for the reasons previously identified. Success can be measured through "hits" made, profiles continuously added, and the prevention of crime. Hits may be from crime scene to crime scene (tying multiple crimes together) or from crime scene to suspect. There were more than 1,700 matches per week in 2002. The suspect identification rate for burglary, in fact, increased from 14 percent to 44 percent when DNA was available at the crime scene and used in the investigation. Also, each crime solved with DNA led to an average of 0.8 other crimes being solved, typically by tying additional offenses to the suspect who had first been identified by DNA (Asplen 2003:20).

Because of the comprehensive legislation guiding the collection of DNA evidence, 8,000 to 10,000 arrestee or suspect profiles were added to the national database every week in 2002. Additionally, 1,000 to 1,500 crime scene profiles were added on a weekly basis. Asplen (2003:29) asserts that the use of DNA in England and Wales is successful because it is not just a:

forensic tool available to law enforcement. Rather, it is considered to be an integrated and routine part of the investigative process. It is not a technology to be used in special or particularly serious cases. It is a process invested in so as to become a routine part of every investigation in which biological material may be left by the perpetrator.

Interests Served By the Myth

So who benefits from the myth that science solves crimes? One possibility is the police establishment. Simply being associated with science helps elevate the professional status of police work. Additionally, solving crimes with science seems efficient, clean, and above reproach, in contrast to the seedier techniques often relied upon by detectives in the past. Thus, scientific crime solving might be thought of as part of the police presentational strategy that helps mystify the public (Manning 1977), or as one of the circumlocutions used by the police to deflect public attention from the morally ambiguous realities of their work (Klockars 1988).

This explanation falls a bit short, though, because many police officials have both resisted the adoption of scientific methods of criminal investigation and continued to express cynicism about the myth. This shows that the police establishment is not monolithic. While the interests of the FBI and some national police leaders might have been served by the myth that science solves crime, many police at the local level took a much more skeptical view of the role of science in criminal investigations, at least until very recently.

Two other distinct beneficiaries are the legal establishment and the scientific community. The legal establishment benefits from the myth that science solves crime because it makes decisions by prosecutors, judges, and juries about guilt, innocence, and punishment seem more objective. The myth makes the legal process seem rational and less like a game that is won by whichever side has the best players. The scientific community benefits from the myth because it ascribes to science a larger and more important role in the adjudication of human affairs. The myth makes a case for the need for more scientists, more labs, and more scientific training for police, prosecutors, and judges.

In truth, though, the myth simply supports a broad set of ideas associated with the Enlightenment. Since the eighteenth century, Western civilization has embraced rationalism, logic, and science as the best means for managing human affairs. We have come to believe that governments, including legal systems and police, should operate logically and scientifically. Most importantly, we want to believe that human conflict and misery can be eliminated through the application of logic and science. We believe that if we study a problem carefully enough we can figure it out and fix it.

Solving crimes provides a challenging test of these Enlightenment ideals. Something bad has happened to a victim—Sherlock Holmes would figure it out with superior logic; the characters on *CSI* figure it out with science. Real-life detectives have traditionally figured it out (if they figured it out at all) by talking to witnesses, encouraging informants to incriminate their friends and associates, and persuading suspects to confess. Most people prefer the Sherlock Holmes/*CSI* myth because it is cleaner, more objective, and more scientific. To admit the truth is not just to admit that injustices occur, but also to accept that they occur in our name

at the hands of agents working for us. The myth is comforting for all of us.

Because the science of crime solving is changing so dramatically, though, it would seem that the myth is truer today than even 10 or 20 years ago. In this sense, it might be best to think of "science solves crimes" as an ideal as well as a myth. As long as the reality of criminal investigation fell so far short of the ideal, it served as a myth, perhaps benefiting the police, legal, and scientific communities, and certainly comforting the public in general. Because it also served as an ideal, though, it provided motivation and direction for scientific and practical developments in crime solving. While it is still true today, despite recent advances, that science does not solve most crimes, that does not mean that it won't be much more effective in the future.

Policy Implications of Belief in the Myth

One might have expected the myth that science solves crimes to have created tremendous pressure on the police and legal systems to produce more and better scientific evidence. The courts have shown growing doubts about confessions, informants, and eyewitness testimony since at least the 1960s, but there has been no systematic attempt to restrict the use of such evidence. The myth (or ideal) does seem to have resulted in modest investments in research, equipment, and crime lab staff over the years, but that has not prevented crime labs from developing serious backlogs of cases or losing experienced scientists to better paying jobs in the private sector.

Perhaps one significant implication of the belief that science solves crimes is a tendency to put too much stock in scientific evidence. Over the past decade, scientific evidence has received severe criticism in a number of notorious and routine criminal trials, including the O.J. Simpson case. Several crime labs, including the FBI's, were found to have performed substandard work, tending to favor the prosecution instead of a neutral standard of justice. A number of scientists were found to have testified inaccurately, either misrepresenting their credentials or misinterpreting their analyses. In 2004, faulty fingerprint identification in the Madrid, Spain, train bombing case caused a Portland, Oregon, lawyer to be jailed for several days (Begley 2004).

These examples demonstrate two things: (1) different branches of science are in different stages of development, leading to results with different degrees of certainty; and (2) science neither tells the truth nor lies—it is interpreted and represented by people (investigators and scientists) who themselves can make mistakes, feel pressure, exaggerate, have their own agendas, and even lie. As the ideal that "science solves crimes" becomes less myth and more reality, this human side of science will probably become a bigger factor in criminal investigation and courtroom trials. Certainly, there is every reason to believe that crime scene investigators and forensic scientists are more objective, dispassionate, and honest in their interpretations of scientific evidence than the average witness, informant, or suspect, but it will be important to overcome our naïveté about the infallibility of science.

References

Asplen, C. H. 2003. The application of DNA technology in England and Wales. Unpublished manuscript. London: Smith Alling Lane PSC.

Bailey, A. F. 2004. State clears a 10-year DNA backlog. *Detroit Free Press* September 1. Accessed online at *http://www.freep.com/news/mich/dna1e_20040901.htm*.

Begley, S. 2004. Despite its reputation, fingerprint evidence isn't really infallible. *The Wall Street Journal* June 4: B1.

Daubert v. Merrell Dow Pharmaceuticals, Inc. 1993. 507 U.S. 904.

Eck, J. E. 1983. *Solving crimes: The investigation of burglary and robbery.* Washington, DC: Police Executive Research Forum.

Federal Bureau of Investigation (FBI). 2004. CODIS mission statement and background. Accessed online at *http://www.fbi.gov/hq/lab/codis/program.htm*.

Franzen, R. 2004. DNA backlog keeps cases cold. *The Oregonian* July 28. Accessed online at *http://www.oregonlive.com/news/oregonian/index.ssf?/base/front_page/1091015902295620.xml*.

Frye v. United States. 1923. 293 Fed. 1013 (DC).

Greenwood, P. W., J. M. Chaiken, and J. Petersilia. 1975. *The criminal investigation process.* Santa Monica, CA: Rand Corporation.

Klockars, C. B. 1988. The rhetoric of community policing. In *Community policing: Rhetoric or reality,* eds. J. R. Greene and S. D. Mastrofski. New York: Praeger.

Manning, P. K. 1977. *Police work: The social organization of policing.* Cambridge, MA: MIT Press.

Miranda v. Arizona. 1966. 384 U.S. 436.

National Institute of Justice (NIJ). 2004. The National Commission on the future of DNA evidence. Accessed online at *http://www.ojp.usdoj.gov/nij/dna/*.

Parker, B., and J. Peterson. 1972. *Physical evidence utilization in the administration of criminal justice.* Washington, DC: U.S. Government Printing Office.

Schwabe, W., L. M. Davis, and B. A. Jackson. 2001. *Challenges and choices for crime fighting technology: Federal and state support for state and local law enforcement.* Santa Monica, CA: Rand Corporation.

Smith Alling Lane. 2004. DNA resource report. Accessed online at *http://dnaresource.com/*.

Swanson, C. R., N. C. Chamelin, and L. Territo. 2003. *Criminal investigation.* 8th ed. New York: McGraw-Hill. ✦

Chapter 14
The Myth That COMPSTAT Reduces Crime and Transforms Police Organizations

James J. Willis,
Stephen D. Mastrofski,
and David Weisburd

COMPSTAT, a technological and management system, is the latest attempt to make the police better organized and more effective at fighting crime (Weisburd et al. 2003; Moore 2003). Heralded as a new "paradigm" or a "revolution" in police organization, COMPSTAT, an abbreviation of "compare stats," or "computer statistics meetings," combines cutting-edge crime analysis and geographic information systems with state-of-the-art management principles. It literally burst onto the scene when it was first implemented in 1994 by then Commissioner William Bratton and Deputy Commissioner Jack Maple of the New York City Police Department (NYPD), and has diffused rapidly across the United States. The first national study of COMPSTAT conducted by the Police Foundation showed that in only five years after COMPSTAT was implemented in New York City, a third of the nation's largest departments (over 100 sworn officers) had already adopted it, and another quarter were planning to do so (Weisburd et al. 2004:6).

COMPSTAT consists of four highly interrelated crime-reduction principles that are designed to make police organizations rational and responsive to management direction: (1) accurate and timely information made available at all levels in the organization; (2) the selection of the most effective tactics for specific problems; (3) rapid, focused deployment of people and resources to implement those tactics; and (4) relentless follow-up and assessment to learn what happened and make subsequent tactical assessments if necessary (Safir n.d.). These and other elements of the COMPSTAT approach are most visibly displayed in the NYPD's twice-weekly COMPSTAT Crime Control Strategy Meetings, during which precinct commanders appear before the department's top echelon to report on crime problems in their districts and what they are doing about them. This all occurs in a data-saturated environment where crime analysts collect, analyze, and map crime statistics to spot trends and to assist precinct commanders with identifying any underlying factors that explain or tie together crime incidents. Top supervisors use this information to quiz precinct commanders on the nature of crime in their beats and to hold them responsible for solving the issues. Any failure to provide a satisfactory response to various inquiries may lead to stern criticism or even removal from command for consistently poor performance.

In this chapter, we critically assess two major COMPSTAT myths. The first credits recent crime drops in the United States to COMPSTAT's effectiveness as a crime control program; the second posits that COMPSTAT results in radical and uniformly positive changes to existing police organization and practice. Next we explore why these myths about COMPSTAT persist, before concluding with some brief comments on prospects for police reform.

The Myth

COMPSTAT has been promoted by its originators and proponents as an effective approach to reducing crime (Bratton 1998; Giuliani 2002; Henry 2002). Since its introduction in New York City, data touting COMPSTAT's success have been collected and publicized in the national media. Between 1993 and 1999, murder and nonnegligent manslaughter in New York declined 66 percent, robbery dropped 58 percent, motor vehicle theft fell 66 percent, and burglary decreased 59 percent (Smith and Bratton 2001:455). Henry presents a similar array of data, the result, he argues, of a "revolution in the way the New York Police Department conducts its business," of which the COMPSTAT process is "an intrinsic part" (Henry 2002:3). Other departments, including New Orleans, Minneapolis, and Philadelphia, have credited COMPSTAT directly with reducing crime in their cities (Anderson 2001). To date there has not been a systematic and rigorous review of the influence of the implementation of COMPSTAT programs, but this has not dampened the spirits of COMPSTAT's believers.

In addition to its purported capacity to reduce crime, claims that COMPSTAT revitalizes and revamps police organizations have added to its appeal, especially among police leaders. Former command officers of the NYPD have implemented COMPSTAT as newly appointed police chiefs in other departments, and other chiefs have adopted it to reform their own departments (Dewan 2004). Acting in unison, COMPSTAT's elements are supposed to form a set of coherent structures and strategies that free police organizations from many of the constraints long associated with bureaucratic dysfunction, including lack of focus and innovation, excessive red-tape, and turf battles. COMPSTAT, it is claimed, improves the police capacity to reduce crime by transforming the organization into a well-oiled machine firing on all its pistons.

The Kernel of Truth

The simple association between COMPSTAT and decreasing crime leads many to believe in the effectiveness of modern police methods. Indeed, COMPSTAT's initial implementation did correspond to a greater drop in New York City's crime rate than the national average. According to Silverman, "During 1994, the overall New York City crime decline was 12 percent, compared to 2 percent nationally, and 17 percent for 1995." Additionally, FBI statistics show that during the first six months of 1995, New York accounted for 61 percent of the nationwide decline in felonies (Silverman 1996:1). Other cities with COMPSTAT programs have also reported falling crime rates.

There is also evidence to suggest, at least in certain respects, that COMPSTAT changes police organizations. The Police Foundation's multistage study identified six key elements that emerged as central to the development of COMPSTAT: mission clarification, internal accountability, geographic organization of operational command, organizational flexibility, data-driven problem identification and assessment, and innovative problem-solving tactics. Using a national survey, researchers compared those departments that had developed a COMPSTAT program to those that were not intending to do so. Results showed that the most significant differences were in the areas of crime control, increased control over managers, and use of data. Departments that claimed to have recently adopted COMPSTAT were more concerned with reducing crime, increasing internal accountability, and conducting crime analysis and computer mapping (Weisburd et al. 2003). Findings from a later stage of this study involving intensive site research at three police departments supported these survey findings. Lowell, Minneapolis, and Newark police were selected because they had copied COMPSTAT from New York's hallmark program and had implemented it fully. These three departments were highly focused on crime, with one department demonstrating its commitment by setting an ambitious goal to cut the city's annual crime rate by 10 percent. COMPSTAT also had a significant influence on middle managers, who exercised considerable decision-making authority and who felt responsible for monitoring crime in their assigned areas, identifying patterns of crime problems and applying solutions to these patterns. Finally, these middle managers relied on timely crime data to make command decisions to a much greater extent than prior to COMPSTAT's implementation (Willis, Mastrofski, and Weisburd 2004b).

The Truth or Facts

While the timing of the crime drop in New York City and elsewhere corresponds approximately to when COMPSTAT was being implemented in cities across the country, it may be nothing more than coincidence, rather than causation. Relying on reported crime rates from the Uniform Crime Reports, COMPSTAT supporters attribute some kind of causal relationship between the two, but to date there has not been a single systematic study assessing

COMPSTAT's influence on crime. In fact, the available evidence suggests there are good reasons to be circumspect about the claims of its supporters. Applying the same descriptive analyses used by COMPSTAT's proponents, Eck and Maguire (2000) challenge the claim that COMPSTAT played an important role in lowering New York City's homicide rate. Their examination of UCR data between 1986 and 1998 shows that the decline in the city's homicides, while noteworthy, began long before COMPSTAT was implemented. They also noted that homicides declined precipitously in other large cities that had not implemented a COMPSTAT program in the early- to mid-1990s. They are led to conclude: "On balance, the data do not support a strong argument for COMPSTAT causing, contributing to, or accelerating the decline in homicides in New York City or elsewhere" (Eck and Maguire 2000:233).

The Police Foundation study was not designed to test whether COMPSTAT reduced crime, but it did examine crime trends before and after the implementation of COMPSTAT in Lowell, Minneapolis, and Newark. Again, a simple prepost test at three sites using a few years of crime data is insufficient to make a determination of the nature and extent of COMPSTAT's influence on crime, but it does raise the question of whether COMPSTAT was the force bringing crime down. An examination of UCR data shows crime was already in decline for at least a year before COMPSTAT was implemented in each city, and the rate of decline was the same or less steep (see Figure 14.1). If COMPSTAT had an influence, we would expect the rate of decline to be steeper after its implementation.

COMPSTAT's accomplishments are even more unclear in Lowell, where crime began to rise two years after its implemen-

Figure 14.1
Crime Rates in Three Cities

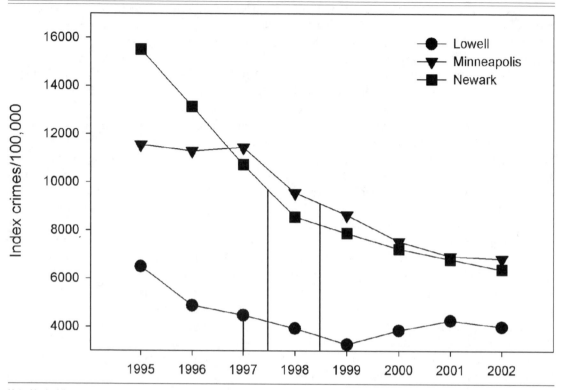

Note: Vertical lines show year that COMPSTAT was implemented.

tation (Willis et al. 2004). Perhaps COMP-STAT was not the force bringing crime down, since a decline had already begun at all three sites; subsequently, the rate of decline did not accelerate, and at one of the sites crime turned upward. This analysis of COMPSTAT's uncertain effects is consistent with Eck and Maguire's (2000) assessment that while it is possible that COMPSTAT did influence crime levels, the balance of available evidence encourages skepticism about the assertions of its advocates.

Regarding its capacity to revolutionize police organizations, a case study of New York City's COMPSTAT program, conducted a few years after its implementation, considered it a resounding success (Silverman 1999). Recent anecdotal accounts express similar views (e.g., Lehrer 2001), but research on COMPSTAT at Lowell, Newark, and Minneapolis suggests a mixed result at odds with the image of COMPSTAT as a transformative mechanism for the delivery of calculable, desirable, and attainable outcomes. Lacking credible evidence to refute these findings, some COMPSTAT followers have dismissed its doubters on ideological grounds (Walsh and Vito 2004). Such an approach is not very convincing, nor is the claim from advocates that skeptical researchers are unable to assess the real potential of COMPSTAT because they have only studied imperfect COMPSTAT programs. These three departments studied by the Police Foundation were specifically selected to allay this type of criticism. As model COMPSTAT programs that were fully operational in departments recognized nationally for their leadership, it is doubtful that the challenges and pathologies these programs experienced were the result of uniquely flawed implementation and operation.

Earlier we noted the most powerful and consistent effects among the three sites that had followed in New York City's footsteps were manifested in the behavior of district commanders. Yet this research also revealed a number of limitations and internal contradictions to COMPSTAT, suggesting what has taken place thus far is not a transformation so much as a transplanting of some elements of progressive management onto fundamentally unaltered organizational structures (Weisburd et al. forthcoming).

First, COMPSTAT's narrow mission conflicted with other core organizational values and undermined officers' commitment to the COMPSTAT goal of crime control. This conflict was experienced most powerfully in Minneapolis, which was the only department to establish a New York–style mission of reducing crime by 10 percent in a year and to reinforce this goal with a specific tactic: aggressive order maintenance facilitated through the practice of directed patrol. At the same time, the department's leadership strongly supported community policing—an approach that generally accords community decision-making, standards of integrity, problem solving, reducing fear of crime, and improving social order—as equally important to fighting crime (Moore 1992:109). Surprisingly, results from a survey distributed at roll call in each site showed that rank-and-file officers in Minneapolis had the lowest buy-in to the redefined COMPSTAT mission (Willis, Mastrofski, and

Weisburd 2004b). Officers' comments revealed high levels of frustration at being caught between the opposing belief systems and approaches of COMPSTAT and community policing. For instance, community partnerships and service competed with crime control through surveillance and law enforcement, and answering calls for service, though valuable for community policing, conflicted with directed patrol.

A second COMPSTAT limitation was that, although its meetings did function effectively as an accountability mechanism, their exclusive focus on middle managers meant that lower-ranking officers did not experience a similarly intense level of accountability. The underdevelopment of this element meant that rank-and-file officers were largely ignorant and unaffected by what went on at department COMPSTAT meetings.

Third, although district commanders did enjoy a larger measure of authority delegated from headquarters, their autonomy was limited by top management's willingness to exercise authority over them, particularly when it came to making critical decisions about department resources. For example, at all three sites, only the chief and his staff had the power to reassign officers between districts and to form task forces.

Fourth, the capacity of each organization to shift resources quickly and decisively to where they were needed most was hindered by traditional features of police organizations (Willis, Mastrofski, and Weisburd 2004). Budget limits impeded managers from working around the constraints of set work shifts by restricting the amount of overtime, and bureaucratic rules and regulations (such as union regulations) limited changes to an officer's shift assignment.

Fifth, little progress had been made in the way data were used. The data analysis employed tended to (a) focus on identifying short-term crime patterns rather than broader long-term crime trends; (b) help with the identification of hot spots, but not with how to select crime strategies once these areas were located; (c) focus disproportionately on what was happening with individual crime cases, and not on longer-term crime patterns and their underlying conditions; and (d) neglect systematic and long-term evaluations of police effectiveness.

And finally, innovation was the exception not the rule. District commanders often relied on tried and tested police strategies, which generally involved stepping up surveillance and enforcement activities.

Some of these limitations on COMPSTAT were due to inadequate changes to existing structures that could have supported a fuller implementation of COMPSTAT. For example, middle managers did not receive additional training in data analysis, and crime analysis units were underresourced. But COMPSTAT's internal contradictions, most noticeably between its accountability and problem-solving structures, appear even harder to resolve. The tremendous pressure on district commanders to take prompt and decisive action interfered with the kind of in-depth analysis that is regarded as a core element of COMPSTAT. The fact that district commanders were expected to come to COMPSTAT with problems already identified and solutions already implemented discouraged a careful and time-consuming analysis of crime data to identify the underlying causes of problems and to assess the effectiveness of responses. The emphasis on accountability also undermined COMPSTAT's innovative problem-solving component by invalidat-

ing the need for brainstorming and increasing the risks of experimenting with new problem-solving strategies. Managers were reluctant to volunteer "helpful" suggestions for fear that they would discredit the people whose feet were being held to the fire of accountability. Furthermore, fear of failure and punishment discouraged managers from pursuing new strategies that might have been more effective than old methods.

In sum, COMPSTAT has been greeted as a way to profoundly transform police organizations in the way they operate. Many consider New York City's pioneering COMPSTAT effort to have introduced a revolution in American policing. But the Police Foundation research at three sites provides a more modest and textured assessment of COMPSTAT's capacity to change existing organizational structures and practices.

Interests Served by the Myth

Although a national survey and a handful of case studies are not adequate to draw conclusions about the influence of COMPSTAT on police practice nationwide, they do suggest there is good reason to be skeptical about the claims of its supporters. In the face of these doubts about COMPSTAT's technical performance, we might ask how and why COMPSTAT has become so popular. Two possible sources of COMPSTAT's appeal are the promise of crime control by highly visible police leaders and politicians, and the attractiveness of empowering police leaders and encouraging innovation in police organization, strategies, and tactics without requiring a revolution in organizational structure. Police leaders who adopt COMPSTAT benefit from the belief that COMPSTAT is the "right" way for police to go about their business and from harnessing the traditional command hierarchy to achieve top management objectives.

Well known police leaders, such as William Bratton, Robert Olson of the Minneapolis Police Department, and John Timoney of the Philadelphia Police Department; highly visible national police-professional associations, including the International Association of Chiefs of Police (IACP); and academic researchers at national conferences have publicized the virtues of COMPSTAT. As a result of this marketing, COMPSTAT has quickly become validated as a necessary feature of progressive police organizations. In response to this pressure to appear cutting-edge and successful, other police organizations have copied those departments that have received recognition for their COMPSTAT programs. It seems likely that incorporating COMPSTAT allows police departments, and particularly police chiefs, to prosper because they gain legitimacy within their own environments. COMPSTAT myths, therefore, are powerful because they are promulgated by widely respected police practitioners and government leaders. They are prevalent because other police organizations that implement COMPSTAT stand to benefit directly from sustaining its rhetoric of success. To the extent that the "rightness" of COMPSTAT makes them believe they are safer in their communities, citizens may also benefit from COMPSTAT's crime-control myth. Press accounts of sophisticated crime technology and increased police accountability help reduce citizen fear by giving the impression that the crime-fighting efforts of local police departments are more effective.

While COMPSTAT did decentralize greater decision-making authority to middle managers in Lowell, Minneapolis, and Newark, it also continued to reinforce the ideal of top-down control. COMPSTAT

meetings provided a rigorous mechanism for disciplining employees and stimulating direct and personal accountability. Moreover, because the top echelon established performance criteria for middle managers, participated in their decisions, and held them accountable, COMPSTAT helped reinforce the traditional command hierarchy of the police organization (Weisburd et al. 2003; Willis, Mastrofski, and Weisburd 2004b). Police departments have traditionally relied on a highly articulated set of rules defining the boundaries of acceptable police practice to ensure internal control. This supervisory system is strongly hierarchical and essentially negative, relying primarily on sanctions for noncompliance with police rules and regulations. COMPSTAT appeals to police administrators and reformers because it increases their control over police organizations with minimal disruption to existing police organizational structures. At the same time, it allows police agencies, at least in theory, to use innovative technologies and problem-solving techniques.

Policy Implications of Belief in the Myth

The most obvious and immediate policy implication is that COMPSTAT will continue to prosper. Its appeal is so widespread that it has spawned similar programs in other local government organizations across the United States. New York's Department of Correction has implemented TEAMS (Total Efficiency Accountability Management System), and Baltimore's CitiStat program applies COMPSTAT's principles of measuring results and holding managers accountable to all of the city's agencies, including its Solid Waste Bureau.

The danger of such uncritical acceptance is that problems associated with

COMPSTAT are ignored, thereby leading to undesirable outcomes. One such outcome is the discord a department creates by assuming COMPSTAT's focus on crime complements its community policing mission; another is the generally superficial nature of problem-solving under COMP-STAT. Community policing and problem-oriented policing are recent and popular policing reforms, but the Police Foundation study suggests these approaches are not wholly compatible with COMPSTAT. Community policing has developed rapidly since its implementation in the 1980s, yet its principle of decentralizing decision-making authority to the lowest possible level in the organization conflicts with COMPSTAT's empowerment of middle managers. COMPSTAT concentrates decision-making power among command staff who issue commands to the rank and file. The centralization of command and control and the limited autonomy of patrol officers are key features of the traditional model of police organizations. As such, COMPSTAT represents a return to a model that has been heavily criticized by community-policing reformers but favored by more traditional police managers.

Problem-oriented policing (POP) has also achieved a high level of acceptability, but COMPSTAT's claim to promote innovation, while simultaneously rewarding standard law-enforcement responses to crime problems, undermines more systematic and rigorous problem-solving efforts. The development of problem-oriented policing beyond a rudimentary level is impeded by COMPSTAT's accountability structure and by COMPSTAT's image as a highly developed, intelligent, and self-reflexive brain controlling all facets of the organization. Since COMPSTAT gives the impression that POP is already taking place, there is a danger that depart-

ments will become complacent in their problem-solving efforts: they will not strive to analyze data to identify the underlying causes of problems, to tailor specific responses to these problems, and to assess the effectiveness of their responses.

The prospect of meaningful police reform requires that any misguided sense of complacency under COMPSTAT be dispelled. Significant improvement in the crime-fighting capacity of the police will demand much more than simple programmatic changes in information collection and management systems. What is needed is a long-term commitment to research to identify which police practices are most promising for controlling crime and disorder. In addition to the pursuit of proven technologies, transformations in the way the police are organized and do business will require a major change in the larger environments in which police organizations operate. At the moment, the police are under a great deal of pressure from politicians and the public to take quick and decisive action when confronting a crime problem. Such an environment, where police are expected to respond to "something-that-ought-not-to-be-happening-and-about-which-someone-had-better-do-something-now," is hostile to the kinds of experimentation and risk-taking necessary for developing knowledge of what works and why (Bittner 1990:249). COMPSTAT's dictum of *doing something now* about crime spikes undercuts a more thoughtful, long-term approach to effective and efficient crime prevention. This transformation in the current police environment is unlikely, given the powerful expectation by members of the public and local politicians that government agencies fix problems immediately. However, there is a chance that practical and inspirational leaders could change widespread cultural beliefs by illuminating the complexity of crime problems, by acknowledging the inadequacies of simplistic solutions, and by buffering the police from criticism when attempting promising strategies that prove unsuccessful (Mastrofski 1998). The reality is that until police are held accountable for what works rather than for what looks right, are allowed to innovate in spite of the risk of failure, and are encouraged to objectively evaluate results, the promise of genuine police reform will remain a myth.

References

Anderson, D. 2001. Crime control by the numbers. Ford Foundation Report. Accessed online: *http://www.fordfound.org/publications/ff_report/view_ff_report_detail.cfm?report_index=264.*

Bittner, E. 1990. *Aspects of police work.* Boston: Northeastern University Press.

Bratton, W. J., with P. Knobler. 1998. *Turnaround: How America's top cop reversed the crime epidemic.* New York: Random House.

Dewan, S. 2004. New York's gospel of policing by data spreads across U.S. *New York Times* April 28, A6:1.

Eck, J., and E. Maguire. 2000. Have changes in policing reduced violent crime? An assessment of the evidence. In *The crime drop in America,* eds. A. Blumstein and T. Wallman. New York: Cambridge University Press.

Giuliani, R. W., with K. Kurson, 2002. *Leadership.* New York: Hyperion Books.

Henry, V. E. 2002. *The COMPSTAT paradigm: Management accountability in policing, business, and the public sector.* New York: Looseleaf Publications.

Lehrer, E. 2001. The police behind America's biggest crime drop. *American Enterprise* (March). Accessed online: *http://www.findarticles.com/cf_dls/m2185/2_12/71004740/p1/article.jhtml.*

Mastrofski, S. D. 1998. Community policing and police organization structure. In *Community policing and the evaluation of police service delivery,* ed. Jean-Paul Brodeur. Thousand Oaks, CA: Sage.

Moore, M. H. 1992. Problem-solving and community policing. In *Modern policing,* eds. Michael Tonry and Norval Morris. Chicago: University of Chicago Press.

———. 2003. Sizing up COMPSTAT: An important administrative innovation in policing. *Criminology and Public Policy* 2:469–494.

Safir, H. n.d. *The COMPSTAT process.* New York: Office of Management Analysis and Planning, NYPD.

Silverman, E. 1996. Mapping change: How the New York City Police Department re-engineered itself to drive down crime. *Law Enforcement News* December 15, 1.

———. 1999. *NYPD battles crime: Innovative strategies in policing.* Boston: Northeastern University Press.

Smith, D. C., and W. J. Bratton. 2001. Performance management in New York City: Compstat and the revolution in police management. In *Quicker, better, cheaper? Managing performance in American government,* ed. D. W. Forsythe. Albany, NY: Rockefeller Institute Press.

Walsh, W., and G. F. Vito. 2004. The meaning of Compstat. *Journal of Contemporary Criminal Justice* 20:51–69.

Weisburd, D., S. D. Mastrofski, A. M. McNally, R. Greenspan, and J. J. Willis. 2003. Reforming to preserve: COMPSTAT and strategic problem solving in American policing. *Criminology and Public Policy* 2:421–456.

Weisburd, D., S. D. Mastrofski, R. Greenspan, and J. J. Willis. 2004. *The growth of COMPSTAT in American policing.* Research in Brief. Washington DC: Police Foundation. Accessed online: *http://www.policefoundation.org/pdf/growthofcompstat.pdf.*

Weisburd, D., S. D. Mastrofski, J. J. Willis, and R. Greenspan. Forthcoming. Changing everything so that everything can stay the same: Compstat and American policing. In *Prospects and problems in an era of police innovation: Contrasting perspectives,* eds. D. Weisburd and A. Braga. Cambridge: Cambridge University Press.

Willis, J. J., S. D. Mastrofski, and D. Weisburd. 2004a. COMPSTAT and bureaucracy: A case study of challenges and opportunities for change. *Justice Quarterly* 21:463–496.

———. 2004b. *Compstat in practice: An in-depth analysis of three cities.* Washington DC: The Police Foundation. Accessed online: *http://www.policefoundation.org/pdf/compstatinpractice.pdf.*

Willis J. J., S. D. Mastrofski, D. Weisburd, and R. Greenspan. 2004. *Compstat and organizational change in the Lowell Police Department: Challenges and opportunities.* Washington DC: The Police Foundation. Accessed online: *http://www.policefoundation.org/pdf/compstat.pdf.* ✦

Section 3

Administration of Justice

Chapter 15
The Myth of Positive Differentiation in the Classification of Dangerous Offenders

Dennis R. Longmire,
Jacqueline Buffington-Vollum,
and Scott Vollum

The Myth

The promise of "scientific criminology" rests in the belief that there are significant and predictable differences between criminals and noncriminals, and that these differences can be discerned through the application of appropriate and available scientific techniques (Gottfredson and Hirschi 1987; Monahan 1981). Taylor, Walton, and Young (1973:156) were in part reacting to this promise when they criticized what they termed the "fallacy of positive differentiation," and what will be referred to throughout this chapter as the "myth of positive differentiation." The promise of positive differentiation suggests that certain sciences can be employed to differentiate "criminals" from "noncriminals" and to categorize the criminals into further subgroups based, in part, on the likelihood of their engaging in future criminality. The commonly cited

distinctions between "classical" and "positivist" criminology include the positivists' belief that criminals are different from noncriminals in some fundamental way. Those differences cause criminality, or are indicators of the cause of criminality, and science and law rather than faith and divine inspiration should be used to differentiate between the two (Rennie 1978).

The notion that criminals represent a unique breed of human being actually predates positivism. Prescientific societies often relied on extreme forms of divination to discern the "good" from the "bad." Barnes (1930) described the different techniques of torture used in primitive (prescientific) societies to help differentiate the guilty from the innocent. The belief that criminality is caused by constitutional or individual characteristics (or is indicated by them) also played a part in "classical" criminology, manifesting itself in deterrence and "rational man" assumptions inherent in the thinking of founders Bentham ([1765] 1970) and Beccaria ([1764] 1963), who both favored legislative reforms that would classify and categorize offenders based on the severity of their offenses and their level of rationality. One of the most important developments in what was termed the "neoclassical" movement was the rational legal principle of *doli incapax*, which recognized certain groups of people as being inherently incapable of formulating *mens rea*, one of the necessary elements of crime (Taylor, Walton, and Young 1973:7; Morris 1982: 70; Miucci 1998). Children, the mentally ill, and the mentally retarded are examples of such groups. In the neoclassical legal spirit, law provides definitions concerning matters of legal infancy, insanity, and mental retardation. People falling into these categories receive special attention from the law including exemption from criminal or civil liability, but are vulnerable to the loss of individual liberties and freedoms in some instances.

Of course, there is no easy way to categorize people into these distinct groups without invoking some level of expertise, and the use of scientific experts in judicial proceedings is a routine matter. There is case law surrounding the definition of expert testimony consistently relying on scientific expertise as the foundation for this definition (see La Morte 2003). Accordingly, the concerns associated with the "myth of positive differentiation" (to be discussed below) apply to these efforts as well. For example, much attention has recently been applied to this problem as a result of the U.S. Supreme Court's ruling that it is unconstitutional to execute mentally-retarded offenders (*Atkins v. Virginia* 2002). While the Court's ruling clearly recognized the mentally retarded as a special group of offenders deserving special exemption from the death sentence, they did not provide any formal definition of "retardation," and instead left it up to each state to work within the parameters of their own definitions. There remains considerable debate among scholars concerning the very meaning of "mental retardation" and how to differentiate between those who are mentally retarded and those who are not (Morgan 2003).

The most important difference between classical and positive criminology is not the belief that differences exist between the "good" and the "bad," or that crime is caused (or the cause is indicated) by some individual or constitutional characteristic attributed to those differences. Rather, it is the application of the paradigm of science to the divination process that sets the two apart. Since the early work of Comte (1830), science has dominated Western culture's "search for criminal man" (Rennie 1978). Early positivist philosophers

qua criminologists, such as Lombroso (1876), Ferri (1901), and Garofalo (1914), believed that science had evolved to a level of sophistication that allowed them to classify and categorize criminals into a taxonomy based on biological, physiological, and social characteristics. This belief remains strong among the general public as well as criminal justice policymakers. Indeed, Lombroso's "epileptoids" and Ferri's "born criminals" were precursors of today's "criminal psychopaths" and "serial murderers." However, the promise of positive differentiation—that scientists can reliably contribute to the categorization of people into any one of these groups—was not delivered by Lombroso and has yet to be realized.

The use of prediction methods in criminal justice has been characterized as "the most pervasive application of social science research in reform of the criminal justice system" (Gottfredson and Tonry 1987:vii). Nowhere is the promise of positive differentiation more apparent than in areas concerning the prediction of future dangerousness and in efforts to differentiate between those who pose a violent threat and those who do not. Criminologists, psychologists, psychiatrists, and other professionals involved in the classification of criminal law violators have staked claim to the possession of specialized skills that enable them to provide expert insights into the criminal mind, which allow for these predictive and preventive endeavors (Gottfredson and Tonry 1987; Monahan 1981; Pfohl 1978). Popular media images of crime, criminality, and criminal justice—both fiction (e.g., films and novels such as *Silence of the Lambs*, and television shows such as *Profiler, Law & Order*, and *CSI*) and nonfiction (e.g., books written by former FBI agents and police officers about their adventures as profilers, and news reports on serial killers, child abductors, and other violent predators)—portray forensic specialists as scientists with extraordinary skills at divining the good from the evil. Although entertaining, these depictions distort the truth. Despite the best efforts of the scientific community, the ability to successfully differentiate between those who are likely to engage in serious crime and those who are not is tenuous at best (Rennie 1978), leaving the promise of scientific positivism more mythical than real. In fact, in the scientific community, the work of criminal profilers and classification experts is frequently judged to be "junk-science" or "quasi-science."

The Kernel of Truth

At best, scientific predictions of the world are made with a combination of various pieces of information in terms of probabilities, not certainties. Scientific principles can be used to increase the level of accuracy of such predictions. Whether the scientist is a meteorologist predicting the course of a storm or a psychologist predicting the future dangerousness of a convicted criminal (Monahan and Steadman 1996), predictions must be articulated in terms of statistical estimations of the likelihood of the predicted event, and can rarely be stated in terms of certainty that such an event will occur. The more developed the scientist's methods of measuring the elements of the world, and the more information he or she is able to reliably collect, the more confidence one can have in his or her predictions.

The best these scientists can do is to assess the relative likelihood of violence based on the accumulation of information collected about an individual. Their estimates, however, are not necessarily driven by any special skills. The old adage "the past is the best predictor of the future"

goes a long way toward characterizing the kernel of truth within most scientific predictions of future behavior. Research consistently demonstrates that people with a history of previous acts of violence have a higher probability of subsequent violence (Monahan 1981). Moreover, social and behavioral scientists have identified demographic (e.g., age, gender, ethnicity), clinical (e.g., substance abuse, impulsivity, psychopathy), and contextual (e.g., level of security in institutions) factors—especially in combination with knowledge of past behavior—that can be used to determine the relative probability that an individual will engage in a criminally violent act in the future. Whether—and the degree to which—this information significantly improves the ability to predict future violence remains a matter of debate.

The Truth or Facts

Prior to the late 1970s and early 1980s, mental health professionals assumed they possessed special expertise in predicting violent behavior and, consequently, asserted their supposed skill (Rubenstein 1988). Accordingly, they were increasingly asked to inform various legal and criminal justice decisions (Shah 1978). Legal professionals immediately began challenging such evidence. In one of the earliest reviews of the literature, Dershowitz (1969: 47) noted that "for every correct psychiatric prediction of violence there are numerous erroneous predictions. That is, among every group of inmates presently confined on the basis of psychiatric predictions of violence, there are only a few who would, and many more who would not, actually engage in such conduct if released." In response, social scientists tested the accuracy of their methods, and a relatively consistent finding emerged: at that time, violence predictions were correct only one out of three times (i.e., of those predicted to be violent, only one of three actually engaged in violent behavior, see Monahan 1981). One estimate of the inaccuracy of predictions of dangerousness reached as high as 95 percent (Ennis and Emery 1978). Although some experts moderated their previous stances, the "one-in-three accuracy" estimate soon became a widely cited statistic and wounded the credibility of professionals offering dangerousness predictions in both the legal and mental health fields. Ennis and Litwack (1974) opined that mental health professionals have no expertise or ability to assess risk, going so far as to suggest that a layperson with access to the necessary information and statistics could do comparably with, and possibly better than, professionals. Ultimately, they concluded such testimony should be barred.

Criticism of mental health professionals' ability to predict future dangerousness came to the forefront in the legal realm in the case of *Barefoot v. Estelle* (1983). With Barefoot facing the death penalty, the American Psychiatric Association submitted an *amicus curiae* brief to the Supreme Court, citing Monahan's estimate and concluding, according to Justice Blackmun, "Psychiatrists simply have no expertise in predicting long-term future dangerousness" (*Barefoot v. Estelle* 1983: 921). Since then, the Court has extended this claim about the lack of expertise to psychologists and other mental health professionals, as well as "even the most highly trained criminologists" (*Schall v. Martin* 1984:278). Nevertheless, the Supreme Court has repeatedly upheld psychiatric predictions of dangerousness in death penalty and other cases, "settling" the issue from a legal standpoint by concluding that "there is nothing inherently unattainable about a prediction of future

criminal conduct" (*Schall v. Martin* 1984: 2417).

In the prediction of violence and future dangerousness, social scientists have relied upon methods that generally fall into two categories: clinical and actuarial. The main difference between these approaches involves the role of human judgment. Most define the actuarial, or statistical, method in terms of its elimination of the human judge, whereby "conclusions are based solely on empirically established relations between data and the condition or event of interest" (Dawes, Faust, and Meehl 1989:1668), and factors are statistically weighted to maximize the power of the instrument used to predict a specified outcome (Krauss and Sales 2001). It also has been characterized as "formal," "mechanical," "algorithmic," composed of explicit decision rules, and "100 percent reproducible" (Grove and Meehl 1996:19). Conversely, the clinical method, which has been the primary mode of assessment and diagnosis for centuries, requires a human judge to measure and/or gather data; to use past training, knowledge, and experience of behavior, mental illness, and diagnosis to interpret information; and to combine and integrate variables to arrive at a prediction of future behavior. Some have additionally defined the clinical approach in terms of the "dynamic" (i.e., changeable) nature of the variables used to make the human judgment. Some have described the clinical method as "informal," "subjective," and "impressionistic" (Grove and Meehl 1996); although others have interpreted this assessment as unduly pejorative, implying arbitrariness and bias (Litwack 2001).

Although the clinical approach has been widely criticized in the literature, it remains the type of risk assessment most widely used in practice by psychiatrists and psychologists, and it possesses some advantages over a pure actuarial approach. First, unlike an actuarial model, which is limited to the few variables that are maintained by the statistical model, clinicians can take into account case-specific information. Moreover, actuarial instruments are less sensitive to changing conditions and protective factors (Rogers 2000), and even if actuarial instruments are used, clinical assessment is still needed to develop and implement treatment interventions. Finally, clinical assessments of dangerousness can take into account the seriousness of the possible harm, as well as an evaluator's degree of confidence. However, social scientists—like all human beings—tend to rely on cognitive heuristics, or shortcuts, in making judgments. Among the errors that plague predictions of violence include relying on prejudicial stereotypes, overattending to information that fits with one's preconceived notions, and accordingly, underattending to disconfirming evidence. What's more, people (including social scientists) are typically more confident than their accuracy warrants (Dawes, Faust, and Meehl 1989). Thus, it has been suggested that "greater accuracy may be achieved if the skilled observer [i.e., social scientist] performs this function [of collecting data] and then steps aside, leaving the interpretation of observational and other data to the actuarial method" (Dawes, Faust, and Meehl 1989: 1671).

Among the most rigorous studies examining predictions of violence was a meta-analysis by Mossman (1994), which directly compared actuarial and clinical predictions of violence. Interestingly, it found the two methods do not differ appreciably in their performance. Reanalyzing 58 previously published data sets, Mossman concluded—contrary to strong arguments in the scientific literature opposed to the clinical method—"Taken together, these data strongly suggest that mental health professionals' violence predictions are substantially more accurate than chance" (1994:793). Moreover, although actuarial methods were found to perform slightly better than clinical prediction, especially with regard to long-term predictions (greater than 1 year), the two methods appeared to function comparably when considering predictions of shorter duration. Ultimately, however, past behavior alone was a better predictor of violence in the future than either clinical prediction or actuarial techniques.

Interests Served by the Myth

There are numerous beneficiaries served by the perpetuation of the myth of positive differentiation. The most obvious includes members of the scientific community who procure jobs in the prediction process, either in providing direct services or in conducting the research upon which services are based. This includes a cadre of specialists in virtually every area of the physical, biological, psychological, social, and behavioral sciences (James 2004). Social workers have even found recent employment as "mitigation specialists" working with defense attorneys representing capital defendants (Orloff 1996; Perry 2003).

Next, all dimensions of the criminal justice apparatus—from the police to the executioner—benefit from the perpetuation of the belief that there are "good" and "evil" people, and that science offers tools that can differentiate between them. The U.S. Supreme Court has consistently provided law enforcement and criminal justice agencies with increased freedom to target special groups in society who are believed to present a threat to the safety and well-being of the community. For example, in *Kansas v. Hendricks* (1997), the Supreme Court sustained a law allowing for the involuntary and indeterminate confinement of "sexually dangerous predators" based on predictions that they pose a future threat to society if not confined. Jails, probation departments, prisons, and parole agencies rely on risk assessments and classification instruments to help separate their charges into different risk groups requiring different levels and intensity of supervision. These assessment instruments were usually recommended and validated through social and behavioral science research (see above).

As Kappeler (2004) notes, the media and government are also common beneficiaries of myths that tend to sensationalize crime and titillate the public. Every medium available derives considerable monetary benefit from the perpetuation of the myths that surround the "ideology of science" (Schwendinger and Schwendinger 1975) coupled with the "dramatization of evil" (Tannenbaum 1938). A more troubling concern arises when the interests of the government become entwined with the interests of the media. Surette (1998:212), in addressing the intricacies of the relationship between media and criminal justice policies, concluded that the association is complex and far reaching. Tonry (2004:60) analyzed the recent development of increasingly punitive penal policies in the United States, noting "the emotional force of ubiquitous mass media coverage of such events as the crimes of Willie Horton, the murders of Megan Kanka and Polly Klaas, and the cocaine-overdose death of Len Bias produced moral panics . . ." and lead to increased calls for punitive penal policies. Christie (1973), along with subsequent work examining the growth of the "criminal justice industrial complex" (Donziger 1996; Sheldon and Brown 2000), clearly

demonstrate the growing nexus of interests between criminal justice, media, and corporate entities.

Policy Implications of Belief in the Myth

The policy recommendations that follow from a belief in the ability to positively differentiate the dangerous from the nondangerous are far reaching and include such legal matters as the involuntary civil commitment of those determined to be incompetent and dangerous to themselves or others; involuntary isolation of people believed to be carrying an infectious disease; pretrial detention of suspects alleged to have committed a crime; and long-term detention, or even execution, of those believed to present a high likelihood of future violence. Supported in part by the belief that science and technology have evolved to a high level of certainty allowing for prediction and classification of risk, moral and legal bases have been used for preemptive or preventive actions. The goal of protecting "us" from "them" underpins the movement toward the use of incapacitative measures.

"Proactive policing," "target hardening," "weed and seed" and "aggressive patrol" all exemplify this approach at the law-enforcement level (Kraska 2004). Laws governing the use of preventive detention in criminal and civil matters have made it an increasingly available option to prosecutors throughout the United States (Tonry 2004). Prison, jail, and other institutional classification procedures have also become more technical and formalized in recent years (Feeley and Simon 1992). This movement reflects what Schwendinger and Schwendinger (1975: 129) call reliance on "technocratic doctrines," requiring the use of "experts or enlightened leaders who are highly informed by advisors." In the spirit of positive differentiation, the development of technical solutions designed to manage more and more specific subgroups of offenders seems to be a logical and most natural consequence.

Kraska provides an interesting analysis of eight different theoretical orientations in criminal justice (2004:11). These orientations include rational-legal, systems theory, due process vs. crime control, political, social construction, system expansion, oppression, and late-modern. Each orientation draws from a unique intellectual tradition and interprets differently the development of criminal justice policies, and thus, focuses on different issues related to the problem of positive differentiation. For example, according to Kraska, criminal justice policies based on the "late-modern" orientation have been associated with the development of "technical management tools of exclusion," "a fetish for safety," and the development of a "complex of controls" (11). He specifically identifies the advancement of "actuarial justice" as one of the five key themes associated with "late-modern" crime-control policies; and the process of positive differentiation has a clear and increasingly important role to play in such a justice system (280–281). Perpetuation of the myth of positive differentiation has contributed to the development of a "culture of security consciousness" (Garland 2001) and a "security ethic" (Bauman 2000) that dominate criminal justice decision-making today. One other salient feature of late-modern thinking associated with the myth is the reliance on "exclusiveness" as an underpinning for justice policymaking. Kraska observes that this exclusiveness plays itself out in two distinct ways: (1) development of policies designed to categorize those who do not contribute to the

conventional, neoliberal free-market system as "dangerous," and (2) implementation of actions designed to maintain "the barrier between the included and excluded" (2004:284).

As long as positive science maintains dominance in the criminological community, positive differentiation will continue to play a role in criminal justice decision-making. Thus, it is incumbent upon those who participate in the community to confront the integrity of this position and qualify the belief that science can contribute significantly to the process of differentiating the dangerous from the pacific. For example, courts should be advised to provide juries and other decision makers involved in the justice process with special instructions concerning the tentative nature (e.g., error rates) of the scientific testimony to be offered in any particular case. Such policies, of course, would require that judges, legislators, and other key criminal justice policymakers also be made aware of the mythical quality of testimony or advice being offered by the "imputational specialists."

If positive differentiation is going to persist, we must encourage that it be driven by principles of compassion rather than punishment. The tools of "imputational specialists," no matter how unrefined, could be put to better use identifying those who are most in need of special services so their lives can be enhanced through the application of available technologies and resources. In 1838, the French Academy of Sciences published the following topic for their annual essay competition:

To seek, by actual observation, in Paris or any other great city, which elements of the population, by their vices, their ignorance, and their poverty, constitute a dangerous class; and to indicate the means by which the Administration, the wealthy, those in comfortable circumstances, and intelligent and hard working laborers might improve that dangerous and depraved class. (H. A. Frégier, as cited in Rennie 1978:3)

Perhaps a similar essay competition could be sponsored today in an effort to turn the purpose of positive differentiation of the dangerous classes away from policies of exclusion and fear and toward policies of compassion and hope for us all.

References

Atkins v. Virginia. 2002. 536 U.S. 304.

Barefoot v. Estelle. 1983. 463 U.S. 880.

Barnes, H. E. 1930. *The story of punishment: A record of man's inhumanity to man.* Montclair, NJ: Patterson Smith.

Bauman, Z. 2000. Social issues of law and order. *British Journal of Criminology* 40:205–221.

Beccaria, C. [1764] 1963. *On crimes and punishments.* Translated by H. Paolucci. Indianapolis: Bobbs-Merrill.

Bentham, J. [1765] 1970. *An introduction to the principles of morals and legislation.* London: Athlone.

Christie, N. 1973. *Crime control as industry: Toward GULAGS, Western style.* New York: Routledge and Kegan Paul.

Comte, A. 1830. *System of positive philosophy.* Paris: Bachelier.

Dawes, R. M., D. Faust, and P. E. Meehl. 1989. Clinical versus actuarial judgment. *Science* 243:1668–1674.

Dershowitz, A. 1969. The psychiatrist's power in civil commitment. *Psychology Today* 2 (February):43–47.

Donziger, S. 1996. *The real war on crime: The report of the national criminal justice commission.* New York: Harper Perennial.

Ennis, B. J., and R. D. Emery. 1978. *The rights of mental patients.* Revised ed. New York: Discuss Books.

Ennis, B. J., and T. R. Litwack. 1974. Psychiatry and the presumption of expertise: Flipping coins in the courtroom. *California Law Review* 62:693–752.

Feeley, M. M., and J. Simon. 1992. The new penology: Notes on the emerging strategy of corrections and its implications. *Criminology* 30: 449–474.

Ferri, E. 1901. *Criminal sociology.* New York: D. Appleton.

Garland, D. 2001. *The culture of control: Crime and social order in contemporary society.* Chicago: The University of Chicago Press.

Garofalo, R. 1914. *Criminology.* Translated by Robert Wyness Millar. Boston: Little, Brown.

Gottfredson, M. R., and T. Hirschi, eds. 1987. *Positive criminology.* Newbury Park, CA: Sage Publications.

Gottfredson, D. M., and M. Tonry, eds. 1987. *Prediction and classification in criminal justice decision making.* Chicago: The University of Chicago Press.

Grove, W. M., and P. E. Meehl. 1996. Comparative efficiency of informal (subjective, impressionistic) and formal (mechanical, algorithmic) prediction procedures: The clinical-statistical controversy. *Psychology, Public Policy, and Law* 2:293–323.

James, S. H. 2004. *Forensic science: An introduction to scientific and investigative techniques.* Boca Raton, FL: CRC Press.

Kansas v. Hendricks. 1997. 521 U.S. 346.

Kappeler, V. E. 2004. Inventing criminal justice myth and social construction. In *Theorizing criminal justice: Eight essential orientations,* ed. P. Kraska. Long Grove, IL: Waveland Press.

Kraska, P. 2004. *Theorizing criminal justice: Eight essential orientations.* Long Grove, IL: Waveland Press.

Krauss, D. A., and B. D. Sales. 2001. The effects of clinical and scientific expert testimony on juror decision making in capital sentencing. *Psychology, Public Policy, and Law* 7:267–306.

La Morte, T. M. 2003. Sleeping gatekeepers: *United States v. Llera Plaza* and the unreliability of forensic fingerprinting evidence under Daubert. *Albany Law Journal of Science and Technology* 14:171–214.

Litwack, T. R. 2001. Actuarial versus clinical assessments of dangerousness. *Psychology, Public Policy, and Law* 7:409–443.

Lombroso, C. 1876. *L'uomo delinquente* (The criminal man). Milan: Hoepli.

Monahan, J. 1981. *Predicting violent behavior: An assessment of clinical techniques.* Beverly Hills: Sage Publications.

Monahan, J., and H. J. Steadman. 1996. Violent storms and violent people: How meteorology can inform risk communication in mental health law. *American Psychologist* 51:931–938.

Morgan, M. H. 2003. Supreme Court of Virginia: *Atkins v. Commonwealth,* 581 S.E.2d 514 (Va. 2003). *Capital Defense Journal* 16:267–272.

Morris, N. 1982. *Madness and the criminal law.* Chicago: The University of Chicago Press.

Mossman, D. 1994. Assessing predictions of violence: Being accurate about accuracy. *Journal of Consulting and Clinical Psychology* 62:783–792.

Miucci, L. 1998. Responsibility and the young person. *Canadian Journal of Law and Jurisprudence* 11:277–309.

Orloff, L. 1996. Social worker as mitigation specialist: The role of the social worker in death penalty cases. Professional Development, Practice and the Profession. National Association of Social Workers, New York City Chapter. Accessed online May 6, 2004: *http://www.naswnyc.org/p2.html.*

Perry, K. 2003. Mitigation pros put best face on accused. *The Cincinnati Post Online Edition* November 12. Accessed online May 7, 2004: *http://www.cincypost.com/2003/11/12/mitig 111203.html.*

Pfohl, S. J. 1978. *Predicting dangerousness.* Lexington, MA: Lexington Books, D.C. Heath and Company.

Rennie, Y. F. 1978. *The search for criminal man: A conceptual history of the dangerous offender.* Lexington, MA: Lexington Books.

Rogers, R. 2000. The uncritical acceptance of risk assessment in forensic practice. *Law and Human Behavior* 24:595–605.

Rubenstein, L. S. 1988. The paradoxes of professional liability. *Hospital and Community Psychiatry* 39:815–820.

Schall v. Martin. 1984. 467 U.S. 253.

Schwendinger, H., and J. Schwendinger. 1975. Defenders of order or guardians of human rights? In *Critical criminology,* eds. I. R. Taylor, P. Walton, and J. Young. London: Routledge and Kegan Paul.

Shah, S. A. 1978. Dangerousness: A paradigm for exploring some issues in law and psychology. *American Psychologist* 33:224–238.

Sheldon, R. G., and B. B. Brown. 2000. The crime control industry and the management of the surplus population. *Critical Criminology* 9:39–62.

Surette, R. 1998. *Media, crime, and criminal justice: Images and realities.* 2nd ed. Belmont, CA: Wadsworth Publishing Co.

Tannenbaum, F. 1938. *Crime and the community.* Boston: Ginn.

Taylor, I. R., P. Walton, and J. Young. 1973. *The new criminology: For a social theory of deviance.* London: Routledge and Kegan Paul.

———, eds. 1975. *Critical criminology.* London: Routledge and Kegan Paul.

Tonry, M. 2004. *Thinking about crime: Sense and sensibility in American penal culture.* New York: Oxford University Press. ✦

Chapter 16
The Myth That the Exclusionary Rule Allows Many Criminals to Escape Justice

Richard Janikowski

The Myth

First announced in *Weeks v. United States* (1914), the exclusionary rule barred admission in federal prosecutions of evidence seized in violation of the Fourth Amendment. The rule originally had three primary purposes: (1) to protect individuals' rights against police misconduct, (2) to prevent police misconduct, and (3) to maintain judicial integrity—for citizens to have faith in the administration of justice, courts should not admit evidence that is tainted by the illegal activities of other criminal justice officials. More recently, the principal purpose of the exclusionary rule has been narrowed to deterring the police from violating people's Fourth Amendment rights.

Applied to federal criminal cases, the exclusionary rule remained relatively uncontroversial for more than three decades. As Justice Brennan noted in his dissent in *United States v. Leon*, "from *Weeks* to *Olmstead* . . . the court plainly understood that the exclusion of illegally obtained evidence was compelled not by judicially fashioned remedial purposes, but rather by a direct constitutional command." As such, the court's reasoning in applying the remedy of exclusion rested upon constitutional grounds, as noted by Pillard's (1999) observation that "legal rights are not mere precatory or aspirational statements, but remediable claims, redressable in courts, for violations." Interestingly, even after the Supreme Court's incorporation of the exclusionary rule to the states in *Mapp v. Ohio* (1961), there was little political or public outcry concerning expansion of the rule from federal to state criminal proceedings. This lack of protest, probably surprising to contemporary audiences, most likely stemmed from the widespread adoption of some form of an exclusionary rule by state legislatures and state courts prior to the decision in *Mapp*.

Some intimations of judicial and political dissatisfaction with the rule can be seen as early as 1926 when Justice (then Judge) Cardozo observed in *People v. Defore* (1926:587) that the criminal must go free "because the constable has blundered." Central to this critique is a belief, raised to the level of truth among politicians and many members of the public, that substantial numbers of criminals are set free to prey again upon society because of the suppression of evidence by "liberal judges." Moreover, while initially little opposition had been voiced to the court's holding in *Mapp*, its decision in *Miranda v. Arizona* (1966) became a platform for attacking both the court and its "activist" jurisprudence, especially—as many polemicists would suggest—in the use of "technicalities" to free obviously guilty defendants. Increasingly, the Warren Court's decisions regarding defendants' rights were subjected to judicial and political criticism, culminating in the court's criminal-procedure jurisprudence becoming a central issue of the 1968 presidential campaign. In essence, the myth regarding the release of guilty persons would change not only the constitutional underpinnings of the exclusionary rule, but the composition and jurisprudence of the Supreme Court.

The Kernel of Truth

Unquestionably, some cases are not prosecuted due to procedural violations; and, in other cases, the suppression of evidence may lead to defendants being found not guilty or to cases being dismissed. No supporter of the exclusionary rule has ever denied that such outcomes occur and that, as a result, application of the exclusionary rule in criminal proceedings carries specific social costs. However, all constitutional rights have costs associated with them. For example, the exercise of free speech can lead to psychological harm to listeners, as evidenced by court decisions allowing American Nazis to march in predominantly Jewish neighborhoods where a number of Holocaust survivors live.

In addition, the exclusionary rule undoubtedly influences the "truth-finding" function of the judicial process. Potential evidence that could be useful, if not critical, to a jury's determination of guilt or innocence is made unavailable to the trier of fact. Supporters of the rule argue there is a need to preserve judicial integrity through suppression of illegally obtained evidence, and to ensure public and law-enforcement respect for the judicial process by avoiding any connection between the courts and lawless official behavior. However, suppression of evidence can lead to public cynicism regarding the judicial process. At the same time, the rule's proponents have been unable to demonstrate empirically that the rule does, in fact, deter police misconduct (Zalman 2002).

The issue of effectiveness in deterring police misconduct becomes critical when weighed against the significant societal costs of lost prosecutions. Observers of police practice, such as Oaks (1970), have proposed elimination of the exclusionary rule, arguing there is no evidence suggesting that the court's decision in *Mapp* had any effect on police practices. These commentators believe that because search and seizure violations continued to occur following the decision in *Mapp,* the rule must have failed in deterring police misbehavior. However, as Zalman (2005:67) has pointed out, Oaks' conclusion (essentially an expression of personal belief), is flawed since the appropriate methodological question should be "whether the number and rates of such violations increased, decreased, or remained level after *Mapp.*" Unfortunately, research directed toward this question has not been conducted, resulting in debate on the issue relying on policy arguments. In addition, difficulties in operationalizing legal deterrence, much less developing rigorous studies of it, will likely prevent meticulous research in the future (Davies 1983). While some observational studies (Uviller 1988) suggest that, overall, police officers attempt to comport their behavior within limits set by courts and Canon's (1982) study of 19 cities revealed some educative effect of the rule on police practices, rigorous empirical evidence is simply unavailable to support or refute the rule's deterrent influence upon law enforcement. Essentially, as Justice Blackmun noted in *United States v. Janis* (1976): "The final conclusion is clear. No empirical researcher, proponent or opponent of the rule, has yet been able to establish with any assurance whether the rule has a deterrent effect even in situations in which it is now applied" (453, fn.22).

Minus such evidence, and without a constitutional directive requiring the rule, the judicially created remedy falters when confronted by evidence of substantial social costs. As a result, a central question concerning the exclusionary rule is the degree to which the "myth of lost cases" surrounding the exclusionary is accurate. Without accurate evidence of the scope of the social impact of the rule, the specter raised by Justice White in *Illinois v. Gates* (1983:257) that "we will never know how many guilty defendants go free as a result of the rule's operation" will continue to preoccupy discussions concerning the exclusionary rule by implying that hordes of guilty individuals are being released by the courts each day.

The Truth or Facts

Unlike research related to the deterrent effects of the exclusionary rule, the empirical evidence that is available almost uniformly demonstrates that few cases are lost due to the exclusionary rule. Opponents of the rule—for example Justice White in *Gates*—tend to rely on a study conducted in California by the National Institute of Justice (NIJ) in 1982. The NIJ study concluded that 4.8 percent of all felony arrests rejected by prosecutors in California between 1976 and 1979 involved search and seizure issues. Moreover, after a review of cases from two prosecutors' offices in the Los Angeles area, the NIJ study (1982:18) concluded that "prosecutors rejected approximately 30 percent of all felony drug arrests because of search and seizure problems." However, a review of the study by Davies (1983) identified serious flaws and demonstrated that the 30 percent figure was misleading. Regarding NIJ's first conclusion, Davies argued that

calculating the number of cases lost, due to search and seizure issues, as a proportion of cases rejected by prosecutors was methodologically inappropriate. Instead, he suggested the study should have examined the percentage of all arrests rejected by prosecutors for search and seizure problems. When this calculation was performed by Davies (1983:617), "data presented in the NIJ study indicate[d] that only 0.8% of all reported felony arrests in California—less than 1%—are declined by prosecutors because of illegal search problems." As to the 30 percent figure, Davies points out that not only is the conclusion based on an analysis of a very small sample, fewer than 150 cases, it also suffers from analytic mistakes. In particular, Davies noted that the study ignored available relevant statewide data which would have improved the estimate. Analysis of this data by Davies (1983:646) demonstrated that "only 2.4% of reported drug law arrests and less than 0.3% of reported arrests for all nondrug offenses combined" were rejected because of issues surrounding an illegal search or seizure.

Additionally, studies conducted by a variety of researchers suggest the influence of the rule on prosecutions is minimal. Zalman (2005), reviewing the available literature, concluded that almost every study has demonstrated that less than 1 percent of cases are dropped because of search and seizure problems. A source of confusion surrounding this issue, however, has been that some studies have not limited their examination of "lost" cases due to search and seizure problems, but have instead focused on the influence of the entire spectrum of due-process issues upon the dismissal of criminal cases. For example, Forst, Lucianovic, and Cox (1978) reported that 168 of 17,534 arrests (1 percent) were rejected by prosecutors in Washington, DC because of due-process issues; critically, only a portion of these cases involved problems of illegal searches or seizures. In the same vein, Brosi (1977), studying five jurisdictions, determined that the rate for prosecutors declining to issue criminal complaints as a result of all due process problems, not just Fourth Amendment issues, varied from a low of 1 percent in Washington, DC to a high of 9 percent in New Orleans. In contrast, research specifically focusing on the dismissal or rejection of cases due to search and seizure problems consistently finds only a very small percentage being dismissed or rejected by prosecutors. The General Accounting Office (1979) found federal prosecutors declining only 0.4 percent of cases because of illegal searches. A review of 7,500 cases in nine counties by Nardulli (1983) revealed that defendants were successful in only 0.69 percent of suppression motions concerning physical evidence. Subsequently, Feeney, Dill, and Weir (1983) determined nonconvictions were the result of search and seizure issues in only 1 percent of cases. Uchida and Bynum's (1991) study of seven cities revealed that only 1.4 percent of defendants won suppression motions involving search warrants. In addition, it is critical to remember that a successful suppression motion does not always mean that the criminal case against the defendant will be dismissed. Defendants can be, and often are, convicted following the suppression of certain evidence. There is nothing in the exclusionary rule that bars prosecutors from proceeding against the defendant with other legally admissible evidence.

A careful review of the empirical literature supports an argument that the myth of significant numbers of cases being lost due to the exclusionary rule is false. Moreover, when violent felonies were examined, Davies (1983) concluded that the number of cases rejected by prosecutors dropped to approximately 0.2 percent. Davies' examination also found that even when all felony arrests were followed through all of the stages of the criminal justice process in California, only 2.35 percent of the cases were dismissed because of problems associated with searches or seizures. While the percentage (somewhere between 2.4 percent and 7.1 percent) was somewhat higher for cases involving drugs, Davies suggested that many of these drug cases may not have involved carefully planned operations, but were instead arrests resulting from suspicion about the presence of drugs that relied on weaker probable cause. Davies cautioned that "lost arrests" should not automatically be equated with "lost convictions," since a substantial proportion of criminal cases result in dismissal of the case, acquittal of the defendant, or a plea bargain reducing the charge from a felony to a misdemeanor. Overall, Zalman (2002:95) concluded:

> unlike the inconclusive result of the exclusionary rule's deterrent effect, research findings of its costs firmly show that fewer than one percent of arrests are lost because of the exclusionary rule. In half of these lost cases, convictions are still obtained because of other evidence. . . . The figures show that the exclusionary rule is not subverting law enforcement.

If these results are accepted as conclusive, then the question turns to whose interests are being served by perpetuating the myth that large numbers of defendants are being released because of the exclusionary rule.

Interests Served By the Myth

Once it was suggested that the exclusionary rule should be applied to state criminal prosecutions, the exclusionary rule became mired in controversy. While Justice Douglas expressed a belief that the Supreme Court's opinion in *Mapp v. Ohio* (1961:670) ended "the storm of constitutional controversy" that was caused by *Wolf v. Colorado* (1949), Kamisar (1983: 566) observed that over the years, the debate "has not only intensified but engulfed the Fourth Amendment exclusionary rule itself." Critics of the rule continue to call for its abandonment (Burger 1964; Wright 1972; Schlesinger 1977; Wilkey 1978), while supporters argue the rule is either a constitutional requirement or a political necessity (Kamisar 1982; Canon 1982). Others suggest limiting the exclusionary rule's application to those instances involving conduct by police that is either willful, malicious, in bad faith, or lacking a reasonable basis (Coe 1975; Ball 1978; Jensen and Hart 1982; Uviller 1982). Some Supreme Court justices have urged reconsideration of the scope and application of the exclusionary rule.

A significant portion of this debate has, for reasons of politics and judicial philosophy, centered on the social-costs theory of the exclusionary rule. The myth became a cornerstone of Nixon's 1968 campaign for the presidency. Adopting a "law and order" platform, Nixon promised to nominate judges to the federal courts who were dedicated to stopping—and even reversing—the tide of what he described as "judicial activism," including the Warren Court's criminal-procedure rulings, which he linked to increases in crime. Nixon found the myth useful, as is illustrated from one of his campaign speeches:

A cab driver has been brutally murdered and the man that confessed [to] the crime was let off because of a Supreme Court decision. An old woman had been murdered and robbed bru-

tally, and the man who confessed [to] the crime was let off because of a Supreme Court decision. And I say, my friends, that some of our courts and their decisions in light of that record have gone too far in weakening the peace forces as against the criminal forces in this country. (quoted in Zalman 2002:15)

Following his victory, Nixon had the opportunity to change the composition of the court. The retirement of Chief Justice Warren allowed President Nixon to nominate Warren Burger as the new chief justice. Burger would bring a new, conservative judicial philosophy to the Supreme Court, and it was expected that he would lead a counter-revolution in the area of criminal procedure. While some commentators, reviewing Chief Justice Burger's tenure on the court, suggested it was the "counter-revolution that wasn't" (Blasi 1983:xi), Weddington and Janikowski (1996:231) argued that a more precise analysis of the decisions of the Burger Court revealed it "provided a launching pad for the counter-revolution—a constitutional missile whose trajectory has accelerated and taken form under Chief Justice Rehnquist." Part of this doctrinal platform involved the creation of a hierarchy of rights with those "perceived to have significant impact on the determination of guilt at trial receiving more scrutiny, and rights which are merely prophylactic or which the court believes may actually impede the quest for accurate fact finding" weakened (Whitebread and Heilman 1987:576).

Policy Implications of Belief in the Myth

The myth of lost cases due to technicalities provided a foundation for the Burger and Rehnquist courts to launch an assault on the scope and applicability of the exclusionary rule. While neither court was ever willing to expressly discard the rule, beginning in Chief Justice Burger's dissenting opinion in *Bivens v. Six Unknown Federal Narcotics Agents* (1971), conservative justices began to undermine application of the rule based on a cost-benefit analysis. In *Bivens* (1971:424) the chief justice argued that the only legitimate foundation for the rule was its effectiveness in deterring police misconduct, and invited the court "to re-examine the scope of the exclusionary rule and consider at least some narrowing of its thrust so as to eliminate the anomalies it has produced." This analysis laid the groundwork for examining applications of the rule within the context of its effectiveness in preventing due-process violations by law enforcement, while balancing these determinations of deterrence against the perceived "social costs" of applying the rule.

Using this balancing approach to launch its attack on the exclusionary rule, the Court, in a series of decisions beginning with *United States v. Calandra* (1974), began to reconsider the conceptual foundation upon which the exclusionary rule had rested. Specifically, the court's new jurisprudential approach, founded upon the myth of lost cases, would purportedly balance the deterrent effect of the exclusionary rule against the cost to government and society of excluding evidence (Whitebread and Slogin 1986).

In *Calandra* (1974:348), the court determined that the primary purpose of the exclusionary rule was "to deter future unlawful police conduct and thereby effectuate the guarantee of the Fourth Amendment against unreasonable search and seizures." Identification of deterrence as the primary focus of the rule allowed the court to conclude that the rule was best understood as a judicially created remedy

"designed to safeguard Fourth Amendment rights generally through its deterrent effect, rather than a personal constitutional right of the party aggrieved." Adopting this formulation allowed the court to develop an analytic framework, weighing the costs to society of excluding evidence compared to any accrued benefits of an increase in the deterrence of police misconduct. Applying the newly formulated test, the court declined to extend application of the rule to grand jury proceedings, concluding that any incremental increase in deterrence was uncertain at best.

Applying *Calandra's* balancing approach, the court announced the "dissipation of taint" exception in *Brown v. Illinois* (1975), reasoning that at some point "the detrimental consequences of illegal police action become so attenuated that the deterrent effect of the exclusionary rule no longer justifies its costs." Subsequently, this doctrinal foundation enabled the court in *Stone v. Powell* (1976) to conclude that the admission of unlawfully obtained evidence at trial did not provide state defendants, previously afforded the opportunity to fully and fairly litigate Fourth Amendment claims, a basis for federal habeas relief. Inspiring the court's holding was the belief that constricting the scope of the exclusionary rule is justified whenever the social costs incurred through exclusion of relevant evidence outweigh any reduction in the rule's deterrent effect. Subsequently, in *Rakas v. Illinois* (1978), the court limited standing to challenge admission of illegally obtained evidence to the actual victim of a search and seizure. Previously, in *Harris v. New York* (1971), the court had precluded even defendants possessing standing from challenging evidence used to impeach their testimony. In both cases, the court determined that any incremental achievement regarding increased deterrence of police misconduct was outweighed by the resulting social costs.

Similarly, in *Michigan v. DeFillippo* (1979), the court, using a balancing approach, refused to suppress evidence obtained by police officers, relying on a statute subsequently found to be unconstitutional. Finally, in *United States v. Leon* (1984:922), the court crafted a "good faith" exception to the exclusionary rule, stating that "the marginal or nonexistent benefits produced by suppressing evidence obtained in objectively reasonable reliance on a subsequently invalidated search warrant cannot justify the substantial costs of exclusion."

As the analysis of the Supreme Court's decisions since *Calandra* reveals, myths have power. The myth that large numbers of guilty defendants are being improperly released through application of the exclusionary rule provided a foundation upon which the court could begin limiting the scope and applicability of the rule. Moreover, it provided the political impetus for conservative presidents since Nixon to change the composition and judicial philosophy of the court. Ultimately, it appears that policy makers can ignore the available evidence regarding the social costs of the exclusionary rule as long as reference can be made to the myth. The myth provides the fuel for the Supreme Court's willingness to limit, if not reverse, the precedents established by the Warren Court.

References

Ball, E. 1978. Federalism and the Fourth Amendment: The "reasonable" exception to the exclusionary rule. *Journal of Criminal Law and Criminology* 69(4):635–657.

Bivens v. Six Unknown Federal Narcotics Agents. 1971. 403 US 388.

Blasi, V., ed. 1983. *The Burger Court: The counter-revolution that wasn't.* New Haven, CT: Yale.

Brosi, K. 1977. *A cross city comparison of felony case processing.* Washington, DC: U.S. Department of Justice, Law Enforcement Assistance Administration.

Brown v. Illinois. 1975. 422 U.S. 590.

Burger, W. E. 1964. Who will watch the watchman? *American University Law Review* 14(1): 1–23.

Canon, B. C. 1982. Ideology and reality in the debate over the exclusionary rule: A conservative argument for its retention. *South Texas Law Review* 23(3):559–582.

Coe, P. S. 1975. The ALI Substantiality Test: A flexible approach to the exclusionary sanction. *Georgia Law Review* 10(1):1–15.

Davies, T. 1983. A hard look at what we know (and still need to learn) about the "costs" of the exclusionary rule: The NIJ Study and other studies of "lost" arrests. *American Bar Foundation Research Journal* 3:611–690.

Feeney, F., F. Dill, and A. Weir. 1983. *Arrests without convictions: How often they occur and why.* Washington, DC: U.S. Department of Justice, National Institute of Justice.

Forst, B., J. Lucianovic, and S. Cox. 1978. *What happens after arrest: A court perspective of police operations in the District of Columbia.* Washington, DC: U.S. department of Justice, Law Enforcement Assistance Administration.

General Accounting Office (GAO). 1979. *Impact of the exclusionary rule on federal criminal prosecutions.* Washington, DC: U.S. General Accounting Office.

Harris v. New York. 1971. 401 U.S. 222 (1971)

Illinois v. Gates. 1983. 462 U.S. 213.

Jensen, D. L., and R. Hart. 1982. The good faith restatement of the exclusionary rule. *Journal of Criminal Law and Criminology* 73(3):916–938.

Kamisar, Y. 1982. How we got the Fourth Amendment exclusionary rule and why we need it. *Criminal Justice Ethics* 1(2):4–15.

———. 1983. Does (did) (should) the exclusionary rule rest on a "principled basis" rather than an "empirical proposition"? *Creighton Law Review* 16(3):565–667.

Mapp v. Ohio. 1961. 367 U.S. 643.

Michigan v. DeFillippo. 1979. 443 U.S. 31.

Miranda v. Arizona. 1966. 384 U.S. 436.

Nardulli, P. 1983. The societal cost of the exclusionary rule: An empirical assessment. *American Bar Foundation Research Journal* 3: 585–609.

National Institute of Justice (NIJ). 1982. *The effects of the exclusionary rule: A study in Cali-*

fornia. Washington, DC: U.S. Department of Justice, National Institute of Justice.

Oaks, D. 1970. Studying the exclusionary rule in search and seizure. *University of Chicago Law Review* 37(4):665–757.

People v. Defore. 1926. 242 N.Y. 13.

Pillard, C. T. L. 1999. Taking fiction seriously: The strange results of public officials' individual liability under Bivens. *Georgetown Law Journal* 88(1):65–105.

Rakas v. Illinois. 1978. 439 U.S. 128.

Schlesinger, S. R. 1977. *Exclusionary injustice.* New York: M. Dekker.

Stone v. Powell. 1976. 428 U.S. 465.

Uchida, C., and T. Bynum. 1991. Search warrants, motions to suppress and "lost cases": The effects of the exclusionary rule in seven jurisdictions. *Journal of Criminal Law and Criminology* 88(1):1034–1066.

United States v. Calandra. 1974. 414 U.S. 338.

United States v. Janis. 1976. 428 U.S. 433.

United States v. Leon. 1984. 468 U.S. 897.

Uviller, H. R. 1982. The acquisition of evidence for criminal prosecutions: Some constitutional premises and practices in transition. *Vanderbilt Law Review* 35(3):501–526.

———. 1988. *Tempered zeal.* Chicago: Contemporary Books.

Weddington, M. M., and R. Janikowski. 1996. The Rehnquist Court—The counter-revolution that wasn't, Part 2: That counter-revolution that is. *Criminal Justice Review* 21(2): 231–250.

Weeks v. United States. 1914. 232 U.S. 383.

Whitebread, C. H., and J. Heilman. 1987. The counterrevolution enters a new era: Criminal procedure decisions during the final term of the Burger court. *University of Puget Sound Law Review* 10(3):571–590.

Whitebread, C. H., and C. Slogin. 1986. *Criminal procedure: An analysis of cases and concepts,* 2d ed. New York: Foundation Press.

Wilkey, M. R. 1978. The exclusionary rule: Why suppress valid evidence? *Judicature* 62(5): 215–232.

Wolf v. Colorado. 1949. 338 U.S. 25.

Wright, C. A. 1972. Must the criminal go free if the constable blunders? *Texas Law Review* 50: 736–745.

Zalman, M. 2002. *Criminal procedure: Constitution and society,* 3rd ed. Upper Saddle, NJ: Prentice Hall.

———. 2005. *Criminal procedure: Constitution and society,* 4th ed. Upper Saddle, NJ: Pearson Prentice Hall. ✦

Chapter 17
The Myth That Harsh Punishments Reduce Juvenile Crime

Donna M. Bishop

Throughout most of its 100-year history, the juvenile court has been a child-centered institution with a mission to protect and treat, rather than punish, young offenders. Cultural ideas about youth that prevailed from the Progressive Era (late nineteenth to early twentieth century) until very recently evoked compassionate responses to adolescents who committed crimes or other forms of misbehavior. Society has long embraced the notion that adolescents are immature in their ability to reason, to make judgments, and to fully appreciate the consequences of their actions. Emotionally and socially, they are also immature: They lack the inner resources to cope well with stress and they are especially vulnerable to peer pressure. Because of their immaturity, juvenile offenders have traditionally been viewed as undeserving of adult-type punishments (Zimring 1981, 1998a, 1998b; Forst and Blomquist 1991; Scott and Grisso 1997).

Adolescence is also a period of rapid change, a time of transition from childhood to adulthood when significant cognitive, emotional, and social development takes place. During this period, young people are especially malleable. Compared to adults, who are more or less fixed in their ways, young people are more receptive to efforts to guide them in positive directions (Scott and Grisso 1997).

These ideas about young people helped to shape a specialized juvenile court. Prior to 1899, juveniles were tried in criminal courts and subjected to the same punishments as adults. In that year, the juvenile court was created to stand as a bulwark against subjecting youth to harsh sanctions and to provide them with programs and services that would help them make the transition to lives as law-abiding and productive adults.

This is not to suggest that the juvenile court's humanitarian ideals have routinely been realized in practice. Tools for diagnosis and assessment have historically been crude, and efforts to provide good interventions have often been misguided. For example, residential programs have sometimes been so underfunded, understaffed, and overcrowded that little in the way of "treatment" could be provided. Deservedly, the juvenile justice system has at times come under heavy criticism. At least until recently, however, criticism has most often led to reinvigorated efforts to achieve the system's rehabilitative mission (through innovations like intensive probation supervision, aftercare, institutional reform, and the adoption of more promising therapeutic techniques).

The Myth

Over the past three decades, a radical shift has taken place in American juvenile justice policy. Instead of focusing on protection and treatment, legislators and public officials have increasingly advocated punishment of young offenders to

140

deter them from reoffending. They have implemented many strategies that threaten the nature and, ultimately, perhaps even the existence of the juvenile court. These include the displacement of probation services by an explicit focus on surveillance and accountability (Beyer 2003), the adoption of determinate and mandatory minimum sentencing ("one size fits all" punishments that are linked to the offense rather than the needs of the offender), the endorsement of punishment-oriented programming (e.g., house arrest, electronic monitoring, military-style boot camps), and the adoption of laws that permit or require the transfer of large numbers of youth (including preteens) to criminal court for prosecution and punishment as adults. All of these shifts rest on the myth that harsh punishments are effective in producing positive behavioral change.

This myth arose for a number of reasons, three of which are especially important. In the 1970s, a series of evaluations was published that were critical of treatment programs. Especially influential was the widely publicized Martinson Report, which drew the conclusion that "nothing works" (Martinson 1974; Lipton, Martinson, and Wilks 1975). Critics of the report responded that the negative results could be explained by methodological problems and weak evaluations, rather than by the absence of effective treatments; but these responses—and even the subsequent retraction of the report's conclusion by its authors—fell on deaf ears. Instead, the public and policy makers became skeptical about the very idea of rehabilitation.

Rising juvenile crime rates also contributed to punitive reforms. Juvenile arrests increased substantially from the mid-1960s until 1980, which reinforced the view that rehabilitation programs were ineffective. Although juvenile crime rates declined in the early 1980s, another upswing followed later in the decade, this one marked by sharp increases in inner-city violence, including homicides committed disproportionately by minority youth (Snyder and Sickmund 1995; Cook and Laub 1998). Images of African American youths wielding guns tapped into racial stereotypes, fueled public fears, and generated what has been described as a "moral panic" (Feld 1977, 2003; Chiricos 2004). Although juvenile violence has declined sharply since 1992 to its lowest level in decades (Snyder 2003), nearly two-thirds of the public falsely believes serious juvenile crime continues to rise (Gallup Poll 2003).

Due in no small part to the explosion of newspaper, magazine, and television coverage of youth violence (Chiricos 2004), ideas about adolescent offenders also shifted (Scott and Grisso 1997). Public perceptions are shaped largely by local television news (Gross and Aday 2003), and both television and the print media give excessive coverage to violent youth crime (especially when the offender is a minority), even when rates are declining (Dorfman and Schiraldi 2001). More important than the volume of stories is their sensationalist nature. Best-selling magazines have printed cover stories with titles such as "Children Without Pity" (*Time* October 26, 1992), "Teen Violence: Wild in the Streets" (*Newsweek* August 2, 1993), "Heartbreaking Crimes: Kids Without a Conscience" (*People* June 23, 1997), "Big Shots: An Inside Look at the Deadly Love Affair Between America's Kids and Their Guns" (*Time* August 2, 1993), and "The Monsters Next Door" (*Time* May 3, 1999). This kind of reporting conflicts with the image of juvenile offenders as misguided and immature, portraying them instead as thugs with little or no moral feeling or human regard. Although only a few scholars have subscribed to this view, those who have were prominently featured in the media. DiIulio and his colleagues, for example, described adolescent offenders as vicious and remorseless "superpredators" (DiIulio 1996; Bennett, DiIulio, and Walters 1996) and warned of the coming of "the youngest, biggest, and baddest generation any society has ever known" (Bennett, DiIulio, and Walters 1996:206). The portrayal of juvenile offenders—even preadolescent ones—as adult-like and evil, legitimated the adoption of harsh, punitive policies.

The Kernel of Truth

When people panic about crime, "common sense" suggests harsh punishment as the solution (Cohen 1972; Gendreau et al. 2002; Chiricos 2004). A recent Gallup poll showed that more than 70 percent of the public believed that toughening penalties for juvenile offenders would make a "major difference" in reducing violent crime (Moon et al. 2000:41). There is clearly some truth to the idea of deterrence. After all, speeding drivers slow down when they see patrol cars. But consider how quickly they speed up again when the threat has passed. When the threat of punishment is clear and imminent, we tend to obey the law. But the threat of punishment is seldom clear and imminent. It is obviously impossible (and undesirable) to have police officers observing us at all times. So the threat of punishment is most often vague and uncertain. It should be no surprise, then, that research provides little support for the idea that threats of even severe punishment are effective in reducing crime.

If the threat of punishment does not deter, common sense still indicates that actually being punished can change people's behavior. Most can recall learning important behavioral lessons as children as a result of being scolded, spanked, or denied privileges by parents. Research shows that parental monitoring and punishment indeed play a vital role in producing prosocial children and adults. So there is clearly some truth to this idea. However, we need to be careful not to generalize from the positive effect that punishment may have had on us while we were growing up, to draw sweeping conclusions about the effectiveness of punishment. The truth is that punishment does not always have the positive consequences we tend to assume.

The Truth or Facts

The effectiveness of punishment depends a great deal on the context in which it is administered (see, for example, Braithwaite 1989, 2000; Braithwaite and Braithwaite 2001). Braithwaite and others caution that the effect of punishment is dependent on who is doing the punishing, what message is communicated to the individual who is punished, and how the punishment is delivered.

Punishment is most effective when it is administered by persons whom we love and respect, and whose opinions and judgments about us matter (Braithwaite 2001:11). Punishment delivered by a police officer, judge, or correctional officer with whom we have no relationship (and toward whom we may have negative attitudes) is much less likely to produce the desired results.

The message communicated to the offender is also consequential. It is important to punish in ways that communicate disapproval of the behavior but that do not reject the individual ("this is a good person who has done a bad act" or "this is a not-so-good person who has done a bad act, but can change"). Effective punishment sends a message that the behavior is wrong, but at the same time teaches and encourages more appropriate behavior and communicates confidence in the individual's capacity to change (Braithwaite and Braithwaite 2001:9). The model of effective punishment is the loving parent: He or she does not threaten to banish the child from the family or suggest that the child is worthless and unforgivable.

Punishment that is ineffective communicates not only that the act is bad, but also that the individual who committed the act is bad. When our whole personhood is attacked, we feel humiliated and tend to defend ourselves by denying the legitimacy of what is being said (not only about us, but about our behavior). We are also apt to react with anger and defiance (see Sherman 1993, 2003). All too frequently, punishments imposed by courts and correctional agencies invoke these counterproductive responses because they are accompanied by messages of rejection.

Finally, how the message is communicated makes a difference. When we treat people with respect, they feel valued. When we afford them an opportunity to be heard, they are more likely to feel they are being treated fairly. When we belittle, nag, insult, when we are blunt and harsh in communicating disapproval, the results are often contrary to what we intend. One of the most consistent findings in criminological research is that children of parents who reject and degrade, and who punish their children harshly, are likely to behave aggressively and violently (Ahmed 2001; Baumrind 1978; Farrington 1989; McCord 1979; McCord, McCord, and Zola 1959; Power and Chapieski 1986; Sampson and Laub 1993; Smith and Thornberry 1995; Stouthamer-Loeber et al. 2001; Strassberg et al. 1994; Wells and Rankin 1988; Widom 1992; Widom and Maxfield 2001).

If harsh, unreasoning, and punitive discipline has negative effects within the family, similar strategies used by the state are likely to backfire as well. A number of studies have shown that offenders are more likely to re-offend if justice officials treat them in ways they perceive as unfair or disrespectful. Paternoster and associates (1997), for example, found that suspects who were treated with respect by police and permitted to relate their version of events, not only felt they had been treated more fairly, but were significantly less likely to reoffend than suspects who were not so treated (see also Sherman 1993). Pfeiffer (1994) reported that defendants randomly assigned to judges who scolded offenders at sentencing had significantly higher rates of recidivism than defendants assigned to judges who did not scold.

Evaluations of punitive correctional strategies (e.g., surveillance, drug testing, electronic monitoring, detention, Scared Straight and its derivatives, boot camps, transfer to criminal court) consistently show that they are not effective in reducing juvenile crime (see, for example, Lipsey 1992; Lipsey and Wilson 1998; Peters, Thomas, and Zamberlan 1997; Petrosino, Turpin-Petrosino, and Finckenauer 2000; for a review and discussion, see Howell 2003). Indeed, many of these programs, especially those in which degradation is a central feature, frequently increase the risk of recidivism. Take transfer, for example. Contrary to reformers' expectations, research consistently shows that transferred youth reoffend more quickly and at higher rates, and commit more serious offenses than similar offenders who are retained in the juvenile system (see, for example, Bishop et al. 1996; Fagan 1995).

Treatment-oriented programs, especially those that incorporate cognitive behavioral therapy and parent/family interventions, are considerably more effective than punishment-oriented ones. There are effective nonresidential treatment programs for minor and first-time offenders as well as effective residential interventions for serious and chronic offenders. In treatment-oriented institutions, young offenders more often develop positive ties to staff, are more receptive to the idea of change, more often learn important social and problem-solving skills, and are more optimistic about remaining law-abiding following release (Street, Vinter, and Perrow 1966; Feld 1977; Poole and Regoli 1983). Recent meta-analyses (studies that examine the effects of multiple programs of the same type) have shown that certain treatment strategies produce substantial reductions in recidivism even among very high-risk offenders (Lipsey and Wilson 1998:336).

Interests Served by the Myth

Despite an almost complete lack of evidence to support it, the myth that harsh punishments reduce juvenile crime continues to flourish. It does so in part because commonsense notions about the efficacy of punishment are deeply ingrained and resistant to change. It does so in part because the public and politicians are skeptical about social science research, especially when the research evidence contradicts popular mythology (Finckenauer and Gavin 1999). And it does so in part because there is a communication gap between criminologists and both policy makers and the media. But there are other reasons for the endurance of the myth. Simply put, the myth serves powerful political and economic interests.

To understand the interests served by the myth, recall the discussion above of the factors that prompted the punitive reforms: (1) the idea that effective treatment programs do not exist; (2) the idea that youth crime, especially violent crime, is increasing; and (3) the idea that adolescent offenders have changed, that they are not the immature and vulnerable children conceived by the founders of the juvenile justice system, but are instead savvy, vicious, and morally impoverished products of a permissive society. Each of these ideas is also a myth and, the more each is reinforced, the greater is the support for punishment as a solution.

Crime and the Media

The myth of rising youth crime and the myth of the superpredator go hand in hand, and both are sustained by the media. Violent crimes receive a grossly disproportionate share of media coverage: More than 25 percent of crime reporting is about murder (Beckett and Sasson 2004) but murders constitute less than one tenth of one percent of all crimes known to the police (Federal Bureau of Investigation 2002). Not only is violence overreported, but also the incidence of particular kinds of violence is exaggerated. Violent crimes most often involve people who are known to each other (spouses, friends, acquaintances), but stranger crime is much more likely to be covered. There is also racial distortion in the coverage. Most violent crime is intraracial, but violent offenses involving black male assailants and white victims are much more likely to receive saturation news coverage. These acts of violence "resonate criminal stereotypes and tap into deeply held racial prejudices" (Chiricos 2004:53; see also Beckett and Sasson 2004; Dorfman and Schiraldi 2001; Feld 2003).

The majority of people depend on the media, especially local television news, to form opinions about crime and crime-control policies (Dorfman and Schiraldi 2001; Gross and Aday 2003). It is little wonder, then, that people exaggerate the level of youth violence or believe the children of today are more dangerous and ruthless than those of the past. It is in the interest of the media to highlight violent crime, especially violence committed by young black males, because this is the kind of crime that the public fears most. This is not to suggest that the media intentionally try to generate fear or champion a punitive crime control agenda, but they exploit fear and inadvertently promote that agenda in the interest of profit. Dramatic accounts of the most feared crimes sell newspapers and magazines. They attract viewers to television news and other crime-related programming, and generate advertising revenues. Violent crime is cheap and easy to report (it does not require in-depth investigative reporting) and it has wide audience appeal (Dorfman and Schiraldi 2001).

The Politics of Crime

The myth of effective punishment also serves political interests. A public that is frightened about violent youth crime responds positively to conservative politicians who propose solutions that appeal to commonsense ideas. The punishment solution is simplistic, intuitive, and wins votes. Playing on public fears of violence, reinforcing the myth of adult-like adolescents, and advocating punitive solutions with catchy sound bites like "adult crime, adult time" unfortunately have become successful strategies for winning elections (Beckett and Sasson 2004).

Advocating a simplistic "get tough" agenda does more than help win elections. Sadly, the "punishment solution" allows politicians to ignore (or remain ignorant of) the good treatment programming that might provide young offenders a much better chance of becoming productive adults. It also provides powerful resistance to dismantling punitive programs whose damaging effects have been demonstrated. Empirical evidence that punitive programs are ineffective is frequently rejected by policy makers because of skepticism about social science research and because belief in the efficacy of punishment is so strong. Finckenauer and Gavin (1999:368) conclude that "It is easier [for legislators] to continue such programs and avoid angering constituents than it is to stop them."

More important still, because the "punishment solution" places responsibility for crime on the immoral choices of individual youths, it diverts public attention from the social and economic conditions that are the underlying causes of violent crime and that, ultimately, must be addressed if crime is to be prevented. However, the interests of the wealthy and the powerful are better served by advocating punishment as a solution than they are by addressing the enduring social and economic problems—poverty, income inequality, inadequate inner-city schools, unemployment, urban decline—that contribute to youth crime (Chiricos 2004).

Policy Implications of Belief in the Myth

The United States has endorsed punishment of children and adolescent offenders to an unprecedented degree, and blurred traditional lines of distinction—philosophically, programmatically, and jurisdictionally—between the juvenile and adult systems. The myth that harsh punishments are effective in reducing youth crime has generated policies that are costly and wasteful. The myth represents a formidable barrier to the development of more humane and effective responses to juvenile crime and, in the end, has done a disservice to victims, offenders, and the public.

Exposing the myth that punishment is an effective strategy to reduce youth crime will depend ultimately on the ability to destroy the myths that support it. Restoring less monstrous conceptualizations of adolescents represents a real challenge. The demonization of youth must be replaced by the realization that the children and adolescents of today are little different than those of a generation ago. Policy makers and the public also need to be made aware that youth violence has declined to its lowest levels in decades. Instead of episodic reporting of individual acts of violence as they occur, the coverage needs to be contextualized to reveal broader crime patterns and trends (Casey Journalism Center on Children and Families 2002). More balanced and responsible media reporting should also include more noncrime stories about youth, as well as thoughtful analyses of youth policy. Additionally, policy makers and the public need to be educated about the counterproductive effects of punishment that takes place in a context devoid of positive attachment and respect, and about the promise of well-implemented, evidence-based treatment programs carried out by professionals who communicate messages of hope rather than messages of rejection. Sadly, because the "punishment solution" and the myths that support it serve powerful interests, the prospects for real change, at least in the short term, appear slim.

References

Ahmed, E. 2001. Shame management: Regulating bullying. In *Shame management through reintegration*, eds. E. Ahmed, N. Harris, J. Braithwaite, and V. Braithwaite. Cambridge: Cambridge University Press.

Baumrind, D. 1978. Parental disciplinary patterns and social competence in children. *Youth and Society* 9:239–276.

Beckett, K., and T. Sasson. 2004. *The politics of injustice.* 2nd ed. Thousand Oaks, CA: Pine Forge Press.

Bennett, W., J. DiIulio, and J. Walters. 1996. *Body count: Moral poverty and how to win America's war against crime and drugs.* New York: Simon and Schuster.

Beyer, M. 2003. *Best practices in juvenile accountability: Overview.* Washington, DC: U.S. Department of Justice, Office of Juvenile Justice and Delinquency Prevention.

Bishop, D. M., C. E. Frazier, L. Lanza-Kaduce, and L. Winner. 1996. The transfer of juveniles to criminal court: Does it make a difference? *Crime and Delinquency* 42:171–191.

Braithwaite, J. 1989. *Crime, shame, and reintegration.* Melbourne: Cambridge University Press.

———. 2000. Shame and criminal justice. *Canadian Journal of Criminology* 42:281–298.

Braithwaite, J., and V. Braithwaite. 2001. Shame, shame management and regulation. In *Shame management through reintegration*, eds. E. Ahmed, N. Harris, J. Braithwaite, and V. Braithwaite. Cambridge: Cambridge University Press.

Casey Journalism Center on Children and Families. 2002. *Coverage in context: How thoroughly the new media report five key children's issues.* College Park, MD: University of Maryland Press. Available online at *http://www.casey.umd.edu.*

Chiricos, T. 2004. The media, moral panics, and the politics of crime control. In *The criminal justice system: Politics and policies*, 9th ed. Eds. G. F. Cole, M. C. Gertz, and A. Bunger. Belmont, CA: Wadsworth.

Cohen, S. 1972. *Folk devils and moral panics.* London: MacGibbon and Kee.

Cook, P., and J. Laub. 1998. The unprecedented epidemic in youth violence. In *Crime and justice: A review of research, vol. 24*, eds. M. Tonry and M. Moore. Chicago: University of Chicago Press.

DiIulio, J. 1996. Help wanted: Economists, crime, and public policy. *Journal of Economic Perspectives* 10:3–23.

Dorfman, L., and V. Schiraldi. 2001. *Off balance: Youth, race and crime in the news.* Washington, DC: Justice Policy Institute.

Fagan, J. 1995. Separating the men from the boys: The comparative advantage of juvenile versus criminal court sanctions on recidivism among adolescent felony offenders. In *A sourcebook: Serious, violent, and chronic juvenile offenders*, eds. J. C. Howell, B. Krisberg, J. D. Hawkins, and J. J. Wilson. Thousand Oaks, CA: Sage.

Farrington, D. P. 1989. Early predictors of adolescent aggression and adult violence. *Violence and Victims* 4:79–100.

Federal Bureau of Investigation (FBI). 2002. *Crime in the United States*. Available online at: *http://www.fbi.gov/ucr/*.

Feld, B. C. 1977. *Neutralizing inmate violence: Juvenile offenders in institutions*. Cambridge, MA: Ballinger.

———. 2003. The politics of race and juvenile justice: The due process revolution and the conservative reaction. *Justice Quarterly* 20: 764–800.

Finckenauer, J. O., and P. W. Gavin. 1999. *Scared straight: The panacea phenomenon revisited*. Prospect Heights, IL: Waveland.

Forst, M., and M. Blomquist. 1991. Cracking down on juveniles: The changing ideology of youth corrections. *Notre Dame Journal of Law, Ethics and Public Policy* 5:323–375.

Gallup Organization, Inc. 2003. *The Gallup poll*. January 9. Available online at: *http://www.gallup.com/*.

Gendreau, P., C. Goggin, F. T. Cullen, and M. Paparozzi. 2002. The common sense revolution and correctional policy. In *Offender rehabilitation and treatment: Effective programmes and policies to reduce re-offending*, ed. J. Maguire. Chicester, UK: Wiley.

Gross, K., and S. Aday. 2003. The scary world in your living room and neighborhood: Using local broadcast news, neighborhood crime rates, and personal experience to test agenda setting and cultivation. *Journal of Communication* 53:411–426.

Howell, J. 2003. *Preventing and reducing juvenile delinquency: A comprehensive framework*. Thousand Oaks, CA: Sage.

Lipsey, M. W. 1992. Juvenile delinquency treatment: A meta-analytic inquiry into the variability of effects. In *Meta-analysis for explanation*, eds. T. D. Cook, H. Cooper, D. S. Cordray, H. Hartmann, L. V. Hedges, R. J. Light, T. A. Louis, and F. Mosteller. New York: Russell Sage.

Lipsey, M. W., and D. B. Wilson. 1998. Effective intervention for serious juvenile offenders: A synthesis of research. In *Serious and violent juvenile offenders: Risk factors and successful interventions*, eds. R. Loeber and D. P. Farrington. Thousand Oaks, CA: Sage.

Lipton, D., R. Martinson, and J. Wilks. 1975. *The effectiveness of correctional treatment: A survey of treatment evaluation studies*. New York: Praeger.

Martinson, R. 1974. What works? Questions and answers about prison reform. *Public Interest* 35:22–54.

McCord, J. 1979. Some child-rearing antecedents of criminal behavior in adult men. *Journal of Personality and Social Psychology* 37: 1477–1486.

McCord, W., J. McCord, and I. K. Zola. 1959. *Origins of crime: A new evaluation of the Cambridge-Somerville Youth Study*. New York: Cambridge University Press.

Moon, M. M., J. L. Sundt, F. T. Cullen, and J. P. Wright. 2000. Is child saving dead? Public support for juvenile rehabilitation. *Crime & Delinquency* 46:38–62.

Paternoster, R., R. Brame, R. Bachman, and L. W. Sherman. 1997. Do fair procedures matter? The effect of procedural justice on spouse assault. *Law & Society Review* 31:163–204.

Peters, M., D. Thomas, and C. Zamberlan. 1997. *Boot camps for juvenile offenders*. Washington, DC: U.S. Department of Justice, Office of Juvenile Justice and Delinquency Prevention.

Petrosino, A., C. Turpin-Petrosino, and J. O. Finckenauer. 2000. Well-meaning programs can have harmful effects! Lessons from experiments of programs such as Scared Straight. *Crime and Delinquency* 46:354–379.

Pfeiffer, C. 2003. Alternative sanctions in Germany: An overview of Germany's sentencing practices. Available online at: *http://www.uplink.com.au/lawlibrary/Documents/Docs/Doc33.html*.

Poole, E. D., and R. M. Regoli. 1983. Violence in juvenile institutions: A comparative study. *Criminology* 21:213–232.

Power, T. G., and M. L. Chapieski. 1986. Child-rearing and impulse control in toddlers: A naturalistic investigation. *Developmental Psychology* 22:271–275.

Sampson, R. J., and J. H. Laub. 1993. *Crime in the making: Pathways and turning points through life*. Cambridge, MA: Harvard University Press.

Scott, E., and T. Grisso. 1997. Adolescent development and juvenile justice reform. *Journal of Criminal Law and Criminology* 88:137–189.

Sherman, L. W. 1993. Defiance, deterrence, and irrelevance: A theory of the criminal sanction. *Journal of Research in Crime and Delinquency* 30:445–473.

———. 2003. Reason for emotion: Reinventing justice with theories, innovations, and research. The American Society of Criminology 2002 Presidential Address. *Criminology* 41:1–38.

Smith, C., and T. P. Thornberry. 1995. The relationship between childhood maltreatment and adolescent involvement in delinquency. *Criminology* 33:451–481.

Snyder, H. N. 2003. Juvenile arrests 2001. *Juvenile Justice Bulletin*. Washington, DC: U.S. Department of Justice, Office of Juvenile Justice and Delinquency Prevention.

Snyder, H. N., and M. Sickmund. 1995. *Juvenile offenders and victims: A national report.* Washington, DC: Office of Juvenile Justice and Delinquency Prevention.

Stouthamer-Loeber, M., R. Loeber, D. L. Homish, and E. Wei. 2001. Maltreatment of boys and the development of disruptive and delinquent behavior. *Development and Psychopathology* 13:941–955.

Strassberg, Z., K. A. Dodge, G. Pettit, and J. E. Bates. 1994. Spanking in the home and children's subsequent aggression toward kindergarten peers. *Development and Psychopathology* 6:445–461.

Street, D., R. D. Vinter, and C. Perrow. 1966. *Organization for treatment.* New York: Free Press.

Wells, L. E., and J. H. Rankin. 1988. Direct parental controls and delinquency. *Criminology* 26:263–285.

Widom, C. S. 1992. *The cycle of violence (research in brief).* Washington, DC: National Institute of Justice.

Widom, C. S., and M. G. Maxfield. 2001. *An update on the "cycle of violence" (research in brief).* Washington, DC: National Institute of Justice.

Zimring, F. E. 1981. Notes toward a jurisprudence of waiver. In *Issues in juvenile justice information and training*, eds. J. Hall, D. Hamparian, J. Pettibone, and J. White. Columbus, OH: Academy for Contemporary Problems.

———. 1998a. *American youth violence.* New York: Oxford University Press.

———. 1998b. Toward a jurisprudence of youth violence. In *Youth violence*, eds. F. Zimring, M. Tonry, and M. Moore. Chicago: University of Chicago Press. ✦

Chapter 18
The Myth That Public Attitudes Are Punitive

Russ Immarigeon

For the past 20 years, county, state, and federal governments have invested heavily in the development of a law enforcement and correctional infrastructure. On the correctional side, this has resulted in mass incarceration (Garland 2003), a greatly expanded prison-industrial complex that includes the construction of record numbers of new and renovated jails and prisons to confine historically high levels of pretrial and sentenced populations of men and women charged with and/or convicted of crimes. One indicator of this trend is that the United States now imprisons well over 2 million men and women, a number that keeps surging even as states—many in the midst of a fiscal crisis—begin to make efforts to stem the tide of penal construction and to release the build-up of prisoners in state and county facilities (Butterfield 2004).

The Myth

One myth behind the rise of toughening criminal sanctions and the increasing use of imprisonment is that public opinion supports it. Put more succinctly, many politicians and policymakers have, over the years, argued that ordinary people— the American public—support measures that imprison criminals for longer periods of time. According to this punitive approach, rehabilitation does not work, and society would be better off with criminals behind bars for as long as possible. At the center of this posture is the belief, or projection, that American citizens are tired of crime and fearful of being in danger of harm. In this environment, legal authorities, such as Joe Arpaio, the Sheriff of Maricopa County, Phoenix, Arizona, or Gerald Hege, the Sheriff of Lexington County, North Carolina, became popular and well known for their "no-frills" approaches to crime and justice that included making prisoners wear "convict-striped" uniforms or pink underwear and routine references to prisoners as "scumbags" (for further details, see Arpaio and Sherman 1996; Elsner 2004).

President Nixon was first to politicize "law-and-order." Since then, politicians, from the national scene to local precincts, have shaped crime and punishment issues within a political framework. In the late 1980s, for example, the infamous "Willie Horton ads" of then–presidential candidate George F. W. Bush showed a black convict swirling ominously through a revolving door from prison to the "free world." The Bush campaign's Willie Horton ads were not the first of their kind, but they were notable, among other things, for their attempt to shape rather than reflect public opinion. Little reference was made to studies or surveys. Even the facts of the Willie Horton case were skewed (see Anderson 1995). Frequently, referrals to public-opinion support for prison-building or tougher criminal sanctions are given with little relationship to the growing, sizable, and important body of research, which assesses the extent of public approval or disapproval for certain measures.

Politicians, who are interested in castigating opponents as "soft-on-crime" to win elections, often justify their "get-tough" proclivities with reference to public opinion. People are fearful, they suggest, and are demanding safety. Consequently, they offer, we must be harsher on criminals. The "get-tough" pitch has been, and remains, a successful strategy for ill-advised, ill-informed, or ill-intended politicians wishing to score a quick, likely electoral victory. They assert that the people want it, and they are going to give them what they want. As an example, a newspaper headline in the *Seattle Post-Intelligencer* recently read, "Pols try to 'out-tough' each other as crimefighters" (Ammons 2004). The article relates how the governor, state legislators, and prosecutors in Washington continue—collaterally if not cooperatively—proposing and passing measures that amplify prison population issues before preparing for the likely outcome of more prisoners for fewer prison spaces.

The emergence of mass imprisonment in the United States is often posited on a multitude of factors, but prominent among them is the belief that public opinion supports such use of incarceration in response to crime and disorder. This chapter challenges this notion based on the following arguments. First, over the past several decades, crime and punishment have become increasingly politicized, marginalizing the perspectives of criminal justice and corrections practitioners, as well as the general public, outside the sphere of influence in criminal justice and correctional policymaking. Second, the role of public opinion in this politicized process is less clear, and certainly not settled. Finally, in some instances, public opinion is given primacy as the driving force behind sentencing and incarceration—notably prison-building and sanction-toughening—policies, while at other times the views and beliefs of American citizens seem either beside the point or simply not important enough for inclusion.

The Kernel of Truth

Arguing that public opinion is not punitive in its reaction or response to crime is not to suggest that Americans do not get angry about crime or that they do not want something done about it. The American public does indeed get anxious about crime and does want something done about it. What remains unclear, however, is what they want done and how they decide or suggest what might be done.

Generally, people—not necessarily just crime victims—are angriest shortly after being personally victimized and when victimization is experienced by others. It is also probable that nonvictim anger lasts longer. For most crime victims, anger subsides and is replaced by more concrete desires for specific things to happen, including meeting offenders to learn why crimes occurred, why they in particular were victimized, and what might be done with offenders to assure their behavior changes.

Early crime victimization surveys and public opinion polls suggest some limitations of surveys that have helped give the impression that the public is more punitive than is actually the case. As one example, in the early 1980s, when the nation's punitive approach to crime was increasing, a report from the American Broadcasting Corporation (MacGillis and ABC News 1983) observed crime was making Americans fearful. Eighty-four percent of Americans felt at the time that crime rates were increasing, even though FBI figures suggested the opposite. Thus, Americans were wrong about crime trends, but their fears were also not necessarily about those activities that were measured through crime statistics. According to the report from MacGillis and ABC News, Americans were actually more fearful of disorder, such as public drunkenness and rudeness, than the major crime categories, such as robbery and theft. While this possibly gives light to why Americans are fearful even when crime is low in their communities, it does not provide everything, especially the remedies to crime that Americans support.

The Truth or Facts

Public opinion on crime and justice in the United States finds support not only for creative approaches to criminal justice, but also for efforts that establish further innovative projects. It is safe to say that public sentiment provides greater support for alternative options than for punitive justice. A key factor in such public support is the implementation of measures that provide for public safety as well as a means of challenging and changing the criminal conduct and misbehavior of persons convicted of crimes. As such, public opinion is not a barrier or drawback to innovative practice. Rather, it seems to encourage such experimentation, as long as it embraces a healthy sense of reality (e.g., the need to reduce the occurrence of crime in neighborhoods, communities, and political jurisdictions). Despite policymaker's beliefs, expectations, or proclamations to the contrary, research has consistently shown over the past few decades that citizens give their support for prison alternatives, such as the use of community service, restitution, and other nonincarceration options, including rehabilitative services and restorative justice.

In the late 1980s, the Public Agenda Foundation and the Edna McConnell Clark Foundation initiated a series of state-specific studies that measured public opinion about crime and punishment.

Unlike previous studies, however, these studies not only asked people their opinions, but also later supplied those surveyed with information about the realities (as opposed to the myths) of various crime and sanctioning issues, thereby creating an informed before-and-after study.

In one study, Alabama residents were initially found fearful of crime and skeptical, even mistrusting, of the criminal justice system (Doble and Klein 1989). While Alabama residents were willing to embrace standard law enforcement and corrections approaches, they nonetheless felt the state's prison system was doing only a fair job. They were familiar with prison overcrowding, although unfamiliar with recent increases in the state's rate of imprisonment. Residents did not view overcrowding as cruel and unusual punishment, and they did not support building new prisons as a viable solution to prison population problems. When informed about how various nonprison options work in practice, Alabama residents reported some interesting views. They did not give much support to "strict probation," preferring options establishing work habits to those merely restricting offenders to a particular time and place. In this vein, they liked community service because of its work ethic. They did not like house arrest because it seemed too easy and nonproductive. They also supported restitution centers in their neighborhoods, especially if violent offenders were screened out. Overall, Alabama residents supported nonprison options because they allowed judges to fit punishments to specific crimes, they provided the potential for rehabilitation, they seemed cost-effective, and they were serious enough to address concerns about public safety. Several years later, another study found similar results in Pennsylvania (Jacobs 1993).

Public opinion polls have occurred, in one form or another, for centuries. But only in recent years has the measurement of citizen attitudes toward crime- and punishment-related issues received much attention from researchers, governmental officials, media representatives, or public policy advocates. In the late 1960s and early 1970s, national opinion surveys were first conducted on such broad matters as capital punishment, fear of crime, police practices, and criminal victimization. Over the past decade, however, with the escalation of public expenditures on criminal justice agencies and institutions, as well as the expansion of local jail and state and federal prisons systems, public opinion polling has begun to probe the depths and dimensions of citizens' attitudes to the relative use of punishment-versus treatment-oriented sentencing options (Flanagan and Longmire 1996). A public opinion survey of Maryland voters, for example, found that twice as many respondents believed too many people were incarcerated, more than one-half (53 percent) felt persons released from prison were more likely than nonincarcerated offenders to commit new crimes, and 86 percent preferred giving judges the option of sending convicted offenders to alcohol- or drug-abuse treatment rather than to prison. Similarly, voters, mostly notably in California where a ballot initiative was approved, have increasingly given support to measures that treat substance abusers instead of simply imprisoning them (McVay, Schiraldi, and Zeidenberg 2004).

Public attitudes toward the circumstances, extent, and consequences of crime are important—although not necessarily determining—factors in the development of public policy and the distribution of public (and perhaps private) funding. It is difficult, though, to measure the nature or to decipher the meaning of these attitudes toward criminality. It is more difficult, still, to describe precisely how, or even if, these attitudes actually influenced the development of policy or the distribution of funds. As Taylor Gaubatz (1995:2) notes, "[P]ublic opinion about crime is not a seamless web. The public that wants a greater use of incarceration also believes that our prisons are not particularly effective; the public that calls for harsher courts also believes that an attack on socioeconomic problems would do more to reduce crime."

The University of Connecticut regularly queries citizens of the state on current social issues. In a report on prison overcrowding released in March 2004, a UConn Poll (based on a sample of 601 residents) found that 51 percent opposed sending prisoners to out-of-state prison facilities to reduce overcrowding, 53 percent opposed building more prisons, 60 percent opposed building prisons in their towns, 61 percent supported reducing mandatory minimum sentences for first-time offenders, 76 percent supported more services for parolees, 84 percent supported sending drug abusers to treatment services rather than jail, and 89 percent supported sending mentally-ill offenders to mental-health facilities instead of prisons.

When asked about the purposes of criminal justice sanctioning, Connecticut residents preferred rehabilitation (41 percent) instead of punishment (24 percent) and protection (22 percent). Fifty-two percent of the state's citizens sampled in this study believed that prisoners have too many rights, but only 32 percent felt they were treated better than they should be. About the same percentage of sampled residents felt that Connecticut's prisoners received sentences that were about the right length (35 percent) or too short (36 percent). Finally, more than two-thirds of those sampled (69 percent) did not agree that rehabilitation for nonviolent offenders was a waste of time and money (see Blint 2004).

Interests Served by the Myth

Public support in the United States for tough-on-crime, law-and-order policies and practices has been nurtured and nudged along by politicians, the media, the prison-industrial complex, and even common sense. Over the course of the last three or four decades, politicians from both major political parties have used hardened positions on crime as a wedge to defeat opponents who were mechanically, but successfully, characterized as being "soft-on-crime." Both in the 1960s and in the 1980s, for example, conservative politicians, especially at the national level, began to raise street crime and drugs—as well as governmental responses to them—as political campaign issues (for example, see Beckett and Sasson 2004:45–72). Subsequently, liberal politicians increasingly took "conservative" positions on crime, especially in the wake of the Willie Horton affair, which was discussed previously.

During this time period, media conglomeration and other corporate shifts within the publishing industry aided, and benefited from, increasingly sensationalistic tabloid coverage of "true crime," which over the long term boosted media profitability. Also, shifts in reporting styles, often associated with the narrowing corporate control of seemingly disparate media outlets, contributed to fast-track selling rather than in-depth coverage of crime—especially violent crime—issues (concerning shifts in reporting sex crimes, see Benedict 1992). On the whole, the hardening political rhetoric about crime (and the need for stiffer punishments) has made for fast-paced, tough-sounding headlines that

have increased the public's fear of crime and abetted the full emergence of a prison-industrial complex.

The fears raised by newspapers and other media outlets, as well as by disingenuous and sharp-tongued politicians, have captivated members of the general public and their "common-sense" of things. Indeed, given the scant information with which to form alternative opinions, the average citizen is hard-pressed to venture beyond get-tough proposals that at least appear to make sense. However, as noted in the previous section, one of the things public-opinion surveys started to show is that, if given adequate information, people are fully capable of changing their minds and forming different opinions, even on topics such as crime (where they seem to hold rock-solid opinions). These polls found that with useful information in hand, citizens could comprehend establishing policies and practices that relied less on incarceration and more on community-based resources (Doble and Klein 1989; Jacobs 1993; Hough and Roberts 1997).

Policy Implications of Belief in the Myth

For much of the past decade and a half, American crime policy has remained unchanged. Community corrections, despite some notable efforts, has also remained unchanged. With the apparent decline in crime in the country, perhaps a window of opportunity exists for community corrections to assert some leadership over the punitive state of affairs that exists today.

Beckett (1997) takes an interesting perspective on the state of contemporary crime policy, noting that the two major crime-policy discourses (i.e., the ways people talk about crime problems and criminal justice operations), have been get-tough and managerial approaches. Both are "cynical sides of the same coin," she says, because they "are fundamentally uninterested in the social causes of criminality or in reintegrating offenders and assume instead that punishment, surveillance, and control are the best response to deviant behavior" (107).

Friedman and Fisher offer some hope for an academic-practitioner partnership. For them,

> the politics of crime has degenerated into a macho posturing that conceals political cowardice. Our elected representatives lack the courage to deal head on with the crime problem as it really is. Whatever voices of reason are likely to be heard will have to come from outside politics. Scholars who study the problem can provide these voices, as can professionals in criminal justice. Working together, academics and professionals must try to persuade a weary public and its wary representatives that marginal increases in deterrent power come at a very high price. (1997:4)

The conundrum facing American crime policy is that public opinion is perhaps weary, as much because it is misperceived as because it is tired of crime. Beckett, along with Friedman and Fisher, urges further review and reconsideration of public opinion as a starting point. Public opinion is, indeed, an important matter meriting additional thought and investigation.

The British Crime Survey (BCS) asks people what they know about crime and punishment, what attitudes they have about judicial sentencers and criminal sentencing, and what sentences victims would like to see offenders receive. Key findings from a recent Home Office Research and Statistics Directorate report include the following:

- People generally have a poor knowledge of crime levels and trends. Knowledge of the criminal justice system is also poor, and this is reflected in attitudes toward sentencers and sentencing practice.

- Most people mistakenly believe that recorded crime is rising, and that a large proportion of crime is violent. Three-quarters thought recorded crime rose between 1993 and 1995, when in fact it fell by 8 percent. A small minority of crimes are violent, but four out of five people substantially overestimated this proportion.

- The majority of people substantially underestimated the proportion of convicted adult male offenders sent to prison. In 1995, 97 percent of adult male rapists, 61 percent of house burglars, and about 70 percent of muggers who were convicted in court were given custodial sentences. Over half of the people underestimated these figures by at least 30 percentage points.

- These misperceptions were partly reflected in people's attitudes towards sentencers and current sentencing practice. Four out of five said that sentencers were too lenient, and the same proportion thought judges were out of touch with the public.

- The proportion of victims favoring imprisonment for their offender has increased over the last twelve years.

- People with lower levels of educational attainment, older people, and those who read tabloid newspapers tended to have less knowledge of crime and criminal justice than others. (Hough and Roberts 1997)

Like British opinion, much of American opinion about criminal justice is based upon false knowledge. "If the public are not made more aware of the true state of affairs in punishment," Roberts and Stalans (1997) suggest, "the result will be the passage of more repressive legislation." As has already occurred, this will have further negative consequences for the viability of community corrections.

Developing Community Corrections With Public Support for Alternatives

Hough and Roberts (1997:4) observe,

The BCS findings suggest that a criminal policy of "playing to the gallery" and extending the use of imprisonment further is not appropriate. Firstly, there was little public support for building more prisons to address prison overcrowding. More importantly, the belief that sentences are too lenient is mainly a reflection of misperceptions about current practice. Finally, such a belief may be so ingrained as to be unaffected by reality—in much the same way that people assume prices are rising, regardless of the actual rate of inflation.

Although these findings hold true in the United States, research alone will not enhance the role of community corrections in local criminal justice systems, especially when the public is poorly informed about the quality and effectiveness of such services. In the mid-1980s, for example, community corrections advocates argued that prison space was scarce (and expensive) and should only be used for the most dangerous offenders. Such a stance raised the possibility of greater reliance on the use of probation. In this context, the California Probation, Parole and Corrections Association (CPPCA) asserted,

If probation is to continue as a local governmental service, probation must take steps now to identify itself to the public it serves as the service that it is. It must further identify itself to the representatives of that public as being a functional and integral part of the justice system. It must further insist that criminal justice be approached politically and economically as a system. This constituency building effort then becomes a part of, and not apart from, probation itself. (CPPCA n.d.:1)

Five Approaches for Community Corrections to Improve Its Image and Demonstrate Its Viability

Market community corrections. Marketing community corrections is not a new idea. The National Institute of Corrections has been urging this approach for many years. Moreover, private foundations, such as the Edna McConnell Clark Foundation, have funded numerous public-opinion surveys in states where they have been attempting to break the overly incarcerative tendencies of local lawmakers. It is clear, from these as well as other academic research efforts, that public opinion is changeable. In short, the public, much like judges given some discretion, responds to concrete information. Given choices, the public is apt to support different options, many of them centered on community corrections. Marketing, it seems, is an obvious first step.

Develop policy briefs. Frightfully, little information about criminal justice practices is available in readily accessible form for the inquisitive citizen or lawmaker interested in learning what choices are available, what works when and how, and so forth. Even potentially eye-opening matters, such as the comparative costs of confinement and community corrections-oriented policies, are left undocumented and undistributed. This is especially alarming because public surveys routinely show that Americans feel that comparative costs are something to consider. Given less-expensive, equally as effective options, the public wisely wants the less-restrictive, less-costly alternative. These facts and figures should be produced in short, concise, understandable policy briefs that are readily distributed to the public, the politicians, and the media.

Develop distribution networks. Beyond having information on hand, the next important step is to distribute it in an effective way. Two vital factors are getting this information to the right places and getting this information there regularly. The "right places" are relatively easy to identify—other criminal justice professionals, judges, the media, state and local political leaders, citizen groups, and even college or university teachers. Information dissemination, however, should not be a one-shot undertaking. People, even in the right places, have short memories, institutional or otherwise. It is wise to make the message obvious, and then obvious again.

Take a proactive stance. The BCS found that tabloid readers had a more distorted perception of criminal justice. The inherent lesson is not so much that tabloid readers are given inaccurate information, but they are given information that appears clear to them. Tabloid papers are good at presenting information in a straightforward fashion. It may be misleading, but it is meted out in bullets. People are clear about what they read in tabloids. Community corrections agencies should develop information that is equally straightforward and to the point. If community corrections has value, it can be asserted in ways that people understand and that speak to people's understanding of how individuals behave and respond to the way they are treated. Research in recent years has clarified many of the benefits of community corrections. It is best to let the public know about it.

Bring professional and political parties together. Community corrections gains little if it keeps what it knows to itself. Repressive and punitive policies succeed in an environment where few options are given, and scarce cover is provided for those who support alternative approaches. Barriers must be broken down between professional and lay worlds, but barriers also exist among professional and political parties. One method of overcoming this obstacle is to bring people together to share information, to explain it, to review it, and to discuss it. Meeting together, in itself, may help bring about the ability to move forward together, instead of in opposition.

These steps are basic ones, and they are but a start. Community leaders and practitioners engaged in the development of community corrections and offender programming generally have more reason to work with public opinion than to fear it. Indeed, they ought to reach out, informing the public as they gain its acceptance and its faith. Often enough, they will find public attitudes urging them to choose rehabilitative and restitution options over punitive ones.

In conclusion, opinion polls that measure public attitudes about crime and justice have become increasingly common, as both the technology of polling and the dependence of political actions on poll results have expanded. In many ways, it is disingenuous to simply report the latest poll survey as news. After all, such findings are generally in line with previous results, with the exception of the stiffening of crime-victim attitudes. But the nature, extent, and implications of these findings are not settled matters, either in the United Kingdom or in the United States. Various media campaigns have been mobilized, with varying degrees of success. But, like many deterrence- and incapacitation-oriented approaches to drunk driving, benefits are apparently short-lived. Consequently, community corrections and program administrators, as well as policymakers and their staff, have much more work to do in establishing a political environment that not only supports community corrections and offender programming, but also demands them.

References

Ammons, D. 2004. Pols try to "out-tough" each other as crimefighters. *Seattle Post-Intelligencer*. Accessed online: *http://seattlepi.nwsource.com*.

Anderson, D. C. 1995. *Crime and the politics of hysteria: How the Willie Horton story changed American justice*. New York: Times Books.

Arpaio, J., and L. Sherman. 1996. *America's toughest sheriff: How to win the war on crime*. Arlington, TX: The Summit Publishing Group.

Beckett, K. 1997. *Making crime pay: Law and order in contemporary American politics*. New York: Oxford University Press.

Beckett, K., and T. Sasson. 2002. *The politics of injustice: Crime and punishment in America*, 2nd ed. Thousand Oaks, CA: Sage Publications.

Benedict, H. 1992. *Virgin or vamp: How the press covers sex crimes*. New York: Oxford University Press.

Blint, D. F. 2004. Prison alternatives supported in poll. *Hartford Courant* March 9.

Butterfield, F. 2004. U.S. correctional population hits new high. *The New York Times* July 26. Accessed online: *http://www.nytimes.com/2004/07/26/national/26parole.html*.

California Probation, Parole and Correctional Association. n.d. *The power of public support: A handbook for corrections*. Sacramento, CA: CPPCA.

Doble, J., and J. Klein. 1989. *Punishing criminals, the public's view: An Alabama survey*. New York: Edna McConnell Clark Foundation and Public Agenda Foundation.

Elsner, A. 2004. *Gates of injustice: The crisis in America's prisons*. Upper Saddle River, NJ: Financial Times Prentice-Hall.

Flanagan, T. J., and D. R. Longmire, eds. 1996. *American view crime and justice: A national public opinion survey*. Thousand Oaks, CA: Sage Publications.

Friedman, L. M., and G. Fisher, eds. 1997. *The crime conundrum: Essays on criminal justice*. Boulder, CO: Westview Press.

Garland, D. 2003. *Mass imprisonment*. Thousand Oaks, CA: Sage Publications.

Hough, M., and J. Roberts. 1997. *Attitudes to punishment: Findings from the British Crime Survey*. London: Home Office Research and Statistics Directorate.

Jacobs, G. 1993. *Punishing criminals: Pennsylvanians consider the options*. New York: The Public Agenda Foundation.

MacGillis, D., and ABC News. 1983. *Crime in America*. Radnor, PA: Chilton Book Company.

McVay, D., V. Schiraldi, and J. Zeidenberg. 2004. *National and state findings on the efficacy and cost savings of drug treatment versus imprisonment*. Washington, DC: Justice Policy Institute.

Roberts, J. V., and L. J. Stalans. 1997. *Public opinion, crime, and criminal justice*. Boulder, CO: Westview Press.

Taylor Gaubatz, K. 1995. *Crime in the public mind*. Ann Arbor: The University of Michigan Press. ✦

Chapter 19
The Myth That the Death Penalty Is Administered Fairly

Brandon Applegate

Compared to other sentences imposed on criminal offenders, the death penalty is relatively rare. At the end of 2002, for example, more than two million people were incarcerated in prisons and jails throughout the United States, and another four million were on probation. In contrast, only 3,557 people were on death row. Still, capital punishment is a critically important aspect of criminal justice. Symbolically, it reflects a belief that under certain circumstances it may be appropriate for the government to take the life of someone who has committed a crime. In practical terms, the death penalty is important because it is the harshest sentence that can be imposed; and once an offender is executed, it is final.

The way capital punishment is administered in the United States changed fundamentally after the Supreme Court's decision in *Furman v. Georgia* (1972). In that case, the Supreme Court ruled that the death penalty, as administered, was unconstitutional, having been imposed arbitrarily and to the detriment of minorities. Most states proceeded to pass new death penalty laws in an attempt to structure discretion in capital cases. In 1976, the Supreme Court decided *Gregg v. Georgia* and two companion cases, upholding statutes that guided the discretion of judges and juries in their decisions regarding when to impose the death penalty.

The court also approved the practice of dividing capital trials into two phases. In the first phase, a defendant's guilt is decided. If a defendant is found guilty, the second phase is undertaken to determine the appropriate sentence. The second, or penalty, phase typically includes deciding on the presence of aggravating and mitigating factors and weighing them. If the aggravating factors outweigh the mitigating factors, the offender is sentenced to death. In 2002, several states amended their laws to assure that juries, not judges, decide on the presence of aggravating factors. The intent of all of these revisions to capital-trial procedures is to produce a system that is not arbitrary, capricious, or discriminatory.

The Myth

According to a Gallup poll conducted in May 2003, 60 percent of Americans think the death penalty is applied fairly. This figure is nine percentage points higher than in June 2000 (Jones 2003).

There are two ways the fairness of a punishment might be considered. The first focuses on the crime as the basis for assessing what level of punishment is deserved. Thus, the harshness of the punishment should fit the severity of the crime committed, and people should not suffer punishment for crimes they did not commit. Although the morality of an execution can be questioned, the death penalty corresponds more closely to murder than most other crime-punishment combinations in the American system of criminal justice. In short, a life is exchanged for a life.

The second aspect of fairness concerns whether a punishment is equally imposed on offenders who are equally deserving. Certain conditions define offenders as legally eligible for the death penalty. Under current capital-punishment laws, this means murder accompanied by aggravating circumstances that outweigh any mitigating circumstances.[1] Thus, differences in the specifics of a homicide situation determine who does and who does not receive a death sentence. For the punishment to be fair, however, extralegal factors, such as the defendant's race, should have no influence on whether capital punishment is imposed. The equal protection clause of the Fourteenth Amendment to the Constitution embodies this consideration: "no state shall . . . deny to any person within its jurisdiction the equal protection of the laws." This chapter largely focuses on this second aspect of fairness.

The Kernel of Truth

Any number of extralegal characteristics might be examined for evidence of discrimination, but perhaps the greatest amount of legal and scholarly attention has been devoted to race. There is some evidence to suggest evenhanded administration of capital punishment with regard to the race of homicide offenders. Data from the Bureau of Justice Statistics show nearly even numbers of whites and blacks currently on death row (Bonczar and Snell 2003). At the end of 2002, 1,931 whites and 1,554 blacks were under sentences of death. Thus, 44 percent of death-row inmates were black, which closely matches the racial distribution of people arrested for murder. Also telling is the fact that, over the past three decades, the growth in the number of whites and of blacks on death row largely parallels each other.

More detailed analyses also have sought to determine whether race influences who receives a death sentence. Two reviews, one by the United States General Accounting Office (GAO) (1990) and one by Baldus and Woodworth (2003), examined studies on how the death penalty has been administered since the decision in *Gregg*. By and large, both reviews reached the same conclusion: the defendant's race is generally not a factor in determining which murderers get the death penalty. At best, the evidence is mixed, with some studies showing that white defendants are more likely to receive a death sentence, and others showing capital punishment is more likely for black defendants. Mostly, however, once the severity of the murder is taken into account, the defendant's race does not matter.

Procedural arrangements also suggest efforts to assure fair application of capital punishment. In 2002, nearly every jurisdiction that authorized the death penalty also provided for automatic appellate review of the conviction and/or sentence in capital cases. The appeal process, which in many jurisdictions goes forward regardless of the defendant's wishes, is meant to verify the fairness of the trial court's decision. It may include determining whether a death sentence was imposed arbitrarily or with prejudice, and whether aggravating circumstances were indeed present. Appellate courts also may conduct proportionality reviews to determine whether a death sentence in one case appears excessive or discriminatory compared to similar cases. Of course, whether these efforts truly result in fair application of death sentences is an empirical question. We now turn to the evidence that shows—convincingly—that fair administration of the death penalty in the United States is a myth.

The Truth or Facts

Mustering the facts on biased application of the death penalty can be complicated for four reasons. First, several discrete components interact to determine who is sentenced to death: whether to charge a defendant with a capital crime, whether to accept a guilty plea in exchange for a lesser sentence, what evidence is introduced, whether the existence of aggravating factors has been proven beyond a reasonable doubt, and so on. Bias may influence any decisions based on these components. Second, these decisions are spread among different people, most importantly prosecutors, judges, and jurors. Third, when disparities are revealed, it is important to consider whether they are truly attributable to extralegal factors or can be explained by differences in legitimate case characteristics. Fourth, the death penalty may be administered unfairly in numerous ways. Discrimination can be shown if similarly situated offenders are more or less likely to receive death sentences based on demographic characteristics. Unfairness also results if errors are made, such as when innocent people are sentenced to death or when there is a gap between how the law indicates capital sentences should be decided and actual decision-making. Below, several sources of unfair application are discussed separately.

Age

At issue is whether a defendant's age influences his or her chances of being sentenced to death. The available evidence suggests that it does. In a study of sentences for more than 5,000 homicides, Williams and Holcomb (2001) found that defendants over 25 years old were more than twice as likely as those 25 or younger to have a death sentence imposed. Their analysis accounted for a number of legally relevant variables, including the number of victims and whether the crime involved another felony. When the researchers restricted their analysis to cases likely to be eligible for capital punishment, offenders over 25 were almost three times more likely to receive the death penalty.

Sex

Capital punishment is almost exclusively reserved for male defendants. In 2002, they made up 98.6 percent of the total offenders under death sentences, and 96.9 percent of people admitted to death row. This situation would be expected if men committed nearly all of the murders in the country, but women account for about 12 percent of all homicides. Data on the proportion of capital (that is, death-eligible) murders committed by women are not available, so it is still possible that men are not overrepresented because of the type of murder they commit.

Studies that take other case characteristics into consideration, however, continue to show an increased chance of the death penalty for male offenders. Brock, Cohen, and Sorensen's (2000) analysis is typical. Female defendants accounted for 12.6 percent of all homicide arrests in their study, but only 1.2 percent of death sentences. Williams and Holcomb (2001) also uncovered gender effects, with male defendants being 2.6 times more likely to be sentenced to death once legally relevant factors were controlled.

Race

When the Supreme Court ruled in *Furman v. Georgia* that the death penalty was administered unconstitutionally, much of the criticism of capital punishment centered on race. Racial discrimination continues to be a central concern and the subject of most of the research on biased application of the death penalty.

As discussed above, the race of the defendant by and large has not been shown to influence who gets a death sentence in studies conducted after *Furman*. Race differences may be observed, but they tend to disappear once other factors are considered. Brock and his colleagues (2000), for example, found that death sentences were 1.4 times more likely for white defendants than expected from the racial distribution of homicide offenders in Texas. Once the seriousness of the offense was controlled, however, the defendant's race had no influence on the chances of a capital sentence.

Still, some evidence suggests that a defendant's race plays some role in particular decisions leading to capital punishment. Baldus and Woodworth (2003) reported that jurors were influenced by the defendant's race in their deliberations about aggravating and mitigating circumstances. After accounting for the influence of 22 legal case characteristics, the researchers found that jurors were 3.8 times more likely to decide that aggravating factors outweighed mitigating factors when the defendant was black. Baldus and Woodworth also reported that when prosecutors strike large numbers of blacks from capital juries, the death-sentence rate for black defendants is 2.6 times higher than for whites.

Also relevant to the discussion of racial bias is the race of the murder victim. On this issue, the evidence is clear: offenders who kill white victims are more likely to be sentenced to death than offenders who kill black victims. The GAO (1990) reported that in 82 percent of the studies it reviewed, the race of the victim influenced the chances that a defendant would be charged with a capital crime or would receive the death penalty. Baldus and Wood-

worth's (2003) review of studies conducted since 1990 revealed an even more consistent pattern of bias. In ten studies, the difference in the rate of charging and sentencing decisions for white and black victims ranged from 2.6 percentage points in Illinois to 29 percentage points in Maryland. In every study, "defendants in white-victim cases are at greater risk of a capital prosecution and of receiving a death sentence than are defendants in minority-victim cases" (Baldus and Woodworth 2003:203). Furthermore, seven of these studies provided additional analyses that accounted for differences in the offender's culpability. The white-victim bias remained in six of the seven studies.

It turns out that the victim-offender racial combination most likely to result in a death sentence is when someone who is black kills someone who is white. In a bivariate analysis of a series of separate decisions, Sorensen and Wallace (1999) found that a prosecutor was significantly more likely to file a first-degree murder charge, file notice to seek the death penalty, and advance the case to a capital trial when the defendant was black and the victim was white. Even when the influence of other case characteristics was taken into consideration—such as prior convictions for violence, multiple victims, and whether the victim was tortured—the significance of race was not eliminated. The probability that a case would advance to a capital trial was 2.5 times greater when a black person killed a white person than with other racial combinations. Thus, not only does the victim's race influence the administration of capital punishment but, when taken in combination, the defendant's race does as well.

Geographic Area

If the severity of punishment is to be based on the offense committed, it is fundamentally unfair for two identical crimes to result in different sentences for the offenders. This is precisely what can happen under present death-penalty practices in the United States. Currently, 36 states, the federal government, and the military have statutes authorizing capital punishment. The remaining 14 states and the District of Columbia do not. Thus, someone who commits an aggravated murder in Texas, for example, can face execution, while someone committing the same murder in Michigan cannot.

States that have the death penalty also vary in the extent to which it is used. Table 19.1 lists the ten states with the largest number of inmates currently on death row, and the ten states with the smallest number. Clearly, there is considerable variation in how many offenders each state has under sentences of death. Five states—California, Texas, Florida, Pennsylvania, and North Carolina—account for more than half of all death-row inmates. It is often true that states with the largest numbers of death sentences have high numbers of murders, but this is not uniformly the case. Colorado, for example, has only 5 inmates on death row, but more murders were committed in Colorado in 2001 than in Ohio, Alabama, Arizona, or Georgia.

Executions also show disparity across jurisdictions with the death penalty. In 2002, 71 death-row inmates were executed in the United States. Twenty-seven jurisdictions that have capital-punishment laws did not carry out any of these executions. On the other hand, Texas accounted for nearly half of the inmates put to death. Texas has also carried out the most death sentences, by far, since 1977—289 executions. The next closest state is Virginia, having executed 87 prisoners. Eight jurisdictions have not executed anyone since they passed post-*Furman*

death-penalty laws. In short, the risk of being sentenced to capital punishment and of actually being executed is zero in jurisdictions without the death penalty. The risk is present in jurisdictions that have the death penalty, and it is much higher in some jurisdictions than in others.

A few researchers also have tried to determine whether the probability of a death sentence varies across geographic areas *within* states. Whether it is unfair for different states to use the death penalty differently could be challenged. A central concept of the American system of government is that the states should have some autonomy to create their own laws; thus, the value of states' rights might supersede the desire for equal punishment of offenders. No such discrepancy is present, however, for the application of capital punishment within a state. The same state statutes govern citizens in all cities and counties; therefore, punishments meted out should be equal throughout the state.

The evidence on whether administration of capital punishment varies within states is not completely consistent but suggests some disparity. In Texas, fewer death sentences were handed down in Dallas and more were imposed in Houston than would be expected based on the number of homicides committed in these areas. Once differences in the severity of murders were considered, however, variations among the major metropolitan areas of Texas largely disappeared (Brock, Cohen, and Sorensen 2000). In contrast, Williams and Holcomb's (2001) analysis of Ohio's death-sentencing patterns showed significant geographic variation, even when other case characteristics were taken into account. Controlling for the possible influence of offender and victim attributes, whether a felony or multiple victims were involved, and other factors,

Table 19.1
Most Active and Least Active Death Penalty States

| | In 2002 | | | |
	On Death Row	Admitted	Executed	Executed 1977–2002
California	614	14	1	10
Texas	450	37	33	289
Florida	366	10	3	54
Pennsylvania	241	9	0	3
North Carolina	206	7	2	23
Ohio	205	7	3	5
Alabama	191	11	2	25
Illinois	159	6	0	12
Arizona	120	1	0	22
Georgia	112	3	4	31
Connecticut	7	0	0	0
Nebraska	7	0	0	3
Montana	6	0	0	2
Colorado	5	0	0	1
New York	5	0	0	0
South Dakota	5	0	0	0
Kansas	5	2	0	0
New Mexico	2	1	0	1
Wyoming	2	0	0	1
New Hampshire	0	0	0	0

Source: Bonczar, Thomas P., and Tracy Snell. 2003. *Capital punishment, 2002.* Washington, DC: Bureau of Justice Statistics.

Williams and Holcomb found that defendants in urban areas were 2.3 times more likely than defendants in rural areas to be sentenced to death. Similarly, Baldus and Woodworth (2003:213) reported that prosecutors in urban areas of Nebraska "advance death-eligible cases to penalty trials at nearly twice the rate of their counterparts in greater Nebraska—59% v. 31%."

Errors in Capital Cases

Nothing could be less fair than sentencing someone to death when there are profound doubts about his or her guilt. At the

end of 2003, Nicholas Yarris was released from death row after 21 years. During his initial trial, blood-type testing of physical evidence supported his guilt in the murder of a 32-year-old woman. In 2000, tests of Yarris' DNA compared with DNA from the crime scene produced no matches, leaving no convincing evidence that he was guilty of the murder (Weinstein 2003).

If an error such as this is attributed to technology that was not originally available or is considered accidental, it is definitely unfortunate but not unfair. The volume of mistakes in capital cases, however, calls into question whether the death penalty is administered fairly. Liebman, Fagan, and West (2000) recently reported on error rates in capital cases between 1973 and 1995. After examining more than 5,700 cases, they observed that the courts "found serious, reversible error in nearly 7 of every 10 of the thousands of capital sentences that were fully reviewed" (Liebman, Fagan, and West 2000:i). Liebman and his colleagues (2000:124) concluded that their findings "reveal a capital punishment system collapsing under the weight of its own mistakes."

The reasons for these errors also indicate that "mistakes" sometimes result from intentional actions, and often result from failures to take action. The explanations for why some people are wrongfully convicted or wrongfully sentenced in capital cases, as summarized by Bohm (2003), include poor police investigations, witnesses who perjure themselves, and confessions that are the product of coercion or manipulation. Bohm also observed that defense attorneys in capital cases are frequently inexperienced and ineffective. Some attorneys fail to investigate or even become acquainted with their clients' cases, some sleep during the trial, and some even fail to call a single witness in their client's defense. In other cases, prosecutors are at fault: withholding evidence that casts doubt on the defendant's guilt, making statements to the jury that might bias them toward imposing a death sentence, striking people from the jury who might hesitate to vote for capital punishment, and other acts of misconduct (Burnett 2002). Under such circumstances, it is surprising that estimates of the percent of people executed who were actually innocent reach only about 5 percent (see Bohm 2003).

Problems With Capital Juries

Recall that in its decision in *Furman*, the Supreme Court ruled the death penalty was unconstitutional because its administration was arbitrary, owing largely to the unfettered discretion of juries. When the revised statutes, which included guidance on what factors juries should consider and how capital sentences were to be decided, were reviewed by the court, it held that on "their face these procedures seem to satisfy the concerns of *Furman*" (*Gregg v. Georgia* 1976:128). Evidence shows, however, that the justices were too optimistic.

Bowers and Foglia (2003) summarized the results from the Capital Jury Project. This effort involved interviews with more than 1,200 people who had served on capital juries in 14 states, and it confirmed many findings of previous studies. Problems with juries and capital-punishment procedures were uncovered in seven general areas. First, jurors tend to make decisions about the appropriate sentence prematurely. Nearly half of the jurors interviewed reported having decided on the sentence before the penalty phase of the trial began and, thus, before they heard about any aggravating or mitigating factors. Second, jurors were selected in such a way that those inclined to impose a death sentence were overrepresented. More than half believed capital punishment was the only acceptable sentence for certain types of murder, and one in ten admitted that the jury-selection process had led them to believe the defendant was guilty and death was the appropriate punishment. Third, jurors did not understand the instructions on how to decide whether a capital sentence was appropriate. Large percentages failed to comprehend that they could consider any mitigating evidence, that mitigation does not need to be proven beyond a reasonable doubt, and that "beyond a reasonable doubt" is the standard of proof required for aggravating factors.

The difficulties observed by Bowers and Foglia (2003) did not end there. A fourth problem was that juries frequently believed—incorrectly—that the law required a death sentence. Fifth, and relatedly, the jurors largely felt that the choice of punishment was out of their hands. When asked, the jurors placed most responsibility for sentencing on the defendant (because of his or her behavior) and the law (because it establishes what punishment applies). Thus, the jurors believed the death penalty was mandatory, which the Supreme Court has held to be unconstitutional because mandatory capital sentences remove all opportunity to consider mitigating factors.

A sixth problem revealed by the Capital Jury Project returns us to the issue of race. Bowers and Foglia (2003:76) noted that "both the racial composition of the jury and the race of individual jurors influence capital decisions." In cases where the defendant was black and the victim was white, death sentences were imposed more than twice as often if the jury included at least five white males. Having at least one black male on the jury cut the chances of a capital sentence nearly in half.

Finally, the Capital Jury Project showed that jurors tend to underestimate the severity of nondeath alternative punishments. In every state, the average estimate of the number of years in prison a juror thought murderers not sentenced to death would serve was less than the mandatory minimum sentence established in that state.

The findings of the Capital Jury Project are wide ranging and convincing. They show that juries' sentencing discretion, in practice, is often not guided by the kind of structure the Supreme Court affirmed in *Gregg*. Furthermore, in every instance of jury problems documented by the study, the process was biased in the direction of more death sentences. Decisions made before hearing evidence, failure to understand how to render a judgment on sentencing, and other problems noted above cannot produce a death penalty system that is administered fairly.

Interests Served by the Myth

The myth that the death penalty is administered fairly promotes retention of this form of punishment. The death penalty can be criticized on several grounds. It is not cost effective, does not deter crime, is immoral, or is unfair. For those who want the option of sentencing murderers to death, the myth of fairness removes one challenge to the legitimacy of this punishment.

Although complex opinion research demonstrates that many Americans prefer life imprisonment over death sentences for most homicide offenders, polls of global attitudes reveal that nearly three-quarters of the public embrace the option of capital punishment in principle. A national poll conducted in May 2003 showed that 74 percent of U.S. citizens favor the death penalty for people convicted of murder (Jones 2003). The myth of fairness furthers the interests of those who wish to retain capital punishment.

Policy Implications of Belief in the Myth

Believing capital punishment is administered fairly means that further efforts to make it fair are unnecessary. Implicitly, the conclusion is that the procedures put in place in the wake of the Supreme

Court's *Furman* decision have resulted in unbiased, rational application of the death penalty. In short, the myth is that the system is not broken and, therefore, it does not need to be fixed.

Believing the death penalty is administered fairly also allows the punishment to continue to be used. Logically, the United States cannot value fair punishment and accept that capital punishment is meted out unfairly, and then continue to sentence offenders to death. Turning away from the evidence, however, allows us to retain our values and the option of executing people for murder. Fear of losing a punishment that appears to be embraced by so many American citizens is strong motivation to disregard the facts.

Ignoring fairness concerns is not the only option, however. Noting errors in death sentencing and the possibility of innocent people being put to death, Illinois' then-governor George Ryan imposed a moratorium on executions in 2000. Illinois' new governor, Rod Blagojevich, has continued the moratorium. These actions demonstrate it is possible to reconsider the quality of justice in capital cases. In most jurisdictions, however, defendants continue to be sentenced to death, and those sentences continue to be carried out despite evidence that the system is not fair.

Note

1. Some crimes other than homicide are specified as death-eligible. For example, federal and some state statutes allow the death penalty for treason or trafficking in large quantities of drugs. Currently, however, no one convicted of a crime other than murder is under a death sentence in the United States.

References

Baldus, D. C., and G. Woodworth. 2003. Race discrimination in the administration of the death penalty: An overview of the empirical evidence with special emphasis on the post-1990 research. *Criminal Law Bulletin* 39:194–226.

Bohm, R. M. 2003. *Deathquest II: An introduction to the theory and practice of capital punishment in the United States*. Cincinnati: Anderson.

Bonczar, T. P., and T. Snell. 2003. *Capital punishment, 2002*. Washington, DC: Bureau of Justice Statistics.

Bowers, W. J., and W. D. Foglia. 2003. Still singularly agonizing: Law's failure to purge arbitrariness from capital sentencing. *Criminal Law Bulletin* 39:51–86.

Brock, D., N. Cohen, and J. Sorensen. 2000. Arbitrariness in the imposition of death sentences in Texas: An analysis of four counties by offense seriousness, race of victim, and race of offender. *American Journal of Criminal Law* 28:43–71.

Burnett, C. 2002. *Justice denied: Clemency appeals in death penalty cases*. Boston: Northeastern University Press.

Furman v. Georgia. 1972. 408 U.S. 238.

Gregg v. Georgia. 1976. 428 U.S. 153.

Jones, J. M. 2003. Support for the death penalty remains high at 74 percent. Gallup News Release (May 19). Accessed online May 24, 2003: *http://www.gallup.com*.

Liebman, J. F., J. Fagan, and V. West. 2000. *A broken system: Error rates in capital cases, 1973–1995*. New York: Columbia University School of Law.

Sorensen, J., and D. H. Wallace. 1999. Prosecutorial discretion in seeking death: An analysis of racial disparity in the pretrial stages of case processing in a midwestern county. *Justice Quarterly* 16:559–579.

U. S. General Accounting Office (GAO). 1990. *Death penalty sentencing: Research indicates pattern of racial disparities*. Washington, DC: U.S. General Accounting Office.

Weinstein, H. 2003. DNA tests clear Pennsylvania capital inmate after 21 years. *Los Angeles Times* December 10:I15.

Williams, M. R., and J. E. Holcomb. 2001. Racial disparity and death sentences in Ohio. *Journal of Criminal Justice* 29:207–218. ✦

Chapter 20
The Myth of Closure and Capital Punishment

James R. Acker

President Bush hopes the execution of Timothy J. McVeigh . . . "will bring closure" for the survivors of the 1995 Oklahoma City bombing, the president's spokesman [Ari Fleischer] said. . . .

(Turner 2001:A12)

I don't think anything can bring me any peace. When I die and they lay me in my grave is when I'll have closure. That's when I'll stop grieving for my daughter.

> Mother of Oklahoma City
> bombing victim, after
> witnessing the execution
> of Timothy McVeigh
> (Bartels 2001:A24)

The Myth

Numerous justifications have been offered in support of capital punishment, many of which date back centuries before the death penalty was brought to colonial America. Some reasons for embracing capital punishment, such as those grounded in religion or strict interpretations of retributive justice, defy rational refutation; they are founded on faith or normative beliefs. Other supporting rationale, including general deterrence, the need to protect society from dangerous repeat offenders, and asserted savings of tax dollars compared to lengthy imprisonment, involve objectively testable premises. These latter, empirically-based arguments almost unexceptionally have been undermined by research, thereby causing death-penalty proponents either to ignore or discount the evidence, or else propose different justifications.

As traditional reasons for supporting capital punishment are weakened or discredited, new ones quickly spring to life or old ones are resurrected after having temporarily lost prominence. Justifying the death penalty in the name of providing "closure" for the family members and loved ones of murder victims is one such currently popular notion. A recent national opinion poll reported that 60 percent of respondents agreed that "The death penalty is fair because it gives satisfaction and closure to the families of murder victims" (Zimring 2003:61). Although references to closure have saturated contemporary media accounts of executions (Gross and Matheson 2003:490), the term first surfaced in the lexicon of capital punishment only in 1989 (Zimring 2003:58). Notwithstanding its recurrent usage, the concept of closure remains remarkably ill-defined.

At a minimum, closure connotes an ending, a sense that an event or stage in life finally has been brought to a close. But surely the term cannot signify the ending of a survivor's grieving or sense of loss in the aftermath of a loved one's murder, a resolution that can only be described as "an illusory hope" (Spungen 1998:239). No one can responsibly maintain that an offender's execution somehow compensates for the death of a child, a spouse, a parent, or any other victim of a homicide. Survivors cannot reclaim their loved ones—the one thing they so desperately want—through criminal punishment, however administered. At the same time, closure must mean something more than the mere termination of legal proceedings, which could be brought about much more swiftly and decisively by imposing virtually any punishment other than death. The concept of closure suggests that some measure of emotional relief, and perhaps satisfaction, is evoked by an execution. In that respect, it represents an uncertain mix of sentiments, including those that justice has been discharged, anger sated, fears comforted, and other deep-seated and perhaps inexpressible feelings released (Bandes 2000). Whatever its precise definition, its unambiguously therapeutic connotations herald closure as a useful and desirable outcome of the capital-punishment process for murder victims' grieving survivors.

The Kernel of Truth

Nothing is more devastating than murder's toll. In addition to the victim's death, life will never again be the same for survivors. Criminal homicide victims in the United States leave behind, on average, seven to ten close relatives (Vandiver 1998:478). A murderer's actions, of course, extend well beyond families to encompass friends, acquaintances, and sometimes entire communities. Historically, legal systems have responded to murder mindful of its catastrophic social consequences. Ancient English law developed an elaborate tariff system that required a slayer and his or her kin to pay monetary damages (known as *wergild*) to the deceased's kin, or else face retaliatory vengeance in the form of a blood feud that could ravage families for generations.

Only gradually did organized government displace private parties in dispensing justice for killings by substituting official punishment for private compensation and feuding (Holdsworth [1936] 1963:35). In some societies, murder victims' survivors continue to be given a direct role in determining punishment. For example, Islamic law allows a victim's family to decide whether the murderer will be executed or instead spared capital punishment through the payment of "blood money"— a settlement called *diyya*—(Postawko 2002:301).

The American criminal justice system evolved from the English tradition and now relies exclusively on impartial judges and jurors to sentence offenders pursuant to legal standards, rather than entrusting crime victims with the power to decide punishment. Some critics have argued that the pendulum has swung too far in the direction of impersonalized justice, and that crime victims, including murder victims' survivors, have been denied a proper voice in prosecution, sentencing, and other decisions affecting criminal cases. An outcry of support for greater legal protections for crime victims swept the nation during the 1970s and 1980s, producing widespread statutory and state constitutional reforms guaranteeing victims the right to be notified about and participate in the legal proceedings important to their cases. With the country awash in the victims' rights movement, the U.S. Supreme Court overturned two of its earlier decisions and ruled that the Constitution permits testimony during capital sentencing hearings about the trauma and other murder-related harms experienced by victims' family members (*Payne v. Tennessee* 1991). The notion that the death penalty helps bring closure to murder victims' families arose during this same time period.

There is no doubt that crime victims for too long were shunted aside or mistreated by many criminal justice officials, who were more intent on disposing of cases according to their own schedules and priorities than providing victims with respectful treatment and support. Through their indifference or insensitivity, the police, prosecutors, judicial personnel, parole boards, and other officials too often unwittingly inflicted a "second wound" on victims of crime. Victims routinely were not apprised, let alone consulted, before critical decisions were made in the cases that so directly affected them. They complained that they felt marginalized, alienated, and that they inexplicably were given fewer rights than the defendants who were accused of committing crimes against them. They felt frustrated and hurt, even "revictimized" by the very system that was supposed to achieve justice for law-abiding people, as well as accused criminals.

Negative sentiments of this nature can be especially pronounced in murder cases, where emotions are particularly raw and case outcomes so consequential. After experiencing the intense grief, pain, anger, fear, and general disequilibrium occasioned by a murder, along with recurrent gruesome reminders of their loved one's death as cases slowly wend through trials and appeals, it is not surprising that victims' family members may be in desperate need of relief. It is understandable that some survivors are passionate supporters of capital punishment, feel cheated when an offender languishes for years on death row pending the completion of appeals (sometimes escaping execution), and report some measure of satisfaction when a death sentence ultimately is carried out. In other words, there is no denying that some murder victims' survivors have a deep psychological and emotional investment in capital punishment, and experience some relief—perhaps "closure"—when the offender who has caused them such a grievous loss is finally executed.

The Truth or Facts

To acknowledge that some victims' survivors may achieve a sense of closure through a murderer's execution is a far cry from providing a general justification for capital punishment based on this rationale. There are many reasons to resist such a generalization, which may not only be wrong but also dangerous. In reality, the capital punishment process is as likely to add further distress, disruption, and psychological damage to murder victims' loved ones as it is to bring them relief.

In the first place, only an infinitesimal percentage of murders culminate in an execution. In 2000, for example, a reported 13,227 arrests were made for murder and nonnegligent manslaughter, but only 229 offenders were added to the nation's death rows, and only 85 were executed (Pastore and Maguire 2002:342; Snell and Maruschak 2002:9, 11). The attrition reflected in these trends is imperfect because of time lags between arrest and sentencing and sentencing and execution; but since homicide rates have declined significantly over the years and the 2000 execution total is the second highest in nearly 50 years (Pastore and Maguire 2002:536), the emerging estimates are actually quite conservative. They suggest that roughly 1.7 percent of arrests for intentional criminal homicide result in a sentence of death, and that executions are even rarer, representing less than one percent (0.64 percent) of annual arrests. Alternatively stated, more than 98 percent of murder victims' survivors will never see the murderer of their loved one sentenced to death, and more than 99 percent will not experience the murderer's execution. Therefore, the promise of closure through an execution is clearly illusory for the overwhelming majority of murder victims' survivors.

There are many reasons why killings so rarely result in an execution. Although all criminal homicide, by definition, involves the death of a victim, a much smaller subset of killings qualify as capital murder. Additionally, prosecutors frequently choose not to pursue capital murder charges or a death sentence even when they can, opting instead to plea bargain or seek only a sentence of life imprisonment in order to conserve resources or because their cases have potential weaknesses. Even when an offender is convicted of a capital crime and a death sentence is sought, juries do not always oblige. For example, juries in federal death-penalty cases have regularly rebuffed prosecutors' efforts to secure capital sentences, returning death sentences in just 46 percent of federal capital trials from 1988 through 2000, and in only 15 percent of capital prosecutions during the first two and one-half years of the Bush administration—2001 through mid-2003 (Liptak 2003). Similarly, it is not uncommon for sentencing judges and juries to reject the death penalty in 50 percent or more of state capital trials, although there is considerable variation both within and between states (Baldus, Woodworth, and Pulaski, Jr. 1990:233; Liptak 2003).

Even if imposed, a capital sentence may never be carried out. Appellate courts reversed convictions and death sentences at a startlingly high rate (68 percent) in state cases in which offenders were sentenced to die between 1973 and 1995. Defendants were not resentenced to death in four out of five cases (82 percent) following reversals (Liebman, Fagan, and West 2000:i).

When a death sentence survives judicial review, there is still the possibility that a condemned offender will be spared through executive clemency. Although most notable because of its rarity in recent years, this discretionary power was invoked by outgoing Governor George Ryan in January 2003 to reduce the death sentences of all 167 condemned prisoners in Illinois to life imprisonment. When executions do occur, they inevitably are years removed from the time of the murder. Currently, the average delay between the imposition of sentence and an execution exceeds ten years (Snell and Maruschak 2002:12).

It strains credulity to justify capital punishment on its presumed ability to bring closure to murder victims' survivors when death sentences are handed out in fewer than 2 percent of intentional killings, later voided in roughly half of the cases in which imposed, and carried out—if at all—over a decade following the murder. Indeed, it would be difficult to design a system that is generally less satisfying to murder victims' survivors. For every family ostensibly gratified by an execution, 99 other families seemingly have reason to feel devalued, frustrated, and disappointed because their loved ones' murderers are not punished by death. And when utilized, the capital-punishment process, with its accompanying harsh glare of publicity, its setbacks and uncertainties, and its agonizingly long duration, cannot be easy for murder victims' survivors to endure. The "second wound" inflicted by the criminal justice system threatens to be intensely acute in the capital punishment context. The cruelest blow of all may ensue when, following years of anticipation, a survivor discovers that the pain of having lost a loved one lingers as strongly as ever after an execution takes place (Henderson 1998:601).

The myth of closure suffers from the further fatal assumption that the offender's execution is a desirable outcome for all murder victims' survivors. It is not. The parents, spouses, children, and siblings of some murder victims stand adamantly opposed to capital punishment (Cushing and Shaffer 2002; King 2003). Other families are divided, sometimes bitterly so, about whether the death penalty should be imposed for the slaying of one of their loved ones (Johnson 2003; King 2003:41, 72, 206). Crime victims are as variable in their reactions and coping mechanisms as any other individuals in any other context. It should not be surprising that their needs, and the best means for satisfying them, also differ. Far too little is known about these complex emotions and interpersonal dynamics to be able to state with assurance that executions bring beneficial closure to murder victims' family members. Such a gross generalization not only lacks supporting evidence, but, if acted on, could inflict further damage on already damaged individuals.

Interests Served by the Myth

The symbolism of closure evokes an image of parents grieving over the brutal murder of their beloved child, a widow anguishing over the slaying of her husband, and a remorseless killer who has manipulatively raised an endless stream of baseless legal claims designed only to thwart justice and keep the executioner at bay. The image evokes both sympathy and anger, and demands a response. The death penalty is the proposed solution. Ultimately, for the reasons previously noted, the promise of capital punishment will most likely prove empty, unfulfilling, or even injurious for past victims of criminal homicide and their survivors. Yet the rhet-

oric of closure remains appealing, because it transcends specific victims of past murders and instead is linked to abstract prospective victims of future homicides. The grieving parents and devastated spouse could be everyman and everywoman; they could be you and me. With our emotions thus laid bare, what is a more natural response to the fear, anger, unmitigated evil of the offender, and sheer monstrosity of the murder of an innocent person, than capital punishment?

Critics of the victims' rights movement have argued that politicians with a law-and-order agenda have much to gain by replacing the impersonal "government" or "state" with the face of a living, and all too vulnerable, human victim of violent crime. By making this substitution, they are able to box opponents of their crime-control policies (e.g., lengthy mandatory prison sentences, and cutting back on procedural safeguards such as the exclusionary rule and Miranda rights) into the difficult position of appearing to be coldly unsympathetic to the plight of injured victims. It is contended, in other words, that individual crime victims have been co-opted, exploited, and used to advance a conservative political agenda that in reality offers neither comfort nor a solution to their most immediate and pressing needs (cf., Dubber 2002; Henderson 1985).

This general strategy, it is suggested, can be asserted with a special vengeance in the context of capital punishment. Zimring (2003:ix) argues,

The proponents of capital punishment have engineered a symbolic transformation over the last two decades. We now tell ourselves that an executing government is acting in the interest of victims and communities rather than in a display of governmental power and dominance.

This symbolic transformation succeeds in giving "the horrifying process of human execution a positive impact that many citizens can identify with: closure, not vengeance" (Zimring 2003:62). With specific reference to the death penalty, Sarat (2001:41) similarly contends that

> The goal of victims and those who take up their cause is to repersonalize criminal justice so that the sentencer has to declare an alliance with either the victim or the offender. Criminal sentencing thus becomes a test of loyalty.

Focusing on the harm suffered by specific victims of murder and their survivors "personalizes death sentencing in just the way revenge personalizes all punishment" (Sarat 2001:52).

Many sincere and well-meaning people doubtlessly support capital punishment based at least in part on their belief that it helps bring closure to the grief-stricken survivors of murder victims. In the politically supercharged world of the victims' rights movement and the death penalty, however, there are skeptics who have put forth—in contemporary discourse about crime and punishment—a competing and less benign explanation for the saliency of closure. They suggest that closure, and its compelling association with relieving the pain and suffering experienced by murder victims' survivors, serves to advance the interests of those whose true priorities lie less with helping the past victims of crime than with implementing increasingly punitive policies consistent with their conservative crime-control agenda.

Policy Implications of Belief in the Myth

If executions are designed to help bring closure to murder victims' families, various legal policy implications follow. For example, some survivors may believe they will achieve even greater closure by directly witnessing the killer's execution. Brooks Douglass was shot and left for dead by two men who broke into his home and murdered his parents when he was 16 years old. He recovered and later was elected to the Oklahoma legislature, where he cosponsored a bill granting murder victims' family members the right to watch the execution of their loved one's murderer. After the law was enacted he stated,

> It is not retaliation or retribution that I seek in witnessing the execution of the man who killed my parents. It is closure. Closure on an era of my life which I never chose to enter. Closure on years of anger and hate. (Goodwin 1997–1998:588)

At least a dozen states now permit the close relatives of murder victims to witness the killer's execution, and corrections officials in many other states have discretion to allow such viewings (Janick 2000: 937). Several victims' family members watched Timothy McVeigh's execution in the federal death house in Terre Haute, Indiana in June 2001, and more than 230 others gathered in Oklahoma City to view the execution via closed-circuit television (Skaret 2002).

Other victim-centered proposals concerning capital punishment also are suggested. For example, noting the impact on murder victims' survivors, federal and state lawmakers have sought to shorten the delays between sentencing and execution by imposing strict time limits on death-penalty appeals. They also have curtailed judicial review of legal claims that were not raised or preserved at earlier stages of the legal process. While such measures might expedite executions and thus promote survivors' efforts to achieve closure, they risk compromising important procedural safeguards and also enhance the likelihood of grave miscarriages of justice. More than a hundred death-sentenced individuals during the past quarter-century have had their capital murder convictions overturned after evidence surfaced of their innocence. Many spent several years on death row and could have been executed had their appeals been expedited (Death Penalty Information Center 2003; Radelet and Bedau 1998). In addition to the consequences for innocent persons consigned to death row, the anguish of murder victims' survivors can only be exacerbated by the realization that the wrong person was convicted while the real killer of their loved one remained at large (Gross and Matheson 2003:505).

A capital punishment system driven by achieving closure for murder victims' survivors has even more radical implications. To provide maximum closure, for the greatest number of survivors, much more aggressive enforcement of death-penalty laws would be required to boost the present paltry ratio of less than one execution per every hundred murders. Capital prosecutions would have to increase dramatically, as would executions, which have not topped a hundred during any year since 1949 (Pastore and Maguire 2002:536). At the same time, murder victims' survivors should logically get much greater say in whether death sentences are sought and carried out, perhaps analogously to the Islamic tradition of allowing victims' families to decide whether a condemned murderer should be spared execution.

Exacerbating this issue are corollary implications for victims who are unmarried, childless, or otherwise leave no close surviving family members. If there are no identifiable survivors for whom closure is an issue, the impetus for seeking and carrying out a death sentence is substantially undercut. As Justice Powell explained while cautioning against the admission in capital sentencing hearings of testimony describing the sense of loss experienced by murder victims' survivors:

> [I]n some cases the victim will not leave behind a family, or the family members may be less articulate in describing their feelings even though their sense of loss is equally severe. . . . Certainly the degree to which a family is willing and able to express its belief is irrelevant to the decision whether a defendant, who may merit the death penalty, should live or die. (*Booth v. Maryland* 1987:505)

It goes without saying that the single-minded pursuit of achieving closure for victims' family members through capital punishment would raise the most serious issues of evenhanded justice and due process of law. An undeniable tension surfaces when laws enacted to serve the general public interest are administered with the needs of specific individuals in mind. The death penalty's principal ostensible benefits, including social protection (deterrence, incapacitation) and justice (retribution), are owed to all of society. Those objectives may cut at cross currents with the individual needs of murder victims' survivors who are struggling to cope with their losses. "Churches and cemeteries, and even therapists' offices are the approved sites for mourning and outrage, not courtrooms" (Sarat 2001:39). Nor should executions be promoted for those purposes.

The death-penalty process is at least as likely to prolong and disrupt the healing of murder victims' survivors as bring them satisfaction. Unlike death sentences, terms of imprisonment are imposed immediately following conviction and have a much greater degree of finality. Nor does imprisonment focus public attention on the offender—sometimes in the form of sympathy and sometimes through demeaningly gleeful celebrations—in the same manner that executions can inspire. Another particularly insidious consequence of relying on executions as a solution for murder victims' survivors is the deflection of energy and resources from initiatives that could provide significantly more meaningful services and support. For far too many unfortunate and grieving family members, the prospect of achieving closure through capital punishment is doomed to be futile and may have outright injurious consequences.

References

Baldus, D. C., G. G. Woodworth, and C. A. Pulaski, Jr. 1990. *Equal justice and the death penalty: A legal and empirical analysis.* Boston: Northeastern University Press.

Bandes, S. 2000. When victims seek closure: Forgiveness, vengeance and the role of government. *Fordham Urban Law Journal* 27:1566–1606.

Bartels, L. 2001. Emotions run deep in OKC: Timothy McVeigh's execution does not end the pain for relatives of bomb victims. *Rocky Mountain News* June 12.

Booth v. Maryland. 1987. 482 U.S. 496, overruled in part by *Payne v. Tennessee* (1991) 501 U.S. 808.

Cushing, R. R., and S. Shaffer. 2002. *Dignity denied: The experience of murder victims' family members who oppose the death penalty.* Cambridge, MA: Murder Victims' Families for Reconciliation.

Death Penalty Information Center. 2003. *Innocence and the death penalty.* Accessed online: *http://www.deathpenaltyinfo.org/article.php?did=412&scid=6.*

Dubber, M. D. 2002. *Victims in the war on crime: The use and abuse of victims' rights.* New York: New York University Press.

Goodwin, M. L. 1997–1998. An eyeful for an eye: An argument against allowing the families of murder victims to witness executions. *Brandeis Journal of Family Law* 36:585–608.

Gross, S. R., and D. J. Matheson. 2003. What they saw at the end: Capital victims' families

and the press. *Cornell Law Review* 88:486–516.

Henderson, L. N. 1985. The wrong of victim's rights. *Stanford Law Review* 37:937–1021.

———. 1998. Co-opting compassion: The federal victim's rights amendment. *St. Thomas Law Review* 10:579–606.

Holdsworth, W. [1936] 1963. *A history of English law.* Vol. II. London: Methuen & Co., Ltd.

Janick, D. 2000. Allowing victims' families to view executions: The Eighth Amendment and society's justifications for punishment. *Ohio State Law Journal* 61:935–977.

Johnson, S. L. 2003. Speeding in reverse: An anecdotal view of why victim impact testimony should not be driving capital prosecutions. *Cornell Law Review* 88:555–568.

King, R. 2003. *Don't kill in our names: Families of murder victims speak out against the death penalty.* New Brunswick, NJ: Rutgers University Press.

Liebman, J. S., J. Fagan, and V. West. 2000. *A broken system: Error rates in capital cases, 1973–1995.* Accessed online: *http://www2.law.columbia.edu/instructionalservices/liebman/liebman1.pdf.*

Liptak, A. 2003. Juries reject death penalty in nearly all federal trials. *New York Times* June 15.

Pastore, A. L., and K. Maguire, eds. 2002. *Bureau of Justice Statistics: Sourcebook of criminal justice statistics, 2001.* Washington, DC: U.S. Department of Justice.

Payne v. Tennessee. 1991. 501 U.S. 808.

Postawko, R. 2002. Towards an Islamic critique of capital punishment. *UCLA Journal of Islamic and Near Eastern Law* 1:269–320.

Radelet, M. L., and H. A. Bedau. 1998. The execution of the innocent. In *America's experiment with capital punishment: Reflections on the past, present, and future of the ultimate penal sanction,* eds. J. R. Acker, R. M. Bohm, and C. S. Lanier. Durham, NC: Carolina Academic Press.

Sarat, A. 2001. *When the state kills: Capital punishment and the American tradition.* Princeton, NJ: Princeton University Press.

Skaret, B. D. 2002. Victim's right to view: A distortion of the retributivist theory of punishment. *Journal of Legislation* 28:349–357.

Snell, T. L., and L. M. Maruschak. 2002. *Bureau of Justice Statistics bulletin: Capital punishment, 2001.* Washington, DC: U.S. Department of Justice.

Spungen, D. 1998. *Homicide: The hidden victims—a guide for professionals.* Thousand Oaks, CA: Sage Publications.

Turner, D. 2001. Bush hopes for 'closure' in McVeigh's execution. *The Buffalo News* May 4.

Vandiver, M. 1998. The impact of the death penalty on the families of homicide victims and of condemned prisoners. In *America's experiment with capital punishment: Reflections on the past, present, and future of the ultimate penal sanction,* eds. J. R. Acker, R. M. Bohm, and C. S. Lanier. Durham, NC: Carolina Academic Press.

Zimring, F. E. 2003. *The contradictions of American capital punishment.* New York: Oxford University Press. ✦

Section 4

Corrections

Chapter 21
The Myth That Punishment Reduces Crime

Raymond Michalowski

The Myth

Stated briefly, the myth of punishment is the belief that punishing criminals reduces crime. This myth is most commonly manifest in three interconnected propositions about crime and punishment:

1. The United State's crime problem is the result of being soft on crime.

2. Increasing the number of people behind bars will decrease the rate of crime.

3. Using prison to demonstrate a zero-tolerance attitude toward lawbreakers will reduce crime by improving the U.S.'s moral climate.

Like all myths, the punishment myth rests on deeply rooted cultural foundations, in this case two secular beliefs and one theological belief.

The first secular proposition is that humans are rational creatures driven by desires to maximize pleasure and minimize pain, and who therefore can be directed away from wrongful behavior by the threat of pain (Bentham 1962). Those who accept this rational-choice explanation for human behavior typically argue that increased punishment will reduce crime when the threat of punishment outweighs the pleasures of crime in the mind of po-tential lawbreakers. From this perspective, the harsher the punishment, the more likely it will deter crime.

The second secular proposition focuses on the ability of the justice system to exert direct control over lawbreakers through penalties such as execution and imprisonment (Zimring and Hawkins 1973). From this standpoint, the best way to reduce crime is to simply remove lawbreakers from society by killing them or sentencing them to lengthy periods of incarceration, thus incapacitating their ability to commit crime—in the latter case, at least against those outside U.S. prisons.

The theological proposition is rooted in the common-founding Abrahamic doctrines of Judaism, Christianity, and Islam, which imagine a world divided into forces of good and evil. Narratives of moral people who were rewarded by the God of Abraham and of wicked people who suffered from God's wrath dominate the Old Testament. Propunishment thinkers such as Bennett, DiIulio, and Walters (1996) argue that these ideas have burrowed into Western consciousness, emerging in the contemporary era as a belief that those who abide by the law are inherently moral and deserving of reward, while those who break it are fundamentally wicked and deserving of punishment. Moreover, because morality and wickedness are understood as underlying qualities of individuals, there is little expectation that the wicked can be redeemed. The grip of Old Testament ideology on modern crime-control policy is clearly reflected by James Q. Wilson, one of the intellectual architects of the "get tough on crime" ideology. Wilson (1975:209) concluded a detailed consideration of the U.S. crime problem by saying that "wicked people exist," and nothing avails except to "set them apart from innocent people."

Of course, few criminologists or other public figures openly articulate a biblical model for the U.S. justice system. However, whenever discussions about crime and criminals utilize the language of good and evil, these discussions are drawing upon the deep cultural inheritance of the vengeful God of Abraham portrayed in the Old Testament. This is the foundation of a belief that the more the United States punishes, the more moral it is as a society, and thus the less crime it will have.

The Kernel of Truth

All cultural myths are based on narratives with meaning that can be adapted to a wide variety of circumstances (Mattingly and Garro 2000). The myth that punishment reduces crime is no different. In the contemporary United States, for instance, people frequently make choices about their behavior. This is evident, for example, in decisions to postpone full-time employment in favor of attending college in order to earn higher salaries in the future; in the carefully calculated decisions of business investors; in the strategic political and military moves of the U.S. government; or in the hundreds of millions of decisions made every day as people decide to do one thing instead of another, to purchase one thing instead of another. So it seems reasonable to assume that this same rationality applies to the decision to commit a crime. After all, if an individual can be deterred from a life of leisure by the threat of poverty, why wouldn't criminals be deterred from crime by the threat of prison?

It would be foolish to say that the threat of punishment does not deter crime. Doubtless, the threat of life in prison without the possibility of parole would be an effective deterrent for parking illegally, or even, for that matter, shoplifting. On a more realistic level, many analysts of white-collar crime suggest prison sentences can be effective deterrents for corporate criminals because of the high degree of rational calculation involved in business-related crimes (Simpson 2002). Certainly, the existence of a functioning justice system that can arrest and punish offenders plays a real role in maintaining social order in modern societies. To confirm this, one need only observe the disorder and crime that emerges when police and judicial systems collapse, as they did in Iraq after the U.S. invasion toppled not only Saddam Hussein, but also all of the Iraqi criminal justice system (Mahajan 2003). The real question, as Zimring and Hawkins (1973) observed, is not whether some crimes are deterred by the threat of punishment, but rather which crimes, how many, and at what costs to society? The same can be said about incapacitation. Undoubtedly, some people in prison would have committed other crimes if they had been free. The question is how much crime is actually averted and at what costs.

As proof that more imprisonment is the way to a safer country, proponents of increased punishment frequently point to the fact that crimes against persons and property began to decline in the 1980s, just as imprisonment rates were increasing (see Figure 21.1). The claimed relationship between crime and punishment, however, is not nearly as straightforward as proponents of more imprisonment claim. Although increases in imprisonment appear to be associated with corresponding decreases in both property and violent crime from 1980 to 1984, the period of steepest increases in rates of imprisonment (1985–1991) coincided with increases in both property and violent crime. As Figure 21.2 shows, annual increases in punishment were often associated with decreases in crime, and at other times with increases in crime. From a statistical standpoint, annual changes in rates of imprisonment show only a weak correlation with annual changes in rates of violent crime. Whether one lags crime behind punishment by one or two years, increases in punishment explain less than 3 percent of changes in rates of violent crime.

The Truth or Facts

The real influence of punishment on crime is much more complex than the partial truths of the punishment myth. Consider the three main arguments for more punishment: deterrence, incapacitation, and moral inoculation.

Deterrence. Many people who endorse increased punishments for criminals in the United States do so because they believe the punishments meted out to lawbreakers are too soft to deter future crimes. The reality is that the United States is the most punitive country in the world. The rate of imprisonment in the United States is not only the highest in the world, it is many times greater than imprisonment rates in other developed, capi-

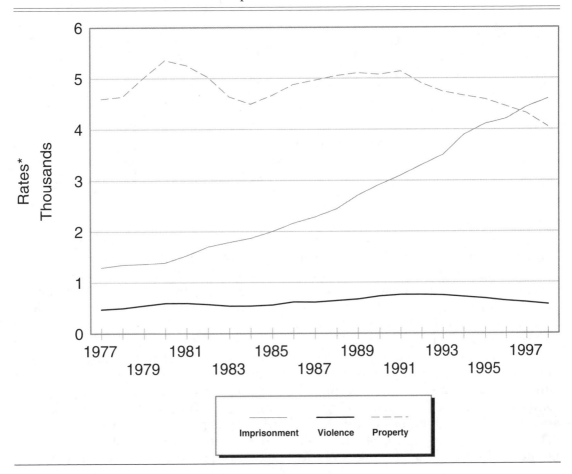

Figure 21.1
Crime and Imprisonment Rates 1977–1998

Figure 21.2
Crime and Punishment Rates Annual Change 1977–1998

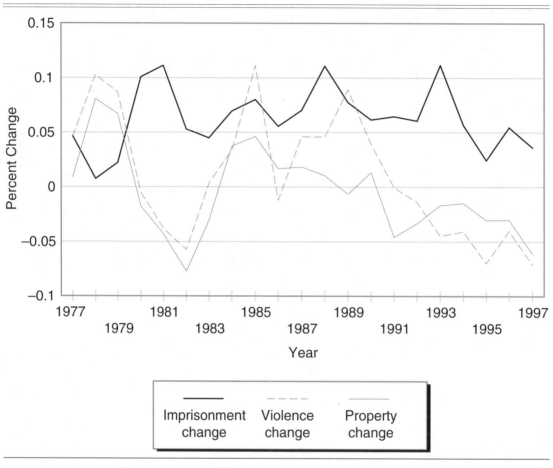

talist nations. As far back as the 1970s, the United States' rate of imprisonment has been two to three times higher than most European countries. By the late 1990s it was more than five times that of England, most countries of western Europe, and Japan. Even countries with long histories of repressive governments such as Russia, China, and South Africa lock up a smaller percentage of their citizens today than the United States, and yet the United States remains one of the most crime-plagued and crime-obsessed nations in the world (The Sentencing Project 1996). Although politicians and other public leaders have

been quick to claim that U.S. courts are too soft on criminals, the simple fact is that if more punishment meant less crime then the United States would be among those countries with the lowest crime rates in the world, not among those with the highest.

The weakness of the belief that more and harsher punishments will deter more crimes is that the deterrent potential of law depends upon the rationality of the lawbreaker. Only if an offender is capable of weighing the gains of crime against the costs of possible punishment will the threat of punishment exert a restraining force. Yet, many of the crimes the public fears the most—violent crimes—are not the result of rational calculation. Violence most often occurs in highly charged emotional situations such as conflicts between intimate partners, turf wars between youth gangs, or crimes that were supposed to be nonviolent but went horribly wrong in the doing, often because the offender panicked. This disconnect between punishment and crime is readily apparent when the relationship between punishment and the decline in murder in the United States is examined.

Homicide rates for adults over the age of 25 began a period of steady decline in 1980. By contrast, homicide rates for adolescents and young adults under 25 years of age rose steadily from the early 1980s until 1994, even though these youthful offenders faced an increased likelihood of prosecution in adult courts if they were juveniles, imprisonment when convicted, and life-without-parole sentences for homicide. Despite this increase in potential punishment, youth violence did not begin to decline until 1994, almost 15 years after adult homicide rates began their steady decline. This suggests that factors other than rates of imprisonment—particularly the crack cocaine epidemic of the 1980s—may better explain the 15-year lag between declines in the rate of adult versus youth homicide.

The rise and decline in youth homicide followed the evolution of markets for illegal drugs, particularly crack cocaine (Brownstein 1996). The emergence of new illegal markets typically leads to increased violence as competing groups battle for control of distribution networks, particularly if the demand is high and the profits lucrative. As some of the groups engaged in this conflict defeat others, becoming larger and more powerful in the process, distribution networks become more organized and less violent. The timing of the rise of youth violence in the 1980s and its decline in 1990s is more consistent with the emergence, conflict, and stabilization of crack markets, first in big cities and somewhat later in smaller ones, than it is with the timing of increases in punishment (Blumstein and Wallman 2000; Cook and Laub 2002).

Equally problematic for the deterrence hypothesis is the fact that adult homicide began to decline before the rise in punishment. The explanation again lies beyond penal policy. A significant component of the overall decline in rates of homicide among adults was a reduction in domestic homicides. Some analysts have suggested that one of the factors behind this reduction was the expansion of hotlines, shelters, judicial protection orders, and other domestic-violence resources in the 1980s and 1990s, which provided assistance to victims of domestic violence (Dugan, Nagin, and Rosenfeld 2003). Although some researchers have suggested that the link between increases in assistance to domestic-violence victims and reductions in domestic homicides is difficult to verify in specific urban settings (Websdale 1999), the decline in domestic homicide at the same time intervention strategies for domestic violence were increasing certainly asks that we consider whether domestic homicide rates may reflect much more than penal policy. Nor were domestic-violence prevention strategies the only changes taking place at the same time that the United States was beginning its late twentieth-century obsession with punishment. In the early 1980s, many cities began deploying rapid-response trauma teams that were better able to keep gunshots, stab wounds, and beatings from developing into homicides. This, along with overall reductions in emergency response times, may have also contributed to the decline in homicide rates that began prior to increases in severity of punishment.

Incapacitation. As a crime-control strategy, incapacitation depends upon the belief that society is divided into law abiding citizens who would never break the law, and criminals who will continue breaking it until they are taken off the streets. This idea that crime is caused by a fixed criminal element underestimates the role of "worker" replacement in many crimes. Replacement is the product of two characteristics shared by different types of crime: first, most crimes are not solitary acts, and second, many crimes are part of markets.

Criminologists have long known that few lawbreakers, whether street or corporate criminals, act alone. Lawbreaking typically emerges out of an interaction within social groups in which people learn the means and motivations for engaging in crime (Sutherland and Cressey 1960). It has also been long understood that crime-inducing social groups select people to be part of the group (Cloward and Ohlin 1960). The arrest and punishment of one member of a crime-generating social group will not necessarily reduce the overall criminal activity within the group's social network. Instead, it will increase the likelihood that someone else will be drawn into the group to fill the vacant space created by the justice system when it removed one or more group members.

Replacement patterns are also influenced by the market nature of certain crimes. Drug dealers, for instance, do not cause drug dealing. A market for drugs causes drug dealing. As drug dealers are arrested and placed behind bars, others will take over their job. As long as there is a demand for illicit drugs, there will be merchants who will try to profit from meeting that demand. The same thing is true in less obvious markets. Burglary, for instance, is an economically profitable crime only if there is a viable market for stolen goods. The stolen goods market, like any market, has limits. If too many stolen televisions, computers, cars, or other items flood the illegal market, or if the store prices of these items drop significantly, their value as stolen goods falls below an attractive profit level, resulting in fewer burglaries. On the other hand, if the value of the stolen goods remains high and their supply low, there will be a corresponding tendency for burglary rates to grow. It is quite possible that the steady fall in burglary rates since the 1990s occurred, in part, because the retail prices of stolen electronics such as stereos, computers, and color televisions—prime targets for burglars in the 1970s and early 1980s—had dropped to a point where they brought a much less attractive return than they did 20 years earlier.

When considering justice policies, it is always important to be aware of unintended effects. Penal policies oriented toward incapacitating offenders may unintentionally increase the number of individuals engaged in criminal activity by increasing the rate of replacement. To the extent that incapacitating offenders creates opportunities for others to take their place, incapacitation may expand, rather than decrease, overall criminality in society.

Moral inoculation. An important element of the punishment myth for many politically conservative thinkers is that the swift and harsh use of the penal system will improve the national moral climate, making the United States a better, safer place. Certainly, the larger the percentage of people who feel morally constrained to abide by the law, the less crime we are likely to have. The real question is whether punishment increases moral sentiments among the public.

Because the idea of moral sentiments refers to an internal, spiritual state of affairs, the actual operations of morality on crime are impossible to observe, and therefore difficult to prove or disprove. Additionally, the reasoning of moral inoculationists tends to be tautological. It goes something like this: Moral bankruptcy is the cause of crime. The United States is suffering from moral bankruptcy, and we know this because of its high rates of crime (Bennett, DiIulio, and Walters 1996). In a perfectly circular fashion, the outcome (high crime) proves the supposed cause (moral bankruptcy), rendering the argument both intellectually and practically worthless.

The important question raised by the moral-inoculation argument is whether increasing punishment leads to improved moral sensibilities in society. Although difficult to prove, there are some reasons to suspect that increasing punishment may coarsen rather than refine moral sentiments in a society. Findings that murders tend to increase shortly after widely publicized executions suggest that some people may take the wrong message from state-authorized violence (Bowers 1988). More than three centuries ago, the English philosopher Jeremy Bentham (1962) observed that when we punish someone, although we may derive benefit from doing so, we are nevertheless doing violence to the person we punish. If we are serious about wanting to make the United States a less violent society, we need to seriously consider whether imposing harsh punishments on all those who break the law sends the wrong message: It is appropriate to do violence to those who bother us.

Interests Served by the Myth

As discussed above, from the late 1970s onward, politically conservative leaders and politicians became increasingly emphatic about the need to increase criminal punishments to protect the public from crime. There is growing evidence that this political rhetoric played an important role in creating the fear of crime, rather than being a response to a fear that already existed (Beckett 1997). The important question is why so many public figures made rhetorical moves in the direction of endorsing the punishment myth. To understand this, we need to put the explosion in punishment in historical context.

The 1960s and 1970s were characterized by significant social change, which challenged the dominant ideology of U.S. society. The widespread introduction of oral contraceptives significantly reduced the fear of pregnancy for women and men, resulting in a sexual revolution that challenged the long established, even if often violated, principle that sex should occur only between people who were married to each other. As beneficiaries of the material influx that followed the end of World War II, many white, middle-class youths began to challenge the work ethic of preceding generations (McWilliams 2000; Allyn 2000). The idea that life should be a long period of unremitting toil for some corporation, followed by a few years of old-age retirement (if one was lucky), was increasingly being replaced in some segments of youth society by a more Dionysian view that the purpose of life was to enjoy pleasure in the present (Riggenbach 1998). The combination of women seeking greater equality (and employers seeking larger and thus more easily exploitable workforces) led to changes in labor laws, which increased the presence of women in previously all-male work settings, as well as to liberalization in laws making it easier for married couples to obtain no-fault divorces. Finally, and perhaps most unsettling for cultural conservatives, the United States was shaken by a powerful tide of civil-rights reforms (Raines 1977). These changes, or more accurately the cultural anxiety they created, played a pivotal role in stimulating the mythology of punishment.

American society is predicated on a deep belief in rationality. Capitalism, the central structural element of U.S. society, rests on the notion of *homo economus*, the idea that people are constantly engaged in the rational calculation of the costs and benefits of any potential action. Likewise, the religious foundations of U.S. culture presume rational individuals are kept away from doing wrong by threats of punishments in hell and promises of rewards in heaven. Proponents of rationality fear pleasure because pleasure is about the present. Rationality is about the future, about what will be the consequences of one choice versus another.

The 1960s and 1970s challenged the dominant role of rationality in U.S. culture. The rise of youth subcultures that seemed more interested in sex, drugs, and rock and roll than in preparing for a life of work; hysterical fears that easier divorce would lead to a break down of the family; and the emerging influence of women and African Americans—who the dominant culture associated with irrationality—seemed to threaten rationality as the centerpiece of the dominant myth of human nature. At the same time, the everyday reality of a diminishing work ethic was also wearing thin. By the late 1970s, the postwar economic boom was over, and good jobs were disappearing faster than they were being created (Gordon, Edwards, and Reich 1982; Harrison and Bluestone 1988). For many adults, hard work was no longer paying off (Davis 1986; MacLeod and Alger 1980). This reality created an additional difficulty for business and governmental leaders who believed the way

out of America's economic slump was to increase worker productivity by getting workers to produce more for less (Kotz, McDonough, and Reich 1994).

Faced with threats to the prominent belief in rationality, social conservatives of all sorts rallied to reinforce the cultural foundation. Most of the changes taking place, however, were either happening beyond the control of lawmakers, or, like laws extending civil rights and women's equality, were changes that could not easily be rolled back. Crime was one area, however, where old-school beliefs could be enforced without fear of significant political backlash.

Because the punishment myth rests heavily on the ideal of rationality, the ideology of rehabilitation, which had dominated penal policy from the 1940s through the 1960s, was not a good ally for promoting a rationalist vision of society. The ideal of rehabilitation rests on psychological and sociological paradigms that treat behavior less as a matter of choice and more as a matter of circumstances beyond the individual's control, which is precisely the opposite of rational-choice explanations of human behavior.

I am not suggesting the cultural leaders, academics, and politicians who spearheaded the legal changes that led to the sharp rise in America's prison populations consciously grasped these connections. What I am suggesting is that for many who cherished established cultural ideals based on rationality, the 1960s and 1970s were a time of confusion and fear. There was a sense in the writings of the time that the culture was coming apart (McDarrah, McDarrah, and McDarrah 2003). Faced with challenges they only vaguely understood, many grabbed at the one solid thing they could, the justice system's ability to punish, and thereby reestablish rationality as a core mythic construct in American culture.

Policy Implications of Belief in the Myth

During the last three decades of the twentieth century, the rate and number of people being sentenced to prison in the United States grew more rapidly than at any time in the nation's history. In 1977, 129 of every 100,000 U.S. residents were serving time in state and federal penitentiaries. Twenty-five years later, by year-end 2002, the rate of imprisonment had more than tripled, to 476 out of every 100,000 U.S. residents. Because the overall U.S. population was growing at the same time, a tripling of the rate of imprisonment resulted in a prison population that was five times larger than it had been 25 years earlier. In 1977, 285,000 people were behind bars in state and federal penitentiaries. By 2002, this figure had grown to 1.4 million prisoners.

From 1998 to 2002, the growth in the imprisonment rate and prison populations slowed to an average of 3 additional prisoners per 100,000 population each year, as compared to an average of 23 additional prisoners per 100,000 population in the previous ten years. During the 1998 to 2002 period, the annual growth in the number of people in prison experienced a similar slowdown: 31,000 additional prisoners per year as compared to 67,000 per year during the previous decade. Although the speed at which the U.S. prison population is growing has slowed somewhat in recent years, it is important to remember that America's prison population is still growing faster now than it did in the years before the imprisonment binge of the 1980s and 1990s (Austin 2001).

Rates of imprisonment and prison populations are only one part of America's penal apparatus. If we add the number of people in local jails to the number serving time in state and federal penitentiaries, the rate of incarceration grows in 2002 to 701 per every 100,000 individuals. If we include the number of people on probation and parole, the rate of penal supervision rises to 2,321 of every 100,000 people—or more succinctly, in 2002, 1 out of every 43 people in the United States was under some form of penal control.

The recent reliance on imprisonment as the penal strategy of choice represents a significant departure from earlier correctional practices. As Figure 21.3 shows, from 1925 until the late 1970s, the rate at which people were incarcerated in the United States grew very little. Overall, the rate of imprisonment appeared so constant that some criminologists had begun to theorize that rates of punishment tend to stabilize over time (Blumstein and Cohen 1973; Hale 1989). Then suddenly, this long-standing pattern shifted dramatically in the direction of increased punishment. This sudden rise in the use of imprisonment in the United States was the direct consequence of the previously discussed "get tough with crime" ideology that came to dominate crime-control rhetoric in the late 1970s and early 1980s.

This move away from rehabilitation and toward punishment as a primary justice-system strategy represented a change in what had been the dominant correctional ideology. For instance, former director of the U.S. Bureau of Prisons Norman Carlson (1974:39) observed that for most of the twentieth century, justice professionals, behavioral scientists, and ordinary citizens understood that the primary purpose of the criminal justice system was to make society safer by rehabilitating offenders. He went on to note that after the 1971 uprising in the state penitentiary in Attica, New York, there was widespread

Figure 21.3
Rate of U.S. Imprisonment 1925–2002

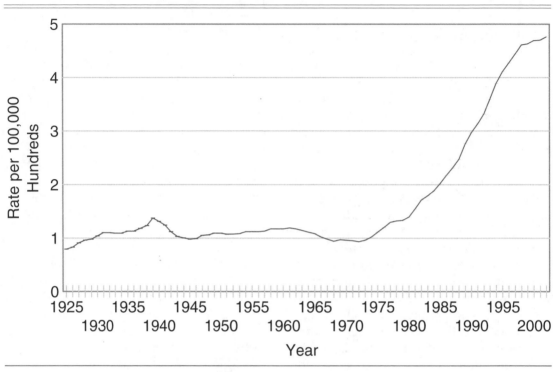

public demand for complete prison reform with even more emphasis on rehabilitation programs. That same year, policy analyst Norval Morris (1974) predicted a future in which postconviction responses to offenders would be increasingly shaped by the goal of rehabilitation. Yet, less than a decade later, the ideal of rehabilitation was politically dead, as legislators around the country scrambled to endorse longer and harsher punishments for criminal offenders (Davey 1998).

The legislative rush to implement the new "get tough" ideology produced two major changes in penal law and policy. The first change was the move by many state legislatures and the federal government to make deterrence, incapacitation, and retribution—instead of rehabilitation—the primary purposes of criminal

sanctions (Austin and Irwin 2000; Chambliss 2000; Currie 1998; Danner 2002; Fogel 1979; Greenberg and Humphries 1980). Guided by the ideology of a "just deserts" model of punishment (Fogel 1979), state and federal politicians began increasing maximum sentence lengths for violent and nonviolent crimes, establishing sentencing guidelines that required a mandatory minimum amount of time be spent behind bars by even the most promising candidates for rehabilitation, and passing strict habitual offender statutes, such as California's "three strikes" law (Currie 1998; Danner 2002; Greenberg and Humphries 1980). These legal changes increased rates of imprisonment by denying judges the discretion to use less punitive options for offenders who in the past might have been given shorter sentences or placed in some form of community supervision, such as probation, mandatory drug treatment, or some other rehabilitative program. They also increased the size of prison populations by ensuring that, not only would more people be sent to prison, but once there they would stay for longer periods of time.

The second important change in justice policy that influenced prison rates and populations was the transformation of the war on crime into a war on drugs (Drug Policy Alliance 2004a, 2004b). By the mid-1980s, police and prosecutors, armed with punishment-oriented, mandatory minimum-sentencing policies, began to focus on drug users and drug dealers, particularly those who were young, male, poor, and not white (Chambliss 2000; Mauer 1999). As a consequence, a significant portion of the rise in imprisonment was driven by a rise in drug arrests and sentences. Overall, drug offenders accounted for 36 percent of the growth in state prison populations and 71 percent of the growth in the federal prison population. Moreover, a substantial proportion of that rise resulted from the significant overrepresentation of young, African-American men among those sentenced to prison on drug-related charges (The Sentencing Project 2002).

There is considerable debate about why this increase occurred, and even more debate about its effects. As noted, the research is fairly clear that changes in penal practices are not a direct reflection of increases in rates of crime (Chiricos and Delone 1992; Michalowski and Carlson 1999). Rather, they respond to changes in beliefs about the need for and the efficacy of punishment, that is, to changes in the mythology of punishment (Box and Hale 1982). In the United States in the late 1970s and early 1980s, conservative public leaders sought political advantage by deploying a mythology of punishment that tapped public fears of social change while creating popular support for a more punitive and less rehabilitative justice system.

It is difficult to determine what will be the long-term consequences of the "imprisonment binge." We do know that tens of thousands of young people that might have otherwise been returned to productive roles in society will now needlessly live out the remainder of their lives bearing both the social stigma and the psychological trauma of imprisonment. It also appears that the centerpiece of the punishment regime—determinate sentencing—is losing both legal and social legitimacy. In 2004, the U.S. Supreme Court in *Blakely vs. Washington* ruled that mandatory-sentencing schemes that allow judges to increase sentences for so-called "aggravating circumstances" are unconstitutional. Also, by 2004, 18 states had substantially revised their mandatory-sentencing schemes in the direction of shorter sentences and fewer mandatory ones. Whether this political momentum will continue, or whether the proponents of the "more-prisoners-equals-less-crime" perspective will mount a successful counterattack remains to be seen. Whatever happens in the short-term, however, it is very likely that future generations will look back on the last third of the twentieth century in the United States as an age when a mythology of punishment triumphed over more humane visions of how society might deal with those who sometimes break the law.

References

Allyn, D. 2000. *Make love, not war: The sexual revolution, an unfettered history.* Boston: Little, Brown.

Austin, J. 2001. *It's about time: America's imprisonment binge.* Belmont, CA: Wadsworth.

Austin, J., and J. Irwin. 2000. *It's about time: America's imprisonment binge.* New York: Wadsworth.

Beckett, K. 1997. *Making crime pay: Law and order in contemporary American politics.* New York: Oxford University Press.

Bennett, W., J. J. DiIulio Jr., and J. P. Walters. 1996. *Body count: Moral poverty and how to win America's war against crime and drugs.* New York: Simon and Schuster.

Bentham, J. 1962. *The works of Jeremy Bentham.* New York: Russell and Russell.

Blakely v. Washington. 2004. __U.S.__, WL 1402697 (June 24).

Blumstein, A., and J. Cohen. 1973. Theory of the stability of punishment. *Journal of Criminal Law and Criminology* 64(2):198–207.

Blumstein, A., and J. Wallman. 2000. *The crime drop in America.* New York: Cambridge University Press.

Bowers, W. J. 1988. Effect of executions is brutalization, not deterrence. In *Challenging capital punishment: Legal and social science approaches,* eds. K. C. Haas and J. A. Inciardi. Newbury Park, CA: Sage Publications.

Box, S., and C. Hale. 1982. Economic crisis and the rising prison population in England and Wales. *Crime and Social Justice* 17:20–35.

Brownstein, H. H. 1996. *The rise and fall of a violent crime wave: Crack cocaine and the social construction of a crime problem.* New York: Harrow and Heston.

Carlson, N. 1974. The federal prison system: Forty-five years of change. *Federal Probation* June:42–43.

Chambliss, W. 2000. *Power, politics, and crime.* Boulder, CO: Westview Press.

Chiricos, T. G., and M. Delone. 1992. Labor surplus and punishment: A review and assessment of theory and evidence. *Social Problems* 39:421–446.

Cloward, R., and L. E. Ohlin. 1960. *Delinquency and opportunity.* Glencoe, IL: Free Press.

Cook, P. J., and J. H. Laub. 2002. After the epidemic: Recent trends in youth violence in the United States. In *Crime and Justice: A Review of Research,* ed. M. Tonry. Vol. 29. Chicago: University of Chicago Press.

Currie, E. 1998. *Crime and punishment in America.* New York: Owl Books/Holt.

Danner, M. 2002. Three strikes and it's women who are out: The hidden consequences for women of criminal justice policy reforms. In *It's a crime: Women and justice,* ed. R. Muraskin. 215–224. Upper Saddle River, NJ: Prentice-Hall.

Davey, J. D. 1998. *The politics of prison expansion: Winning elections by waging war on crime.* Westport, CT: Praeger Press.

Davis, M. 1986. *Prisoners of the American dream: Politics and economy in the history of the U.S. working class.* London: Verso.

Drug Policy Alliance. 2004a. *What's wrong with the drug war?* Accessed online: *http://www. drugpolicy.org/drugwar/.*

———. 2004b. *Race and the drug war.* Accessed online: *http://www.drugpolicy.org/communities/ race/.*

Dugan, L., D. Nagin, and R. Rosenfeld. 2003. Exposure reduction or retaliation? The effects of domestic violence resources on intimate partner homicide. *Law and Society Review* 37(1): 169–198.

Fogel, D. 1979. *We are living proof: The justice model for corrections.* Boston: Anderson Publishing Company.

Gordon, D. M., R. Edwards, and M. Reich. 1982. *Segmented work, divided workers: The historical transformation of labor in the United States.* New York: Cambridge University Press.

Greenberg, D., and D. Humphries. 1980. The cooptation of fixed sentencing reform. *Crime and Delinquency* 26:206–225.

Hale, C. 1989. Unemployment and imprisonment and the stability of punishment hypothesis: Some thoughts using cointegration and error corrections models. *Journal of Quantitative Criminology* 5:169–186.

Harrison, B., and B. Bluestone. 1988. *The great u-turn: Corporate restructuring and the polarizing of America.* New York: Basic Books.

Kotz, D. M., T. McDonough, and M. Reich. 1994. *Social structures of accumulation: The political economy of growth and crisis.* New York: Cambridge University Press.

MacLeod, C., and H. Alger. 1980. *Farewell: The end of the American dream.* New York: Seaview Books.

Mahajan, R. 2003. *Full spectrum dominance: U.S. power in Iraq and beyond.* New York: Seven Stories Press.

Mattingly, C., and L. C. Garro. 2000. *Narrative and the cultural construction of illness and healing.* Berkeley: University of California Press.

Mauer, M. 1997. *Americans behind bars: U.S. and international rates of incarceration, 1995.* Washington, DC: The Sentencing Project.

———. 1999. *Race to incarcerate.* New York: The New Press.

McDarrah, F. W., G. S. McDarrah, and T. S. McDarrah. 2003. *Anarchy, protest, and rebel-*

lion: And the counterculture that changed America. New York: Thunder's Mouth Press.

McWilliams, J. C. 2000. *The 1960s cultural revolution.* Westport, CT: Greenwood Press.

Michalowski, R., and S. Carlson. 1999. Unemployment, imprisonment and social structures of accumulation: Historical contingency in the Rusche Kirchheimer Hypothesis. *Criminology* 37(2):217–250.

Morris, N. 1974. *The future of imprisonment.* Chicago: University of Chicago Press.

Raines, H. 1977. *My soul is rested: The story of the civil rights movement in the deep south.* New York: Penguin Books.

Riggenbach, J. 1998. *In praise of decadence.* Amherst, NY: Prometheus Books.

Sentencing Project. 2002. *U.S. prison populations: Trends and implications.* Washington, DC: The Sentencing Project, Briefing Sheet.

Simpson, S. 2002. *Corporate crime, law, and social control.* New York: University of Cambridge Press.

Sutherland, E. H., and D. Cressey. 1960. *Criminology,* 6th ed. Chicago: Lippincott.

Websdale, N. 1999. *Understanding domestic homicide.* Boston: Northeastern University Press.

Wilson, J. Q. 1975. *Thinking about crime.* New York: Basic Books.

Zimring, F. E., and G. Hawkins. 1973. *Deterrence: The legal threat in crime control.* Chicago: University of Chicago Press. ✦

Chapter 22
The Myth That Imprisonment is the Most Severe Form of Punishment

Peter B. Wood

The Myth

The general public, state and federal lawmakers, and criminal justice policymakers voice considerable agreement with the idea that, aside from the death penalty, the most severe punishment the criminal justice system can impose is imprisonment in a state or federal prison. The notion of a continuum of criminal justice sanctions typically places probation at the low end of the severity scale and imprisonment at the high end, with a variety of alternative sanctions (such as community service, intensive-supervision probation and parole or ISP, day fines, house arrest, etc.) between the two extremes. Ideally, as one moves up the scale toward imprisonment, the presumed severity of sanctions increases.

A review of public perceptions of punishment in the U.S. reveals that the public knows very little about the many sentencing alternatives, and tends to focus exclusively on imprisonment when thinking about sentencing (Roberts et al. 2003). The myth that imprisonment is the most severe sanction seems to rest primarily on opinions and attitudes expressed by the public and policymakers. Adding to the myth is that virtually all descriptions of criminal justice sanctions portray the aforementioned continuum of severity with probation at one end and imprisonment at the other (Petersen and Palumbo 1997; Morris and Tonry 1990; Von Hirsch and Ashworth 1992; NIJ 1993, 1995). The development of a continuum of sanctions—and a ranking of their presumed severity—has been the responsibility of legislators and criminal justice policymakers who generally have no reliable means for rating the severity of the sanctions they propose. Punishments devised by legislators and practitioners are rarely if ever based on experiential data, and depend primarily on guesswork by persons with no direct knowledge of what it is like to serve various sanctions (Morris and Tonry 1990). Under these circumstances, the conventional belief that correctional punishment is bound by probation at one extreme and imprisonment at the other deserves to be questioned. It is by no means clear that the continuum envisioned by policymakers mirrors that of prison inmates who know the experience of both prison and alternatives. The issue centers on the question of whose opinion is used to determine which sanctions are more severe than others, and whether convicted offenders calculate the same costs and benefits in the same fashion as policymakers. From a marketing viewpoint, it makes sense that the consumers of the product (offenders who serve the sanctions) evaluate the product (correctional sanctions) to truly understand how the product is experienced. In the absence of such knowledge, we are left with what policymakers and the public think about how offenders experience correctional punishments—which derives from a preconceived notion that prison is the most severe punishment.

The Kernel of Truth

Most people would agree that, aside from rare and sporadic use of the death penalty, a prison term of many years is the most severe sanction our criminal justice system can impose. Research shows that 70 to 90 percent of prison inmates would prefer an alternative (depending on the alternative) to four months in a medium-security prison (Wood and Grasmick 1999). Thus, it can rightly be argued that for many inmates imprisonment is the most severe punishment that we have regularly used. But this view of prison as the most severe sanction fails to take into account the importance of punishment duration, that there are punishments aside from prison that can be experienced as more punitive, that people can experience the same punishment in very different ways, and that most people sentenced to prison do not serve long prison terms. Certainly no one would claim that 20 years of house arrest is less severe than one year of minimum-security imprisonment of the sort experienced by Martha Stewart, for example.

The Truth or Facts

Despite the widespread belief of the public and policymakers that prison and probation define the extremes of criminal punishment, there is a small but growing body of research suggesting this vision of a sentencing continuum may be flawed (May et al. 2005; Wood, May, and Grasmick 2005; Wood and May 2003; Wood and Grasmick 1999; Petersilia and Deschenes 1994a, 1994b; Spelman 1995; Crouch 1993; Apospori and Alpert 1993; Petersilia 1990; McClelland and Alpert

1985). This research has focused on how convicted offenders perceive and experience the severity of correctional punishments. Depending on the specific sanction, the studies show that up to one-third of offenders will refuse to participate in the alternative even if it means a shorter duration of imprisonment. Reasons for choosing imprisonment over alternative sanctions include: (1) the manner in which alternatives are administered—particularly concerns about abusive or antagonistic personnel who run the programs, (2) the likelihood of program failure and revocation to prison after investing time and effort in the alternative, and (3) the belief held by many offenders that serving time in prison is easier than many alternative sanctions. Interestingly, few inmates view the formal rules and responsibilities of the alternatives as a serious obstacle. For example, Wood and Grasmick (1999) found that reasons such as, "Programs like those in this survey are too hard to complete," "Program rules are too hard to follow," and "Serving time in prison is less hassle because the programs have too many responsibilities" are among the least important reasons for avoiding alternative sanctions. The available research suggests that alternatives may be perceived by many offenders as a significant gamble and that inmates' assessment of this gamble influences many of them to rate alternative sanctions as more punitive than prison. This is manifested in two ways. Either offenders would choose prison over any duration of an alternative, or they would not serve as much of an alternative as they would prison. These concerns are apparently significant enough to generate considerable rejection of alternatives by offenders who would rather serve out their time in prison. By definition, if offenders would rather serve time in prison than any duration of an alternative, or would serve a longer duration of prison than the alternative, they perceive the alternative as more severe than imprisonment.

Consider some of the evidence. Petersilia (1990) noted that nearly one-third of nonviolent offenders given the option of participating in Intensive Supervision Probation (ISP) chose prison instead. They felt that working everyday, submitting to random urinalysis, and having their privacy invaded were more punitive than a prison term. Many also stated they would likely be caught violating conditions and revoked back to prison. Petersilia and Deschenes (1994a, 1994b) determined that inmates viewed one year in jail as equivalent to one year in prison, while five years of ISP were ranked as more punitive than one year in prison, but not as harsh as three years in prison. Similarly, Wood and Grasmick found that about 30 percent of male inmates refused to participate in any duration of ISP to avoid four months of imprisonment, and more than 20 percent chose a year of imprisonment over any duration of ISP. As noted by Wood and Grasmick (1999:31), "For many inmates, prison is the lesser of two evils." In another study conducted by William Spelman, an inmate maintained, "Probation [ISP] has too many conditions. If you can't meet them, you end up in jail anyway. I'd rather just do the time and pay off my debt to society that way." The inmate added, "On probation, you're on a short leash. If you cross over the line, they give you more time. The longer it lasts, the more chances you have to mess up. If you break [probation conditions], you'll do longer than a year in jail" (Spelman 1995: 126). For these offenders, ISP is viewed as more punitive than imprisonment.

Studies using offenders from Oklahoma, Indiana, and Kentucky found that none of the offender groups ranked prison as the most severe sanction (see Table 22.1). Observe that in the Oklahoma study (Wood and Grasmick 1999), seven of the alternative sanctions were ranked more severe than prison, with prison viewed as more punitive than only community service and regular probation. The Indiana study (Wood and May 2003) showed that for African-American probationers, prison is ranked as the tenth most severe sanction, surpassing only regular probation in terms of perceived severity. In contrast, white probationers ranked prison as the third most severe sanction, which suggests a significant racial difference in the perceived severity of prison. Finally, in the Kentucky study, the interaction of race and prior prison experience generated significantly different severity rankings, as African Americans with prior prison experience ranked prison as the seventh most punitive punishment, while white first-timers ranked it as the third most punitive sanction (Wood, May, and Minor 2004).

As noted above, offenders receiving identical punishments may "perceive the severity of their punishment to be very different due to differences in their age, race, sex, prior punishment history, or other factors" (Spelman 1995:132). In general, African-American offenders (Spelman 1995; Crouch 1993; Wood and May 2003), men (Wood and Grasmick 1999), older offenders (Spelman 1995; Crouch 1993; May et al. 2005), unmarried offenders (Petersilia and Deschenes 1994b), offenders without children (Petersilia and Deschenes 1994a), drug offenders (Spelman 1995), and those with a greater number of prior convictions (McClelland and Alpert 1985) are more likely to rate prison as less punitive than their counterparts. These differences are explored below.

Gender

Women are less likely than men to choose prison to avoid alternative sanc-

Table 22.1
Severity Rankings of Correctional Sanctions Based on a 12 Month Index

Severity Ranking	All* Respondents	Male*	Female*	Black**	White**
Most Severe	Boot Camp	Boot Camp	Boot Camp	Boot Camp	County Jail
	County Jail	County Jail	County Jail	County Jail	Boot Camp
	Day reporting	Intermittent Incarceration	Intermittent Incarceration	Electronic Monitoring	**Prison**
	Intermittent Incarceration	Day Reporting	Day Reporting	Day Fine	Day Fine
	Halfway House	Halfway House	Halfway House	ISP	Electronic Monitoring
	ISP	Electronic Monitoring	Electronic Monitoring	Halfway House	Intermittent Incarceration
	Electronic Monitoring	ISP	ISP	Intermittent Incarceration	Halfway House
	Prison	**Prison**	**Prison**	Day Reporting	ISP
	Community Service	Community Service	Community Service	Community Service	Day Reporting
	Regular Probation	Regular Probation	Regular Probation	**Prison**	Community Service
Least Severe				Regular Probation	Regular Probation

*From Wood and Grasmick. 1999. Survey of nonviolent inmates in eight Oklahoma correctional facilities. This ranking excludes day fine, which is a function of the offender's income, the amount of the fine, and the duration of the sanction (how many days/months). As inmates, these offenders have no probability of a steady income.

tions. The pattern of women being more amenable to alternatives holds with the exception of electronic monitoring (EM) and halfway house placement, in which case women are less willing to participate in those sanctions (Wood and Grasmick 1999). This discrepancy may be a function of the restrictions associated with the sanctions. For example, the description of halfway-house placement presented to inmates stated that no visitors were allowed—a restriction that would restrict mothers' contact with children. In the case of EM—an incapacitating punishment designed to restrict physical movement—women may have wanted greater flexibility in their schedules to attend to the needs of children. Given the unpredictable nature of childcare, many women may view the requirements of some alternatives as too restrictive. Still, available research indicates that, with two notable exceptions, women view imprisonment as more severe than do men, and are more willing to serve alternatives.

Race

Crouch (1993) suggests that African Americans may adjust to prison more easily than other groups, perhaps because a large proportion of inner-city, African-American males are imprisoned and they routinely find friends and relatives already in prison who can provide them with information, material goods, and protection. The urban underclass lifestyle makes the potential violence and deprivation of a prison term seem less threatening to blacks compared to whites:

Because the ghettos from which many African-Americans come are often unpredictable and threatening environments, they learn to emphasize self-protection and to develop physical and psychological toughness. This toughness protects African-American prisoners and enables them to dominate others behind bars, especially whites—it suggests that race and ethnicity may influence how offenders view the relative costs of punitiveness of criminal sanctions. (Crouch 1993:71)

For these reasons, it is believed that given a choice between prison and a range of alternative sanctions, African-American males would choose prison more often than would white males.

There are additional reasons to expect that African-American males are more likely than white males to choose prison over a range of alternative sanctions. African-American males (more than white males) may tend to feel that they will be subject to abuse or harassment under alternative sanctions, and thus may feel they are more likely to be revoked back to prison. This implies that African-American males and white males entertain a different risk assessment when it comes to evaluating whether participation in an alternative is a gamble they are willing to take. Rather than viewing prison as less punitive than alternatives, it is therefore possible that prison contains less uncertainty; and many offenders (black and white) may wish to serve out their terms and be released rather than invest time and effort in an alternative sanction involving potentially abusive program officers and a high likelihood of program violation and revocation. Questions remain, however, about whether such risk assessments vary by race, and if so, why.

Only four previous studies explored race difference in perceptions of sanction severity. Petersilia and Deschenes (1994a, 1994b; both from the same research study) failed to find a significant race difference; however, Crouch (1993:67) observed that "being African-American is the strongest predictor of a preference for prison" and Spelman (1995:122) found that "the most important predictor of preference for a jail term is the offender's race." Wood and May (2003) found that African-American probationers were more likely than whites to choose prison over alternatives; and among offenders who were willing to serve alternatives to avoid prison, whites would serve longer durations of them. African-American offenders were two to four times as likely as whites to choose prison rather than serve any amount of a given alternative sanction (Wood and May 2003).

Age

Age appears to influence both the decision to choose imprisonment over alternative sanctions and the amount of an alternative that offenders are willing to serve to avoid imprisonment. Older inmates are more likely to reject alternatives and choose prison instead, and older offenders will not serve as much of an alternative as will younger ones (May et al. 2005). There are several possible explanations for this finding. First, older offenders may view alternative sanctions as more of a gamble than younger ones. They may feel that the chances of revocation are too high and realize that if they fail to complete the sanction they will be revoked back to prison to serve out their original sentence, extending their time under correctional supervision. Consequently, they may feel that their total time under correctional supervision may be shorter if they avoid alternative sanctions and go directly to prison to serve out their term. Another explanation is that older offenders are more likely to have been sentenced to prison than younger ones, may be more familiar with and less fearful of incarceration, and may now view prison as less severe. They may see alternatives as more of a hassle, and feel more comfortable serving their time incarcerated rather than in the community. Third, older offenders are more likely to be experienced convicts who hold alternatives in disdain. They may view those willing to subject themselves to the supervision and restrictions of alternatives as "punks" who are fearful of prison, and who are willing to subject themselves to "institutionalized embarrassment" to avoid doing time. For many older offenders, alternatives are a "copout" of sorts, and carry a stigma of being reserved for younger and weaker offenders.

Prison Experience

Offenders with more prison experience are less willing to serve alternative sanctions and more likely to prefer to serve prison time instead (May et al. 2005). This contradicts the idea of the traditional probation to prison severity continuum. If prison is perceived by inmates as significantly more punitive than alternatives, then persons with more prison experience should be more willing to serve alternative sanctions—and to serve longer durations of them—to avoid imprisonment. However, this is not the case. Offenders who have acquired knowledge and experience about living in prison appear less fearful of prison than those without such experience. For them, prison is less of an unknown, and for some it may be seen as easier than an alternative sanction—particularly if they perceive the alternative as involving an unacceptable degree of supervision, mistreatment, and a high likelihood of revocation. Particularly among inmates with experience serving time, im-

prisonment becomes familiar, while the outcome of involvement in alternatives is less certain and less attractive. In contrast, persons without prior experience in prison may be more fearful of it, and will opt to do the alternative—and a longer duration of it—to avoid prison. While this may seem strange to those not familiar with serving time, it has been noted that most offenders would rather do a longer prison term, for example, than a short jail sentence (Fleisher 1995). Fleisher cites an offender who states he would rather do three or four years at a state penitentiary before doing one year in the county jail. Fleisher goes on to note, "Prison isn't a risk that worries street hustlers. Things such as limited freedom, loss of privacy, violence, and variant sexual activity, which might frighten lawful citizens, don't frighten them" (1995:164).

Interests Served by the Myth

There appear to be several interests that benefit from maintaining the myth. Politicians who want to appear to be tough on crime routinely emphasize their support for harsh punishment policies based on the belief that imprisonment is the most severe correctional sanction available, and most if not all felony offenders deserve it. As noted previously, the public has little knowledge about sanctions other than imprisonment, and supports the notion that prison is the most severe sanction. Certainly such a "tough on crime" platform would be undermined if it became known that imprisonment is widely regarded among offenders as less severe than several alternative sanctions.

Parties associated with the prison-industrial complex are committed to the imprisonment myth, and to continued growth in the prison system. Corrections is a $50 billion per year industry. In 2000, private prison companies (PPCs) contributed nearly $1.2 million to 830 candidates in 14 southern states during their respective election cycles (Bender 2002). The major contributors were Corrections Corporation of America (CCA), Wackenhut, Cornell Corrections, and Correctional Services Corporation. These and other PPCs focused their contributions largely on legislative races in 14 states. Companies gave more than 70 percent of their contributions to winning candidates. Another 20 percent went to incumbents who did not run. Thus, more than 90 percent of contributions went to winning or incumbent politicians. Much of the money went to influential members of key committees, where unfavorable policies were more easily altered, stalled, or even killed. In committee, policies draw less scrutiny than if they go to the floor for debate. These politicians repaid their contributors by blocking legislation that would have been harmful to the interests of PPCs.

Private prison companies have fared well during the imprisonment binge. Annual revenues at CCA increased from $14 million in 1986, the year it became a publicly traded company, to $120 million in 1994, the year it was represented on the NYSE (Mattera et al. 2001). Wackenhut was created in 1988 and saw its revenues grow from $19 million in 1989 to $84 million in 1994 when it made an initial public offering of its stock (Mattera et al. 2001). Although these increases have slowed a bit over the past 5–6 years, several 20-year federal contracts for new facilities have been let, and each promises significant profits over the next few years. According to analysts, these federal contracts could be worth more than $750 million over the next ten years (Mattera et al. 2001). Further, in 2001, the INS and the U.S. Marshals Service renewed a total of five contracts with CCA worth more than $50 million per year (Mattera et al. 2001). Despite a decreasing crime rate, and concerns that states will seek to reduce the inflow of inmates into their correctional systems to control costs, it appears that the private prison industry will continue to be lucrative into the near future.

The prison-industrial complex has become so profitable that many industrial sectors vie for a piece of it. Prison construction budgets for the United States are now about $7 billion per year, and Wall Street firms compete to underwrite prison construction with enormous bond issues (Sarabi 2000). Financial intermediaries buy bonds and securities from private prison companies, state agencies, or state and county governments, and resell them to investors, a market niche worth about $3 billion per year (Sarabi 2000). Phone companies compete to provide collect-call services to inmates. These companies may charge rates up to six times the free-world rates—plus an automatic "connect fee" between $1.50 and $3 per inmate call (Sarabi 2000). MCI was recently forced to admit it had been improperly charging California inmates an even higher rate than its contract called for. California, like most states, receives a kickback from phone companies who run prison phone systems. Profits from contracts with MCI and GTE netted the state of California more than $16 million in 1998 alone (Sarabi 2000).

One intriguing interest is the small towns that specialize in imprisoning offenders. Florence, Arizona, recorded a 2000 census population of 17,054—11,830 of whom are inmates. Florence, with only 5,224 residents, boasts two state prisons, three private prisons, and a U.S. Immigration and Naturalization Service detention center. Florence has the highest percentage of prison inmates of any town of more than 10,000 (nearly 70 percent). Since the Census now counts inmates as residents, Florence has twice paid the Census Bureau to do special recounts to update its population. The increase means millions of extra dollars in state and federal funding. Florence's prison bonus in state and federal funds now amounts to more than $4 million per year. Florence now houses prisoners from as far away as Washington, DC—transferred there by CCA (Kulish 2001).

In Gatesville, Texas, numerous prisoners depress per-capita wages and make the community eligible for additional cash from state and federal poverty programs. In Gatesville, 9,095 inmates (58 percent of the total town population) helped push the city's per capita income below the state poverty level, which qualified the town for a $4.2 million state grant in 1997 that it used to upgrade water lines and build new roads (Kulish 2001). By 2000, Malone, New York, benefited significantly from state and federal dollars as 5,000 of its population of 15,000 consisted of prison inmates. The prisons brought 1,600 jobs to Malone, one-third of the new employees live in town, the rest in nearby towns in the same county. Annual payroll for the three facilities amounts to $67 million, and there are new pharmacies, discount stores, and fast-food outlets. The local hospital has added a dialysis unit and a cancer-treatment center, and the golf course has added another 18 holes. As of September 2000, the county unemployment rate dropped to its lowest level since 1975 (Duke 2000).

If it were commonly perceived that imprisonment was not the most severe sanction, the use of imprisonment might decline, threatening the interests of many of the above-mentioned parties. However, given the profits to be made, it is possible that even incontrovertible proof refuting the myth would fail to alter commitment to the expanding prison-industrial complex.

Policy Implications of Belief in the Myth

A widespread acceptance and philosophical commitment to the myth that imprisonment is the most severe form of punishment is the foundation upon which the imprisonment binge of the past 25 years rests. If legislators believe that imprisonment is the most severe sanction, then in a law-and-order climate, they will advocate more imprisonment and longer sentences. Policies such as mandatory minimums, Truth-In-Sentencing, and Three Strikes rest on the myth, and are supported by the belief that the majority of offenders deserve as much imprisonment as can be justified. An associated belief that prison is a general or specific deterrent helps validate these policies. One might claim that lawmakers and the general public have enjoyed a love affair with imprisonment that will be difficult to end. If it were commonly perceived that imprisonment is not the most severe sanction, support for its widespread use might erode, encouraging efforts to explore greater use of less costly noncustodial sanctions.

A growing body of research now demonstrates that many offenders (or significant categories of them) perceive a variety of intermediate sanctions to be as punitive (or even more punitive) than imprisonment. Consequently, the claim that prison is the most severe sanction for all offenders is questionable—as is the primary justification for the continued U.S. prison build-up and the huge associated financial costs. Recognition by practitioners and policymakers that many offenders perceive certain community-based sanctions as onerous may (1) allow a significant number of offenders who would otherwise be sentenced to prison to be placed into community-based sanctions that have a roughly equivalent punitive bite, and (2) encourage courts to place some offenders who would otherwise be sentenced to token probationary supervision into intermediate sanctions that place more intrusive controls on their behavior (Morris and Tonry 1990; Von Hirsch and Ashworth 1992). Such policy-related outcomes "would give both the appearance and reality of fairness to the community and to the convicted offender" (Morris and Tonry 1990:32).

References

Apospori, E., and G. Alpert. 1993. Research note: The role of differential experience with the criminal justice system in changes in perception of severity of legal sanctions over time. *Crime and Delinquency* 39:184–194.

Bender, E. 2002. *A contributing influence: The private-prison industry and political giving in the south.* Helena, MT: The National Institute on Money in State Politics.

Crouch, B. M. 1993. Is incarceration really worse? Analysis of offenders' preferences for prison over probation. *Justice Quarterly* 10: 67–88.

Duke, L. 2000. Building a boom behind bars: Prison construction boom transforms small towns. *The Washington Post* September 8.

Fleisher, M. S. 1995. *Beggars and thieves: Lives of urban street criminals.* Madison: University of Wisconsin Press.

Kulish, N. 2001. Annexing the penitentiary. *The Wall Street Journal* August 9. Accessed online at: *http://www.grassrootsleadership.org/ Articles/Article5_spr2002.html.*

Mattera, P., M. Khan, G. LeRoy, and K. Davis. 2001. *Jail breaks: Economic development subsidies given to private prisons.* Washington DC: Good Jobs First, The Institute on Taxation and Economic Policy.

May, D. C., P. B. Wood, J. L. Mooney, and K. I. Minor. 2005. Predicting offender-generated exchange rates: Implications for a theory of sentence severity. *Crime and Delinquency* 51: 373–399.

McClelland, K. A., and G. Alpert. 1985. Factor analysis applied to magnitude estimates of punishment seriousness: Patterns of individual differences. *Journal of Quantitative Criminology* 1:307–318.

Morris, N., and M. Tonry. 1990. *Between prison and probation: Intermediate punishments in a rational sentencing system.* New York: Oxford University Press.

National Institute of Justice. 1993. *Intermediate sanctions: Research in brief.* Washington DC: U.S. Government Printing Office.

———. 1995. *National assessment program: 1994 survey results.* Washington, DC: U.S. Government Printing Office.

Petersilia, J. 1990. When probation becomes more dreaded than prison. *Federal Probation* 54:23–27.

Petersilia, J., and E. P. Deschenes. 1994a. What punishes? Inmates rank the severity of prison vs. intermediate sanctions. *Federal Probation* 58:3–8.

———. 1994b. Perceptions of punishment: Inmates and staff rank the severity of prison versus intermediate sanctions. *The Prison Journal* 74:306–328.

Petersen, R. D., and D. J. Palumbo. 1997. The social construction of intermediate punishments. *The Prison Journal* 77:77–92.

Roberts, J. V., L. J. Stalans, D. Indermaur, and M. Hough. 2003. *Penal populism and public opinion: Lessons from five countries.* New York: Oxford University Press.

Sarabi, B. 2000. America's internal colony. Western States Center Views. *Western States Center* Spring/Summer.

Spelman, W. 1995. The severity of intermediate sanctions. *Journal of Research in Crime and Delinquency* 32:107–135.

Von Hirsch, A., and A. Ashworth, eds. 1992. *Principled sentencing.* Boston: Northeastern University Press.

Wood, P. B., and H. G. Grasmick. 1999. Toward the development of punishment equivalencies: Male and female inmates rate the severity of alternative sanctions compared to prison. *Justice Quarterly* 16:19–50.

Wood, P. B., and D. C. May. 2003. Race differences in perceptions of sanction severity: A comparison of prison with alternatives. *Justice Quarterly* 20:605–631.

Wood, P. B., D. C. May, and H. G. Grasmick. 2004. Gender differences in the perceived severity of boot camp. *Journal of Offender Rehabilitation* 40(3/4).

Wood, P. B., D. C. May, and K. I. Minor. 2004. The effects of race and prison experience on perceptions of sanction severity. Paper presented at the 2004 American Society of Criminology Annual Meeting, Nashville, TN. ✦

Chapter 23
The Myth of Prisons As Country Clubs

Marilyn McShane,
Frank P. Williams III,
and Beth Pelz

The Myth

Many people believe prisons tend to coddle inmates and supply various amenities for their use. It is not unusual to hear someone say, "I would like to have someone paying for my room and board and free recreation." The general myth is that some prisons are like county clubs, with services and leisure activities that many citizens cannot afford in their own lives. The essence is that prisons are camps in which inmates live the easy life, not having to do anything to support themselves, while being taken care of by the government. This is usually accompanied by an expression of dismay that those sentenced to prison are not really being punished.

This general country-club myth is actually a collective set of beliefs representing a number of more specific concerns about the way prisons are operated and what amenities are available to inmates. The elements of the myth suggest prisoners live a life of leisure, paid for by taxpayers. Inmates can watch television, engage in various games and interesting recreation, lift weights, and even participate in arts and crafts. Or, conversely, they can lie around all day doing nothing in their spacious cells, if that is what they want to do. They are served tasty and well-prepared food, have excellent free medical care, and generally are deferred to by the correctional staff. They receive training in desirable employment skills for which ordinary citizens must pay. In short, prisoners enjoy services and privileges not available to law-abiding citizens.

The country-club myth seems to be driven by two assumptions about prisons. First is that merely being sentenced to, and required to serve time in, prison is not punishment. Many people believe that for punishment to take place, inmates must be required to perform work at hard labor and suffer conditions that deprive them of all but basic necessities. Otherwise, prison is not a deterrent. Second, many people assume large correctional budgets are a product of the privileges and amenities provided inmates.

The Kernel of Truth

Historically, prisons developed in rural areas where large tracts of land were available for farming, animal husbandry, and factories and industries. The remote settings were a benefit not only because of the lack of competition for land or resources, but also because there were few complaints about the presence of inmates, possible escapes, and effects on land values. Consequently, as urban development spread to these once outlying areas, people began to notice the prison landscaping, perhaps creating some fuel to the myth of a "country club" setting. Indeed, part of the country-club myth has to do with the attractiveness of the facility as well as how it is operated. The landscaped areas of a prison are generally well tended, with clipped hedges and mown grass, no trash and weeds, and sidewalks carefully edged. It is not much of an exaggeration to say some prison grounds can rival the manicured look of exclusive resorts.

The unprecedented growth in state and federal prison populations as a result of the war on drugs has led officials to scramble for space and facilities to house prisoners. While state and federal prison growth has mushroomed, there has been no corresponding growth of funds to build new prisons. Consequently, the preferred funding plan has been to construct new prisons based on the most economical designs or, in cases where existing government facilities were available, the conversion of those facilities to prisons. The best candidates for conversions are facilities with sufficiently large holding capacities, such as unused military facilities (for example, the federal prison camps at Eglin Air Force Base in Florida and Maxwell Air Force Base in Alabama), state hospitals, and old hotels (for example, the California Rehabilitation Center is housed in an old hotel). Some of these adapted facilities came with pools, recreation areas, tennis courts, and even golf courses, giving further support to the country-club myth.

Because of movies and television shows, the public is aware of recreation activities behind bars—there has even been a movie about a football game (*The Longest Yard*). Images of inmates working out with weight-training equipment are a mainstay of crime-related television series. At the same time, it is true that prison recreation may include organized and informal games (sports, physical fitness, table games, intramural competition), hobbycrafts, music programs, movies, and stage shows. Each prison endeavors to provide a minimum number of hours of recreation per week for each inmate, adding more fuel to the myth.

Where costs are concerned, prisons are indeed expensive propositions. Over the past couple of decades, budget crises in many jurisdictions led to concern over prison spending. Surrounding commentary often gives the impression that too much money is spent on prisoners. Newspapers are prone to provide comparisons of areas where state budgets are being spent and even to make comparisons of the cost of keeping an inmate in prison as opposed to sending someone to college for a year. Because many states, in their efforts to drive down prison costs, turned to private prisons, there may be another contributing factor to the country-club prison myth: a misunderstanding about private prisons. Normally, the term "private" is associated with better and more attractive facilities (for example, private country clubs) . Therefore, it is reasonable to assume that some people may associate a private prison with a country-club image.

The Truth or Facts

The myth that prisons are similar to country clubs cannot be supported by any of the actual structural, operational, or philosophical components of current correctional systems. Some aspects of prison mythology are supported by a lack of understanding prisons and prison life. A misunderstanding of budgets and costs provides other support. Finally, there is support from beliefs about what prisons should do as opposed to what they must do according to judicial interpretations of the Constitution.

The Country-Club Look

The country-club look is associated with a few minimum-custody facilities that have been converted from existing governmental properties, such as old hospitals, mental institutions, hotels, and unused military facilities. The monies appropriated for the conversion of these facilities into prisons only allowed for the most basic and quickly installed security upgrades. Rarely was it deemed cost effective to remove preexisting amenities. In most cases, inmates do not have access to any of the preexisting recreational features. If used at all, they tend to be reserved for correctional staff and their families who live near the facilities.

While the public and the media are fascinated by glimpses of some of these converted facilities, they are less likely to see the construction of the new fortress-like, solid concrete, supermax facilities built in most states. In these facilities, as well as in many of the maximum-security prisons, inmates spend 23 hours per day in their cells and are manacled or shackled whenever they move even briefly outside their cells.

The well-manicured grounds are another part of the country-club look. All of the labor—the mowing, trimming, and painting—that enhances the facility is done by inmates. In fact, more inmates are available for work than there are jobs to perform. In some cases, one inmate will mow the lawn on Tuesday, and another inmate will mow the same lawn on Thursday. Picking up trash, edging, weeding, and repairing cracks in the sidewalk all seem to give an institution a pristine look; however, the appearance is a direct consequence of too many workers and not enough work, or of a need to keep scores of unskilled offenders busy.

Minimum-security federal prisons with their dormitories and well-manicured grounds are simply less-expensively constructed prisons with minimal surveillance and hardware. To provide more security than necessary, given the overwhelming majority of nonviolent inmates, would be a waste of money. Even if a few

inmates walk away from these minimum-custody facilities, they are such low-risk prisoners that the savings from not increasing security offsets any potential harm they may cause. In fact, a recent survey of prison wardens revealed that most of them believed that half of their prisoners could be released without having a negative effect on public safety (Schiraldi and Greene 2002).

Costs

The United States spends a huge amount of money on incarceration. State, local, and federal jurisdictions spend about $40 billion dollars on incarceration each year. This means that states use approximately one out of every fourteen general-fund dollars on prisons (Schiraldi and Greene 2002). No doubt it makes citizens frustrated to see valuable resources that could go to education, health, transportation, and housing used to lock people up. Although some people may imagine their tax dollars buying a lavish prison lifestyle, very little of that money is used directly on inmates. For example, the average amount spent on each prisoner's food per day in 2000 was $3.62 (Camp and Camp 2002:105–106).

Also, what the data are less likely to reveal is that a prison budget is almost entirely spent on personnel and not on prison amenities. Four of every five dollars spent on prisons are for employee salaries and building maintenance (DiMascio 1997). Correctional officers, support staff, administrative and clerical salaries, benefits, and retirement costs make up the greatest share of any correctional system's budget.

The total costs of corrections can be misleading to the public in another way as well. A state's correctional budget most often includes parole costs, and may even include probation costs. In addition to the country's incarcerated population, there are an additional 3.8 million people on probation and more than 750,000 under parole supervision (BJS 2002). Thus, the correctional budget includes the costs of incarcerated offenders, as well as the costs to supervise offenders in the community.

In addition, the amount of money each state budgets for corrections is not predicated on the number of inmates. In fact, a greater number of inmates often means that less is spent on each inmate per day. For example, South Carolina reports that budget cuts have reduced the amount spent on each inmate from $46 per day to $35 per day (Buisch 2003). Because prison expenses have increased over time, a decrease in the amount allocated per prisoner requires the elimination of basic operational services.

The move toward private prisons has been an attempt to cut costs even further by subcontracting some of the burden of building, maintaining, and operating expensive prison facilities. Because private corporations that own or operate private prisons are businesses run under the capitalist system, their primary goal is to make money. Many of them, in the pursuit of profits, have not provided inmates with adequate medical care, employed correctional workers with insufficient skills, and cut corners wherever possible. In the long run, most states have discovered that subcontracting private prisons are not true cost-saving measures (see Chapter 25). For inmates, a private prison is often far from a country-club facility.

On the whole, recent cost cutting has made prisons not only tougher and more dangerous places, but also the lack of basic services has forced many of them to operate in violation of the U.S. Constitution. For example, in 2002, the entire adult correctional departments in 10 states were under court orders to reduce overcrowding or improve other conditions of confinement and, in another 12 states and the District of Columbia, one or more institutions were under court orders for the same reasons. In short, correctional budgets frequently do not allow for the constitutional operation of prisons, much less the provision of amenities.

Not all prison operations are financed from taxes. What many people do not realize is that federal prisoners must pay a portion of their incarceration costs as directed by Public Law 102-395, Section 111 and 18 U.S.C. 4001, which sets out a "cost of incarceration fee"—usually equal to the average cost of one year of confinement (Federal Bureau of Prisons 1999). Some states have similar requirements.

Recreation and Leisure

Recreational activities (sports, physical fitness, table games, intramural competition, hobby-crafts, music programs, movies, and stage shows) must follow uniform policies and time frames for participation, be properly supervised, and involve detailed reporting procedures. Federal guidelines for inmate recreation require that the objectives include reducing the number of medical problems by increasing healthy lifestyle activities and decreasing idleness with constructive occupations (Federal Bureau of Prisons 2002). In short, the primary purpose of prison recreation is cost-effective control, rather than mere social enjoyment.

In a study of Orange County, Florida residents, Applegate (2001) found that 87 percent of the respondents felt most of the prison amenities available for inmates should be retained as long as inmates earn the money for them working within the prison. This is, in fact, how amenities are usually financed. Virtually no taxpayer- or state-funds are used in the support of inmate recreation in any state or federal facility. The sports and recreational activities provided are quite modest, and only in a few minimum-custody federal facilities are areas for tennis, shuffleboard, or other country-club-image activities found. These are mostly tolerated because the equipment cost is low, and the activities involve low levels of inmate contact and easy supervision.

There are practical problems with inmates financing their own prison amenities, however. First, there are usually not enough work programs for all inmates, thus earning money in prison can be difficult. Second, an accounting system that pays inmates in a timely fashion and places funds into usable inmate accounts is difficult to maintain. The usual solution to these problems is to create collective inmate funds garnered from profits on the sale of telephone services and commissary items. These funds are then used to purchase recreational equipment such as balls, baskets, and nets for team sports and the necessary tools and supplies for arts, crafts, and music.

Personal Amenities

While there are certainly some facilities where inmates have some amenities, conditions overall meet very basic constitutional standards. That is, they are simply one step better than cruel and unusual, and the courts make it difficult to complain about general conditions. In one case, an inmate filed a grievance alleging overcrowding, excessive noise, insufficient storage space, inadequate heating and cooling, improper ventilation, unclean and inadequate restrooms, unsanitary dining facilities and food preparation, and housing that mixed mentally- and physically-ill inmates. To win his case, the inmate not only had to show that those conditions existed but was further required to show prison officials were deliberately indifferent to the needs of inmates.

In some prison facilities, it is safer to have individuals isolated and preoccupied rather than mixing in the general population. In these cases, individual or cell-mounted television sets may be appropriate. These television sets are black and white, housed in very strong enclosures, and receive very few channels. It is not only the televisions themselves that create the myth, but the way they are used also seems to undermine peoples' need to see prisoners engaged in punitive activity, not leisure. However, the reality is that television is really employed to help prison staff. That is, television watching is used as a management tool in the same way parents use their children's television watching as a form of babysitter. Idle inmates tend to create problems and become much more labor intensive for prison staff. By allowing them to watch television, inmates are more controllable and the number of correctional staff can be reduced—making prisons less expensive.

Further, the structuring of group television activities is a socialization exercise in any prison. It is a privilege that must be earned and may be withdrawn to coerce socially acceptable behavior. The group must vote on the selection of shows, and democracy prevails. This ability to sit together through prearranged and officially sanctioned viewing is something even the American family has abandoned as too difficult.

Privileges

A study by Wunder in 1995 revealed that inmate privileges have been decreasing over time. Sixty percent of corrections officials surveyed indicated that some privileges had been curtailed over the past

·years, and almost three-quarters said inmates had the same or fewer privileges over the past ten years. In the federal system, reductions in privileges have been more severe. The "No-Frills Prison Act" of 1996 allowed the U.S. Attorney General to set standards for federal facilities that included prohibiting coffee pots, televisions, and hot plates in cells, and eliminating unmonitored phone calls and all types of electronic equipment. Many states have followed this trend. A survey of prison wardens by Johnson, Bennett, and Flanagan (1997) found that three dozen different types of prison programs were eliminated, such as literacy and GED classes, certain types of physical training, and some forms of visitation. Other services eliminated included access to legal resources and AIDS treatments, clearly not what the "no-frills" concept meant to do.

Prisons as Punishment

There is an underlying belief that time in prison, by itself, is not punishment. Many people believe that to achieve punishment, something else must be done to inmates. This belief is partly the result of the assumption that offenders are "sentenced to prison at hard labor." This is generally not true. The typical sentence is to be incarcerated in a state institution, nothing more or less. In the few jurisdictions that have laws with language equivalent to "at hard labor," prison management is forced to violate those laws because either there is not enough work for all inmates or there is not nearly enough correctional officers to supervise the working inmates. Requiring inmates to labor while in prison is impractical and expensive.

Simply being confined in prison is punishment enough. Sociologists have long written about the deprivations in "total institutions" (Clemmer 1940) and the "pains of imprisonment" (Sykes 1958; see also Wheeler 1961; Toch 1977; Johnson 1987). Prison writers have attempted to describe this conflicting world of isolation and crowding, solitude and exposure. Santos (2003:190), for example, writes about the reality of incarceration as it pertains to privacy:

> Prisoners have no rights to privacy. All mail is potentially censored before leaving an institution, and telephone calls are recorded. When guards are assigned to posts where they have free time—they frequently listen to tape recordings of an individual's telephone conversations.

Interests Served by the Myth

Politicians use the image of "country club" prisons as a way to direct public emotions against a common and popular enemy—criminals. For many people, the Watergate scandal tarnished the image of honest government. Ironically, Watergate also gave the public its first images of the federal facilities to which the convicted politicians were sent. Some people were angry about the obvious disparate treatment of white-collar criminals, like the Watergate offenders, and minority prisoners at Attica, Joliet, and Folsom—prisons which the public saw as a result of riots and civil-rights protests.

A related interest may be that political conservatives hope to ignite public outcry and divert attention from more substantial issues to one that is easy to win consensus on—prisoners are evil and deserve to be deprived of all but the most basic things. The country-club prison also gives the public a simplistic reason for the failure of prisons to significantly reduce recidivism and crime. The message is that by coddling prisoners rather than harshly punishing them, a disincentive for law-abiding behavior is created. However, research shows that people are more realistic about corrections and prisons and less punitive than politicians think they are (Gottfredson and Taylor 1984). Studies show backing for inmate-support services related to rehabilitation and other amenities, as long as they are paid for by the inmates themselves and not by taxes (see Applegate 2001; Lenz 2002).

Policy Implications of Belief in the Myth

The myth of county-club prisons directly influences the safety of those employed behind the walls. Those who work in prisons and jails argue that prison management should be allowed to decide how best to regulate inmate conduct through the award of privileges and access to resources within each facility. Instead, current efforts to make prison life more punitive, which some refer to as the "penal harm" movement (Clear 1994), may actually increase the daily risks faced by correctional staff. The lives of thousands of prison personnel depend on their ability to design and operate their own safe, viable measures of supervision and control. Nonetheless, outsiders with little knowledge of prisons continue to micromanage prisons, with assumptions based less on the realities of prison life than on emotion, rumor, and myth.

Political attempts to appear tough on crime are often more easily accomplished by appearing tough on criminals instead. The broad-based social improvements people favor, including school improvements, community treatment programs, and alternative job- and skill-training efforts are perceived as prohibitively expensive and are not pursued. Instead, politicians believe there is general support for

simply making prisons tougher for those who have been caught, which often appears to cost nothing at all. For example, attempting to pander to public pressure, some sheriffs and wardens have created old-fashioned chain gangs to work on public projects. However, the high cost of supervising such crews outside the facilities and the provision of the necessary work and health related resources make these ventures impractical from an insurance standpoint alone. Only a small number of inmates have participated in these projects.

In another example, legislators passed the 1995 Prison Reform Litigation Act, which was intended to limit the number of lawsuits filed by inmates as well as the ways and means by which they could access courts. At the same time, politicians were demanding that correctional officials remove recreation and programmatic opportunities within prisons. This meant that, while appearing to get tough with prisoners, officials were also eliminating ways inmates could complain about these increasingly restrictive measures. Ironically, the passage of the Act has drawn hundreds of lawsuits challenging the constitutionality of this measure (Butler 1999).

Depriving inmates of activities and resources will not save money. In fact, harsher, more austere, fortress-like construction will only cost more. Attempts to make prisons more punitive will only lead to costly consequences such as disturbances, riots, lawsuits, and, potentially, mental illness.

References

Applegate, B. 2001. Penal austerity: Perceived utility, desert, and public attitudes toward prison amenities. *American Journal of Criminal Justice* 25(2):253–268.

Buisch, M. 2003. Budget cuts present challenge to many state correctional agencies. *Corrections Today* 65(7):101–105.

Bureau of Justice Statistics. 2002. Accessed online: http://www.ojp.usdoj.gov/bjs/.

Butler, J. 1999. The prison litigation reform act: A separation of powers dilemma. *Alabama Law Review* 50:585.

Camp, C. G., and G. M. Camp. 2002. *The 2001 corrections yearbook: Adult systems.* Middletown, CT: Criminal Justice Institute, Inc.

Clear, T. 1994. *Harm in American penology: Offenders, victims, and their communities.* Albany, NY: States University of New York Press.

Clemmer, D. 1940. *The prison community.* Boston: Christopher Publishing Company.

DiMascio, W. 1997. *Seeking justice: Crime and punishment in America.* New York: Edna McConnell Clark Foundation.

Federal Bureau of Prisons. 1999. Policy statement number 5380.06. Washington DC: U.S. Department of Justice, Federal Bureau of Prisons. Accessed online at: *http://www.bop.gov/DataSource/execute/dsPolicyLoc.*

———. 2002. Policy statement number 5370.10. Washington DC: U.S. Department of Justice, Federal Bureau of Prisons. Accessed online at: *http://www.bop.gov/DataSource/execute/dsPolicyLoc.*

Gottfredson, S., and R. Taylor. 1984. Public policy and prison population: Measuring opinions about reform. *Judicature* 68(4/5):190–201.

Johnson, R. 1987. *Hard time: Understanding and reforming the prison.* Belmont, CA: Wadsworth.

Johnson, W., K. Bennett, and T. Flanagan. 1997. Getting tough on prisoners: Results from the National Corrections Executive Survey, 1995. *Crime and Delinquency* 43:24–41.

Lenz, N. 2002. Luxuries in prison: The relationship between amenity funding and public support. *Crime and Delinquency* 48(4):499–525.

Santos, M. 2003. *Profiles from prison: Adjusting to life behind bars.* Westport, CT: Praeger.

Schiraldi, V., and J. Greene. 2002. Reducing correctional costs in an era of tightening budgets and shifting public opinion. *Federal Sentencing Reporter* 14(6):332–336.

Sykes, G. 1958. *Society of captives: A study of maximum security prison.* Princeton, NJ: Princeton University Press.

Toch, H. 1977. *Living in prison: The ecology of survival.* New York: Free Press.

Wheeler, S. 1961. Socialization in correctional communities. *American Sociological Review* 26:697–712.

Wunder, A. 1995. The extinction of inmate privileges. *Corrections Compendium* June. ✦

Chapter 24
The Myth That Prisons Can Be Self-Supporting

Mary Parker

The Myth

The myth that prisons can be self-supporting, or the "myth of self-sufficiency" has haunted institutional corrections since its inception. The philosophies that support incarceration as a principal sentence for crime have religious roots based on the idea that institutional corrections can both reform an incarcerated offender and, at the same time, produce goods and services to support itself. The original operating structure of the prison, which was drawn from monasteries and nunneries, supported this possibility—that men and women could be brought together for the common goal of reforming themselves under one "household," which could not survive without common labor from its residents. The primary problem with the philosophy was that, unlike monasteries and nunneries, the men and women who are sent to prison do not want to be there, have not developed a common unity and goal, and do not care whether the correctional institution succeeds or fails (Foucault 1977).

The intensity of the desire for self-sufficiency is demonstrated by the early debates of the Philadelphia Society for Alleviating the Miseries of Public Prisoners and the Boston Prison Discipline Society. Each of these organizations ardently supported a different model of incarceration. The Philadelphia Society supported the "Pennsylvania system" or "separate system" of confinement; the Boston Society championed the "Auburn system" or "congregate system" of confinement. Once the design battles were fought, the real debate ensued over how much labor each type of incarceration could extract from the inmates housed within its walls. The Auburn system became the predominate model for incarceration in the United States because it was cheaper to build, and its philosophy—which supported group labor by inmates—was thought to be a more feasible method for achieving self-sufficiency.

The obsession with prison self-sufficiency was particularly strong during the industrial period of institutional corrections (from the 1900s to the 1930s). This period saw the first real increase in the institutional correctional population, an increase so great that crowding became an issue. The number of incarcerated offenders overwhelmed many government entities that were required to financially support them. Once again, the idea of harnessing a large number of able-bodied men and women who were confined in prisons to produce goods for sale on the open market proved irresistible to policymakers. These efforts were eventually thwarted, however, because of the passage of several federal laws designed to protect free world, union jobs by restricting the sale of inmate-made goods on the open market.

For example, the Hawes-Cooper Act of 1929 allowed states to block the importation of prison-made goods. The Ashurst-Sumners Act of 1935 prohibited the interstate transportation of prisoner-made goods to states where such products were prohibited, and required labels on all prisoner-made products sold in interstate commerce. As amended in 1940, it further prohibited the interstate transportation of prisoner-made products, except agricultural commodities and goods produced for states and their political divisions. The Walsh-Healey Act of 1936 (amended in 1979) added additional controls by prohibiting the use of inmate labor to fulfill general government contracts that exceeded $10,000.

After implementation of these laws, the possibility of prison self-sufficiency was doomed. With so few markets, the best prisons could do was to create small, specialty work opportunities for inmates that occupied their time and provided services or goods to public agencies and nonprofit organizations. For example, many states primarily engage prisoners in building or assembling furniture. A problem is that current manufacturing capacity for prison-made furniture is at maximum capacity in most states. So, if the goal is self-sufficiency of prisons, expansion of prison industry is necessary, but such expansion is difficult because of legal restrictions limiting the market. This problem is exacerbated because to expand, states would have to expend additional moneys, again on the prospect of self-sufficiency in a limited market. Expansion of existing manufacturing programs and the creation of new manufacturing lines must take into account potential markets and short- and long-term payouts in much the same way as private industry. The important difference is that the market for prison-made goods will never be an open market, so any expansion must be tempered with the reality of an involuntary work force, a limited manufacturing capacity, and a limited market for goods made.

The Kernel of Truth

Prisons do have enormous human-capital potential, and if it were possible to harness it institutional corrections could potentially contribute to the costs of operating prisons. The possibilities for prison industry are unlimited in a theoretical sense. Ideally, prisons would not only hold people who commit crimes but would actively treat, educate, vocationally train, and utilize the skills of those offenders to improve institutional corrections and society. If prisons were allowed to expand into high-tech teaching and training programs to produce marketable ex-offenders based on the education and skills acquired in prison, the possibility of contributing to the cost of incarceration would be feasible. However, the concept of "least eligibility" and the general public sentiment against such an investment prevents the achievement of such a goal in prison (Rothman 1971). Least eligibility refers to the concept that life in prison (treatment, education, training, food, medical care, etc.) should never be better than the life of the lowest working segment of society. Based on this premise, prison industry, which is the best chance at self-sufficiency, will never be cutting edge enough to contribute substantially to the costs of incarceration.

The general public, while supportive of basic human rights in prison, does not support better quality, more expansive treatment, education, and training than is available in society. The idea that a young man who works hard and stays out of trouble cannot afford to go to college or acquire a vocational skill, while a young man who never worked a day in his life and ends up in prison can emerge with a college degree or a skill that is highly sought after, is unacceptable to society. Finally, prisons generally cannot even utilize the existing skills and talents of incarcerated offenders unless they are applicable to existing prison-industry options, which they typically are not.

The Truth or Facts

Prisons have never been self-sufficient in providing the basic human necessities to inmates. The only circumstances under which prisons have approached self-sufficiency are those times when either the prison system did not provide those incarcerated with even the basic necessities of life (food, clothing, shelter), or when states leased or sold inmates to private entities (individuals or companies) who paid the state a fee and were then free to do as they wished with the inmates. Many were beaten, abused, and some even died at the hands of their "owners." Neither of these sets of circumstances proved the viability of self-sufficiency, since under neither sets of circumstances did the state attempt to provide even the most basic services to those incarcerated in its prisons.

Currently, prisons are not self-sufficient because of barriers to free trade of inmate goods and the basic level of services prison systems are required to provide those who are incarcerated. As already discussed, the first barrier is the inability to engage in free trade. Given the current legal restrictions on trade, the ability of prison systems to generate sufficient funding is limited. However, this does not mean prison-industry programs cannot help prisons survive. In many states with large industrial or agricultural programs, the profits from such enterprises are used to secure bonds to build new prisons and expand existing prisons, or they may be used to pay off bonds early.

In other states, cooperative arrangements with private businesses exchange prison-made goods and services for recreational and security equipment for prisons. The best current example of this type of arrangement is the agreements between telecommunication companies and prison systems to provide telephone services to incarcerated offenders. The initial investment by the company in many cases is tremendous (running fiber optic lines to multiple rural prisons throughout a state), but the profit over the term of the contract can far outweigh any initial investment. With this type of contract, state departments of correction generally receive a percentage of the overall profits, which they then reinvest into the maintenance, operation, and improvement of correctional facilities under their care.

Prisons will never be self-sufficient unless society's entire concept of sentencing and the use of incarceration as a punishment option changes. Since the beginning of correctional history, society has sent corrections mixed messages about what it wants prisons to do. Mixed messages are still being sent: calls for longer and tougher sentences followed by expectations for prison staff to produce a better person upon release. If self-sufficiency is the goal, institutional corrections can no longer be pulled in different directions. Long-term decisions must be made that support the possibility of creating a cost-effective prison model that meets the minimum standards required by the courts and society. The public must be willing to greatly reduce the number of offenders sent to prison while supporting rehabilitation efforts of treating, educating, and training offenders who are sent to prison. Society must abandon concepts like "least eligibility" and endorse offering high-quality, intensive, and extensive services in prison—services that may be better than those same services offered in the free world. Society must also open the free market to prison-made goods to encourage private/public partnership ventures, such as those currently under way with the Prison Industry Enhancement (PIE)

Certification Program—a federally certified industry program that allows private industry to use prison labor on prison sites within the general guidelines of the program. Although the PIE program works, in its present form it is much too restrictive to promote self-sufficiency within institutional corrections. In addition to welcoming prison made goods into the free market, the public must be willing to welcome incarcerated offenders into their communities as workers, and eventually welcome offenders who have completed their terms in prison back into society. These are the initial steps that must be taken to even explore the viability of correctional self-sufficiency.

Interests Served by the Myth

Whenever corrections threatens to arise as a political issue, the myth of self-sufficiency emerges to divert the public's attention from the larger questions of what corrections is supposed to do for society, and how corrections is to accomplish it. The idea that corrections will continue to absorb greater amounts of the average state budget is abhorrent to the general public. However, until the public embraces a goal for corrections that allows prisons to focus on those most feared and violent amongst criminals, the costs will continue to rise and any hope of mitigating cost will be lost.

There is a need for more rational sentencing policy. Too often, sentencing policy is the result of a lone lawmaker's personal quest for justice. For example, an increase in a particular drug-crime penalty was enacted in one southern state because the legislator who sponsored the change felt so passionately about his cause that he cried in committee. Even though his legislative colleagues did not believe an increase in the penalty to require offenders to serve 70 percent of their sentences before becoming eligible for parole was the right thing to do, they passed it anyway.

The myth also keeps alive the debate over opportunities for inmates. Many feel the opportunity to get a GED education, acquire college credit, receive vocational training, and have real work opportunities while in prison should not be a part of incarceration. They believe if all incarcerated inmates worked long hours at menial jobs, prison would be self-supporting. Until society is ready to make incarcerated offenders market-ready, sufficiency will not be possible. Work in prison must be promoted as a skill-based goal, not just an occupier of time or menial labor. Many prisons utilize inmates to support the institutional operation—they cook the food, do the laundry, clean the floors, and mow the yards or work in the fields (especially in southern prisons)—but until inmate labor encompasses skills that are in demand in the free world, correctional budgets will continue to grow.

Finally, the myth of self-sufficiency serves to maintain a clear and continuous divide between security and treatment components of incarceration. In prison, security is essential, while many in society consider treatment to be optional. The confusion is created by policymakers' insistence on treating security and treatment as separate functions of incarceration. This arbitrary division between security and treatment perpetuates the erroneous belief that treatment is an add-on function that could be eliminated without any adverse consequences. Most people wrongly assume security alone controls prisons. The reality is that security and treatment complement each other; both are necessary to keep prisons under control.

Policy Implications of Belief in the Myth

Policymakers continue to underfund corrections based on a deep-seated hope that prisons will somehow find a way to support themselves if money is denied them long enough. The myth of self-sufficiency sustains this hope. As long as the fallacy of self-sufficiency is allowed to remain a possibility, policymakers will hang on to it to use whenever funding of corrections reaches a point of crisis. Even the slight possibility of self-sufficiency fosters the hope that prison costs could be reduced, and constitutional standards maintained. This hope has clouded the issues of institutional corrections. Currently, there are more than 2 million individuals incarcerated in the United States. With continued growth at the current rate, the incarcerated population will reach 3 million inmates soon. It is unlikely that states or the federal government can support that kind of sustained growth without major shifts in budget priorities (Austin and Irwin 2001).

When policymakers gather to discuss corrections, the multiple goals of corrections typically overtake the real discussion and turn it into a garbled rhetoric of self-fulfilling wishes. On the rare occasion when the din of rhetoric subsides, clear voices of reason can be heard. Unfortunately, these voices are usually speaking a language foreign to the policymakers and legislators. To overcome the attendant attitude of caution, ignorance, individual prejudice, etc., it is important that the myth of self-sufficiency be understood. The long-term policy implication is that the myth continues to promote corrections as a second-class function of government. As long as the myth remains, attention can be diverted from long-term correctional issues.

Finally the myth of self-sufficiency allows policymakers to keep corrections as a second-class function of government as long as the possibility of self-sufficiency can be touted by an opponent of correctional funding. Even though the myth is blatantly false, it persists and manages to confuse the larger issue of the real purpose of incarceration.

References

Austin, J., and J. Irwin. 2001. *It's about time: America's imprisonment binge,* 3rd ed. Belmont, CA: Wadsworth Publishing.

Foucault, M. 1977. *Discipline and Punish: The Birth of the Prison.* Vintage Publishing.

Rothman, D. J. 1971. *The discovery of the asylum: Social order and disorder in the new republic.* New York: Little, Brown and Company. ✦

Chapter 25
Correctional Privatization and the Myth of Inherent Efficiency

Curtis Blakely and John Ortiz Smykla

The Myth

One of the most widely held myths in corrections is that the private sector operates prisons more efficiently than does the public sector. Furthermore, advocates of prison privatization assume the competitive marketplace motivates the private sector toward efficient operations. This, in turn, is believed to translate into substantial savings. Others believe the private sector operates more efficiently because it is unencumbered by bureaucratic red tape and more sensitive to wasteful practices. The myth of "inherent efficiency" suggests that the private sector manages and spends its resources and capital more prudently, does not reduce inmate provisions, and that cost savings are not the result of reductions in employee pay or staffing levels.

Proponents of privatization argue that the private sector can reduce prison-operating expenses by 20 percent. However, measuring and substantiating savings are difficult for at least three reasons. First, facilities differ in ways that confound cost comparisons. Second, differences between public- and private-sector accounting procedures make the identification of comparable costs difficult. Finally, although several studies comparing public and private correctional costs have sought to overcome these and other difficulties, few have succeeded (McDonald et al. 1998).

For purposes of this inquiry, we focus only on the third proposition of the myth, that cost reductions are not due to changes in staff pay or staffing levels. The other two propositions are difficult to examine because little information about prisoner services and resource management is available. While we recognize that inmate services and amenities are important components of institutional efficiency, we believe the more valid test lies in those factors closely related to a facility's employees. This position is supported by a number of scholars who suggest that tests of operational savings must focus on staffing and employee issues (Bloomer 1997; Brister 1996).

The Kernel of Truth

Our focus on labor costs is framed by a number of studies, several of which are reviews of existing research. Pratt and Maahs (1999) conducted a meta-analysis of 33 cost-effectiveness evaluations of private and public prisons. Their findings reveal that the daily cost to house an inmate within a privately operated facility was $2.45 less than it was to house an inmate in a public facility. Although this finding supports the belief that incarceration by the private sector is less expensive, the promise of double-digit savings or the alleviation of financial burdens on state corrections budgets did not materialize to the extent previously believed. Furthermore, Pratt and Maahs discovered that the more effective predictions of operating costs are a facility's economy of scale, its age, and its security level.

The Truth or Facts

Currently, more than 2 million people are behind bars in the United States, an increase of 28 percent in less than a decade (Harrison and Beck 2003). The most recent data reveal that the largest increase in type of confinement used within the United States is in the private sector (Stephan and Karberg 2003). Regardless of whether the unit of analysis is the number of confinement facilities, number of inmates, rated capacity, or number of staff, the increases were dramatically higher for private sector confinement from 1995 through 2000 than they were for federal or state confinement facilities (see Table 25.1). Explaining these increases, however, remains a mystery because as Gaes and colleagues (1998) point out, a coherent theory of why privately operated prisons are increasingly being utilized to supplement existing government facilities has yet to emerge.

In 2000, almost 78,000 adults were sentenced to confinement in private correctional facilities in 30 states, Puerto Rico, and the District of Columbia (Austin and Coventry 2001; Stephan and Karberg 2003), an increase of 511 percent from 1995. Texas had the most facilities (43), followed by California (24), Florida (10), and Colorado (9). In 2000, the Bureau of Prisons privatized 3,300 beds, with an estimated value of $760 million over 10 years. In 2001, the Immigration and Naturalization Service and the U.S. Marshal's Service renewed five private contracts worth approximately $50 million each (Caplan 2003). Of the 15 or so private-corrections firms operating in the United States, the largest in 2003 was Corrections Corporation of America (CCA). CCA con-

Table 25.1
Number of Confinement Facilities*, Inmates, Rated Capacity, and Staff in Federal, State, and Private Prisons, 1995 and 2000

		1995	2000
Number of confinement facilities	Federal	75	84
	State	1,056	1,023
	Private	29	101
Number of inmates in confinement facilities	Federal	80,221	110,974
	State	899,376	1,055,746
	Private	12,736	77,854
Rated capacity	Federal	64,500	83,113
	State	891,826	1,090,225
	Private	19,294	105,133
Number of custody/ security staff	Federal	10,048	12,376
	State	207,647	243,352
	Private	3,197	14,589

Source: Stephan, J. J., and J. C. Karberg. 2003. *Census of state and federal correctional facilities, 2000.* Washington, DC: U.S. Department of Justice.

* Confinement facilities are institutions in which less than 50 percent of the residents are regularly permitted to leave, unaccompanied by staff, for work, study, or rehabilitation.

trolled more than 50 percent of the private correctional market. Only Texas, California, the Federal Bureau of Prisons, New York, and Florida had prison systems larger than CCA.

The United States General Accounting Office (GAO) examined the operating costs of private and public prisons. The GAO detected little difference, or mixed results, and ultimately "could not conclude whether privatization saved money" (1996). The U.S. Marshals Service, which uses hundreds of governmental facilities to house its inmates, found that privately operated jails were costing 24 percent more than were their public counterparts (Gerth and Labaton 1995). More recently, Austin and Coventry (2001) examined cost savings in some of the better known comparative studies in the field of private corrections. Their findings suggest that rather than the fabled 5 to 20 percent savings attributed to private-sector operations, actual savings were closer to 1 percent, with most of that being achieved through lower labor costs. Costs associated with labor are what we turn to next.

A traditional disadvantage to public employment has been its relatively low pay in comparison to the private sector. The question of whether this advantage holds true in the field of prison operations has been overlooked. To start, salary and fringe benefits of prison staff account for approximately 70 percent of a facility's operating expense (Austin and Coventry 2001:16; Bates 1999:5; Greene 2000:4; Welch 2000:82). Therefore, the keys to containing or reducing labor costs are to provide the lowest possible wage to the least number of employees, while supervising a maximum number of inmates. This statement suggests that salary, inmate-to-staff ratios, and capacity levels prove especially insightful when considering the myth of cost-containment. We discuss each beginning with salary levels.

In 1998, the average salary for a correctional officer working in a private prison ranged from $15,919 to $19,103 per year (Camp and Camp 1998). In comparison, the average salary for a correctional officer working in a public prison ranged from $21,246 to $34,004 per year, a range difference of $3,184 to $12,758. In 2000, Camp and Camp reported that the median entry-level salary for a correctional officer working in a private prison was $17,628, while the median entry-level salary for a publicly employed correctional officer was $23,002. Median maximum salaries were $22,082 and $36,328, respectively. It is therefore safe to say that, on average, the private sector pays its correctional officers less than does the public sector.

Private prisons also operate with fewer staff. Austin and Coventry (2001:52) found that private prisons operate with 15 percent fewer staff than does the public sector. For example, lawmakers in North Carolina learned that CCA planned to hire only 68 corrections officers to supervise 528 inmates instead of the 141 officers the state employed (Neff 1998). Using the starting salary ($21,246) of a public correctional officer as a test of savings, CCA would have saved $1.5 million in annual operating expenses in the North Carolina facility due to a higher inmate-to-officer ratio. Similar findings have been observed in juvenile facilities where the private sector maintains an average of approximately 3.9 juveniles per staff member compared to the public's ratio of 1.7 to 1 (Armstrong and MacKenzie 2003). Although some of the difference in staffing ratios might be attributed to the relatively new age of private facilities and the use of technology, corrections is a labor-intensive business, and the private sector simply employs fewer staff per inmate than does the public sector. Next we consider the effects that reduced pay and staffing levels have on a prison's employees. We begin with a discussion of employee turnover.

Turnover refers to the number of correctional officers or staff leaving a prison within one year. To consider turnover, we examine both correctional-officer turnover and staff turnover. The literature on correctional-officer turnover reveals that the turnover rate for correctional officers in private prisons is almost three times what it is in public prisons, 53 percent versus 16 percent, respectively (Thompson 2002). Welch (2000:82) even found a turnover rate of 100 percent in one private prison. Reasons for correctional-officer turnover are shown in Table 25.2. The data suggest that correctional officers in

Table 25.2
*Reasons for Correctional Officer
Turnover in Private and Public Prison*

	Private prison	Public prison
Resigned	71.0%	63%
Retired	0.6%	15%
Dismissed/Other	28.4%	22%

Source: Camp, C. G., and G. M. Camp. 1998. *The corrections yearbook 1998*. Middletown, CT: Criminal Justice Institute.

private prisons resign their jobs more frequently than do their public counterparts.

A high staff turnover rate directly benefits company owners and stockholders, especially if the cost of new staff training remains low. Research has shown that the private sector offers fewer hours of pre-service training to corrections officers than does its public counterparts, 149 hours versus 250 hours, respectively (Thompson 2002). Thus, if one were to assume that training new corrections officers is an expense associated with high turnover, then reducing the number of training hours would also lower private correctional costs and contribute to higher profit margins.

Turnover rates also influence retirement benefits. High turnover rates mean correctional officers do not stay on the job long enough to receive retirement benefits. Although no information is currently available about the type and amount of benefits provided by the private sector, Table 25.2 shows correctional-officer turnover is higher in the private sector than it is in the public sector.

All of this leads us to challenge the myth that the private sector can and does operate its facilities in a more efficient manner. Instead, cost savings can be attributed to less salary and salary advancement, fewer employees, high turnover rates, and fewer employees receiving re-

tirement packages. Thus, when based upon an assessment of factors associated with employee pay and staffing levels, we see a violation of the third proposition of inherent efficiency that savings must not be the result of pay reductions or a reduction in the number of employees retained by a facility. By relying upon reduced pay and fewer employees, and by failing to present these factors as substantially contributing to reduced operating costs, the private sector is able to promote itself and its services as being more efficient. The promotion of this myth ensures the private sector continues to gain increasing shares of the correctional market without revealing that its cost savings are the result of reductions in employee pay and staffing levels.

Interests Served by the Myth

We believe the myth persists because the politics of misinformation, and the beneficiaries of this misinformation are private-prison administrators, former public-prison administrators, staff, shareholders, government officials, and politicians who are able to profit from the government's insatiable need for additional correctional space. By perpetuating the myth, the private sector ensures it survives, expands operations, and reaps financial rewards in terms of profit-sharing programs, stock valuation, and continued employment.

Consider what happened in Tennessee and Florida. In 1985, a former Tennessee governor and the CCA cofounder and chairman of the state republican party were good friends. The governor backed a plan to hand over the entire state prison system to CCA for $200 million. The state legislature rejected the plan as too risky, but not before it was discovered that the governor's wife and the Speaker of the

House in Tennessee's General Assembly were CCA stockholders. The governor's wife earned $100,000 profit when she converted her CCA stock to a blind trust (Bates 1998).

In 1986, CCA won a contract to operate the Silverdale Work Farm near Chattanooga for $21 per inmate per day, $3 less than the county was spending. Not long afterwards, however, a crackdown on drunk drivers flooded the work farm with new inmates. The county soon found itself $200,000 over budget. "The work farm became a gold mine [for CCA]," (Bates 1998: 3). When the contract came up for renewal, county commissioners voted to remain with CCA. One commissioner had a pest-control contract with CCA and later went to work for CCA as a lobbyist, another did landscaping at the prison, and a third ran the moving company that settled the warden into his new home. CCA also put the son of the county employee responsible for monitoring the Silverdale contract on the payroll at its Nashville headquarters.

Conflict of interest over privatization has also spilled over into higher education. In 1999, the Florida Ethics Commission found that a University of Florida criminologist, Charles Thomas, had a considerable financial stake in the success of private prisons and fined him $20,000 for conflict of interest. The crux of the issue involved Thomas being the director of the Private Corrections Project, which was housed within the Center for Studies in Criminology at the University of Florida. The Commission ruled that Thomas' published research and media quotations in support of private prisons did not reveal that he was a trustee of the CCA-offshoot, Prison Realty Trust, of which he owned 30,000 shares, and from which he received $12,000 a year, $1,000 for each board meeting, $500 for each

meeting of subcommittees, and a summer salary of $25,000 (from an organization to which CCA was a large contributor). His co-authors were also affiliated with the same industry-funded organization.

In April 2004, Florida's *St. Petersburg Times* reported that Governor Bush asked his inspector general to investigate whether the Correctional Privatization Commission (CPS), the state agency that oversees private prisons in Florida, violated the law by hiring a former state corrections secretary as a consultant (James 2004). CPS paid him $64,000 to oversee the commission's efforts to bid for two of the state's five private prison contracts. Florida state law prohibits the commission from hiring anyone who worked in the previous two years for the state department of corrections to discourage conflicts of interest between public and private prisons.

Quick fixes and simple solutions have been a part of corrections management since the eighteenth century, when the Quakers first believed solitary confinement and a religious curriculum would reduce crime. Not much has changed since the eighteenth century. It matters little that there is sound research on which to build policy. Perception, rather than fact, often dominates. As a result, correctional policies are often based on image rather than research. Had results from randomized experimentation in the Kansas City Preventive Patrol Experiment, the Minneapolis Domestic Violence Experiment, or ISP (Intensive Supervision Probation and Parole) guided public policy, the criminal justice system would be much different today. However, results from these and other scholarly inquiries have had little overall influence. Evaluation research counts for little in guiding criminal justice policy. The facts in this myth are clear—most, if not all, of the savings that jurisdictions enjoy through privatization are due to cuts in staffing and staff pays.

Policy Implications of Belief in the Myth

To consider the policy implications of this myth, at least three observations should be made. First, cheaper does not necessarily mean better. Jurisdictions should ensure all contracts specify that the quantity and quality of services to be provided meet or exceed those provided by the contracting jurisdiction. Second, legal and contractual issues pertaining to use of force, public access to private prison records, and the impact of bankruptcy laws on private contractor insolvency continue to provoke discussion. Jurisdictions that consider these issues early within the contracting process will certainly be better prepared to ensure they receive the best possible service for their money. Finally, there is strong public employee opposition to private prisons by a number of influential organizations, such as the National Sheriff's Association (NSA) and the American Federation of State and County Municipal Employees (AFSCME). AFSCME provides web access to many antiprivatization documents on its website (*http://www.afscme.org*). This site and others like it continue to raise questions and identify issues that warrant further discussion.

Whether or not private prisons save money, sustained growth within the private sector is likely to increase for a number of reasons. First, many of the leaders in the private prison movement come from the public sector, and can use their influence to obtain additional contracts. Second, the private sector, while hesitantly admitting that savings might not be as much as expected, argue that they still provide a valuable service. Such a state-

ment is difficult to counter. Third, as interest continues to increase in the privatization of education, social security, social services, and various public utilities, and as claims of success (real or imagined) are publicized, it will become increasingly difficult to discontinue experimentation with correctional privatization. Fourth, some private providers might develop a coherent theory explaining why private ownership might provide better rehabilitation services for special prison populations (the elderly, mentally challenged, drug abusers, and those with HIV/AIDS and TB). Finally, if prison populations again rise, legislators will have little alternative but to turn to the private sector for solutions to the many challenges they will encounter.

While double-digit savings may have failed to materialize, it is unlikely that hidden labor costs will eventually be the demise of private corrections. The number of private prisons is likely to increase, but not at the pace exhibited during the past two decades. Public opinion may be the determining factor on how much of the corrections profession will be outsourced to private providers. The evolution from public to private management will continue to be painful to correctional traditionalists.

References

Armstrong, G., and D. MacKenzie. 2003. Private vs. public juvenile correctional facilities: Do differences in environmental quality exist? *Crime and Delinquency* 49:542–563.

Austin, J., and G. Coventry. 2001. *Emerging issues on privatized prisons*. Washington, DC: U.S. Department of Justice, Bureau of Justice Assistance.

Bates, E. 1998. Private prisons. *The Nation* January 5. Accessed online: *http://www.druglibrary.org/schaffer/media/thenation_0105bate.htm*.

———. 1999. Private prisons. *The Nation* June 7. Accessed online: *http://www.thenation.com/doc.mhtml?i=19990607&s=bates*.

Bloomer, K. 1997. America's newest growth industry. *These Times* March 17.

Brister, R. C. 1996. Changing of the guard: A case for privatization of Texas prisons. *The Prison Journal* 76:310–330.

Camp, C. G., and G. M. Camp. 1998. *The corrections yearbook 1997*. Middletown, CT: Criminal Justice Institute.

———. 2000. *The corrections yearbook 2000*. Middletown, CT: Criminal Justice Institute.

Caplan, J. 2003. Policy for profit: The private-prison industry's influence over criminal justice legislation. *ACJS Today* 26:15.

Gaes, G. G., S. D. Camp, and W. G. Saylor. 1998. Appendix 2: Comparing the quality of publicly and privately operated prisons: A review of research. In *Private prisons in the United States: An assessment of current practice*, eds. D. McDonald, E. Fournier, M. Russell-Einhorn, and S. Crawford. Boston: Abt Associates.

Gerth, J., and S. Labaton. 1995. Prisons for profit. *New York Times* November 24.

Greene, J. 2000. Prison privatization: Recent developments in the United States. Paper presented at the International Conference on Penal Abolition. Accessed July 15, 2004 online: *http://www.grassrootsleadership.org/Articles/j_greene.html*.

Harrison, P., and Beck, A. J. 2003. *Prisoners in 2002*. Washington, DC: U.S. Department of Justice, Bureau of Justice Statistics.

James, J. 2004. Inquiry to view prisons hiring. *St. Petersburg Times* April 27.

McDonald, D., E. Fournier, M. Russell-Einhorn, and S. Crawford. 1998. *Private prisons in the United States: An assessment of current practice*. Boston: Abt Associates.

Neff, J. 1998. Lawmakers want to let a private-prison company double the capacity of the facilities it is building. *News and Observer Publishing Company* February 6.

Pratt, T., and J. Maahs. 1999. Are private prisons more cost-effective than public prisons? A meta-analysis of evaluation research studies. *Crime and Delinquency* 45:358–371.

Stephan, J., and J. C. Karberg. 2003. *Census of state and federal correctional facilities, 2003*. Washington, DC: U.S. Department of Justice.

Thompson, K. 2002. AU law, corrections, prisoners' rights expert to participate on task force to combat prison privatization *AU News* July 26. Accessed online: *http://www.american.edu/media/*.

U.S. General Accounting Office (GAO). 1996. *Private and public prisons: Studies comparing operational costs and/or quality of service*. Washington, DC: U.S. General Accounting Office.

Welch, M. 2000. The role of the immigration and naturalization service in the prison-industrial complex. *Social Justice* 27:73–88. ✦

Chapter 26
The Myth That the Focus of Community Corrections Is Rehabilitation

Mark Jones

The Myth

Community corrections is the subfield of corrections consisting of programs in which offenders are supervised and provided services outside jail or prison. It consists of such programs as diversion, restitution, probation, parole, halfway houses, and various provisions for temporary release from prison or jail. One popular myth about community corrections is that it is concerned almost solely with rehabilitation, but the history of community corrections, especially both probation and parole, is a mixture of attempts to control and assist offenders in the community. American probation has its genesis in the 1840s. John Augustus, a Boston shoemaker and dedicated foe of alcohol use, began making trips to local courts in 1841, volunteering to take offenders accused of petty crimes such as drunkenness and prostitution under his supervision for 30–60 days, and to report their progress to the court. If Augustus presented a positive report to the court, the judge would either dismiss the charges or impose a minimal punishment, such as

court costs, which Augustus would often pay himself. Augustus's efforts, and a growing sentiment toward diverting juveniles from incarceration, spawned similar pretrial intervention and probation supervision efforts throughout the United States for adults and juveniles during the nineteenth century. Thus, probation has a strong historical tie with the rehabilitative ideal.

Parole has a different history. Unlike probation, it was not a U.S. invention. In 1840, Alexander Maconochie assumed charge of Great Britain's penal colony on Norfolk Island, located 900 miles off the coast of Australia. In the belief that providing an incentive for good behavior would make the prison more orderly and act as a rehabilitative measure, Maconochie instituted a graduated-release system for prisoners, culminating in conditional release, referred to as *ticket-of-leave*. Walter Crofton, who oversaw British penal facilities in Ireland, adapted Maconochie's system several years later. American penologists studied Crofton's system; chief among them was Zebulon Brockway, a Michigan prison warden. Brockway instituted a similar system at the Elmira Reformatory in New York in the 1870s, except conditional release was called parole, a term historically associated with war prisoners who were released upon an agreement not to resume battle.

Viewing parole's history from this standpoint might lead one to believe that parole's primary concern has been with rehabilitation and the control of prison populations, but that is only part of the story. Before parole, early prison release decisions in the United States were in the hands of governors, who had the power to grant pardons or commutations of sentence. Some governors grew tired of pressure from prisoners' family members to commute the sentences of relatives or constituents of powerful legislators, and some governors were subject to bribes and manipulation by virtue of possessing such power. As a result, parole boards were created to make prison-release decisions in a supposedly less arbitrary and politically charged manner. Parole, therefore, was instituted as much for the purposes of political reform as it was to control prison populations and recently released inmates.

An ancillary myth about community corrections is that rehabilitation and enforcement are diametrically opposed and cannot coexist. The truth is that rather than seeing rehabilitation and enforcement as complete opposites, like a continuum, one should view them in a circular fashion, as starting out with opposing ideals but accomplishing similar objectives. For example, while community corrections officers may view mandatory substance-abuse treatment as a means of assistance, offenders may view it as a punishment because counseling may be inconvenient, unpleasant, and intrusive. One rather exceptional case demonstrates this idea. Johnson (2003) relates the story of a young man placed on probation for sexual assault. Fearing he would fail a urine test (a form of substance-abuse treatment), the young man left the state. He eventually returned, but was given stricter conditions of probation, one of which was to avoid alcohol intoxication. After failing a breathalyzer test, the young man's probation officer ordered him to take Antabuse, a drug that induces sickness if the taker consumes alcohol. The Antabuse, which was designed to forcibly curb his craving for alcohol, supposedly had unpleasant side affects, which prompted him to see a physician who recommended antidepressant medication. The young man eventually committed suicide, driven in part by the fear that he

could not live up to the terms of his sentence, all of which were supposed to help him. Although Johnson's explanation for the young man's problem appears too simplistic—i.e., probation drove him to suicide—it demonstrates the maxim that government usually does its greatest degree of harm when trying to help someone.

The Kernel of Truth

The idea that rehabilitation is an integral part of community corrections contains more than a kernel of truth. Many agents view rehabilitation as a large part of their mission, many attempts to rehabilitate are present, and it is a vital part of community corrections' history. The array of rehabilitative tools offered or brokered through community corrections is quite large and diverse. Common rehabilitative measures include: (1) substance-abuse counseling, (2) anger management, (3) vocational training and rehabilitation, (4) mental-health treatment, (4) education, and (5) life-skills training. Some community corrections agencies administer these services directly, but the more common approach is for community corrections agencies to recommend or require offenders to seek these services from other agencies, with the officer's primary task being to monitor compliance and progress with the service.

Klockars (1974) identified four philosophical orientations in community corrections work. One is the *law enforcer,* who is concerned with strict enforcement of the conditions of release and acts quickly against those who commit violations. The second is the *therapeutic agent,* whose primary or sole concern is rehabilitation. The third is the *timeserver,* who has no real philosophical orientation, but merely goes through the motions of doing the job. The fourth is the *synthetic officer*, who represents a blend of the other three orientations. The truth about community corrections is that most officers represent the synthetic orientation, without adhering strictly to law enforcement or to a rehabilitative ideal, but striving to provide a mixture of both.

The Truth or Facts

During the 1980s, some researchers suggested that probation officers had adopted a law-enforcement orientation toward their work (Harris, Clear, and Baird 1989). The truth is the law-enforcement orientation was already present, especially in parole. In his study of the history of parole in California, Simon (1993) maintains that parole has always been concerned with controlling lower-class criminal offenders, with a lesser concern for rehabilitation.

The extent to which orientation, law enforcement, or rehabilitation holds greater sway in a community-corrections agency depends on a number of factors. The first factor in the orientation debate centers around legal constraints on an agency. In some states or jurisdictions, probation or parole officers are not allowed to recommend jail or prison sentences for certain types of violations. For instance, several years ago, Arizona enacted a law prohibiting the incarceration of offenders convicted of first-time misdemeanor marijuana possession. All such offenders were placed on probation. By law, courts were not allowed to incarcerate these offenders, regardless of how many violations they committed. Therefore, probation officers found themselves virtually handcuffed with these offenders because they could not use the threat of incarceration as leverage against them. The result was that probation officers quickly rec-ommended early termination of these cases, thinking it futile to keep people under supervision that they could not control.

The second factor are the stated goals and mission of the agency. In some states, community-corrections services are administered by a corrections department, some by the judiciary, and some by state-welfare or social-service agencies. Being housed in a social-welfare agency might be an indication that rehabilitation is an overriding goal of the agency, whereas being housed in a corrections department might indicate that law enforcement holds greater sway.

The organizational culture is also an influencing factor. While the overall mission of a community-corrections agency is important, what may be more important is the day-to-day work environment and attitudes within the workgroup. While two agencies in neighboring counties may be housed administratively in the same statewide department, the people within a certain work environment, especially the middle managers, may have different orientations toward their work and their mission. Managers, judges, and officers in one county may be oriented very strongly toward law enforcement; while managers, judges, and officers in the neighboring county may have a stronger orientation toward rehabilitation.

Finally, and perhaps the most important factor, is the individual officer. One finds a great diversity of attitudes toward the purpose of community corrections within individual agencies and among individual officers. Some officers may be oriented toward law enforcement while some may be oriented toward rehabilitation. In practice, public safety is a much easier sell than rehabilitation; therefore, community-corrections agencies have adopted public safety as their overriding objective. Crime and fear of crime victimization consistently rank high on the list of public concerns, as indicated by pollsters (Reddick 2003). A result of the concern with crime has been more police officers, more people in prison, more people on probation, and the abolition of parole in some jurisdictions. Between 1980 and 2002, the percentage of Americans in prison increased more than 350 percent, although this acceleration has slowed in recent years (Bureau of Justice Statistics 2003). The truth about community corrections is that its agents are in the business of catching people breaking rules and locking them up.

Another truth about community corrections is that most officers do not have the expertise to offer rehabilitation services. The typical requirement for becoming a probation or parole officer is a four-year degree from an accredited college or university, with preference usually, but not always, given to those with degrees or backgrounds in criminal justice, social work, counseling, or some related discipline. The majority of community-corrections officers do not have the expertise needed to provide quality rehabilitative services such as drug counseling. The best that most community-corrections officers can offer is monitoring an offender's compliance with rehabilitative requirements.

In addition, with caseloads ranging in size from 50 to 500, it is ludicrous to expect quality treatment from anyone, regardless of his or her qualifications. Given the size of caseloads, very few officers can provide the quality of service of a full-time service provider. One example from the author's experience as a probation officer illustrates the frustration officers often encounter when trying to provide their own rehabilitation service while administering a large caseload. Another officer had a degree in social work and was well trained in substance-abuse counseling. She was one of the few people in the office who had such expertise. Unfortunately, she spent most of her day completing paperwork on recently sentenced offenders, explaining their conditions of supervision, writing delinquent reports for those who violated the terms of release, going back and forth to court and staff meetings, and documenting every conversation she had with clients on her caseload. She did not have opportunities to spend the time necessary to deliver quality counseling to her probationers. When she did try to make the time, she grew frustrated with the backlog of paperwork and the offenders waiting for her in the lobby. She eventually resigned herself to just going through the bureaucratic motions of probation work, not because of apathy but because time constraints offered her no other choice.

The transformation of community corrections' mission is even reflected in the appearance of many officers. The historical image of the community-corrections officer is either the crusading therapeutic agent or the seasoned bureaucrat. In many agencies today, probation and parole officers are barely distinguishable from plainclothes police officers. They may openly display a badge, carry and be trained in technologically advanced weapons, and possess the overall bearing of a law enforcer, not a social worker. Many probation and parole officers are also discovering an unintended benefit of carrying a gun and badge—offers of free and discounted meals in restaurants—which introduces an entirely new set of ethical questions to community-corrections work.

Nowhere is the enforcement ideal exhibited within community corrections better than electronic house arrest. Harvard researchers developed early electronic house arrest mechanisms in the 1960s as a means of monitoring released mental patients. Interest in electronic monitoring was revived in the 1980s, based on three factors: (1) the realization that home visits at night and on weekends could not insure an offender would stay at home; (2) the need for a viable solution to jail and prison crowding that would help insure public safety; and (3) the efforts of a New Mexico judge who, frustrated with sending people to prison who did not belong there, and equally frustrated with placing people on probation who viewed the sanction as a joke, contracted a computer salesman to develop a mechanism for tracking offenders' movements in the community (Jones 2004; Ross and Jones 1997). Since the 1980s, the electronic house-arrest industry has mushroomed, and private vendors have greatly increased the effectiveness of their products, with community-corrections agencies eager to embrace these technological supervision aids. Electronic house arrest represents the embodiment of the control aspect of community corrections. Its sole purpose is to monitor an offender's whereabouts. It does not offer any form of treatment or assistance. The object is simple: Protect the public from an offender by keeping that offender at home. Although officers who supervise these offenders may attempt to rehabilitate them in other ways, the electronic monitoring device does not address underlying personal factors that may lead the offender into crime, such as drug problems, psychological or psychiatric maladies, or family problems (an irony given that many offenders have problems with their home life, and the device is designed to keep them in that environment).

Electronic house arrest and intensive supervision have made community corrections punitive. In fact, in some instances, community corrections has become so punitive that offenders opt to forego community-corrections supervision in favor of serving a prison or jail sentence. A 1996 study found that 10 to 15 percent of North Carolina probationers chose prison over community corrections. One of the leading predictors of choosing incarceration over probation was being under intensive supervision; another predictor was having to pay a hefty fine or restitution (Jones 1996).

Interests Served by the Myth

The primary interests served by the community corrections–rehabilitation myth are an ideology and the people who benefit from it—the practitioners who support rehabilitation. That ideology is based in large measure on the ideal of positivism, which is the belief that human behavior is the result of social, psychological, or biological factors and can be treated through scientific means (Jones 2004). According to that ideal, crime to some extent is "curable." Those who support the rehabilitative ideal argue that incarceration focuses primarily on punishment, whereas community corrections focuses on rehabilitation.

Private corporations also have an interest in this myth. Some of these corporations sell products, such as electronic house-arrest equipment, that are designed to assist the public-safety goals of community corrections; however, many offer rehabilitative-type services and products, including the types of common rehabilitative services listed previously. Rehabilitation-type services are often more labor intensive and expensive; therefore, these corporations can make more money from selling rehabilitative services than from public-safety products.

Finally, some politicians and other punishment advocates can use the rehabilitative ideal to mask their real intentions. These people are able to put a humane spin on otherwise punitive policies by emphasizing rehabilitation. This strategy, at least to some extent, may appease both sides in the "punishment versus rehabilitation" debate. The reality is that community corrections is increasingly becoming more punitive, even though it continues to emphasize its rehabilitation components.

Policy Implications of Belief in the Myth

Belief in the myth that community corrections focuses on rehabilitation has several practical consequences. First, if true rehabilitative efforts are attempted in an environment that stresses public safety, the rehabilitative programs are likely to fail. If this occurs in community corrections, money may be wasted on half-hearted or disingenuous efforts at rehabilitation.

Additionally, community-corrections personnel may become demoralized when they discover that what they do is mostly law enforcement and not the counseling that they wanted to do and went to school to learn. At a time when community-corrections agencies are having a difficult time retaining qualified personnel, a work environment that emphasizes public safety while publicly holding out the ideal of rehabilitation places stress on community corrections personnel. This may create excessive turnover in agencies and inflated personnel hiring and training costs.

The myth creates problems for colleges and universities as well. During the 1960s and 1970s, most colleges and universities that offered community-corrections courses operated under the assumption that probation and parole officers focused on rehabilitation. Because community corrections is placing greater emphasis on public safety and the enforcement aspects of community corrections, textbook writers and those who teach community corrections, perhaps in fairness to their students, should focus less on training students in the therapeutic aspects of community corrections, and emphasize the issues of public safety, risk management, and legal liability.

References

Bureau of Justice Statistics. 2003. Prison Statistics. Accessed online: *http://www.ojp.usdoj. gov/bjs/prisons.htm.*

Harris, P., T. R. Clear, and S. C. Baird. 1989. Have community supervision officers changed their attitudes toward their work? *Justice Quarterly* 6(2):233–246.

Johnson, B. 2003. Grieving mom reflects on son's struggle with probation. *Denver Post* November 29.

Jones, M. 1996. Voluntary revocations and the 'elect to serve' option in North Carolina probation. *Crime and Delinquency* 42(1):36–49.

———. 2004. *Community corrections.* Prospect Heights, IL: Waveland.

Klockars, C. B. 1974. A theory of probation supervision. *Journal of Criminal Law, Criminology and Police Science* 63(4):550–557.

Reddick, C. 2003. Casebanking as a budget response. *Community Corrections Report on Law and Corrections Practice* 10(6):81, 91–92.

Ross, D. L., and M. Jones. 1997. Electronic monitoring and boot camp in North Carolina: Comparing recidivism. *Criminal Justice Policy Review* 8(4):383–403.

Simon, J. 1993. *Poor discipline: Parole and the social control of the underclass, 1890–1990.* Chicago: University of Chicago Press. ✦

Chapter 27
The Myth That Correctional Rehabilitation Does Not Work

*Francis T. Cullen
and Paula Smith*

When a person breaks the law, what should the government and its criminal justice system do? A common response might be, "Catch and punish the offender." But embedded in any answer is an amalgamation of philosophical and practical issues that have implications for the values that define us as Americans and for our ability to achieve a safer society. Thus, the response of how to react to a lawbreaker is hardly simple. And, perhaps not surprisingly, the answer Americans have offered to the question of what to do with offenders has changed—sometimes dramatically—over our distant and recent history.

On one level, most Americans would agree that criminals should be punished to compensate for the harm they have caused. In making this suggestion, they are arguing that a core purpose of the criminal justice system is to achieve justice—to balance the harm caused by the offender against the pain suffered by the victim. This philosophical justification for punishing offenders is sometimes called "retribution" and sometimes called "just deserts." If justice were our only concern,

then we would stop our analysis at this point and focus our attention exclusively on how best to achieve this goal of justice. However, as a people, we want the criminal justice system to achieve something else: We also want the system to control or reduce crime, to make the community safer. This mission is called a "utilitarian" goal because the purpose of sanctioning offenders is not just an end in and of itself (justice) but involves the use of the penalty to achieve a broader end (crime control).

Of course, this raises the problem of how best to control crime. Most readers of this chapter have lived all, or much, of their lives at a time when federal, state, and local governments have told us that the best strategy to halt lawbreaking is to "get tough on crime." Indeed, virtually every election is punctuated by politicians competing over who, once in office, will put more offenders behind bars for longer periods of time. Although not the purpose of this chapter, we will pause to note that this "get tough" approach has produced mixed results. Most research indicates that imposing stiff prison sentences on offenders does little to reduce recidivism (it may even increase reoffending) and prevents only a modest amount of crime by keeping them off the streets (i.e., by "incapacitating" them) (Clear 1994; Cullen et al. 2002b; Currie 1998; Spelman 2000). Commentators have also noted that reductions in crime have only been achieved at an enormous financial cost, robbing the government's treasury of money that might have been devoted to other pressing social needs.

There is, however, another possible perspective on how to make offenders brought into the criminal justice system less criminally oriented when they leave the system: to rehabilitate them. This approach can be defined in this way (see Cullen 2002:255):

> Rehabilitation is a planned correctional intervention that targets for change the factors known through scientific studies to cause crime. The goal is to reduce recidivism and, where possible, to improve other aspects of an offender's life.

Thus, when done correctly, rehabilitation involves subjecting an offender to a program specifically designed to change the person. This planning should include knowledge of what criminology has shown are the factors that are, or are not, related to a person's reoffending. The intervention should focus on altering these factors so that the offender will be less at risk of returning to crime. In the process, rehabilitation has the potential not only to make an offender less criminal, but also to help the person live an improved life (e.g., to be more educated, more employable, better able to sustain family relationships). Note that "get tough" approaches mainly wish to inflict pain or discomfort on offenders and do not seek to improve them as persons or as community citizens.

Although it might seem strange in today's political environment, until three decades ago, most public officials in the United States—as well as most criminologists—would have argued that rehabilitation should be the main goal of the criminal justice system. In fact, the place of rehabilitation in our nation's crime policies and culture is long-standing and, in a way, fundamental. Indeed, in the 1820s, America was the first nation to create a prison system; it is instructive that these newly invented institutions were called "penitentiaries." The purpose of placing inmates in cells was not merely to remove them from society but to allow them to contemplate their waywardness, to do penance, and to build moral character— that is, to change who they were and to have them emerge from their time behind bars as reformed individuals (Rothman 1971). In the 1900s, the term "corrections" eventually was selected to describe the state's reactions to offenders. Thus, after an offender is convicted, this person is said to be entering the "correctional system." Prisons are spoken of as "correctional institutions"—and not as "punishment" or "justice" institutions. Offenders not sent to prison are said to be subject to "community corrections." The language of corrections, of course, embodies the goal of rehabilitation: We are to "correct" and not simply to punish offenders.

However, within a relatively short period of time—from the late 1960s into the mid-1970s—the previously accepted ideal of rehabilitation came under a withering attack. It suddenly became fashionable to proclaim that attempting to treat offenders was a failed enterprise. As discussed below, a key pillar of this shift in thinking was the emergent belief—based in part on a famous study—that "nothing works" to rehabilitate offenders. Thus, if correctional programs were hopelessly flawed— if they had no utility—it was not reasonable to continue to support rehabilitation as a goal.

This attack on rehabilitation, though damaging, was not completely successful. To be sure, many public officials and criminologists embraced the "nothing works" idea—a fact that had disquieting consequences for correctional policy and practice. But many of those working in correctional agencies continued to try to keep treatment services alive and to help offenders. Most significantly, although support for rehabilitation declined somewhat, a silent majority among the public continues to support treating offenders as a purpose of corrections (Cullen, Fisher, and Applegate 2000). One recent national study, for example, found that 88 percent of the respondents agreed that "it is important to try to rehabilitate adults who have committed crime and are now in the correctional system." When the same item was asked with regard to rehabilitating juveniles, 98 percent agreed (Cullen et al. 2002). These findings show that rehabilitation remains a vital part of our nation's belief system. The significance of this insight will be explored later.

This chapter is divided into five parts. First, we will explore the origins of the myth that "nothing works" to rehabilitate offenders. In the second section, we will argue that the idea that criminals cannot be reformed is based, in part, on a kernel of truth—on the reality that many previous treatment programs have been ineffective. In the third section, however, we explore why the "nothing works" idea is a myth. We attempt to show that the existing empirical evidence demonstrates both that interventions can be effective and that promising strategies exist for effecting change in offenders. The fourth section explores the interests that helped to nourish the growth of the "nothing works" myth. The fifth and final section will examine the policy implications of "nothing works" mythology—its dangers and where next to proceed in pursuing a more beneficial future for corrections in America.

The Myth

In the early 1970s, Robert Martinson was part of a research team given the task of reviewing the existing research literature to determine the effectiveness of correctional programs (Lipton, Martinson, and Wilks 1975). Martinson did not start out as a doubter of rehabilitation; but as the results of the team's evaluation accumulated, he became increasingly pessimistic that they would find any intervention that would reliably reform offenders. Indeed, he began to question whether, within the confines of prisons and community supervision, it would ever be possible to change criminals for the better.

Martinson became so skeptical of the rehabilitation enterprise that he took it upon himself in 1974 to publish, as a single author, an unauthorized article that appeared in *The Public Interest*. In a way, this work had the trappings of a typical academic article reporting the results of a research project. Thus, Martinson noted that the team's project involved a review of 231 evaluation studies, published between 1945 and 1967, that compared outcomes for a treatment group with outcomes for a control group. He then offered a rather dry, scholarly-like summary. "With few and isolated exceptions," concluded Martinson, "the rehabilitative efforts that have been reported thus far have had no appreciable effect on recidivism" (1974a:25).

In and of itself, this assertion was not revolutionary. Several other researchers had already reached similar conclusions. But unlike his predecessors, Martinson did not use his findings on the ineffectiveness of existing programs to call for a renewed commitment to construct treatment interventions that were more scientifically based and implemented in a way that they could achieve behavioral change. He took a very different path, raising a more fundamental question: "Do all these studies lead irrevocably to the conclusion that nothing works, that we haven't the faintest clue about how to rehabilitate offenders and reduce recidivism?" (1974a). Martinson stopped short of explicitly saying that nothing could ever work in corrections, but his point was clear. Not long thereafter, he was interviewed in a segment on *60 Minutes* where he echoed his deep reservations about treatment. And in another forum, he admitted that, although his work did not contain the statement that "rehabilitation is a 'myth,'" it was a "conclusion I have come to" (1974b:4).

The review by Martinson and his colleagues was, at the time, a state-of-the-art piece of scholarship (Lipton, Martinson, and Wilks 1975). But most writings in the world of academia—including the best of studies—are greeted not with unanimous praise but with a measure of scrutiny and skepticism. If Martinson's writings had been closely inspected—as they were by only a few scholars (see, e.g., Palmer 1975)—observers would have discovered that the results were not as clear-cut as they had been portrayed. Thus, only about a third of the studies included measures of both treatment programs and recidivism (as opposed to a program such as probation or an outcome measure such as adjustment to prison). Across these studies, about half actually showed that recidivism was reduced (Palmer 1975). Many treatment interventions that have subsequently proven to be the most effective (e.g., cognitive behavioral programs) either were not analyzed separately or were not included in the study (Cullen and Gendreau 2000). In short, Martinson's research should have been a sobering reminder that many things done in the name of rehabilitation border on quackery (Latessa, Cullen, and Gendreau 2002). However, in suggesting that "nothing works" or that "nothing could ever work" to rehabilitate offenders, Martinson was reaching far beyond his data.

It is noteworthy that Martinson's study was not subjected to withering analysis but rather was quickly and uncritically accepted as the final word on rehabilitation. "Nothing works" thus became a doctrine—something that virtually all policy makers and criminologists accepted as being true. We will argue that "nothing works" should be considered a myth because it is inaccurate, but that is an issue for later in this chapter. For now, the discussion turns to why so many people involved in crime and corrections accepted Martinson's study and the "nothing works" doctrine as true. Again, other studies had been published previously that had questioned the effectiveness of rehabilitation, but they had been largely ignored. Now, things were different. That difference was that many of those concerned about corrections were ready to hear an antirehabilitation message. Times had changed and so had their thinking.

Thus, the decade spanning the mid-1960s to the mid-1970s was a period of major, if not cataclysmic, changes in American society. The nation was rocked by the Civil Rights Movement and violence against protesters, urban riots, assassinations of a president and major public figures, the increasingly unpopular Vietnam War and massive antiwar demonstrations, the shootings of students at Kent State University, and Watergate and repeated revelations of corruption in high places in society. Taken together, these events had many enduring effects on America. What was particularly noteworthy was the extent to which people who experienced these events lost confidence in the government and worried about its agents abusing their powers. Indeed, opinion polls showed a dramatic loss in trust in the state, so much so that it was labeled a "confidence gap" (Lipset and Schneider 1983).

This deep mistrust of the government had important ramifications for rehabilitation because the whole treatment enterprise hinged on giving state officials the freedom to make decisions over the lives of offenders. Rehabilitation was created to mirror medicine. The "medical model" meant that doctors would diagnose what was wrong with a patient, give each patient an individualized treatment, and then stop treating the patient only when the person was cured. In a like matter, under the rehabilitative ideal, judges were not to punish the crime but rather were supposed to prescribe individualized sanctions for each offender. Based on presentence reports from probation officers, the judge would decide whether or not to imprison the offender. Once incarcerated, the inmate's release would depend not on what crime he or she had committed but on when he or she was rehabilitated. A parole board would make that decision. When in the community, a probation or parole officer would watch over offenders—helping to reform them but, if need be, sending recalcitrant supervisees to prison for more intensive interventions (Rothman 1980).

The legitimacy of this medical model of individualized treatment hinged on the belief that judges, prison wardens, parole boards, and probation and parole officers would not only be well trained (like doctors) but also have the offender's best interests at heart (again, as doctors are supposed to have for their "patients"). But what if people no longer believed this to be the case? What if judges were suspected of disregarding the treatment needs of offenders and of unfairly putting minorities and the poor in prison? What if prison wardens were now believed to be more interested in coercing conformity from inmates than in reforming them? What if parole boards were populated by political hacks who had no business deciding who is cured? And what if prisons were now believed to be inherently inhumane—viewed as dreary dumping grounds for society's outcasts rather than as carefully designed therapeutic communities?

In the turmoil of the times, these beliefs struck people as likely to be true. People were inclined to doubt the goodness and competence of judges and correctional officials; they were more likely to see them as self-interested, discriminatory, coercive, and poorly trained. And why not? If government officials could discriminate against minorities in the larger society, could authorize the beatings and shootings of protesters (or look the other way), could lie to the American public about a war, and could break the law in corrupt ways, why would we not also believe that the last thing they were really up to in the correctional system was rehabilitation (Cullen and Gilbert 1982)?

In this context, Martinson's "nothing works" doctrine was not so much a study that changed minds, but rather a document that confirmed what many people were already thinking and "knew to be true." It was as though many correctional observers jumped from an uncritical acceptance of rehabilitation to an uncritical acceptance of this new antitreatment doctrine. It is important to realize that Martinson's study and the reservations people then harbored about corrections were not foolish; they had one foot in reality—just enough to "make sense." The problem, however, was that they went too far: It is just not true that offenders cannot be rehabilitated, and it is just not true that the problems with the correctional system ever were, or are, chiefly due to rehabilitation (Allen 1981).

The Kernel of Truth

As just intimated, there was ample reason for Martinson and fellow criminolo-

gists to find fault with correctional rehabilitation programs. First, in the 1960s
and early 1970s, empirical criminology
was in its infancy and, as a result, scholars' understanding of the predictors of recidivism was limited. Obviously, if the
causes of reoffending were only vaguely
known, it would have been difficult to determine accurately what a program
should target for reform. Second, having
no valid theory of crime—or, in some
cases, no theory whatsoever—many programs were based on forms or modalities
of treatment that had little chance of
transforming high-risk offenders into
prosocial citizens. Third, in many cases,
there was little commitment within corrections to implement intervention programs effectively. Sometimes, this failure
of intervention was due to a lack of resources, sometimes to a lack of will, and
sometimes to a lack of knowledge. Even
today, these failures in criminological
knowledge and in implementation remain—so much so that many of the interventions currently in vogue have rightly
earned the label of "correctional quackery" (Latessa, Cullen, and Gendreau
2002).

The difficulty with the "nothing works"
doctrine, however, was not the assertion
that many programs were irresponsibly
ineffective but rather the larger claim that
all rehabilitation programs were inherently flawed—that offender treatment
would never work. Although the task of
changing offenders into law-abiding citizens is daunting, it simply is not accurate
to claim that offenders are so intractably
different from the rest of us and so firmly
criminal that they are beyond redemption. As discussed in the sections ahead,
such thinking is not only incorrect criminology but also dangerous in its policy
implications.

The Truth or Facts

Why "Nothing Works" Is a Myth

Thus far, we have proceeded on the assumption that "nothing works" is not a de-
fensible doctrine but an indefensible
myth. On the broadest level, the science of
behavioral change has demonstrated that
all sorts of creatures—pigeons, rats, dogs,
and even humans—can change their conduct. This is not to say that change is easy
or that it is easily achieved. But research
demonstrates that interventions can help
troubled or challenged individuals improve their lives in areas ranging from
mental health to educational difficulties
to developmental challenges (Lipsey and
Wilson 1993). It would be an odd occurrence if the only category of humans unable to change were criminals.

As noted, a few scholars took issue with
Martinson's work when it appeared. The
most decisive critique was leveled by
Palmer (1975), who recalculated Martinson's data. He found that 48 percent of the
studies with measures of recidivism
showed that the treatment intervention
actually reduced reoffending. Other reviews of the treatment literature reached
similar results, and the debate was at least
kept alive (see also Gendreau and Ross
1979, 1987).

A turning point in the debate over the
effectiveness of rehabilitation was the application of a statistical technique called
"meta-analysis." At its core, meta-analysis
takes all studies reviewed by an author
and computes what the average influence
on recidivism is across all the studies (sort
of like calculating a player's batting average across all games in a season). When
this technique was used to assess evaluation studies of rehabilitation programs,
the results indicated that the overall influence of correctional treatments was posi-

tive: On average, the effect size was about 0.10. In concrete terms, this meant that if the recidivism for offenders was normally 55 percent (as found in control groups in studies), the treatment group's recidivism rate would be 45 percent (Cullen and Gendreau 2000). This difference was not astoundingly large, but it did reveal through a more precise statistical method that rehabilitation programs had worthwhile effects and held promise. "It is no exaggeration," observes Lipsey (1999: 614), "that meta-analysis of research on the effectiveness of rehabilitation programming has reversed the conclusion of the prior generation of reviews on this topic." In short, meta-analysis illuminated that "nothing works" is best considered a myth.

One more key to this empirical debate was subsequent research into the question of whether all treatment programs have the same effects (homogeneity of effects) or whether some programs are more effective than others (heterogeneity of effects). The latter turns out to be the case. This finding of heterogeneity is important because it means that, whereas some programs have no influence on recidivism (or may even increase it), other programs can have much larger, positive impacts. Indeed, research has found that reductions in recidivism for some programs can be 25 to 30 percent. The significant point is that these effective programs tend to share common characteristics; they tend to obey what has been called the "principles of effective intervention" (Andrews and Bonta 2003; Cullen 2002; Cullen and Gendreau 2000).

What Does Work: The Principles of Effective Intervention

The likelihood of achieving a successful outcome (i.e., reducing offender recidi-

vism) as a result of program efforts is greatly increased when careful attention is paid to the principles of effective intervention (Andrews and Bonta 2003). Recent research suggests that these principles are applicable to a wide range of correctional populations—including juvenile offenders, mentally disordered offenders, sex offenders, and violent offenders—and, on the basis of more limited evidence, to females and minority groups (Andrews and Bonta 2003; Gendreau and Goggin 2000). In what follows, the basic characteristics underlying "appropriate" correctional treatments are introduced—namely, the principles of risk, need, and responsivity. It is important to note that this area of inquiry has matured to the extent that detailed expositions of these principles now exist, and the reader is encouraged to consult additional sources for more extensive reviews (e.g., Andrews 1995; Andrews 2001; Cullen 2002; Gendreau 1996; Gendreau, Cullen, and Bonta 1994).

The Risk Principle. The term risk refers to measurable attributes of offenders and their situations that have been empirically validated as the most robust predictors of future criminality. There are two broad categories of predictors in this regard: (1) static, or immutable, risk factors (e.g., criminal history); and (2) dynamic, or malleable, risk factors (e.g., procriminal associates and substance abuse). A plethora of research demonstrates that it is possible to distinguish high-risk offenders from low-risk offenders on the basis of these risk factors using actuarial assessments (see Andrews and Bonta 2003; Van Voorhis 2000).

The measurement of risk has obvious implications for security and release decisions, and thus facilitates two of the most fundamental utilitarian goals of the criminal justice system: to protect society and to manage safe institutions (Clear 1988; Levinson 1988). It also has important implications, however, for the rehabilitation of offenders. Research indicates that high-risk offenders are more likely to derive greater benefits from treatment than low-risk offenders (Andrews and Bonta 2003). The risk principle, then, states that the most intensive levels of treatment should be delivered to high-risk offenders. It is not cost-effective to subject low-risk offenders to intensive services, and in fact some studies have found increased post-treatment recidivism rates among low-risk offenders (see Andrews, Bonta, and Hoge 1990).

The Needs Principle. Dynamic risk factors are typically referred to as criminogenic needs, and are prime treatment targets given their amenability to change. In short, the needs principle states that the likelihood of future criminality is substantially reduced when dynamic risk factors, or criminogenic needs, are altered. Several meta-analyses (e.g., Gendreau, Little, and Goggin 1996) have identified the following criminogenic needs as the most robust predictors of recidivism: (1) procriminal attitudes, values, beliefs, rationalizations, and cognitions; (2) immediate interpersonal and social support for procriminal behavior (i.e., procriminal associates); (3) personality and temperamental factors, including poor self-control, impulsiveness, restless aggressive energy, and adventurous pleasure seeking; (4) problematic circumstances in the domains of home, education, employment, and leisure activities; and (5) substance abuse. The most effective interventions are "multi-modal" in that they are equipped to address a number of these criminogenic needs (Andrews 2001).

Meta-analyses have also demonstrated that other attributes once regarded as important treatment targets (e.g., low self-esteem, depression, and anxiety) are relatively weak predictors of future criminality. As a consequence, addressing these attributes in treatment produces very little change in offender recidivism (Gendreau, Little, and Goggin 1996).

The Responsivity Principle. With remarkable consistency, the results of meta-analyses indicate that the most effective interventions are behavioral in nature (e.g., radical behavioral, social learning, or cognitive behavioral) (e.g., Andrews et al. 1990; Gendreau, Little, and Goggin 1996). That is, effective programs emphasize positive reinforcement contingencies for anticriminal behavior (the principle of general responsivity). In contrast, ineffective programs are based on psychodynamic, nondirective, phenomenological, or physical-disease treatments, as well as "get tough" and "punishing smarter" strategies.

Other factors, if addressed, have also been shown to affect how well an offender responds to treatment. To enhance the effectiveness of interventions, the styles and modes of service delivery should be matched to the learning styles and abilities of the offender (the principle of specific responsivity). There are two broad categories of specific responsivity factors: (1) internal responsivity factors, or cognitive, personal, and social-personal offender characteristics (e.g., intelligence, anxiety, and attention deficit disorder); and (2) external responsivity factors, or counselor characteristics (e.g., interpersonal competencies) and setting considerations.

Interests Served by the Myth

The challenge to rehabilitation as the guiding correctional philosophy was precipitated chiefly by political liberals. Although once the staunchest supporters of offender treatment, the loss of confidence in the government in the 1960s and beyond caused political liberals to forsake rehabilitation as just another ideology that gave the state unwarranted and abusive power in the lives of vulnerable Americans. In their view, rehabilitation was a benevolent ideology that merely served to allow judges and correctional officials to victimize offenders. For this reason, political liberals favored a system whose only goal was to "do justice"—not to try the supposedly pointless goal of rehabilitating the wayward, but rather to limit the government's role to punishing lawbreakers in a fair and humane way (Cullen and Gilbert 1982). Discrediting offender treatment thus seemingly served their political interests.

This position, however, was politically naive and fraught with difficulties. Thus, once political liberals rejected rehabilitation, they legitimated the idea that the main goal of corrections should be to punish offenders. Political liberals favored short sentences, seeing any time spent in prison as a severe penalty. But this idea had two problems. First, it was not at all clear why offenders who repeatedly harmed others should receive short sentences. Second, the liberals were mainly concerned with curtailing injustice and thus with being fair to offenders. Political conservatives used this concern to paint liberals as unconcerned about victims. "Crime" thus became an issue in which liberals seemed to side with "superpredators" and "chronic offenders," while conservatives seemed to side with victims and decent folk. By portraying the issue in such stark and simplistic terms, conservatives persuaded many Americans that they were the party who could restore "law and order" and keep people safe. They earned political support as a result.

The notion that "nothing works" to reform offenders ultimately served the interests of political conservatives in an additional way. Again, conservatives asserted that only they—not "bleeding heart left-wingers" who wanted to "do justice"— had the credentials to protect society by "getting tough" with the dangerous criminals previously allowed to roam the streets of our communities. These views coincided with the increasing extent to which the undercurrent of racial politics informed policy debates. As America's prisons became increasingly populated by minorities, it became easier for right-wing politicians to imply that their policies would protect white Americans from a group of intractably criminal black Americans who were beyond rehabilitation and should be incapacitated for a very long time. The infamous "Willie Horton" campaign advertisement in the 1988 presidential contest signified this strategy to capitalize on racial fear with a promise of using mass imprisonment to afford protection to "us" from "them." By contrast, rehabilitation—which might include the type of prison furlough program given to Willie Horton—was portrayed as another ill-conceived liberal social welfare policy that pandered to undeserving, if not dangerous, minorities at the expense of the heretofore silent ("white") majority.

Policy Implications of Belief in the Myth

The Dangers of the "Nothing Works" Myth

As numerous commentators have noted, "ideas have consequences." In this case, the spread of the idea that rehabilitation "does not work" and is merely an excuse to treat offenders unfairly had disturbing effects. Indeed, America has been in a "post-rehabilitation" era for three decades, and the results are not encouraging. Four untoward consequences can be briefly identified.

First, the decline of rehabilitation has coincided with an era of reckless punitive rhetoric and unprecedented harshness in the treatment of offenders. This "penal harm" movement, as Clear (1994) calls it, may have occurred even if rehabilitation had not been attacked. But, clearly, discrediting offender rehabilitation made it more difficult to challenge a punishment approach. After all, if rehabilitation does not work, the only option is to punish offenders.

Second, as noted, the "nothing works" idea gave credence to the notion that offenders were a separate category of people—a dangerous class of "superpredators" or "career criminals" who were beyond redemption. Again, the policy option seemed obvious: Such people needed to be incarcerated, preferably for lengthy periods of time.

Third, the services provided to offenders have diminished. The logic follows that if offenders cannot change, then there is no reason to offer them education, job training, or counseling. In fact, according to this logic, such programs soften offenders' lives in prison and may make them less fearful of future imprisonment. Accordingly, policies were put forward to make life in prison even more miserable by diminishing the quality of basic amenities (e.g., food, housing arrangements), restricting recreation (e.g., television), forbidding comforts such as air conditioning, reintroducing chain gangs, and eliminating college education opportunities.

Fourth, as we moved away from rehabilitation, an array of punitive interventions became acceptable—intensive supervision in the community, boot camps, scared straight programs, mandatory sentences, the waiver of juveniles to adult court—that have little chance of reducing crime and, oftentimes, increase recidivism (Cullen et al. 2002b; Cullen, Wright, and Applegate 1996). These programs robbed offenders of a chance to reform, but they also possibly exposed the community to victimizations that need not have occurred.

In short, the "nothing works" doctrine had no demonstrable positive influence in the lives of offenders, and almost certainly made the lives of many offenders worse. As noted, the public likely paid a price as well: Many offenders who might have been reformed were not, and went on to commit crimes that could have been prevented.

Beyond the "Nothing Works" Myth

For three important reasons, the time has come to dispel fully the myth that "nothing works" in correctional rehabilitation. First, as has been shown, the empirical evidence is clear that treatment programs can achieve significant reductions in recidivism, especially with high-risk offenders. Martinson's study was a worthy scholarly effort, but it was based on a review of evaluation research conducted four decades ago, used a simple count of studies rather than meta-analysis to draw conclusions, and did not cover many of the types of interventions shown to be effective. To be sure, implementing effective programs is a daunting challenge (Lin 2000). Even so, there is a growing knowledge base that holds a blueprint for how to change the behavior of offenders; it should be followed.

Second, there is a high cost to ignoring this knowledge on effective interventions (Van Voorhis 1987). Rehabilitation programs often are portrayed as giving services to undeserving people (criminals) and as offering an excuse to be soft on crime. As noted, however, the research is now clear that many of the current "get tough" interventions imposed on offenders have actually endangered public safety. Phrased differently, the most effective way to benefit not only offenders but also potential future victims is to implement effective programming in corrections. Rehabilitation should be a key element in the family of strategies used to prevent crime and victimization.

Third, the American public wants a balanced approach to corrections. Opinion polls are clear in showing that Americans are punitive toward offenders (Cullen, Fisher, and Applegate 2000). But these surveys are equally clear in revealing that Americans are not exclusively punitive. Rather, although members of the public favor exacting a measure of justice and incarcerating dangerous offenders, they also reject the idea that corrections should merely be about inflicting pain on and warehousing offenders. Instead, Americans also want corrections to "correct"— to reform those brought under legal supervision. They desire to have a correctional system that both protects society as best it can and seeks to achieve a nobler purpose of "doing good" and improving the lives of offenders. This is a moment when the collective judgment of the American public is wise and welcomed (Cullen, Fisher, and Applegate 2000); policy makers should pay attention.

References

Allen, F. A. 1981. *The decline of the rehabilitative ideal: Penal policy and social purpose.* New Haven, CT: Yale University Press.

Andrews, D. A. 1995. The psychology of criminal conduct and effective treatment. In *What works: Reducing reoffending—Guidelines from research and practice,* ed. J. McGuire. Chichester, UK: John Wiley and Sons.

———. 2001. Principles of effective correctional programs. In *Compendium 2000 on effective correctional programming,* Vol. 1., eds. L. L. Motiuk and R. C. Serin. Ottawa, Ontario: Correctional Service of Canada.

Andrews, D. A., and J. Bonta. 2003. *The psychology of criminal conduct,* 3rd ed. Cincinnati: Anderson.

Andrews, D. A., J. Bonta, and R. D. Hoge. 1990. Classification for effective rehabilitation: Rediscovering psychology. *Criminal Justice and Behavior* 17:19–52.

Andrews, D. A., I. Zinger, R. D. Hoge, J. Bonta, P. Gendreau, and F. T. Cullen. 1990. Does correctional treatment work? A clinically relevant and psychologically informed meta-analysis. *Criminology* 28:369–404.

Clear, T. 1988. Statistical prediction in corrections. *Research in Corrections* 1:1–39.

———. 1994. *Harm in American penology: Offenders, victims, and their communities.* Albany: State University of New York Press.

Cullen, F. T. 2002. Rehabilitation and treatment programs. In *Crime: Public policies for crime control,* 2nd ed., eds. J. Q. Wilson and J. Petersilia. Oakland, CA: ICS Press.

Cullen, F. T., B. S. Fisher, and B. K. Applegate. 2000. Public opinion about punishment and corrections. In *Crime and justice: A review of research,* Vol. 27, ed. M. Tonry. Chicago: University of Chicago Press.

Cullen, F. T., and P. Gendreau. 2000. Assessing correctional rehabilitation: Policy, practice, and prospects. In *Criminal justice 2000: Volume 3—Policies, processes, and decisions of the criminal justice system,* ed. Julie Horney. Washington, DC: U.S. Department of Justice, National Institute of Justice.

Cullen, F. T., and K. E. Gilbert. 1982. *Reaffirming rehabilitation.* Cincinnati: Anderson.

Cullen, F. T., J. A. Pealer, B. S. Fisher, B. K. Applegate, and S. A. Santana. 2002a. Public support for correctional rehabilitation in America: Change or consistency? In *Changing attitudes to punishment: Public opinion, crime and justice,* eds. J. V. Roberts and M. Hough. Devon, UK: Willan Publishing.

Cullen, F. T., T. C. Pratt, S. L. Miceli, and M. M. Moon. 2002b. Dangerous liaison? Rational choice as the basis for correctional intervention. In *Rational choice and criminal behavior: Recent research and future challenges,* eds. A. R. Piquero and S. G. Tibbetts. New York: Macmillan.

Cullen, F. T., J. P. Wright, and B. K. Applegate. 1996. Control in the community: The limits of reform? In *Choosing correctional interventions that work: Defining the demand and eval-*

uating the supply, ed. A. T. Harland. Thousand Oaks, CA: Sage.

Currie, E. 1998. *Crime and punishment in America.* New York: Metropolitan Books.

Gendreau, P. 1996. The principles of effective intervention with offenders. In *Choosing correctional interventions that work: Defining the demand and evaluating the supply,* ed. A. T. Harland. Thousand Oaks, CA: Sage.

Gendreau, P., F. T. Cullen, and J. Bonta. 1994. Intensive rehabilitation and supervision: The next generation in community corrections? *Federal Probation* 58 (March):72–78.

Gendreau, P., and C. Goggin. 2000. Correctional treatment: Accomplishments and realities. In *Correctional counseling and rehabilitation,* 4th ed., eds. P. Van Voorhis, M. Braswell, and D. Lester. Cincinnati, OH: Anderson.

Gendreau, P., T. Little, and C. Goggin. 1996. A meta-analysis of the predictors of adult offender recidivism: What works! *Criminology* 34:575–607.

Gendreau, P., and R. R. Ross. 1979. Effective correctional treatment: Bibliotherapy for cynics. *Crime and Delinquency* 25:463–489.

———. 1987. Revivification of rehabilitation: Evidence from the 1980s. *Justice Quarterly* 4: 349–407.

Latessa, E. J., F. T. Cullen, and P. Gendreau. 2002. Beyond correctional quackery: Professionalism and the possibility of effective treatment. *Federal Probation* 66 (September): 43–49.

Levinson, R. 1988. Development in the classification process. *Criminal Justice and Behavior* 15:24–38.

Lin, A. C. 2000. *Reform in the making: The implementation of social policy in prison.* Princeton, NJ: Princeton University Press.

Lipset, S. M., and W. Schneider. 1983. *The confidence gap: Business, labor, and government in the public mind.* New York: Free Press.

Lipsey, M. W. 1999. Can rehabilitative programs reduce the recidivism of juvenile offenders? An inquiry into the effectiveness of treatment with juvenile delinquency? *Virginia Journal of Social Policy and Law* 6:611–641.

Lipsey, M. W., and D. B. Wilson. 1993. The efficacy of psychological, educational, and behavioral treatment. *American Psychologist* 48: 1181–1209.

Lipton, D., R. Martinson, and J. Wilks.1975. *The effectiveness of correctional treatment: A survey of treatment evaluation studies.* New York: Praeger.

Martinson, R. 1974a. What works? Questions and answers about prison reform. *Public Interest* 35 (Spring):22–54.

———. 1975b. Viewpoint. *Criminal Justice Newsletter* 5 (November 18):4–5.

Palmer, T. 1975. Martinson revisited. *Journal of Research in Crime and Delinquency* 12:133–152.

Rothman, D. J. 1971. *Discovery of the asylum: Social order and disorder in the new republic.* Boston: Little, Brown.

———. 1980. *Conscience and convenience: The asylum and its alternatives in progressive America.* Boston: Little, Brown.

Spelman, W. 2000. What recent studies do (and don't) tell us about imprisonment and crime. In *Crime and justice: A review of research,* Vol. 27, ed. M. Tonry. Chicago: University of Chicago Press.

Van Voorhis, P. 1987. Correctional effectiveness: The high cost of ignoring success. *Federal Probation* 51 (March):59–62.

———. 2000. An overview of offender classification systems. In *Correctional counseling and rehabilitation,* 4th ed., eds. P. Van Voorhis, M. Braswell, and D. Lester. Cincinnati, OH: Anderson. ✦

Index

DATE DUE

OC 2 7 08		
	WITHDRAWN	

DEMCO 38-296